CBT Case Formulation as Therapeutic Process

Giovanni Maria Ruggiero
Gabriele Caselli • Sandra Sassaroli
Editors

CBT Case Formulation as Therapeutic Process

Springer

Editors
Giovanni Maria Ruggiero
"Psicoterapia Cognitiva e Ricerca,"
Cognitive Psychotherapy School
and Research Center
Milan, Italy

Sigmund Freud University
Milan, Italy

Sigmund Freud University
Vienna, Austria

Sandra Sassaroli
Sigmund Freud University
Milan, Italy

Sigmund Freud University
Vienna, Austria

"Studi Cognitivi," Cognitive Psychotherapy
School and Research Center
Milan, Italy

Gabriele Caselli
Sigmund Freud University
Milan, Italy

Sigmund Freud University
Vienna, Austria

Department of Psychology
London South Bank University
London, UK

ISBN 978-3-030-63586-2 ISBN 978-3-030-63587-9 (eBook)
https://doi.org/10.1007/978-3-030-63587-9

This Springer imprint is published by the registered company Springer Nature Switzerland AG
The registered company address is: Gewerbestrasse 11, 6330 Cham, Switzerland

Dedicated to Tom Borkovec, Ana Catina, Raffaele Papa, Don Bannister, Francesco Rovetto, Marcantonio Spada, and Adrian Wells who mentored the editors

Foreword

It is a rarity to witness such a wide array of experts come together to offer us insights into case formulation in the cognitive and behavioural therapy approaches. I commend the editors of this book for the timeliness of this publication. Over the last 20 years (if not longer), there has been a gradual erosion of case formulation skills as training programmes have increasingly shifted to focusing on developing intervention skills at the expense of forging formulation skills. The capacity to formulate the complexity of clinical presentations has, as a result of this shift, been increasingly lost. The central message of this work is that the shared case formulation is the cardinal, unifying and distinctive tool for the effective delivery of any cognitive and behavioural therapy approach. Indeed, as all the authors argue, the shared case formulation offers an unparalleled foundation for the effective management of the therapeutic alliance and relationship, which is key for positive outcomes in treatment.

The book begins with the emergence of the earlier shared case formulation approaches exemplified in Beck's Cognitive Therapy and in Victor Meyer's Behaviour Therapy. Some insightful commentaries follow describing the central role of working models and goal setting in Cognitive Therapy and the idea of the case formulation (based on Meyer's approach) as part of environmental and behavioural circumstances that must be altered to achieve therapeutic change.

The book progresses to showcase and discuss Albert Ellis' Rational Emotive Behavior Therapy case formulation (which anticipated metacognitive formulations) as well as Schema Therapy where strong interpersonal factors rooted in development bring to stereotypical and inflexible relational models. The metacognitive therapy case formulation is then introduced with its central focus on the function of conscious executive choice that can become dysfunctional because of metacognitive biases. This is followed by a review of case formulation in Acceptance and Commitment Therapy and its roots in Meyer's functionalist conception of case formulation. Finally, process-based case formulation in Cognitive-Behavioural Therapy is presented integrating standard Cognitive Therapy into a process framework by formulating the case around fundamental biopsychosocial processes in target-specific situations with specific clients.

The book then leads us to discover constructivist approaches to case formulation, which assume that sharing the case formulation is the outcome of an explorative process and not an initial and targeted treatment step. A series of commentaries and reflections presented by several authors provide a rich resource and insight into this case formulation in constructivism. As we near the end of the book, case formulation models that emphasize the role of the therapeutic relationship are reviewed by several distinguished authors in the field. The book then introduces an integrated model to case formulation in the cognitive and behavioural therapies which conceptualizes psychological dysfunction as emerging from the combination of the negative evaluation of events and relational patterns combined with a rigid stance to the management of themes emerging from these events and relational patterns. The closure to the fascinating journey of this book brings us to the most recent developments in case formulation integrating online E-mental health applications.

In conclusion, this book attempts to present the full complexity of what a shared case formulation entails by providing invaluable insights from leading clinicians and researchers in the field. I have no doubt that this book will provide something of interest for anyone who has the ambition to learn about the most important tool in psychological treatment: case formulation.

London, UK
August 2020

Marcantonio Spada

Foreword

One cannot avoid the impression that to modern medicine, patients' own assessments are of little to no interest. New technical achievements promise that in the future it will be possible to utterly do without it: Patients get a medical "check-up", nothing is asked of him or her; the objective clinical reports speak for themselves. After the begin of a consultation, studies show that it takes general practisers' an average 11–14 s to break in a patient who tells his or her story (Wilm et al., 2004). Based on the legitimacy of its science, the medical authority monologises on the suffering patients entrusted it with. It is against this disciplinary background that the special feature of psychotherapy's founding history stands out: Sigmund Freud—a truly "strange" doctor who does nothing but listen to his patients. In psychoanalysis, Freud (1926, p. 12) writes, "nothing else [...] happens between doctor and the patient except that they talk to each other". The patient talks about himself and he also talks about things that are difficult to be said to another person. Just as in daily conversations where we strive to remove barriers of conversations to get our dialogue partner to say what he or she wants to say, the psychoanalyst strives to create conditions under which it becomes easier for patients to reveal "secrets" lying heavy on them (Bernfeld, 1941).

But enough of Freud and psychoanalysis! After all, this book is a collection of texts on Cognitive Behavioural Therapy. It addresses and negotiates the functional role of the instrument of Shared Case Formulation in the process of Cognitive Behavioural Therapy. And yet it seems to me that the essence of the individual contributions and commentaries also is of a more general interest. In addition, although the main focus is on Cognitive Behavioural Therapy, there are three chapters devoted to case formulation in the psychodynamic model.

I want to briefly sketch the train of thought that has been occupying my friend Hans Werbik from Erlangen and me for months. What interests us is the question of how to adequately understand the data generated by psychological research. The starting point of our considerations is what is known in the history of psychology as "introspection". Upon closer inspection, it turns out to be a basically interactive procedure framed by the researcher's objective: a game of questions and answers between the experimenter and the subject on the stage of the experimental psychological laboratory. The reports that emerge are thus not data from the perspective of the first person, but from the perspective of the second person. Of course, this applies to questionnaires also: Just as in the case of introspection, they are neither data from the perspective of the first nor data from the perspective of the third person, but ground on a special form of interaction between researcher and subject—A test person provides answers to questions that are relevant for the researcher, i.e. questions that per se have nothing to do with the respondent's subjective relevancies. This is a strongly restricted, utterly asymmetrical, "monologic" form of a "conversation". If we can show that much, perhaps even most, of the data in psychology is based on such a monologic relationship, is it possible then to think of psychological data that is based on a more dialogical relationship between researcher and subject? What would be the consequences for such an expanded methodology of psychology? Various models of psychotherapy provide a first point of contact: In addition to the dialogical procedure in the psychoanalytic setting, there is also the procedure of Shared Case Formulation in Cognitive Behavioral Therapy that is in the heart of the analysis in this book. In the future, it will be interesting to see whether and how the Milan group will use the data emerging from the therapeutic process as empirical material for psychological research.

Vienna, Austria Gerhard Benetka
August 2020

References

Bernfeld, S. (1941). The facts of observation in psychoanalysis. *The Journal of Psychology, 12*, 289–305.

Freud, S. (1926). *Die Frage der Laienanalyse [The question of lay analysis]*. Wien, Austria: Internationaler Psychoanalytischer Verlag.

Wilm, S., Knauf, A., Peters, T., & Bahrs, O. (2004). Wann unterbricht der Hausarzt seine Patienten zu Beginn der Konsultation? [At which point does the geral practitionerinterrupt his patients at the beginning of a consultation?]. *Zeitschrift für Allgemeine Medizin, 80*, 53–57.

Arthur Freeman Memorial Statement

This book features one of Arthur Freeman's last scientific contributions. In the third chapter, he comments on his ideas about case formulation in CBT therapy. A few weeks after submitting his contribution, he died from the after-effects of a long fight with cancer. Art Freeman was a significant figure both in the foundation and in the development of classical CBT, and he played a seminal role in the broadening of its applicability to treat many clinical problems and populations, and in the comparison of CBT with other therapeutic orientations. Art was always helpful, friendly, personable, connected, funny and passionate about growth and knowledge.

Finally, it is intriguing that he could rise above his rebellious youth, complete his education and make significant contributions to the academic literature. Art was the ultimate disseminator of CBT and a great presenter. Is there an area of CBT that he did not write about? Publishing one of his later writings in this book is, we feel, an excellent way to honour him.

Albert Ellis Institute
New York, NY, USA
St. John University
New York, NY, USA

Raymond DiGiuseppe

Cognitive Behavioural Specialization School
"Psicoterapia Cognitiva e Ricerca", Milan, Italy
Sigmund Freud University
Milan, Italy
Sigmund Freud University
Vienna, Austria

Giovanni Maria Ruggiero

Contents

Contributors

Wouter Backx Nederlands Instituut voor RET en CGT, Haarlem, The Netherlands

Barbara Barcaccia Scuole di Psicoterapia Cognitiva, Roma, Italy

Sapienza Università di Roma, Roma, Italy

Andrea Bassanini MeP—Mindfulness e Psicoterapia, Milano, Italy

Società di Psicoterapia Cognitivo Comportamentale CBT-Italia, Milan, Italy

Antonino Carcione "Terzo Centro di Psicoterapia Cognitiva" Third Centre of Cognitive Psychotherapy, Rome, Italy

Scuole di Psicoterapia Cognitiva, Roma, Italy

Gabriele Caselli Sigmund Freud University, Milan, Italy

Sigmund Freud University, Vienna, Austria

Department of Psychology, London South Bank University, London, UK

Raymond DiGiuseppe St. John University and Albert Ellis Institute, New York, NY, USA

Maurizio Dodet "Laboratorio di Psicologia Cognitiva Post-razionalista", Cognitive Psychotherapy Center, Rome, Italy

Kristene Doyle Albert Ellis Institute and St. John University, New York, NY, USA

Christiane Eichenberg Faculty of Medicine, Sigmund Freud University, Wien, Austria

Benedetto Farina Università Europea di Roma, Rome, Italy

"Centro Clinico Janet" Cognitive Psychotherapy Center, Rome, Italy

Guillem Feixas Institut de Neurociències, Universitat de Barcelona, Barcelona, Spain

Institut d'Estudis Catalans, Barcelona, Spain

Arthur Freeman Philadelphia College of Osteopathic Medicine, Philadelphia, PA, USA

Francesco Gazzillo Department of Dynamic and Clinical Psychology, Sapienza University of Rome, Rome, Italy

Stefan Hofmann Department of Psychological and Brain Sciences, Boston University, Boston, MA, USA

Steven D. Hollon Department of Psychology, Vanderbilt University, Nashville, TN, USA

Mariano Ruperthuz Honorato Andrés Bello University, School of Psychology, Santiago del Cile, Chile

Marco Innamorati Università degli Studi di Roma "Tor Vergata", Rome, Italy

Francesco Mancini Scuole di Psicoterapia Cognitiva, Roma, Italy

Università Guglielmo Marconi, Roma, Italy

Nicola Marsigli Institute for Behavioral and Cognitive Psychology and Psychotherapy (IPSICO), Florence, Italy

Gabriele Melli Institute for Behavioral and Cognitive Psychology and Psychotherapy, IPSICO, Florence, Italy

Paolo Migone Psicoterapia e Scienze Umane ["Psychotherapy and the Human Sciences"], Parma, Italy

Paolo Moderato IULM University, Milano, Italy

Fabio Monticelli "Centro Clinico Janet", Cognitive Psychotherapy Center, Rome, Italy

Claudia Perdighe Scuole di Psicoterapia Cognitiva, Roma, Italy

Eckard Roediger Institut für Schematherapie, Frankfurt, Germany

Saverio Ruberti Società italiana di Terapia Comportamentale e Cognitiva (SITCC), Rome, Italy

Giovanni Maria Ruggiero "Psicoterapia Cognitiva e Ricerca," Cognitive Psychotherapy School and Research Center, Milan, Italy

Sigmund Freud University, Milan, Italy

Sigmund Freud University, Vienna, Austria

Angelo Maria Saliani Scuole di Psicoterapia Cognitiva, Roma, Italy

Università degli Studi dell'Aquila, L'Aquila, Italy

Diego Sarracino Department of Psychology, University of Milano Bicocca, Milano, Italy

Sandra Sassaroli Sigmund Freud University, Milan, Italy

Sigmund Freud University, Vienna, Austria

"Studi Cognitivi," Cognitive Psychotherapy School and Research Center, Milan, Italy

Antonio Scarinci Azienda Sanitaria Locale Viterbo; "Studi Cognitivi" Cognitive Psychotherapy School and Research Center, Milano, Italy

Antonio Semerari "Terzo Centro di Psicoterapia Cognitiva" Third Centre of Cognitive Psychotherapy, Rome, Italy

Scuole di Psicoterapia Cognitiva, Roma, Italy

George Silberschatz University of California, San Francisco, CA, USA

Avigal Snir Department of Psychological and Brain Sciences, Boston University, Boston, MA, USA

Peter Sturmey The Graduate Center and Queens College, City University of New York, New York, NY, USA

Raffaella Visini Società italiana di Terapia Comportamentale e Cognitiva (SITCC), Rome, Italy

Kelly G. Wilson The University of Mississippi, Oxford, MS, USA

David A. Winter University of Hertfordshire, Hertfordshire, UK

Shared Case Formulation as the Main Therapeutic Process in Cognitive Therapies

Giovanni Maria Ruggiero, Gabriele Caselli, and Sandra Sassaroli

Contents

The Core Assumption of the Book

Case formulation may be the purloined letter of the therapeutic process in standard cognitive behavioral therapy (CBT) or other CBT approaches. It is the object that has escaped most careful investigations, although it has been visibly displayed on the mantel, as it were. In CBT approaches, clinicians have devoted themselves—not

G. M. Ruggiero (✉)
"Psicoterapia Cognitiva e Ricerca," Cognitive Psychotherapy School and Research Center, Milan, Italy

Sigmund Freud University, Milan, Italy

Sigmund Freud University, Vienna, Austria
e-mail: gm.ruggiero@milano-sfu.it

G. Caselli
Sigmund Freud University, Milan, Italy

Sigmund Freud University, Vienna, Austria

Department of Psychology, London South Bank University, London, UK

S. Sassaroli
Sigmund Freud University, Milan, Italy

Sigmund Freud University, Vienna, Austria

"Studi Cognitivi," Cognitive Psychotherapy School and Research Center, Milan, Italy

G. M. Ruggiero et al. (eds.), *CBT Case Formulation as Therapeutic Process*,
https://doi.org/10.1007/978-3-030-63587-9_1

without reason nor with bad results—to look for irrational beliefs and cognitive biases, sometimes at the price of underrating the explicit sharing case formulation by taking it for granted (Kuyken 2006, p. 12).

The basic assumption of this book is that case formulation is the initial move and main operational tool of CBT approaches by which a therapist manages the entire psychotherapeutic process. The idea is that, in CBT, case formulation incorporates both the specific cognitive and behavioral interventions of the treatment and the non-specific components, including the negotiation of the therapeutic alliance and the management of the therapeutic relationship. In addition, this book assumes that, in CBT approaches, case formulation is a procedure incessantly and openly shared between the patient and therapist from the beginning to the end of treatment. This book aims to show how this aspect is increasingly becoming the hallmark of standard CBT approaches because it is in line with CBT's basic principles. This attitude implies full confidence in the conscious agreement between therapists and patients, transparent cooperation, and an explicit commitment to the CBT model of clinical change.

In summary, the objectives of this book are to:

- Conceptualize shared clinical case formulation as the core and distinctive intervention of the main forms of CBT because it is intrinsically linked to CBT's basic tenets;
- Describe the shared case formulation procedures in CBT approaches to show how, in many of them, this process allows the therapist to manage both CBT-specific and non-specific features of the therapeutic process;
- Review the historical development of the main forms of CBT to show the way in which shared case formulation emerges is a truly unifying and distinctive feature of CBT approaches; and
- Explore the use of case formulation in some relational and psychodynamic approaches close to CBT approaches by discussing similarities and differences.

Of course, case formulation is present in psychotherapeutic approaches beyond CBT. Despite many similarities, it is important to distinguish CBT approaches from other psychotherapeutic treatments in which conscious cognition is an important variable but is neither the cardinal mediator of emotional suffering nor the main target of therapeutic intervention. This theoretical difference also becomes a theoretical divide in the conception and management of shared case formulation during the therapeutic process between CBT and non-CBT approaches.

This book attempts to qualify CBT approaches as treatments in which—by definition—the therapeutic process occurs with full conscious sharing (Dobson and Dozois 2001); it also distinguishes these approaches from other models in which the therapeutic process occurs by not establishing this full sharing from the beginning and conceiving it as a goal to be achieved and a final outcome of the treatment. This latter aspect involves exploring mental states and relational patterns that are not immediately accessible to the consciousness, as happens in psychodynamic psychotherapies (Gabbard 2017) or by looking for personal and existential meanings that are fully constructed only at the end of a long exploratory process, which is a component of constructivist psychotherapies.

For the sake of clarity, we must notice that there are some constructivist approaches (also called constructive approaches) that were born in the CBT domain and in a broad sense belong to this clinical field, but differ in—among many other things—the conception of case formulation. These are the constructivist approaches that target hermeneutic, emotionally charged, and "tacit" cognition (Guidano 1991; Guidano and Liotti 1983; Mahoney 2003; Neimeyer 2009) and may partially diverge from other CBT approaches that favor therapeutic work over shared case formulation. For this reason, the term "constructivist approaches" is sometimes used in this book as distinct from CBT approaches, although we remain aware that they belong to the CBT domain.

Summing up, we propose that this way of sharing case formulation is one of the main qualifying features of many CBT approaches. This particular approach involves unceasingly sharing the case formulation with the patient in three aspects:

1. Formulation of the explanatory model of emotional suffering;
    (a) Formulation of the rationale for the treatment strategy proposed to the patient; and
    (b) Monitoring of therapeutic progress and its feedback action on the treatment strategy, which allows, when necessary:
        i. Reformulation of the case;
        ii. Renegotiation of the goals of therapy; and
        iii. Changing the treatment plan according to the new formulation and new rationale.

This emphasis on the conscious sharing of case formulation as a tool to obtain full patient cooperation allows us to explain another core feature of many CBT approaches: The patient is a fully active agent in his or her treatment, because the therapeutic model and the rationale of the intervention can be shared with him or her from the beginning. This possibility to manage case formulation in a relentlessly shared way derives from the CBT tenet that dysfunctional states are reasonably accessible to consciousness and significantly tractable at the level of consciousness (Dobson and Dozois 2001).

Even the CBT attention to the patient's specific disorders, problems and symptoms—although shrinking with the emergence of transdiagnostic models (Hayes and Hofman 2018)—would originate from the principle of the shared case formulation: The CBT therapist starts from problem areas defined during case formulation, including the symptoms for which the patient seeks effective and reasonably immediate solutions.

Shared Case Formulation and Therapeutic Alliance

This book also promotes the idea that the principle of shared case formulation can offer CBT approaches a specific terminology to deal with the so-called common and unspecific therapeutic processes, namely the management of the therapeutic alliance and relationship (Asay and Lambert 1999). It is not a coincidence that, in the above-mentioned psychodynamic and constructivist models, cognition is conceived as inseparable from relational experience to such an extent that they consider the relationship as the real significant mediator of the therapeutic change (Bara 2018; Gabbard 2017). Adopting an operationally CBT-specific terminology for the concepts of alliance and therapeutic relationship such as "**shared case formulation**" without borrowing words from approaches that obey different principles allows one to remain focused on the historical proposal of CBT. It also encourages the conceptualization of the therapeutic alliance in terms that are consistent with the principles of CBT approaches (Bruch 1998, 2015; Sturmey 2008, 2009). In CBT approaches, alliance and relationship are an important pre-condition of the therapeutic process but are not a unit of analysis for the change process. This observation is not coincidental; rather, it is significant for maintaining the distinction between CBT approaches and relational models that increasingly; this distinction suggests the resolutive aspects of the therapeutic process are to be found in the therapeutic relationship as, for example, in the case of Wampold and Imel's model (Wampold and Imel 2015). It is therefore not just a matter of terminology: Words are important and reflect the nature of the theoretical model.

Case Formulation in CBT and Non-CBT Approaches

From a historical point of view, a divergence of development in CBT and non-CBT case formulation seems correct. Regarding CBT, behavioral therapies have historically used the term case formulation, as reported by various scholars focused on the history of this term (Bruch 1998, 2015; Eells 2007, 2011, 2015; Sturmey 2008, 2009). Of these, Bruch and Sturmey tell the story from a CBT point of view: They highlight how the term case formulation was initially conceived by Victor Meyer (1957) and finally introduced into CBT approaches in 1985 by Turkat (1985, 1986). Moreover, the term was present in the work of other theorists and clinicians belonging to the CBT domain, such as Shapiro (1955, 1957), Lazarus (1960, 1976), Wolpe (1954), Yates (1958), and Kanfer and Saslow (1969). Meyer's contribution stands out because it introduces to CBT an element of alliance, while for the other authors, case formulation did not contain in itself the element of agreement and sharing with the patient (Meyer and Turkat 1979).

Outside the CBT domain, Eells aimed to outline a more atheoretical story of case formulation. However, Eells did not ignore the contribution of CBT, given that Eells' handbook entrusts to Persons and Tomkins (2007) the account of the development of CBT case formulation. The atheoretical tradition followed by Eels appears to be more recent, as is clear if we pay attention to the years of publication of the cited texts: It begins with Weerasekera (1996), followed by McWilliams (1999) and Eells (2007). At present, there are many case formulation models outside the CBT line sown by Meyer, such as plan analysis by Caspar (1995, 2007), the mode model by Fassbinder et al. (2019), the formulation of maladaptive patterns by Critchfield et al. (2019), and the dynamic formulation focused on motives, defenses, and conflicts by Perry et al. (2019).

Contents of the Chapters and Structure of the Book

The following chapters of this book develop this program; some chapters, written by the three editors **Giovanni Maria Ruggiero**, **Gabriele Caselli**, and **Sandra Sassaroli**, deal with case formulation in either CBT or non-CBT therapeutic orientations, while other chapters are critical comments on the main assumptions of the book delivered from experts in specific therapeutic orientations. For example, the chapter on case formulation in standard cognitive therapy (CT) is followed by a comment from Arthur Freeman, a clinician and researcher in the CT area.

Hereafter, we briefly summarize the content of the chapters and note the names of the authors who comment on them. After this introductory chapter, the second chapter deals with the emergence of shared case formulation in Beck's CT (Beck 1963, 1964; Beck et al. 1979; Clark and Beck 2010) and in Victor Meyer's behavioral approach. The chapter describes how Aaron T. Beck uses the components of his cognitive diagram—central beliefs, intermediate beliefs, and coping strategies—to provide the patient with a psychopathological interpretation and therapeutic reworking of the reported problematic situations by questioning them. Moreover, in CT, the diagram is fundamental to managing the therapeutic relationship by conceptualizing distorted interpersonal beliefs and increasing therapist empathy (Beck 2005).

The first commentary on this chapter is written by **Arthur Freeman** (chapter "The Conceptualization Process in Cognitive Behavioral Therapy. Commentary on Chapter "Case Formulation in Standard Cognitive Therapy"") who describes the conceptualization process of CBT in eleven steps, from the need to develop a working model of the patient's problems to the collaborative work with the patient to refine the conceptualization. **Steven Hollon** (chapter "Case Formulation in Standard Cognitive Therapy: A Commentary on Chapter "Case Formulation in Standard Cognitive Therapy"") confirms many of the theoretical assumptions of the commented chapter from his unique viewpoint as a scholar who significantly contributed to the development of CBT, and explains how cognitive therapists manage the developing relationship across different clients in a manner that is wholly guided by the cognitive conceptualization. Nonspecific processes are relatively secondary with less complicated clients, whereas with more complicated clients they instantiate the case formulation in terms of the "three-legged stool": current life events, childhood antecedents, and therapeutic relationship. **Angelo Saliani**, **Claudia Perdighe**, **Barbara Barcaccia**, and **Francesco Mancini** (chapter "Commentary to Chapter "Case Formulation in Standard Cognitive Therapy": The Use of Goals in Cognitive Behavioral Therapy Case Formulation") introduce the role of goals in CT case formulation, which are often overlooked and may allow treatment of the problem of motivation from a cognitive viewpoint. It is fascinating to notice how goals and motivations represent a cognitive answer to the problem of the difficult detachment of some patients from their biased beliefs, an answer that makes it possible to conceive the subjective and emotional rationality that keeps patients stuck in their symptoms, an answer related to but distinct from the metacognitive model that we subsequently encounter.

Chapter "Case Formulation in the Behavioral Tradition: Meyer, Turkat, Lane, Bruch, and Sturmey" deals with the use of the shared case formulation in the behavioral tradition. This section owes much to the comprehensive and convincing description from Michael Bruch (2015) of the development of the concept of case formulation by Meyer (1957) and Turkat (1985, 1986). Meyer shares the case formulation with the patient in a way that is itself part of those environmental and behavioral circumstances that must be altered to achieve therapeutic change. The commentary for this chapter is written by **Peter Sturmey** (chapter "Some Thoughts on Chapter "Case Formulation in the Behavioral Tradition: Meyer, Turkat, Lane, Bruch, and Sturmey" *Case Formulation in the Behavioral Tradition: Meyer, Turkat, Lane, Bruch, and Sturmey* by Giovanni Maria Ruggiero, Gabriele Caselli and Sandra Sassaroli"), a major scholar in the behavioral tradition. He addresses four points: what is meant be "sharing a case formulation"; what is the relationship between case formulation and therapeutic relationship; what is the behavioral the conception of cognition and meta-cognition in behavioral case formulation; and, finally, what is the self-managed life?

Chapter "How B-C Connection and Negotiation of F Allow the Design and Implementation of a Cooperative and Effective Disputing in Rational Emotive Behavior Therapy," written by the editors in cooperation with **Diego Sarracino**, discusses how in Albert Ellis' rational emotive behavior therapy (REBT; DiGiuseppe et al. 2014; Ellis 1962; Ellis and Grieger 1986), the therapist uses three specific steps from the basic ABC DEF procedure of REBT—namely the B–C connection, D rationale, and F negotiation—to formulate the patient's problems, regulate the therapeutic process, and manage the therapeutic alliance. The healthy attitude is not to have negative thoughts but rather to tolerate them and not take their demands seriously and awfulize aspects. This REBT attitude anticipates metacognitive procedures. It is this unceasing sharing of the rationale of the therapy that allows the REBT therapist to show empathy and respect toward the patient. **Raymond DiGiuseppe** and **Kristene Doyle** (chapter "Commentary to Chapter "How B-C Connection and Negotiation of F Allow the Design and Implementation of a Cooperative and Effective Disputing in Rational Emotive Behavior Therapy." REBT's B-C connection and Negotiation of F") and **Wouter Backx** (chapter "Commentary to Chapter "How B-C Connection and Negotiation of F Allow the Design and Implementation of a Cooperative and Effective Disputing in Rational

Emotive Behavior Therapy." Commentary on Chapter "How B-C Connection and Negotiation of F Allow the Design and Implementation of a Cooperative and Effective Disputing in Rational Emotive Behavior Therapy": REBT Provides a firm Basis for Case Formulation by Employing an Ongoing, Implicit and Hypothetico-Deductive form of Data Collection in Critical Collaboration, Negotiation and an Equal Relationship with the Client"), who are among the major heirs of Albert Ellis' legacy, comment on this hypothesis. DiGiuseppe and Doyle expand on several points made in the commented chapter, including the importance of a solid therapeutic alliance and strategies to attain this, common factors in psychotherapy as they relate to REBT, the often overlooked and/or underrecognized behavioral consequences of irrational beliefs, important aspects of assessment and how it contributes to case conceptualization, how REBT in most cases involves a simultaneous process of assessment and treatment, a method that often deviates from many other CBT approaches, and important considerations of cognitive process and content domain. On the other hand, Backx emphasizes how in REBT the case formulation process is implicit and ongoing and the hypothetico-deductive method is used. While in chapter "How B-C Connection and Negotiation of F allow the Design and Implementation of a Cooperative and Effective Disputing in Rational Emotive Behavior Therapy" the editors have focused on the B–C connection, D rationale, and F negotiation, Backx stress that it takes place as well during the search for the critical A, the accurate IB (Irrational Belief), and during the formulation of the EB (Effective New Belief). The whole approach is built upon critical collaboration, negotiation and equality between client and therapist.

Chapter "Case Formulation in Process-Based Therapies," written by the editors in cooperation with **Andrea Bassanini**, discusses case formulation in more recent CBT approaches focused on cognitive processes. In schema therapy (ST; Arntz and van Genderen 2009; Young et al. 2003), the case is formulated in terms of cognitive patterns of the self that are not purely cognitive (as in Beck's CT). Further, this approach shows a strong interpersonal aspect rooted in the development of the patient and conceptualized in the so-called "modes" that are stereotypical and inflexible relational models. ST organizes case formulation in terms of schemata and modes to manage its therapeutic strategy. In the metacognitive therapy model (MCT; Wells 2008; Wells and Mathews 1994), case formulation is focused on the function of conscious executive choice that can become dysfunctional because of metacognitive biases. Given the importance of the concept of choice in MCT (Mathews and Wells 1999), case formulation in this model is, by definition, fully shared with the client on a conscious and collaborative level. The acceptance and commitment therapy model (ACT; Hayes and Strosahl 2004) belongs to the so-called "third wave" process of cognitive therapies and can be conceptualized as a reincarnation of Meyer's functionalist conception of case formulation in which the therapeutic task is focused on evaluating and sharing with the patient his or her mental functioning in order to plan the treatment (Hayes and Strosahl 2004). Finally, process-based CBT (PB-CBT; Hayes and Hofman 2018) integrates the standard CT approach into a process framework by formulating the case around fundamental biopsychosocial processes in target-specific situations with specific clients. **Avigal**

Snir and **Stefan Hofmann** comment on the description of case formulation in PB-CBT (chapter "Commentary on Chapter "Case Formulation in Process-Based Therapies": Process Based CBT as an Approach To Case Conceptualization") and describe how PB-CBT works under the assumption that the symptom is maintained and is also maintaining a network that is maladaptive and resilient for change; PB-CBT aims to help the client replace a maladaptive network with an adaptive one, to strengthen processes that promote well-being and experiences that goes in line with the clients' values and ambitions. **Paolo Moderato** and **Kelly Wilson** comment on the description of case formulation in ACT (chapter "Clinical Behavior Analysis, ACT and Case Formulation. A Commentary on Chapter "Case Formulation in Process-Based Therapies"") and stress how it is deeply rooted in Behavior Analysis. The basic points of Behavior Analysis are psychological flexibility, non-mentalistic assumption, functional analysis, and values. Psychological flexibility is an overarching complex repertoire of skills that allow clients to be open to the experience of the present moment and to direct their lives. Non-mentalistic assumption implies that ACT processes are behavioral patterns in context and shouldn't be cognitivized. Functional analysis is helpful to assess the patient's patterns of behavior that in many occasions were useful and functional and are maintained by strong contingencies of reinforcement but can be very harmful and dysfunctional in different contexts**.** In ACT the term values refers to patterns of activities that give our lives meaning. Regarding the rise of PB-CBT, the authors suggest that it could be a new version of the functional analysis integrated within multi-level, multi-dimensional evolutionary science. **Eckard Roediger**, **Nicola Marsigli** and **Gabriele Melli** in ST (chapter "Schema Therapy, Contextual Schema Therapy and Case Formulation: Commentary on Chapter "Case Formulation in Process-Based Therapies"") describe how schema therapy combines cognitive theory and developmental concepts. The impact of early childhood need frustrations leads to biased cognitive schemata. The focus on aversive early childhood experiences and resulting schemas broadens the scope of conventional cognitive case formulations into the very early childhood years. The experiential interventions used in Schema Therapy add an emotional dimension to the initial cognitive framework, by bringing the clients in touch with significant childhood experiences. All of these models introduce a second level of metacognitive processes in mental activity that allows the conceptualization of the difficulties of patients who are seemingly less able to detach from their biased cognitive contents. In addition, ST adds a developmental level in which cognitive biases are learned during the personal life of the patient, while ACT considers a motivational component: values.

Chapter "Strengths and Limitations of Case Formulation in Constructivist Cognitive Behavioral Therapies" is devoted to constructivist approaches. The central hypothesis of the chapter is that, in constructivist models, sharing case formulation is the outcome of an explorative process and not an initial move that sets the rules of the game. Of course, constructivism has contributed to the development of the practice of case formulation in the CBT domain: It introduced the concept of personal meanings with Bruner (1973) and Kelly (1955), and then transformed it into a clinical concept with Guidano (1991), Mahoney (2003), Neimeyer (2009), and other constructive thinkers and clinicians (Neimeyer and Mahoney 1995). On the other hand, as noted above, constructivist approaches that target hermeneutic, emotionally charged, and "tacit" cognition (Guidano 1991; Guidano and Liotti 1983; Mahoney 2003; Neimeyer and Mahoney 1995) may diverge from more standard CBT approaches in the use of case formulation. The most promising developments rooted in this tradition are the models of metacognitive and interpersonal therapy (MIT; Dimaggio et al. 2007; Semerari et al. 2014), which integrates interpersonal and metacognitive concepts, and dilemma focused therapy (DFT, Feixas and Compañ 2016). DFT is derived from Kelly's personal construct theory (Kelly 1955) and psychotherapy (Winter and Viney 2005) and proposes an interesting case formulation procedure based on a dilemmatic conception of the constructs of the self and of significant others. The comments on this chapter are written by many clinicians and theorists of the constructivist tradition: **Guillem Feixas** and **David Winter** (chapter "A Constructivist Pioneer of Formulation. A Commentary on Chapter "Strengths and Limitations of Case Formulation in Constructivist Cognitive Behavioral Therapies"") discuss how George Kelly introduced the notion of formulation in his personal construct psychology and its associated form of psychotherapy. The process of assessing and sharing the formulation, in which the clinician attempts to construe the construction processes of the client using a set of diagnostic constructs, is an example of what Kelly termed sociality. **Antonio Semerari** and **Antonino Carcione** (chapter "Commentary on the Presentation of the Metacognitive Interpersonal Therapy Model in Chapter "Strengths and Limitations of Case Formulation in Constructivist Cognitive Behavioral Therapies"") explain how their MIT is a treatment specific to relatively difficult patients with complex personality and psychotic disorders. Owing to their relational difficulties, these patients can activate problematic interpersonal cycles during treatment, in which the therapist is involved. In turn, relational difficulties are related to reduced metacognitive skills. **Benedetto Farina** (chapter "The Role of Trauma in Psychotherapeutic Complications and the Worth of Giovanni Liotti's Cognitive-Evolutionist Perspective (CEP): Commentary on Chapter "Strengths and Limitations of Case Formulation in Constructivist Cognitive Behavioral Therapies"") discuss how Liotti's cognitive-evolutionist perspective is a cognitive psychotherapeutic perspective focused on the treatment of psychopathology resulting from abusive and, more specifically, neglectful family and interpersonal contexts. CEP attempts to solve the problems and obstacles that developmental trauma generates on a relational, cognitive, and metacognitive level in psychotherapy and to provide theoretical and practical solutions to the relational difficulties of psychotherapy, in particular in the therapeutic alliance. **Maurizio Dodet** (chapter "The Case Formulation in the Post-Rationalist Constructivist Model. Commentary on Chapter "Strengths and Limitations of Case Formulation in Constructivist Cognitive Behavioral Therapies"") explains how the core of radical post-rationalist constructivism is the exploration of the self and of its identity and continuity processes. The model has a vision of the individual as an autonomous complex system builder of meanings, generating a feeling of continuity and unity central to the maintenance of a stable identity. An emotional disorder represents the attempt to maintain this feeling of continuity and unity of identity.

Fabio Monticelli (chapter "Case Formulation and the Therapeutic Relationship from an Evolutionary Theory of Motivation. Commentary to Chapter "Strengths and Limitations of Case Formulation in Constructivist Cognitive Behavioral Therapies"") clarifies some fundamental principles of the clinical use of the case formulation and the therapeutic relationship from an evolutionary theory of motivation (ETM) viewpoint. From an ETM perspective, the case formulation is conceived as a dynamic, concrete, and intensely emotional and relational element. It is formulated and shared with the patient at the beginning of the therapy—as happens in other cognitive behavioral treatments—but it is subject to continuous verification, especially during relational events. **Raffaella Visini** and **Saverio Ruberti** (chapter "Emotion, Motivation, Therapeutic Relationship and Cognition in Giovanni Liotti's Model: Commentary on Chapter "Strengths and Limitations of Case Formulation in Constructivist Cognitive Behavioral Therapies"") explain how Liotti based much of this relational elaboration on the construct of the interpersonal motivational system, using it as a privileged tool for the identification and exploration of universal rules based on innate and phylogenetically grounded principles which guide and orient intersubjective dynamics. Evolutionary, motivational and biological aspects are necessary in order to understand human emotional experiences and relational behavior. In Liotti's cognitive evolutionary orientation, the shared formulation of the case can be considered one of the effective interventions, but it does not in itself constitute the main instrument of therapeutic intervention and the therapeutic relationship. All of these theorists and clinicians seem interested in exploring the level of mental activity attentive to perceptual, non-verbal, relational, and traumatic-based aspects, which are emotional and not controlled by rational calculation and voluntary faculties.

Chapter "Case Formulation as an Outcome and Not an Opening Move in Relational and Psychodynamic Models" deals with case formulation models that emphasize the role of the therapeutic relationship, whether psychodynamic (e.g., Mitchell and Aron 1999) or constructivist (Bara 2018; Liotti and Monticelli 2014). The possible assumption of these models is that the case formulation cannot be completely shared at the beginning of treatment but is rather an outcome of the therapeutic process. These conceptions consider the therapeutic relationship as the unit of analysis for the disorder and as the field in which the psychopathological mechanism acts and the therapeutic process is applied. The consequence is that relational models share case formulation as the final result of an explorative path. This hypothesis is also applicable to modern psychodynamic models such as the control mastery theory (Silberschatz 2013), which includes a formulation procedure that can only be fully understood and shared after the client has unconsciously tested the therapist by recreating previous interpersonal experiences in the therapeutic relationship. Passing the tests creates conditions that allow the patient to acquire new emotional experiences that will help to disconfirm dysfunctional beliefs. The first commentary on this chapter is written by **Francesco Gazzillo** and **George Silberschatz** (chapter "Commentary to Chapter "Case Formulation as an Outcome and not an Opening Move in Relational and Psychodynamic Models": Plan Formulation vs. Case Formulation: The Perspective of Control-Mastery Theory") who clarify how in the Control-Mastery Theory (CMT) perspective both clinicians and researchers talk about *plan formulation* and not case formulation. The *plan formulation* includes the description of the adaptive *goals* that patients wish to achieve by disproving their unconscious *pathogenic beliefs*, and that derive from early attempts to deal with *traumatic and adverse developmental experiences*. In addition, in order to master their traumas, patients aim to disprove their pathogenic beliefs by unconsciously posing *tests the therapists*. Last, the *plan formulation* includes a description of *new experiences* or *insights* patients would like to have in order to better understand their problems. **Marco Innamorati** and **Mariano Ruperthuz Honorato** (chapter "Some Historical and Theoretical Remarks about Psychodynamic Assessment. Commentary on Chapter "Case Formulation as an Outcome and not an Opening Move in Relational and Psychodynamic Models"") discuss how the difference of attitude, with respect to case formulation, is tied to many factors, like the general setting of therapy and the theorists' epistemological attitude, which can be more or less realist, or, on the contrary, more or less hermeneuticist or constructionist. Single theorists' beliefs about the effect of case formulation are also important. They are, linked to the beliefs about *when* or even *if* it is possible to verbalize a case formulation to the patient. **Paolo Migone** (chapter "Case Formulation in Psychoanalysis and in Cognitive-Behavioral Therapies: Commentary on Chapter "Case Formulation as an Outcome and not an Opening Move in Relational and Psychodynamic Models"") writes that in psychodynamic therapy, case formulation is always present; it can be conceived in terms of understanding the patient's history, his or her life narrative. In a way, interpretation itself (a central concept of psychoanalysis) can be seen as a case formulation, i.e., the explanation to the patient of the meaning of his/her symptoms, the reason why he or she asked for help. The commentary discusses why case formulation at the beginning of the therapy is questionable in the treatment of difficult patients both in psychoanalysis and in cognitive behavioral therapies. These comments develop the theme of the non-rational mental states already explored in the previous chapters, taking it to the further level of the unconscious states of the psychodynamic models.

Chapter "The Empirical State of Case Formulation: Integrating and Validating Cognitive, Evolutionary and Procedural Elements in the CBT Case Formulation in the LIBET Procedure" presents a case formulation model by the editors of this book; it explores the possibility of integrating standard CBT, developmental, and process elements in case formulation. The model is called *Life Themes and Plans: Implications of Biased Beliefs Elicitation and Treatment* (LIBET; Sassaroli et al. 2017a, 2017b). The emotional disorder is conceptualized on two axes: (1) A negative evaluation of events and relational patterns, called "painful life themes," learned in significant experiences and relationships evaluated as intolerably painful and formulated in terms of self-beliefs, a concept based both on Kelly's personal constructs (Kelly 1955) and Beck's core belief concepts (Beck 1963); and (2) a rigid and one-dimensional management of life themes achieved by using avoidant, controlling, and/or impulsive coping strategies called "semi-functional plans," privileged even at the cost of renouncing to a significant degree areas of personal, relational, emotional, cognitive, and behavioral development. There is a third process level that keeps themes and plans dysfunctionally active. The LIBET procedure is both a process and a developmental response to the problem of conceptualizing and formulating the case in patients who show irrational and seemingly uncontrollable mental states, and it is aptly commented on by constructivist scholar **David Winter** (chapter "Commentary on Chapter "The Empirical State of Case Formulation: Integrating and Validating Cognitive, Evolutionary and Procedural Elements in the CBT Case Formulation in the LIBET Procedure": A Constructivist Perspective on LIBET"). His commentary endorses the use of shared case formulation as main therapeutic tool, and discusses the role of personal meanings and constructions, and their level of awareness. In addition, the capacity of the axes of the LIBET procedure of case formulation to describe the adaptive value of clients' constructions in certain areas of their lives, or at particular times, is acknowledged. On the other hand, the commentary critically remarks on the occasional difficulty of completely shedding a rationalist cognitive approach.

Last, **Christiane Eichenberg** (chapter "New Dimensions in Case Planning: Integration of E-mental Health Applications") discusses the most recent technological developments in case formulation and planning: the integration of online E-mental health applications. This paper treats the integration of digital support into psychotherapy, its impact on past case formulations, and recommendations on effective implementation of digital technology in the psychotherapeutic field. In the final section are discussed the empirical evidence on the inclusion of E-mental health in the case formulation. In the final afterword (chapter "Now's the Time: CBT Shares Case Formulation more (But not *too*) Easily"), the three editors themselves briefly discuss how the core assumptions of this book can be influenced by and profit from the observations and criticisms presented in the commentaries.

References

Arntz, A., & van Genderen, H. (2009). *Schema therapy for borderline personality disorder.* Chichester: John Wiley & Sons Ltd.

Asay, T. P., & Lambert, M. J. (1999). The empirical case for the common factors in therapy. In M. A. Hubble, B. L. Duncan, & S. D. Miller (Eds.), *The heart and soul of change: What works in therapy* (pp. 23–55). Washington, DC: American Psychological Association.

Bara, B. (2018). *Il terapeuta relazionale [The relational therapist].* Torino: Bollati Boringhieri.

Beck, A. T. (1963). Thinking and depression: I. Idiosyncratic content and cognitive distortions. *Archives of General Psychiatry, 9*, 324–333.

Beck, A. T. (1964). Thinking and depression: II. Theory and therapy. *Archives of General Psychiatry, 10*, 561–571.

Beck, A. T., Rush, A. J., Shaw, B. F., & Emery, G. (1979). *Cognitive therapy of depression.* New York, NY: Guilford Press.

Beck, J. S. (2005). *Cognitive therapy for challenging problems: What to do when the basics don't work.* New York, NY: Guilford Press.

Bruch, M. (2015). *Beyond diagnosis: Case formulation in cognitive behavioural therapy.* Chichester/New York, NY: John Wiley & Sons Ltd.

Bruch, M. H. (1998). Cognitive-behavioral case formulation. In E. Sanavio (Ed.), *Behavior and cognitive therapy today: Essays in honor of Hans J. Eysenck* (pp. 31–48). Kidlington, Oxford: Pergamon.
Bruner, J. (1973). *Going beyond the information given*. New York, NY: Norton.
Caspar, F. (1995). *Plan analysis: Toward optimizing psychotherapy*. Boston, MA: Hogrefe & Huber Publishers.
Caspar, F. (2007). Plan analysis. In T. D. Eells (Ed.), *Handbook of psychotherapy case formulation* (pp. 251–289). New York, NY: Guilford Press.
Clark, D. A., & Beck, A. T. (2010). *Cognitive therapy of anxiety disorders: Science and practice*. New York, NY: Guilford Press.
Critchfield, K. L., Panizo, M. T., & Benjamin, L. S. (2019). Formulating key psychosocial mechanisms of psychopathology and change in interpersonal reconstructive therapy. In U. Kramer (Ed.), *Case formulation for personality disorders* (pp. 181–201). London: Academic.
DiGiuseppe, R., Doyle, K. A., Dryden, W., & Backx, W. (2014). *A Practioner's guide to rational emotive behavior therapy*. New York, NY: Oxford University Press.
Dimaggio, G., Semerari, A., Carcione, A., Nicolò, G., & Procacci, M. (2007). *Psychotherapy of personality disorders: Metacognition, states of mind and interpersonal cycles*. London: Routledge.
Dobson, K. S., & Dozois, D. J. A. (2001). Historical and philosophical bases of the cognitive-behavioral therapies. In K. S. Dobson (Ed.), *Handbook of cognitive-behavioral therapies* (pp. 3–39). New York, NY: Guilford Press.
Eells, T. D. (2007). *Handbook of psychotherapy case formulation*. New York, NY: Guilford Press.
Eells, T. D. (2011). *Handbook of psychotherapy case formulation* (2nd ed.). New York, NY: Guilford Press.
Eells, T. D. (2015). *Psychotherapy case formulation*. Arlington, VA: American Psychological Association.
Ellis, A. (1962). *Reason and emotion in psychotherapy*. New York, NY: Stuart.
Ellis, A., & Grieger, R. M. (Eds.). (1986). *Handbook of rational-emotive therapy* (Vol. 2). New York, NY: Springer.
Fassbinder, E., Brand-de Wilde, O., & Arntz, A. (2019). Case formulation in schema therapy: Working with the mode model. In U. Kramer (Ed.), *Case formulation for personality disorders* (pp. 77–94). London: Academic.
Feixas, G., & Compañ, V. (2016). Dilemma-focused intervention for unipolar depression: A treatment manual. *BMC Psychiatry, 16*, 235. https://doi.org/10.1186/s12888-016-0947-x.
Gabbard, G. O. (2017). *Long-term psychodynamic psychotherapy: A basic text*. Arlington, VA: American Psychiatric Pub.
Guidano, V. F. (1991). *The self in process: toward a post-rationalist cognitive therapy*. New York, NY: Guilford Press.
Guidano, V. F., & Liotti, G. (1983). *Cognitive processes and emotional disorders: A structural approach to psychotherapy*. New York, NY: Guilford Press.
Hayes, S. C., & Hofman, S. G. (2018). *Process-based CBT. The science and core clinical competencies of cognitive behavioral therapy*. Oakland, CA: Context Press, New Harbinger.
Hayes, S. C., & Strosahl, K. D. (2004). *A practical guide to acceptance and commitment therapy*. New York, NY: Guildford Press.
Kanfer, F. H., & Saslow, G. (1969). Behavioural diagnosis. In C. M. Franks (Ed.), *Behaviour therapy: Appraisal and status*. New York, NY: McGraw-Hill.
Kelly, G. A. (1955). *The psychology of personal constructs: Vol 1 and 2*. New York, NY: Norton.
Kuyken, W. (2006). Evidence-based case formulation: Is the emperor clothed? In N. Tarrier (Ed.), *Case formulation in cognitive behaviour therapy. The treatment of challenging and complex cases* (pp. 28–51). Hove/New York, NY: Routledge.
Lazarus, A. A. (1960). The elimination of children's phobias by deconditioning. In H. J. Eysenck (Ed.), *Behaviour therapy and the neuroses*. Oxford: Pergamon.
Lazarus, A. A. (1976). *Multimodal behavior therapy*. New York, NY: Springer.

Liotti, G., & Monticelli, F. (2014). *Teoria e clinica dell'alleanza terapeutica. Una prospettiva cognitivo-evoluzionista [Therapeutic alliance theory and clinic. A cognitive-evolutionary perspective]*. Milano: Raffaello Cortina editore.

Mahoney, M. J. (2003). *Constructive psychotherapy: A practical guide*. New York, NY: Guilford.

Mathews, G., & Wells, A. (1999). The cognitive science of attention and emotion. In T. Dalgleish & M. Power (Eds.), *Handbook of cognition and emotion* (pp. 171–192). New York, NY: Wiley.

McWilliams, N. (1999). *Psychoanalytic case formulation*. New York, NY: Guilford.

Meyer, V. (1957). The treatment of two phobic patients on the basis of learning principles. *The Journal of Abnormal and Social Psychology, 55*(2), 261.

Meyer, V., & Turkat, I. D. (1979). Behavioral analysis of clinical cases. *Journal of Behavioral Assessment, 1*(4), 259–270.

Mitchell, S. A., & Aron, L. E. (1999). *Relational psychoanalysis: The emergence of a tradition*. Hillsdale, NJ: Analytic Press.

Neimeyer, R. A. (2009). *Constructivist psychotherapy. Distinctive features*. London: Routledge.

Neimeyer, R. A., & Mahoney, M. J. (Eds.). (1995). *Constructivism in Psychotherapy*. Washington, DC: APA Press.

Perry, J. C., Knoll, M., & Tran, V. (2019). Motives, defences, and conflicts in the dynamic formulation for psychodynamic psychotherapy using the idiographic conflict formulation method. In U. Kramer (Ed.), *Case formulation for personality disorders* (pp. 203–224). London: Academic.

Persons, J. B., & Tomkins. (2007). Cognitive-behavioral case formulation. In T. D. Eells (Ed.), *Handbook of psychotherapy case formulation* (pp. 290–316). New York, NY: Guilford Press.

Sassaroli, S., Caselli, G., Bassanini, & Ruggiero, G. M. (2017a). Procedure e protocollo di terapia LIBET seconda parte: fasi del protocollo e caso clinico Antonia A [LIBET therapy procedures and protocol second part: protocol phases and clinical case Antonia A]. *Psicoterapia Cognitiva e Comportamentale, 32*, 331–344.

Sassaroli, S., Caselli, G., Redaelli, C., & Ruggiero, G. M. (2017b). Procedure e protocollo di terapia LIBET – prima parte: le procedure ABC-LIBET, laddering e disputing [LIBET therapy procedures and protocol first part: ABC-LIBET procedures, laddering, and disputing]. *Psicoterapia Cognitiva e Comportamentale, 23*, 73–92.

Semerari, A., Colle, L., Pellecchia, G., Buccione, I., Dimaggio, G., Nicolò, G., Procacci, M., & Pedone, R. (2014). Metacognitive dysfunctions in personality disorders: correlations with disorder severity and personality styles. *Journal of Personality Disorders, 28*, 751–766.

Shapiro, M. B. (1955). Training of clinical psychologists at the institute of psychiatry. *Bulletin of the British Psychological Society, 8*, 1–6.

Shapiro, M. B. (1957). Experimental methods in the psychological description of the individual psychiatric patient. *International Journal of Social Psychiatry, 111*, 89–102.

Silberschatz, G. (Ed.). (2013). *Transformative relationships: The control mastery theory of psychotherapy*. London: Routledge.

Sturmey, P. (2008). *Behavioral case formulation and intervention: A functional analytic approach* (Vol. 89). Chichester/New York, NY: Wiley.

Sturmey, P. (Ed.). (2009). *Clinical case formulation: Varieties of approaches*. Chichester/New York, NY: Wiley.

Turkat, I. D. (1985). *Behavioural case formulation*. New York, NY: Plenum.

Turkat, I. D. (1986). The behavioural interview. In A. R. Ciminero, K. S. Calhoun, & H. E. Adams (Eds.), *Handbook of behavioural assessment* (2nd ed.). Chichester/New York, NY: Wiley.

Wampold, B. E., & Imel, Z. E. (2015). *The great psychotherapy debate: The evidence for what makes psychotherapy work* (2nd ed.). New York, NY: Routledge.

Weerasekera, P. (1996). *Multiperspective case formulation: A step towards treatment integration*. Florida, FL: Krieger Publishing Company.

Wells, A. (2008). *Metacognitive therapy for anxiety and depression*. London: Guilford Press.

Wells, A., & Mathews, G. (1994). *Attention and emotion: A clinical perspective*. Hove/Hillsdale, NJ: Erlbaum.

Winter, D. A., & Viney, L. L. (Eds.). (2005). *Personal construct psychotherapy. Advances in theory, practice and research*. London: Whurr Publishers.

Wolpe, J. (1954). Reciprocal inhibition as the main basis of psychotherapeutic effects. *AMA Archives of Neurology & Psychiatry, 72*, 205–226.

Yates, A. J. (1958). The application of learning theory to the treatment of tics. *The Journal of Abnormal and Social Psychology, 56*, 175–182.

Young, J. E., Klosko, J. S., & Weishaar, M. (2003). *Schema therapy: A practitioner's guide*. New York, NY: Guilford.

Case Formulation in Standard Cognitive Therapy

Giovanni Maria Ruggiero, Gabriele Caselli, and Sandra Sassaroli

Contents

The Standard Model of Cognitive Therapy

This chapter deals with the case formulation applied to Beck's cognitive therapy (CT; Beck 1963, 1964; Beck et al. 1979) that, among the cognitive behavioral therapy (CBT) approaches, is the model that has received the most reliable confirmation of effectiveness. For the sake of clarity, it has to be noted that in the UK and sometimes in other European countries, CT is called standard cognitive behavioral therapy (standard CBT; Clark and Beck 2010), leading to the risk of terminological

G. M. Ruggiero (✉)
"Psicoterapia Cognitiva e Ricerca," Cognitive Psychotherapy School and Research Center, Milan, Italy

Sigmund Freud University, Milan, Italy

Sigmund Freud University, Vienna, Austria
e-mail: gm.ruggiero@milano-sfu.it

G. Caselli
Sigmund Freud University, Milan, Italy

Sigmund Freud University, Vienna, Austria

Department of Psychology, London South Bank University, London, UK

S. Sassaroli
Sigmund Freud University, Milan, Italy

Sigmund Freud University, Vienna, Austria

"Studi Cognitivi," Cognitive Psychotherapy School and Research Center, Milan, Italy

G. M. Ruggiero et al. (eds.), *CBT Case Formulation as Therapeutic Process*,
https://doi.org/10.1007/978-3-030-63587-9_2

confusion between the broad and general domain of the many cognitive behavioral approaches, also called "CBT approaches" and the particular form of CT, also called "standard CBT." For instance, in the domain of all CBT approaches in a broad sense there are also the models of Ellis' rational emotive behavior therapy (REBT; DiGiuseppe et al. 2014; Ellis 1962; Ellis and Grieger 1986) and the many so called constructivist psychotherapies (Feixas and Compañ 2016; Guidano and Liotti 1983; Guidano 1991; Mahoney 1995, 2003; Neimeyer 2009; Neimeyer and Mahoney 1995; Winter and Viney 2005). These cousin models of CT/standard CBT will be discussed in their specific chapters of this book, respectively 6 and 15. In this chapter, therefore, we always use the term "CT" to refer to either CT or standard CBT, while the term "CBT" refers only to the general domain of all CBT approaches.

Of course, the CBT approaches are grouped in the same domain because they show significant commonalities. CT, REBT, and constructivist psychotherapies have all historically adopted the clinical cognitive principle that emotional disorders are dependent on automatically distorted mental contents that can be modified through conscious verbal reattribution. A canonical definition can be found in Dobson and Dozois (2001), according to which the historical CBT approaches share three fundamental principles:

1. The mediational role of cognition, which states that there is always a cognitive processing and evaluation of internal and external events that may influence an individual's response to such events;
2. The possibility that cognitive activity is reasonably accessible to the consciousness and can be monitored, evaluated, measured, and re-elaborated in a limited time through conscious choices in an explicitly negotiated collaboration between patient and therapist;
3. The behavioral change can be mediated and encouraged by these cognitive evaluations and can therefore be considered an indirect sign of cognitive change.

However, these commonalities, although noteworthy, were not so significant as to determine procedures common to all CBT approaches for the management and conception of case formulation. To understand how these three models use case formulation, it is crucial to highlight several of the differences apparent among CT, REBT, and constructivist psychotherapy. In fact, there are other features that are common to some CBT approaches, albeit not to all of them.

As an instance, an aspect absent in REBT but present in both CT and constructivist psychotherapies is that both these traditions have organized their clinical work around biased cognitive contents focused mainly on the self (Wells and Mathews 1994: p. 2), such as the core self-beliefs of CT (Beck 1995: p. 169, 2011: p. 233) and the personality organizations outlined in the constructivist tradition (Guidano and Liotti 1983; Mahoney 2003). In both traditions, we can observe the emergence of a taxonomy of core variables focused on the self that plays a structural role in providing guidance, coherence, coordination, and integration to mental states (Bandura 1977, 1988; Markus 1977; Markus and Nurius 1986; Markus and Sentis 1982; Neisser 1967). On the other hand, an aspect absent in the constructivist approaches but present in both CT and REBT is that, while CT and REBT have tended to

Table 1 Comparison of cognitive therapy (CT), rational emotive behavior therapy (REBT), and constructivist psychotherapy

Emphasis on	CT	REBT	Constructivist psychotherapy
Self-knowledge	X	–	X
Conscious knowledge	X	X	–

emphasize the conscious aspect of cognition, most constructivist cognitive psychotherapies have also shown interest in tacit, perceived, and experienced knowledge not represented in the internal discourse and not easily verbalized (Guidano 1987, 1991; Mahoney 1995, 2003). Table 1 summarizes the differences and similarities between these three historical CBT approaches.

Self-Beliefs, Collaborative Empiricism, and Sharing the Case Formulation

The structural key role attributed to the negative core self-beliefs in the CT model play a key role in its case formulation conception and in its sharing procedure. It plausibly helped Beck to formalize the CT procedures in amenable and user-friendly ways for use by clinicians. However, this advantage was acquired at the price of increasing the risk of conceiving the therapeutic process as the mechanical discovery of biased self-beliefs, in which the active part is fully entrusted to the therapist while the role of the patient may (at least seemingly) look passive, reducing his or her role to being instructed to take note of the cognitive biases and abandon them as an automatic effect of the instruction. The assessment of dysfunctional mechanisms partially risked not being used as a shared tool for conscious and active change—especially by the patient—and the monitoring of clinical work, but as a tool for modification that inadvertently encouraged locking the patient in a passive position. This effect—although always avoided by Beck, who unsurprisingly spoke of collaborative empiricism from the very beginning (Hollon and Beck 1979)—may be implied in the CT theoretical approach that emphasizes the structural role of self-beliefs. It is not coincidental that, notwithstanding the widespread agreement regarding the central role of collaborative empiricism in CT, there has been little theoretical analysis of the construct, as noted by Tee and Kazantzis (2011).

A possible consequence of the insufficiently explored definition of collaborative empiricism may be that in Beck's initial works, the aspect of sharing the case formulation procedure is present but not always sufficiently emphasized. Perhaps the need to share the case in CT—and in other CBT approaches as well—seemed to be a step that could be taken for granted in the implementation of the formulation process itself. This reduced emphasis on the shared component in the implementation of case formulation exposes CT to an accusation of rationalism, suggesting that its process occurs through the non-shared imposition of a software that has to be implanted in the patient's mind and that can work without his or her active cooperation. It is a typical accusation by several constructivist theorists who have argued that CT procedures are too didactical and mechanically directive and are therefore at risk of undermining the therapeutic alliance (Guidano 1987, 1991; Mahoney 1995, 2003).

It is not coincidental that Tee and Kazantzis (2011) have responded to this criticism by arguing that Beck's collaborative empiricism "is not simply willing participation by the client nor agreement on tasks or goals. Rather, the cognitive therapist aims to engage the client in a genuine sharing of the work of goal setting and creative authorship of therapeutic tasks, progressively encouraging the client to take the lead role in these activities as far as is practicable" (Tee and Kazantzis 2011, p. 49). Therefore, collaborative empiricism is a "stylistic fulcrum that permits the helping alliance to thrive" (Stein et al. 2006, p. 359).

Moreover, Tee and Kazantzis (2011) argue that collaborative empiricism may act as a specific change process in CT, as well as the classical CBT principle of cognitive mediation: Direct changes in clients' beliefs. In fact, belief change is plausibly more likely to happen if the rationale for change comes from a collaborative task, rather than from didactic illustration by the therapist (Dattilio and Padesky 1990). Tee and Kazantzis (2011) have also argued that a possible theoretical ground for their clinical hypothesis can be found in the model of Self-determination theory by Deci and Ryan (2002). This model states that people's behaviors are regulated on a continuum ranging from intrinsic and autonomous regulation to external regulation and that intrinsic regulation is more likely to lead to significant change. Accordingly, collaborative empiricism clearly parallels the concept of intrinsic regulation.

This definition of collaborative empiricism by Tee and Kazantzis seems to be in line with the concept of shared case formulation discussed in this book. Moreover, from our point of view shared case formulation advances one step forward by being a more operational and specific concept for CBT approaches than that of collaborative empiricism. As an instance, from an operational viewpoint sharing with the patient the case formulation (that means sharing a model of the emotional disfunctions, of the rationale of the behavioral change, and of the interventions) have much in common with the factors of change proposed in the Self-determination model: A meaningful rationale for behavior change, the possibility of active participation and exercising of choice, and the acceptance and acknowledgment of negative feelings (Markland et al. 2005).

From Case Formulation to Shared Case Formulation

In spite of the aforementioned clinical problems, Beck deserves credit for including shared case formulation in the CT procedure from its origins, although he gave it a different name. In chapter "Commentary to Chapter "How B-C Connection and Negotiation of F Allow the Design and Implementation of a Cooperative and Effective Disputing in Rational Emotive Behavior Therapy." REBT's B-C Connection and Negotiation of F" of his *Cognitive Therapy and Emotional*

Disorders, Beck (1976) describes his procedure of analysis of problematic situations and introduces the term "formulation" several times. Faced with the objection of the patient's possible resistance, Beck fully agrees that the patient can respond to this initial formulation with the two opposite attitudes of skepticism or condescension. Beck remarks that these difficulties, although present, should not be underrated or exaggerated. The nature of the therapeutic alliance in CT is neither that of immediate adherence nor of continuous and devious sabotage. In reality, it is only natural that sometimes the patient would assume a critical and waiting position; this attitude should not be confused with a more or less unconscious sterile opposition. Understanding should be sought in an initial arrangement in which the patient agrees to test the proposed model and its capacity to generate well-being. The patient is encouraged not to adhere to an abstract and naive dependence of emotion on rationality but rather to trust more his or her capacity of executive mastery of mental states guided by rational reasoning.

Beck insists that it is necessary to negotiate an agreement between the patient's and therapist's expectations (Beck 1976). The difficulties listed by Beck can ultimately be reduced to one: the tension between the patient's hope for emotional relief without active engagement and the therapist's task of encouraging the patient to seek relief through active engagement. In the CT procedure, the patient's hope of passively finding relief is not attributable to more or less unconscious resistance but to erroneous beliefs about mental functioning. The patient underrates his or her capacity to master mental functioning. The core then becomes the active sharing with the patient of the aware knowledge of cognitive and behavioral dysfunctionality, and then sharing the case formulation.

Over time, a growing awareness appears to have emerged in the CBT literature that it is necessary to explicitly instruct the therapist to share the formulation of the case with the patient. CT manuals have increasingly emphasized the need to manage the treatment by sharing case formulations in order to effectively implement the assessment and reformulation of negative core self-beliefs. As an instance, in the classic manuals of CT by Judith Beck (Beck 1995, 2011), we find a definition as well as a detailed and operational description of the therapeutic use of shared case formulation. The main tool in the CT of case sharing is the Cognitive Conceptualization Diagram (CCD, Beck 2011, p. 200). In CT, the therapist uses the components of the CCD—core beliefs, intermediate beliefs, and coping strategies—to provide the patient with a psychopathological interpretation and a therapeutic re-qualification of the reported problematic situations by questioning him or her. The term "sharing" emphasizes the therapist's task of constantly communicating and discussing any emerging aspects of the formulation with the patient and using it as a tool to manage the direction of the therapeutic process. Moreover, in CT the diagram is fundamental in managing the therapeutic relationship in so-called complex cases, i.e. cases that undermine the therapeutic alliance. Beck (2011) suggests that the problem in complex cases should be addressed at the relational level, and the CCD can be used to conceptualize relational obstacles to therapy and find solutions for relational difficulties using a careful analysis of distorted interpersonal beliefs.

Shared Case Formulation and Therapeutic Alliance

Therefore, in CT, and also in other CBT approaches (but not in all of them), the explicit sharing of case formulation can be the clinical tool that allows us to manage the therapeutic alliance and relationship in a specific CBT manner. In fact, in the therapeutic tradition of CBT approaches, while the alliance and relationship were mentioned and not underrated, they were not considered to be the theoretical center of therapy. In the worst scenario, the alliance was mentioned only in order to indicate a particular situation of non-cooperation of the patient that must be clinically managed through good practice interventions. Another tradition refers to collaborative empiricism in the CBT literature as the foundation for the alliance (Dattilio and Hanna 2012; Kazantzis et al. 2013; Tee and Kazantzis 2011). Collaborative empiricism parallels Bordin's conception of the alliance that comprises the client-therapist "bond" and "agreement" on the goals and tasks of therapy (Dattilio and Hanna 2012). However, Bordin's "agreement" seems to reveal a lesser degree of both active participation of the patient and shared contribution with him or her in comparison to the CT conception. As written previously, Bordin's working alliance focuses on sharing the tasks and goals of therapy (Bordin 1979, p. 254), while Beck's collaborative empiricism focuses on sharing "the work of goal setting and creative authorship of therapeutic tasks" (Tee and Kazantzis 2011, p. 49).

However, in the common principles of the CBT approaches proposed by Dobson and Dozois (2001), the theoretical and clinical link between case formulation and therapeutic relationship is implied, although not explicitly mentioned (Knapp and Beck 2008). In fact, it follows from those principles that the therapeutic change occurs in a type of collaboration and alliance between therapist and patient that allows the patient to be informed and encouraged to share the formulation of his or her own case and the rationale and objectives of the treatment. This clinical need of the therapist's and patient's full awareness from the very beginning of the therapeutic process implies that in CBT approaches, and particularly in CT, there is a characteristic conception of the use of case formulation. In the CT and CBT approaches closest to it, case formulation can be an operational tool with which the therapist manages the entire psychotherapeutic process, including CT-treatment-specific interventions, as well as non-specific ones, such as the therapeutic alliance and relationship.

Shared Case Formulation: Clinical Examples

Assessment. At this point, we introduce a practical illustration of the management of case formulation in the CT procedure, i.e. through the shared assessment of the CCD. A practical illustration is the best way to highlight the operationally shared character of the formulation procedure. It is not our intention to provide an exhaustive and detailed description of the entire process of assessing emotional disorders according to the CT procedure; this task is much better performed by Judith Beck (2011) in her manual. We prefer to illustrate and comment on the CT procedure by highlighting and analyzing some of the procedure's steps that are most useful to promote formulation sharing. Of course, these steps are presented and interpreted from our viewpoint and cannot be considered a didactic illustration of the CT procedure.

To achieve this shared agreement, Beck J. uses a simple and straightforward approach, quickly explaining to the patient that the problem depends on the thoughts and ideas that upset him or her, followed by an invitation to actively examine them (Beck 2011, p. 19). This direct approach may appear to be simplistic and is one of the causes of the accusation of rationalism. However, it is not as simple as it first appears: Behind this invitation, there is an immediate encouragement to the patient to detach from such thoughts and start thinking of themselves as beings distinct and separate from their beliefs. This is already a preliminary sharing of the case formulation. Indeed, the most common mistake of patients is the position of merging with their own thoughts, so the person thinks they are wholly resolved in what they think.

CCD fulfillment begins with the identification of problematic situations. In this initial step, we can already identify an element of sharing that should not be overlooked. CT therapy, in fact, tends to be applied to specific problems or disorders and therefore starts from the request to start from typical problematic situations and not from vaguely described problems.

Can you tell me a specific situation in which your problem/disorder occurred?

In the CT setting, this question is not necessarily accompanied by an immediate explanation of its rationale. On the other hand, in a CBT approach that emphasizes the role of shared case formulation, the therapist is encouraged to share with the patient an explanation of why it is preferred to start by assessing a specific situation. Of course, sharing can be done immediately or after an appropriate interval if the therapist perceives a need for a prolonged and relaxed report by the patient without initial interruptions. In both cases, the therapist who pays attention to share the case formulation could say something like this:

In our approach, we prefer to start from specific situations defined in time and space because the treatment is set on specific problems, although of course we will also look for patterns that are repeated in different situations.

The next step is one of the most characteristic strategic actions of CBT approaches: the assessment of automatic thoughts carried out with the classic question:

What was going through your mind at that moment?

Once again, in a CBT approach that emphasizes sharing the case formulation and treatment rationale, this question should be asked to ascertain automatic thoughts and make the patient more aware of the link between thoughts and mental states. This link is not one-sided and mechanical; rather, it comprises encouraging an increase in the ability to executively master mental states. As in the case of the identification of problematic situations, the rationale must be clarified to the client in order to encourage sharing at each step. Therefore, something like the following can be relayed to the patient at the appropriate time:

In this approach, becoming aware of what is going through your mind at the moment of emotional distress is important. We believe that it is precisely in those momentary thoughts to which we often give little importance that there is the key to both understand the reasons of the emotional suffering and get the possibility of getting out of it.

This sharing communicates to the patient that dysfunctional thoughts are processed in an automatic mode, in which the patient takes for granted the notion that no executive control can be exercised. This intervention suggests the idea that, in reality, executive control is possible.

A hard step then follows, but it may be an opportunity for another shared clarification of the treatment rationale. The patient sometimes responds by not reporting the thoughts that went through his or her head at the moment of the problematic situation. Instead, they might report other subsequent or previous thoughts, or even interpretations he or she is having during the session. These thoughts are sometimes incongruously reasonable—incongruously because at that moment it is not yet useful to produce functional alternatives given that their appearance makes it hard to assess significant dysfunctional thoughts. Instead of reporting dysfunctional beliefs, the patient provides a kind of early questioning of little therapeutic value. For example, he or she might report something like this:

Actually, I know that I worry too much and probably nothing I fear will happen.

This statement, however, must not be devalued: It must be validated and put aside momentarily:

It is important that you are aware that perhaps your fears are exaggerated. This thought, however, is perhaps not what went through your mind when you were upset. Now let's focus on what was going through your mind at that very moment and that didn't help you.

This step can be useful in order to reiterate the rationale of reporting what exactly went through the patient's mind at the problematic moment:

Let's try to understand together why in this approach being aware of what goes through your head at the moment of emotional distress is particularly important. The fleeting thoughts that we do not pay attention to in the moment of emotional distress are the object of our work; by remembering them better and understanding that we can work them out in order to feel better.

The next step is just as significant; it is the *down arrow* procedure, i.e. the assessment of the meaning of automatic thoughts, carried out by asking what the reported thoughts mean or imply in more personal terms.

And what does that mean to you? What's the problem with that?

This question brings us closer to the core belief about the self, which can either emerge spontaneously or be explicitly asked for by the therapist:

So how do you see yourself in that situation? You are ...

In this case, the procedure must not be expressed in a mechanical way. It can once again provide an opportunity to share with the patient the rationale of the CT approach, namely that emotional reactions are related to cognitive states processed in dysfunctional terms (Beck 2011, pp. 159–161). This way of connecting thoughts about the self, the world, and emotions has sometimes been accused of abstract intellectualism, but it can also be conceived as a validation that normalizes the patient's emotions. For example, you could tell the patient:

The point is to understand that fearing this situation implies that you judge yourself as an inadequate person and/or that the world is a dangerous place. This meaning is what turns a tolerable unpleasant feeling into an intolerable anxiety. In other words, you use emotions not to relate to situations but to judge yourself: because you are worried then you see yourself as stupid or fragile. This chain of thoughts should no longer be considered as an unchangeable object but as something you can work out.

When the patient learns the concept of the maladaptive interpretation of emotional states, he or she also learns that emotions are not necessarily dysfunctional *per se*. Rather, they can read them as a definition of the self or of the world and not as a signal of a problematic scenario. For example, anxiety is not used as a signal of a possible risk but as an evaluation of a supposed personal inadequacy: If I have anxiety, then I am not up to it.

From this viewpoint, the definition of a dysfunctional mental state in the CT model, including the emotional state, welcomes the constructive criticism that has rejected the rationalistic definition of maladaptive states as erroneous evaluations of reality. The constructivist theory is right: Dysfunctionality is better defined as a maladaptive and rigid application of personal meanings that *per se* are neither wrong nor right (Guidano 1987, 1991; Mahoney 1995, 2003). It is important to understand how this normalizing intervention is best carried out by integrating it with the sharing of the case formulation, in the following terms:

The problem is not feeling anxiety but how you use it. The problem is using anxiety to make evaluations about yourself. How do you consider yourself in this situation where you have anxiety?

In this passage, what matters is that, in contrast to the patient's viewpoint in which situations generate emotions, the CCD visually represents a reversed perspective: The core beliefs and the coping strategies are above while the situations are below. In this way, the patient is encouraged to overturn the relationship between mental states and situations. The patient is then invited to reflect on how the subjective hardness of situations may depend on a thought of personal inadequacy and not vice versa. The question that introduces this topic may be as follows:

Now let's think. If you think in some way that you are inadequate (core beliefs) and that consequently (assumptions) you must avoid exposing yourself (coping strategy), what will you think in daily situations and how will you face them?

Followed once again by a generalization of the pattern:

You could apply this way of reworking thoughts to other scenarios as well. The idea would be that every thought should not be taken for granted just because it has crossed our minds but can be critically examined. You can work on that.

In the same natural way, we can introduce the phase of *questioning*:

Now that we have assessed which thoughts are not helping you, we can also question them. Every time we have a thought we take it as true. What if we question it instead? What if we don't take it as true?

But most of all:

What if the therapy consists not only of understanding and reworking these thoughts, but of learning to recognize and to rework them by yourself?

The procedure must be repeated for the assessment of emotions and behaviors, especially safety behaviors. Emotions must be understood by connecting them to thoughts:

Do you see the relationship between what you feel, what you think, and what you do? In this case, between anxiety, thoughts of inadequacy, and a tendency to avoid certain situations?

We can further stress this point:

Once again, it is important not only that you understand this connection but also that you learn to actively seek out these connections on your own. In this way, you can learn to master your mental states.

This statement implies that psychological disorders comprise biased versions of normal emotions and behaviors and are not a condition of insanity.

From what you're telling me, you're suffering from anxiety. This anxiety makes sense and we'll find its meaning together. It's not to be understood as some kind of disease.

In other words, the therapist helps the patient to conceive his or her symptoms in human terms, as dysfunctional forms of mental states that are meaningful and in themselves normal.

You're anxious because you're worried about something. We'll figure out what you're worried about. However, we also have to understand the use you make of your anxiety, the way in which your anxiety can become an obstacle.

Same with the behavior:

And when you feel this anxiety, what do you do?

And after the patient's response:

If I may summarize, it seems to me that when you feel this anxiety you tend to avoid situations.

Such behavior, which we call avoidance, could in turn be understood as a kind of illness. It must therefore be reformulated as a behavior that may make sense.

Avoidance in itself is not wrong. Sometimes it can be useful. It can be a wise behavior that indicates awareness of one's limits. The problem, however, is the mechanical use of this behavior.

In this way, we provide the patient with a model in which his or her "disease" corresponds to emotional states that are used as obstacles and not as signals for appropriate behaviors. It may be useful to add:

I would like you to keep these two variables in mind: emotions as obstacles and not as signals and behaviors as understandable but rigid reactions.

And further:

Whenever you feel the emotional distress that brought you into therapy, you may ask yourself: What is the emotion that I am using as an obstacle and what behavior am I tempted to put into action mechanically?

The relentless sharing of case formulation, as well as the treatment rationale serves to build what in other orientations is called a therapeutic alliance. Beck herself reports that the first principle of CT is a constantly evolving formulation of patients' problems (Beck 2011).

After problem situations have been ascertained in the lower half of the CCD, they will be combined into a unitary model in the upper half, in which we find core beliefs, intermediate beliefs, and coping strategies. As is well known, in core beliefs the meanings of automatic thoughts are summarized in general thoughts about the self, the world, relationships, or the future.

Although CT is focused on the here and now, Judith Beck added a focus on relevant childhood data in which the therapist seeks to understand with the patient how core beliefs were born and maintained and what events in life (especially childhood events) might be related to the development and maintenance of a belief (Beck 2011, pp. 32–35). This developmental procedure—even if more abstract— adds a level of awareness that is useful in CT questioning.

Furthermore, in this case, the core of shared case formulation remains that every step is implemented in order to increase the patient's awareness of the treatment's formulation and rationale. It is easy to lose this awareness because too many steps may seem obvious in the eyes of the therapist and are therefore not shared with the patient. During the assessment of relevant childhood experiences, the patient could be told:

Your anxiety or tendency to avoid problematic situations may be related to past experiences. Somehow you have learned in past moments that anxiety means something hopelessly negative about yourself and that it is preferable to avoid situations of this kind.

Judith Beck's practical use of the CCD helps us to understand how case formulation in the CT model is not just a theoretical framework. Rather, it is a concrete intervention that allows the therapist to establish a therapeutic alliance in emotional terms, namely by creating an atmosphere of trust, cooperation, and pragmatic terms and sharing with the patient a general hypothesis of his or her psychological distress and the treatment mechanism. When the therapist shares the case formulation with the patient, it should not be presented as a theory of the mind working without the patient's consent but as a common working hypothesis that establishes a set of rules. It describes the patient's ongoing attempt to deal with the emotional and external limitations of his or her development. Therefore, the following is inappropriate:

NON-SHARED FORMULATION: *Your distress depends on a series of biased thoughts that this therapy will change.*

In reality, the following is appropriate:

SHARED FORMULATION: *My job is to encourage and help you to understand the connection between your distress and the thoughts that do not help you, to question them in order to detach from them and look for other more helpful thoughts.*

Questioning. The next step is the classic CT *questioning* and all the other cognitive techniques of change. The risk is—once again—implementing them in an unshared manner. Good *questioning* or good motivation for behavioral exposure is not sufficient. It is, however, necessary to make the patient fully aware that the therapeutic goal is not to passively receive the new rational belief that the feared scenario is either unlikely (which is not even always true) or at least tolerable (which is more probable). Rather, it is crucial to become aware of the mind's ability to question negative thoughts and detach from them.

What matters is not that I show you how unlikely it is that the feared event would happen or that all in all you are capable of tolerating negative states, but that you realize that you can be aware of your negative thoughts and stop giving them credit just because they have crossed your mind.

Monitoring clinical progression. Monitoring clinical progression is the last element that should be performed in a fully shared rather than a mechanical and passive way. By monitoring the progression, the therapist and patient continuously refocus on case formulation, which increasingly clearly becomes the real measure of therapeutic progress. Not coincidentally, the monitored variables are the adherence to *core beliefs* and *coping strategies*, evaluated according to scales from 1 to 10, in order to evaluate the degree of detachment as a clinical index of progress.

Shared Case Formulation as a Theoretical Shift Towards Functionalism

In this final section of the chapter, we suggest that case formulation as a shared operation between therapists and patients has become clinically important because some limitations of the structuralist self-centered conception of CT have emerged. Shared case formulation has favored and encouraged a theoretical shift of CT towards functionalism. This functionalist perspective of CT enables one to conceptualize the alliance and the therapeutic relationship around the pivot of sharing case formulation.

A first argument in favor of this hypothesis is that the shared case formulation can be conceived as a process managed by mental functions, at least from an operational—if not theoretical—viewpoint: The patient is encouraged to understand that his or her mental states derive from executive choices that can be governed cognitively. The therapist then explains to the patient how his or her mental states derive from beliefs about him- or herself, life, the world, others, and the future. These beliefs are, after all, ways of consciously formulating how the mind works.

The same idea also applies to the sharing of the treatment rationale. Sharing with the patient the rationale of a *questioning* intervention, pro and con analysis, and behavioral exposure does not imply faith in a mechanical action of a rational tool on the emotional experience. Rather, it indicates the choice to consciously activate a series of mental functions that can be mastered together, and that the patient has so far largely chosen to neglect to activate—considering them uncontrollable by default. It is clear that by reasoning in this way, the true mechanism of therapeutic action turns out to be more functionalist and metacognitive than structuralist and cognitive. Due to its simplicity, it cannot be denied that the CT procedure is effective in setting the patient's disposition in the direction of mastery rather than passivity.

It is true that case formulation in the clinical model of CT is a theoretical simplification. Reducing mental states to verbal cognitive content is questionable, just as it is questionable to reduce the relationship among thoughts, emotions, and behaviors to a one-way direction. The mind-body system and the set of mental states and behaviors are a continuum and so are not easily reducible to verbalizations. Clearly, executive control of behaviors—and even more so of emotional states—is a complex process that only partially occurs at the conscious executive level. It is also true, however, that this process is partially controllable, and to a greater extent than we think, in everyday life. The real basic principle of cognitive psychotherapy may no longer be that this process is entirely controllable by executive consciousness but rather that it is controllable to a greater extent than the patient believes. Emotional distress also depends on the extent to which the patient underestimates this power. From this viewpoint, the cognitive principle must be rethought, transforming the relationship between thoughts and emotions into a metacognitive distortion of low mastery of mental states.

It is not easy to reconstruct the development of clinical knowledge that has led to the current highly explicit and shared case formulation using the CT diagram or other tools. We certainly know that Aaron T. Beck's training was psychoanalytic (Rosner 2014a, 2014b) and that Beck continued to consider the early stages of development of his model as belonging at least in part to the psychodynamic world, as reported in his 1984 work in which he defines a continuum between CT, behavioral therapy, and psychoanalysis and unexpectedly states that his attention to consciousness came from psychoanalysis, or rather from the particular psychoanalysis he knew (Beck 1970a, 1970b, 1970c, 1971). In fact, the American psychoanalysis in which Beck was trained was influenced by both the neo-Freudian ego-psychology current developed by both Anna Freud (1936/1966) and Hartmann, Kris, and Loewenstein (Hartmann 1964; Hartmann and Loewenstein 1964; Hartmann et al. 1946); this favors conscious ego functions at the expense of the unconscious ego and id, and the interpersonal tradition dating back to Alfred Adler and Otto Rank and arriving at Karen Horney and Harry Sullivan, which emphasizes the importance of understanding and treating patients' conscious experiences and the need to treat the meanings that patients attribute to the events in their lives. CT focused on intrapsychic processes rather than manifest behavior is more a legacy of these neo-psychoanalytic theories.

On the other hand, it is true that Beck's therapeutic procedures are more similar to behavioral therapy (Rosner 2014a, 2014b). In fact, we also know that from the 1970s onwards, Beck approached the behavioral world and combined the concepts borrowed from psychoanalysis with behavioral functional analysis. As is widely known, functional behavioral analysis is an assessment procedure that searches for an explanatory model of patients' behaviors in terms of antecedents and consequences which either influence or retroactively condition it.

Admittedly, the rationale of functional analysis is in turn metacognitive because it presupposes that the person, once aware of his or her functional model, can modulate the interactions with the behavioral antecedents and consequences. However, even the neo-analytical model is metacognitive in its own way; this model influenced Beck because its basic assumption is that conscious mental states can modulate unconscious mental drives once a person becomes aware of them. In both cases, it is believed that it is possible to move from the automatic management of behavioral sequences or drives to executive management via a metacognitive analysis. The final result is the fully shared formulation contained in the manual signed by Judith Beck (2011).

However, while in functional analysis the content of variables is always open, in CT's CCD, the content of the cognitive mediator is predetermined, tending to be conceptualized in terms of beliefs about the self, the world/environment (including interpersonal relationships), or the future. Over time, beliefs about the self have gained a prominent role within the cognitive triad of CT (Wells and Mathews 1994: p. 2). This final prevalence of pattern theory about the self is also attributable to the influence of the clinical applications of Bandura's (1977, 1988) fundamental work on self-efficacy (Maddux and Kleiman 2012) and Neisser's (1967) and Markus' (1977) models of the self. In summary, positive self-judgements about the ability to manage and control events and emotional reactions are considered largely responsible for emotional well-being and effectiveness in daily life, while negative self-judgements are what make us depressed or anxious (Williams 1996). Self-beliefs are stable, hierarchically superordinate organizations of knowledge because they integrate and summarize a person's thoughts, feelings, and experiences (Markus and Sentis 1982), including their physical characteristics, social roles, personality traits, and areas of special interest and ability (Markus and Nurius 1986).

It is also possible that the emphasis in Beck's CT on the self depends on the influence of Bandura, Neisser, and Markus in cognitive science, as well as Beck's own psychoanalytic background. In this psychodynamic paradigm, it is assumed that the human mind possesses conscious adaptive functions called ego functions that are not influenced by aggressive and libidinal conflicting drives (Rosner 2014a, 2014b). In short, the ego plays a key organizational role in mental activity that seems to be similar to the role played by self-beliefs in Beck's CT.

The concept of self-knowledge likely helped Beck formalize his procedures in ways that are more understandable and manageable to clinicians. Furthermore, Beck's crucial advantage was his commitment to the development of replicable protocols applicable to psychiatric diagnoses of emotional disorders (Rush et al. 1977).

Subsequently, Beck's CT model has been applied to a wide range of emotional disorders such as panic disorder (Clark 1986), social phobia (Clark and Wells 1995), post-traumatic stress disorder (Ehlers and Clark 2000), eating disorders (Fairburn et al. 1999), and obsessive-compulsive disorder (Salkovskis 1985). These scholars both borrowed Beck's "psychodynamic" treatment for verbal reattribution focused on personal beliefs (Rachman 2015) and strongly reintroduced the behavioral element grounded on the work of Meyer and Turkat (1979). British behaviorism merged with Beck's CT (Marks 2012) due to Meyer's efforts to develop appropriate case formulation procedures (Bruch 2015; Rachman 2015). In turn, Beck also increased the behavioral components in its model (Beck et al. 1979, 1985). Therefore, a standard CT clinical model was born that has the basic principle that emotional disorders depend on biased automatic cognitive processes that can be changed through verbal reattribution in therapy (Beck 1976; Clark et al. 1999; Clark and Beck 2010; Dobson and Dozois 2001; Ellis and Grieger 1986; Kazdin 1978; Kelly 1955; Mahoney 1974; Meichenbaum 1977; Rachman 1977). It was a sort of psychotherapeutic counterpart of the anthropological reflections about the executive brain and of the civilized mind (Goldberg 2001). In this way, Beck consolidated his success and managed to characterize his CT approach as the standard one. The disadvantage of this success, however, is that the functional analysis model has been overshadowed by the cognitive assessment of Beck's CT on which it was modeled.

References

Bandura, A. (1977). Self-efficacy: Toward a unifying theory of behavioral change. *Psychological Review, 84*, 191–215.

Bandura, A. (1988). Self-efficacy conception of anxiety. *Anxiety Research, 1*, 77–98.

Beck, A. T. (1963). Thinking and depression: I. Idiosyncratic content and cognitive distortions. *Archives of General Psychiatry, 9*, 324–333.

Beck, A. T. (1964). Thinking and depression: II. Theory and therapy. *Archives of General Psychiatry, 10*, 561–571.

Beck, A. T. (1970a). The core problem in depression: The cognitive triad. *Science and Psychoanalysis, 17*, 47–55.

Beck, A. T. (1970b). Cognitive therapy: Nature and relation to behavior therapy. *Behavior Therapy, 1*, 184–200.

Beck, A. T. (1970c). Roles of fantasies in psychotherapy and psychopathology. *Journal of Nervous and Mental Disease, 150*, 3–17.

Beck, A. T. (1971). Cognitive patterns in dreams and daydreams. In J. H. Masserman (Ed.), *Dream dynamics* (pp. 2–7). New York, NY: Grune and Stratton.

Beck, A. T. (1976). *Cognitive therapy and the emotional disorders*. New York, NY: International Universities Press.

Beck, A. T., Emery, G., & Greenberg, R. L. (1985). *Anxiety disorders and phobias: A cognitive perspective*. New York, NY: Basic Books.

Beck, A. T., Rush, A. J., Shaw, B. F., & Emery, G. (1979). *Cognitive therapy of depression*. New York, NY: Guilford Press.

Beck, J. S. (1995). *Cognitive therapy: Basics and beyond*. London/New York, NY: Guilford Press.

Beck, J. S. (2011). In London (Ed.), *Cognitive therapy: Basics and beyond* (2nd ed.). New York, NY: Guilford Press.

Bordin, E. S. (1979). The generalizability of the psychoanalytic concept of the working alliance. *Psychotherapy: Theory, Research & Practice, 16*, 252–260.

Bruch, M. (2015). *Beyond diagnosis: Case formulation in cognitive behavioural therapy*. Chichester/New York, NY: John Wiley & Sons Ltd.

Clark, D. A., & Beck, A. T. (2010). *Cognitive Therapy of Anxiety Disorders: Science and Practice*. New York, NY: Guilford.

Clark, D. A., Beck, A. T., & Alford, B. A. (1999). *Scientific foundations of cognitive theory and therapy of depression*. New York, NY: Wiley & Sons.

Clark, D. M. (1986). A cognitive approach to panic disorder. *Behaviour Research and Therapy, 24*, 461–470.

Clark, D. M., & Wells, A. (1995), A cognitive model of social phobia. In R.G. Heimberg, M. Liebowitz, D. Hope, D. e F. Scheier (Eds.), *Social phobia: Diagnosis, assessment, and treatment* (pp. 66–93). New York, NY: Guilford.

Dattilio, F. M., & Hanna, M. A. (2012). The collaborative relationship in cognitive-behavioral therapy. *Journal of Clinical Psychology, 68*, 146–158.
Dattilio, F. M., & Padesky, C. A. (1990). *Cognitive therapy with couples*. Sarasota, FL: Professional Resource Exchange.
Deci, E. L., & Ryan, R. M. (Eds.). (2002). *Handbook of self-determination research*. Rochester, NY: University of Rochester Press.
DiGiuseppe, R., Doyle, K. A., Dryden, W., & Backx, W. (2014). *A Practioner's guide to rational emotive behavior therapy*. New York, NY: Oxford University Press.
Dobson, K. S., & Dozois, D. J. A. (2001). Historical and philosophical bases of the cognitive-behavioral therapies. In K. S. Dobson (Ed.), *Handbook of cognitive-behavioral therapies* (pp. 3–39). New York, NY: Guilford.
Ehlers, A., & Clark, D. M. (2000). A cognitive model of post-traumatic stress disorder. *Behaviour Research and Therapy, 38*, 319–345.
Ellis, A. (1962). *Reason and emotion in Psychotherapy*. New York, NY: Stuart.
Ellis, A., & Grieger, R. M. (Eds.). (1986). *Handbook of rational-emotive therapy* (Vol. 2). New York, NY: Springer.
Fairburn, C. G., Shafran, R., & Cooper, Z. (1999). A cognitive behavioural theory of eating disorders. *Behaviour Research and Therapy, 37*, 1–13.
Feixas, G., & Compañ, V. (2016). Dilemma-focused intervention for unipolar depression: A treatment manual. *BMC Psychiatry, 16*, 235. https://doi.org/10.1186/s12888-016-0947-x.
Freud, A. (1936/1966). Ego and mechanisms of defense. In *The writings of Anna Freud* (Vol. 2, Rev. ed.). New York: International Universities Press
Goldberg, E. (2001). *The Executive Brain: Frontal Lobes and the Civilized Mind*. Oxford: University Press, Oxford.
Guidano, V. F. (1987). *Complexity of the Self*. New York, NY: Guilford Press.
Guidano, V. F. (1991). *The self in process: toward a post-rationalist cognitive therapy*. New York, NY: Guilford Press.
Guidano, V. F., & Liotti, G. (1983). *Cognitive processes and emotional disorders: A structural approach to psychotherapy*. New York, NY: Guilford Press.
Hartmann, H. (1964). *Essays on Ego psychology*. New York, NY: International Universities Press.
Hartmann, H., Kris, E., & Loewenstein, R. M. (1946). Comments on the formation of psychic structure. *The Psychoanalytic Study of the Child, 2*, 11–38.
Hartmann, H., & Loewenstein, R. M. (1964). *Papers on psychoanalytic psychology. Psychological issues monograph*. New York, NY: International Universities Press.
Hollon, S. D., & Beck, A. T. (1979). Cognitive therapy of depression. In P. C. Kendall & S. D. Hollon (Eds.), *Cognitive-behavioral interventions: Theory, research, and procedures* (pp. 153–203). New York, NY: Academic.
Kazantzis, N., Beck, J. S., Dattilio, F. M., Dobson, K. S., & Rapee, R. M. (2013). Collaborative empiricism as the central therapeutic relationship element in CBT: An expert panel discussion at the 7th International Congress of Cognitive Psychotherapy. *International Journal of Cognitive Therapy, 6*, 386–400.
Kazdin, A. E. (1978). *History of behavior modification: Experimental foundations of contemporary research*. Baltimore, MD: University Park Press.
Kelly, G. A. (1955). *The psychology of personal constructs: Vol 1 and 2*. New York, NY: Norton.
Knapp, P., & Beck, A. T. (2008). Fundamentos, modelos conceituais, aplicações e pesquisa da terapia cognitiva [Cognitive therapy: foundations, conceptual models, applications and research]. *Brazilian Journal of Psychiatry, 30*, s54–s64.
Maddux, J. E., & Kleiman, E. M. (2012). Self-efficacy. In C. R. Snyder & S. J. Lopez (Eds.), *Handbook of positive psychology* (pp. 89–101). New York, NY: Oxford University Press.
Mahoney, M. J. (1974). *Cognition and Behavior Modification*. Cambridge, MA: Ballinger.
Mahoney, M. J. (1995). Theoretical developments in the cognitive and constructive psychotherapies. In M. J. Mahoney (Ed.), *Cognitive and constructive psychotherapies. Theory, research,*

and practice (pp. 103–120). Springer and American Psychological Association: New York, NY, Washington, D.C.
Mahoney, M. J. (2003). *Constructive psychotherapy: A practical guide*. New York, NY: Guilford.
Markland, D., Ryan, R. M., Tobin, V. J., & Rollnick, S. (2005). Motivational interviewing and self-determination theory. *Journal of Social and Clinical Psychology, 24*, 811–831.
Marks, S. (2012). Cognitive behaviour therapies in Britain: The historical context and present situation. In W. Dryden (Ed.), *Cognitive behaviour therapies* (pp. 1–24). New York, NY: Sage Publishing.
Markus, H. (1977). Self-schemata and processing information about the self. *Journal of Personality and Social Psychology, 35*, 63–78.
Markus, H., & Nurius, P. (1986). Possible selves. *American Psychologist, 41*, 954–969.
Markus, H., & Sentis, K. (1982). The self in social information processing. In J. Suls (Ed.), *Social Psychological Perspectives on the Self* (pp. 41–70). Hillsdale, NJ: Erlbaum.
Meichenbaum, D. H. (1977). *Cognitive behavior modification*. New York, NY: Plenum Press.
Meyer, V., & Turkat, I. D. (1979). Behavioral analysis of clinical cases. *Journal of Behavioral Assessment, 1*, 259–270.
Neimeyer, R. A. (2009). *Constructivist psychotherapy. Distinctive features*. London: Routledge.
Neimeyer, R. A., & Mahoney, M. J. (Eds.). (1995). *Constructivism in Psychotherapy*. Washington, DC: APA Press.
Neisser, U. (1967). *Cognitive Psychology*. Englewood Cliffs, NJ: Prentice-Hall.
Rachman, S. (1977). The conditioning theory of fear acquisition: a critical examination. *Behaviour Research and Therapy, 15*, 375–387.
Rachman, S. (2015). The evolution of behaviour therapy and cognitive behaviour therapy. *Behaviour Research and Therapy, 64*, 1–8.
Rosner, R. I. (2014a). Aaron T. Beck's drawings and the psychoanalytic origin story of cognitive therapy. *History of Psychology, 15*, 1–18.
Rosner, R. I. (2014b). The "Splendid Isolation" of Aaron T. Beck. *Isis, 105*, 734–758.
Rush, A. J., Beck, A. T., Kovacs, M., & Hollon, S. (1977). Comparative efficacy of cognitive therapy and pharmacotherapy in the treatment of depressed outpatients. *Cognitive Therapy and Research, 1*(1), 17–37.
Salkovskis, P. M. (1985). Obsessional-compulsive problems: a cognitive behavioural analysis. *Behaviour Research and Therapy, 23*, 571–583.
Stein, D. J., Kupfer, D. J., & Schatzberg, A. F. (Eds.). (2006). *The American Psychiatric Publishing textbook of mood disorders*. Washington, DC: American Psychiatric Publishing.
Tee, J., & Kazantzis, N. (2011). Collaborative empiricism in cognitive therapy: A definition and theory for the relationship construct. *Clinical Psychology: Science and Practice, 18*, 47–61.
Wells, A., & Mathews, G. (1994). *Attention and emotion: A clinical perspective*. Hove/Hillsdale, NJ: Erlbaum.
Williams, J. M. G. (1996). Depression and the specificity of autobiographical memory. In D. Rubin (Ed.), *Remembering Our Past: Studies in Autobiographical Memory* (pp. 244–267). Cambridge: Cambridge University Press
Winter, D. A., & Viney, L. L. (Eds.). (2005). *Personal construct psychotherapy. Advances in theory, practice and research*. London: Whurr Publishers.

The Conceptualization Process in Cognitive Behavioral Therapy. Commentary on Chapter "Case Formulation in Standard Cognitive Therapy"

Arthur Freeman

Contents

CBT Conceptualization Process and Patient's Life Goals

In 1977, the late Dr. Michael J. Mahoney called Cognitive Behavior Therapy (CBT) as the barbarians at the gates. The basic psychodynamic establishment saw CBT as simplistic, mechanistic, overly prescriptive, technique focused, and while being logical, lacked the essence of being psychological, and lacking in the elegance of the psychodynamic formulations. These mistaken notions are used as reasons to deride CBT.

In this comprehensive chapter, the case formulation methodology of CBT is described and discussed in detail, comparing and contrasting with Rational Emotive Behavior Therapy and the Constructivist approach of Mahoney, Guidano, and Liotti. The conceptualization process is one of model-building and is among the most sophisticated skills of the therapist. Whenever an artist create a painting they start with a basic outline or sketch of the goals and plan for the creation.

What is interesting is that the ability to develop a conceptual framework for the patient's problems, strengths, challenges, and perceived threats is the key to effective CBT. Rather than trying to apply specific techniques (or classes of techniques) to help the patient develop a more adaptive style requires the clinician do several things, which are:

- First, the clinician needs to develop a working model of the patient's problems.

A. Freeman (✉)
Philadelphia College of Osteopathic Medicine, Philadelphia, PA, USA

G. M. Ruggiero et al. (eds.), *CBT Case Formulation as Therapeutic Process*,
https://doi.org/10.1007/978-3-030-63587-9_3

- Second, the therapist -working collaboratively with the patient- needs to refine and sharpen the conceptualization.
- Third, the patient's input and feedback is an essential issue in that it reflects how the patient sees and understands their life issues.
- Fourth, the therapist and patient develop specific targets for change that can help the patient to alter their present style to one that is more adaptive.
- Fifth, the therapist and the patient establish a direction and symptom cluster upon which to focus.
- Sixth, through a series of cognitive and behavioral experiments the patient works to alter their present life picture.
- Seventh, the patient and therapist evaluate the success of the experiments and make any mid-course alterations to the patient's life direction.
- Eighth, the therapist and the patient explain the data gleaned from the experiments.
- Ninth, second and third experiments, collaboratively developed can be introduced to gather further data.
- Tenth, the therapist establishes the therapeutic atmosphere based on the patient's life experience and both stated and implied therapeutic goals.
- Finally, the patient can assess their new set of actions and goals.

The patient must be socialized to the CBT model, discuss the therapist's role, the patient's role in therapy, the patient's expectation of therapy, a setting of therapeutic boundaries, assessment of the patient's therapeutic and life skills, and the time parameters and constrains for the therapy The therapeutic focus and the conceptual framework must focus on the patient's goals. The patient, in accord with their goals must learn how to process thoughts, feelings, and actions and the interaction between the seemingly disparate.

Essentially, the patient can make the sequential steps needed for them to more closely approximate their life goals. They learn to ask themselves the question, "is this where I want to be? Is this the direction that I want to take? Does this set of actions get me more (or less) of what I would like for myself, my relationships, my family, my work, and my friendships. The conceptualization helps the therapy to be more proactive than reactive in the therapy work.

Two key constructs are moderation and structure. The patient needs to be moved from an extreme view toward a more moderate view, and they learn to structure both the therapy, overall, and the session, in particular. This structure helps the patient gain greater control of their life-goals and the focus of their desired life changes.

Both therapist and patient can check on the purpose and value of the conceptualization in a very direct manner by asking three questions. First, does the conceptualization as developed explain the patient's past behavior? Second, does the conceptualization make sense of the patient's present behavior? And third does the conceptualization help to predict future behavior?

Elements of the CBT Approach

In many ways, the term "Cognitive Behavioral" is a misnomer (and has also become a target for criticism). It implies that CBT examines the way in which people process information (cognitive) and how this processing both influences, and in some cases, directs how one acts (behavioral), In point of fact the CBT approach examines how what one thinks and perceives will influence how they feel. In addition, CBT includes neurological and biological influences, general and specific skill deficit, and behavior.

Our experience has been that many of the so-called psychological problems are the result of a lack or poorly developed skills which can be taught, learned and practiced. For example, I recall when my youngest son started school we placed him in a private school inasmuch as when he was ready for kindergarten he had learned to read, knew his numbers, etc. Rather than have him bored by a repetition of his already mastered skills we enrolled him in a private school. At the end of each day, every boy in the school had to "check-out" with a teacher. They were required to state their name (My name is Aaron Freeman. And then, had to hold eye-contact with the teacher and say, "have a good day. And shake the teacher's hand) If the child lost eye contact, the teacher would gently point this our. "Aron, look at me. Have a good day. When he mastered that he got into my car and we drove home. What is interesting is that for many years, when introducing my three sons to another adult, it is Aaron who would step forward and introduce himself. These early social skills have eventuated in my eldest son being a computer academic, my middle son working for a large corporation and Aaron owning his own business where his social skills have served him well.

The CBT approach seeks to address four elements. What is the style, content, and goals of evaluation both internal and external events. While the CBT therapist accepts that some thoughts are not easily or immediately accessible to consciousness, and the cognitive shifts can be used as indirect signs of change. The therapist and patient want to first explore the patient's *phenotyp*e (that which is viewed and evaluated by others, *the genotype*, the basic constitutional factors, the s*ociotype*, how the individual interacts with others, and the *schematype,* the influence of the patient's schema. It is this last element that is at the heart of the CBT approach. The patient's schema (also termed rules or requirement. These rules most often derive from family of origin. They may be family rules, cultural rules, gender-related rules, age-related rules, geographic rules, group dictated rules, and religious rules. These schema serve as a filter for life experience and for how one responds to the schema. The earlier the schema is acquired, the credibility of the rule-maker or rule-enforcer, the more powerful the rule and the greater effect on the individual. If, for example, a child learns that they lacked value (You are no good), intelligence (You are stupid, (social skills (don't you know how to greet people), they may carry those rules as part of broader rules or as simple negative self-statements.

Beck and others developed the idea that rather than view problems in their totality, the targeted issues needed to be broken up to smaller, more workable elements.

The CBT therapist starts with identifying the approximate time/ setting of the experience, a description of the experience, the patient is then asked what thoughts, ideas, percepts they have regarding the experience. A key ingredient is the attachment of both the emotion and the level of the emotion. The initial assessment of the emotion becomes the baseline against which change can be assessed. This is followed by the patient identifying the nature of the distortions and how believable they see the ideas to be. (This also serves as a baseline). The patient is then encouraged to challenge the negative ideas and distortions and the changes in emotion, if any, can be assessed.

Unlike the REBT approach (discussed later in this volume) the CBT therapist does not debate, confront, challenge or try to dispute the patient's ideas. The technique is the Socratic Dialogue which uses a questioning format to help the patient to identify their thoughts. The questioning format is very much like the examination procedures used in school examinations. This helps to make the questioning format familiar to the patient. For example, After the therapist teaches and demonstrates the Socratic Dialogue the patient can learn to use it on themselves. (1) The answer to the question might require a long example. (2) Some questions require a brief description and answer, (3) The answer can be a true/false answer. (4) The use of the missing word (when you think those thoughts, it makes you feel…? (5) The use of a matching strategy (which of these pieces go together? (6) The use of metaphor (7) The use of story, fable, myths, or literature references.

Probably the most useful and economic intervention is the use of the "Critical Incident technique." Rather than long stories and the retelling of previous experience, the patient can be asked, "Tell me one incident that will shown me exactly what you experienced. Each critical incident has to have a moral. The therapist can ask, "What did you learn from that experience?

The chapter stresses the importance differentiating between the working alliance and the alliance and the working relationship. The alliance is the sum of the goals of therapy and the working relationship is the way in which the patient and therapist interact. Clearly they are related but are, at the same time, different, each being an important part of the overall therapeutic alliance. If there was a key word to describe this chapter it would be that it is comprehensive and offers a concise review of the conceptualization process in Cognitive Behavior Therapy.

Reference

Mahoney, M. J. (1977). Cognitive therapy and research: A question of questions. *Cognitive Therapy and Research, 1*, 5–16.

Case Formulation in Standard Cognitive Therapy: A Commentary on Chapter "Case Formulation in Standard Cognitive Therapy"

Steven D. Hollon

Contents

Case Formulation in Standard Cognitive Therapy and Nonspecific Processes: The Three-Legged Stool

There is much of value in the chapter "Case Formulation in Standard Cognitive Therapy" on case formulation by Ruggiero, Caselli, and Sassaroli. Their basic point is that cognitive therapy uses case formulation as the main operative tool by which it handles the whole therapeutic process including both strategies both specific to cognitive therapy and the nonspecific factors such as the therapeutic alliance and the therapeutic relationship. With that premise I wholly agree.

That being said, we handle nonspecific processes quite differently than more traditional therapies; we "hit the ground running" in the sense of working to bring about rapid symptom change from the first session onward and get to know the patient in the process, rather than getting to know the patient (and them to know us) first before we start to work on symptom change (DeRubeis and Feeley 1990; Feeley et al. 1999). The metaphor that I like to use is that we "go to war" with our patients against their disorders and get to know one another "in the foxhole" as we work to provide symptomatic relief.

S. D. Hollon (✉)
Department of Psychology, Vanderbilt University, Nashville, TN, USA
e-mail: steven.d.hollon@vanderbilt.edu

G. M. Ruggiero et al. (eds.), *CBT Case Formulation as Therapeutic Process*,
https://doi.org/10.1007/978-3-030-63587-9_4

We also vary what we do in terms of the extent to which we explicitly focus on and talk about the developing relationship across different clients in a manner that is wholly guided by the evolving cognitive conceptualization. This is best instantiated by the concept of the "three-legged stool" introduced to deal with clients with depressions superimposed on personality disorders (Beck and Freeman 1990). The original version of cognitive therapy that I learned in the 1970s focused largely current life issues and addressed childhood antecedents only in later sessions when the client was largely asymptomatic (Beck et al. 1979). The nature of the therapeutic relationship was only addressed if there were problems in the therapy (missing sessions or not doing homework). As the Center for Cognitive Therapy matured, there was a marked shift in the nature of the clients that were treated; patients who were uncomplicated and easy to work with got better and went away whereas patients who were more interpersonally challenging tend to hang on and frustrate successive groups of trainees. What we learned to do with such clients was to touch on each leg of the stool with respect to any item that got put on the agenda; how best to deal with issue in their current life (current life concerns), when did they first start to respond in a similar fashion in similar situations in terms of thoughts, feelings, and behaviors (childhood antecedents), and did the way we worked on the topic together stir up any thoughts or feelings that might be of concern (therapeutic relationship).

The Cognitive Conceptualization Diagram in Complex Cases

For these more complicated patients, this work is guided by a cognitive conceptualization that evolves across the early treatment sessions and that is often instantiated in the form of a cognitive conceptualization diagram (CCD). The CCD has space at the bottom for three different thought records across three different situations but adds a particularly important component when it asks for the meaning of the automatic thought in each (this is essentially using the "downward arrow" to explore the meaning system of the client). These meanings tend to be relatively uniform across different situations and different specific automatic negative thoughts (usually either "I am incompetent" or "I am unlovable" for depressed patients) and correspond nicely to the beliefs that sit at the core of their depressogenic schemas. These core beliefs are likely about the self (especially in depression), the world (often other people and especially relevant in social anxiety), and the future (again with respect to depression a sense of hopelessness that things will not work out and that gratification will not be obtained).

The step above the core beliefs are the earlier life experiences (usually childhood antecedents) in which the client first developed his or her core beliefs. Identifying these events (facilitated by asking about the first time that the client ever felt this way or believed this about him or herself) is useful because they often involve an inference that was drawn from the perspective of a child that may not seem so compelling now that the client is an adult. Ross (1977) talks about three strategies that help a person move beyond his or her existing beliefs: (1) evidential disconfirmation; (2) replacement of an existing belief system (or reinterpreting an existing belief); and (3) "process insight" in which the individual is helped to recognize the logical errors that led to the adoption of that erroneous belief. Recognizing how the client came to generate his or her core beliefs helps them gain "process insight" (most of us are more mature as adults and would not have drawn the same causal inferences from life events as we did as a child) and facilitates reinterpreting existing beliefs in a more "adult" fashion.

The next step down from the core beliefs are the underlying assumptions (aka conditional beliefs) that help guide a person through the world given that they buy into the validity of the core belief. Someone who thinks that he or she is unlovable may buy into the notion that "if I put my partner's desires above my own in all things than she/he will not desert me" or "if I do not take chances in my career then people will see not see that I am incompetent." In essence, these are "cut your losses" conditional beliefs, "if...then" statements that guide someone through life while decreasing the odds of getting what one really wants out of living.

The next step down from the core beliefs and underlying assumptions (located in the middle of the form) brings us to the compensatory strategies. This is the most interesting category on the CCD and a particularly interesting addition to cognitive theory. Compensatory strategies are the things that people do (they are mostly overt behaviors but can be cognitive events as well) that operationalize the "if...then" statements (the way they try to cut their losses in life) that flow from their core beliefs. Not everyone engages in (or gets in trouble from) their compensatory strategies but for patients with personality disorders they are the primary source of their distress. Others do not know you from your affects or your cognitions but they do know you from your behaviors and the behaviors that clients with personality disorders engage in to compensate for their perceived inadequacies often have the effect of turning other people off. The narcissist compensates for his or her underlying sense of inadequacy by being boastful or self-centered, the person with an avoidant personality compensates for his or her belief that he or she will be rejected by making plans then backing out at the last minute, and the person with borderline personality disorder looks to others to regulate his or her affect and then flips back and forth between idealizing and dismissing the object of their affection. From the perspective of people with personality disorders, they are only doing what they must to get by in life, but from the perspective of the people with whom they interact, it is the way they behave (the compensatory strategies) that creates problems in the relationship.

Compensatory strategies are essentially analogous to safety behaviors in the anxiety disorders in the sense that clients see these behaviors as protecting them from the inevitable consequences of what their core beliefs and underlying assumptions lead them to believe they will face. In fact, they keep the client from learning that those underlying beliefs are not as true as they seem and, in the case of compensatory behaviors for patients with personality disorders, the very things that cause negative reactions in the people with whom they interact.

This is where the CCD and the three-legged stool come in. For patients with personality disorders, the therapist is well-advised to get out in front of the process as soon as he or she can (preferably from the first session on) since the client will react to the therapist in the same way that he or she reacts to everybody else; compensatory strategies will be on full display because they are driven by underlying assumptions that in turn are driven by core beliefs. The nature of the therapeutic relationship will be shaped by the necessity to identify these behaviors as soon as they start to emerge (and they will emerge) and casting them in light of the larger cognitive conceptualization. In essence, patients with depression superimposed on personality disorders have no other way of thinking about themselves; depressions come and go but personality disorders linger on. Laying out a CCD helps clients understand just why they are doing what they are doing and why they are feeling what they are feeling. The CCD provides a "road map" for how clients can test the beliefs that underlie their problematic behaviors and provides a way for the therapist to use the session to test those underlying beliefs.

Aaron T. Beck's Training

This whole approach is a throwback to Beck's dynamic training. When I was in Philadelphia we used to watch him work with clients and most of the time we could follow what he was doing. There is always coherence among thoughts, feelings, physiology, and behavior (at least behavioral impulses) in any given situation and Beck was masterful in how he helped clients lay that coherence out. But there were times when we could not anticipate where he was going and why he asked the questions that he did. That was because he was generating a cognitive conceptualization in his head and tying current beliefs and behaviors to earlier experiences that shaped the core beliefs and underlying assumptions that drive the compensatory strategies and that in turn subvert relationships.

There is always someone in the session who knows exactly what the most compelling experiment is to run to test the client's core beliefs and that is the client him or herself. That most compelling test is to drop the compensatory strategy (née safety behavior) and act in a way that is inconsistent with his or her underlying assumptions and (below that) core beliefs. That is the same strategy that has proven so successful in the treatment of the anxiety disorders; patients with panic disorders are encouraged to do whatever they can to bring on the heart attack (or psychotic decompensation) and if they are still standing (or sane) thirty minutes later then the catastrophic cognition clearly cannot be true. For patients with personality disorders, the therapeutic relationship itself becomes a vehicle for testing the validity of the underlying assumptions and core beliefs. Much of dynamic treatment focuses on generating a transference neurosis so that the client can work through the infantile fantasies seen as driving difficulties and desires in the adult. In cognitive therapy, we do not go so far as to encourage a transference neurosis, but we do go to the "third leg of the stool" and use the client's reactions to us as therapists to identify and dispense with their compensatory strategies so as to uncover and test their underlying assumptions and core beliefs.

I do not necessarily complete a CCD with every client, although I do generate one in my head. Relatively uncomplicated depressions and anxiety disorders do not necessarily need that degree of explicit structure to understand what they do and why they do it. But for patients with depressions superimposed on personality disorders (or with chronic depressions) it is the key to efficacious treatment.

Two Clinical Cases

I am a huge fan of and do trainings several times a year for Increasing Access to Psychological Therapies (IAPT) in the United Kingdom (Clark 2018). Despite the incredible successes that have been achieved in that program (remission rates have risen from the mid-30s to over 50% over the last decade), there are limits to the number of sessions that therapists can provide that do not serve more complicated clients well. In the trainings that I do, I focus on two clients, both severely depressed, but one relatively uncomplicated and the other with a history of trauma that left her functioning in a fashion consistent with borderline personality disorder. I likely would not have bothered to lay out a CCD with the first client even if it had been enunciated by that time (see Hollon and Beck 1979) but would have been lost without it with the second. What I encourage the IAPT therapists to do is to lay out a CCD with clients like the second client so that they have a "road map" to take with them when they move on to their next therapist (as they almost invariably will do). That ensures that the therapy process goes on without interruption despite the fact that it might have to continue with another therapist. The less complicated patient that I worked with fully remitted with 20 sessions across twelve weeks; the more complicated patient took several hundred sessions across the course of several years to fully remit, but fully remit she did. She would not have done as well as she did if we had not developed a CCD that guided everything we did and had we not used the therapeutic relationship to allow her to test the consequences of dropping her compensatory strategies (lying, dissimulating, and manipulating to get what she wanted rather than asking for it directly). Our sessions served a "practice trials" for learning to engage in the same assertive behaviors in relationships in her outside life when it really mattered.

Ruggiero, Caselli, and Sassaroli (in press) are absolutely correct when they say that the case formulation is the main operative tool that handles both nonspecific and specific processes in cognitive therapy. Nonspecific processes are relatively secondary with less complicated clients (with such clients I think of myself as a glorified "auto mechanic" who simply helps clients get their cars running again) whereas with more complicated clients it is the case formulation instantiated as the CCD and the "three-legged stool" (current life events, childhood antecedents, and therapeutic relationship) that is absolutely essential to success in treatment.

References

Beck, A. T., & Freeman, A. (1990). *Cognitive therapy of personality disorders* (1st ed.). New York: Guilford Press.

Beck, A. T., Rush, A. J., Shaw, B. F., & Emery, G. (1979). *Cognitive therapy of depression*. New York: Guilford Press.

Clark, D. (2018). Realizing the mass public benefit of evidence-based psychological therapies: The IAPT Program. *Annual Review of Clinical Psychology, 14*, 159–183.

DeRubeis, R. J., & Feeley, M. (1990). Determinants of change in cognitive therapy for depression. *Cognitive Therapy and Research, 14*, 469–482.

Feeley, M., DeRubeis, R. J., & Gelfand, L. A. (1999). The temporal relation of adherence and alliance to symptom change in cognitive therapy for depression. *Journal of Consulting and Clinical Psychology, 67*, 578–582.

Hollon, S. D., & Beck, A. T. (1979). Cognitive therapy of depression. In P. C. Kendall & S. D. Hollon (Eds.), *Cognitive-behavioral interventions: Theory, research, and procedures* (pp. 153–203). New York: Academic.

Ross, L. (1977). The intuitive psychologist and his shortcomings: Distortion in the attribution process. In L. Berkowitz (Ed.), *Advances in experimental social psychology* (Vol. 10, pp. 173–220). Orlando, FL: Academic.

Commentary to Chapter "Case Formulation in Standard Cognitive Therapy": The Use of Goals in Cognitive Behavioral Therapy Case Formulation

Angelo Maria Saliani, Claudia Perdighe, Barbara Barcaccia, and Francesco Mancini

Contents

A. M. Saliani
Scuole di Psicoterapia Cognitiva, Roma, Italy

Università degli Studi dell'Aquila, L'Aquila, Italy
e-mail: saliani@apc.it

C. Perdighe
Scuole di Psicoterapia Cognitiva, Roma, Italy
e-mail: perdighe@apc.it

B. Barcaccia
Scuole di Psicoterapia Cognitiva, Roma, Italy

Sapienza Università di Roma, Roma, Italy
e-mail: barbara.barcaccia@uniroma1.it

F. Mancini (✉)
Scuole di Psicoterapia Cognitiva, Roma, Italy

Università Guglielmo Marconi, Roma, Italy
e-mail: mancini@apc.it

G. M. Ruggiero et al. (eds.), *CBT Case Formulation as Therapeutic Process*,
https://doi.org/10.1007/978-3-030-63587-9_5

The Role of Goals in Case Formulation

In the formulation of a standard cognitive behavioral psychotherapy (CBT) case, the pathogenic role of dysfunctional (or irrational) *beliefs* (or ideas) is central (Beck 1976; Ellis 1962). The patient suffers because he or she believes that he or she is worth nothing, or that nobody loves him or her or that he or she is selfish, and so on. The mind of human beings, however, is not limited to believing and knowing. The mind also creates representations of what *it wants* and what it does *not want*. Standard CBT seems to neglect—at least in its explicit formulation—the role played by mental representations that are different from beliefs, which we could define as representations of the will: the *goals* or *purposes* (from now on: goals). With this term we refer to the motivations of the individual, his or her plans and mental structures, well described in the work of Miller et al. (1960), without which beliefs would play a mere epistemic function (Castelfranchi and Miceli 2004). More specifically, if we consider the field of psychopathology, it becomes necessary to underline the fundamental role played by a special type of goal: the overinvested *anti-goals*, the states, the scenarios, the unintended facts experienced by the patient as catastrophic, terrible, unacceptable. If every time a patient reveals his or her automatic thoughts to us we do not sense what he or she cares about, what he or she *wants*, and what he or she really does *not want*, how could we understand the reason why a belief causes him or her painful emotions and hinders his or her well-being? For example, if a person believes that having sex exposes him or her to the risk of poor judgment, but he or she does not care much about sex or poor judgments, the belief will not lead him or her to any particular emotional reactions: it would merely and coldly represent a viewpoint. On the other hand, if that person pursues an intense sex life, but does not want in any way to run the risk of a sexual failure (i.e., he or she has the overinvested anti-goal of avoiding any sexual failure and feeling humiliated because of it), then that belief will probably systematically hinder the natural pursuit of a desire and cause suffering. Hence, it becomes pathogenic.

CBT uses two main types of formulation of pathogenic beliefs. One type expresses them through statements, or simple propositions ("I'm ugly," "I'm not brilliant," "I'm selfish," "I'm fragile," "I'm unpleasant," "everyone hates me," "everyone is better than me," etc.), and inferences like "if...then...," in which a premise brings to a consequence:

- *if I get engaged to a girl other than the one my mother wants, my mother would feel betrayed;*
- *if I share my viewpoint, I would be ignored;*
- *if I buy the car of my dreams, my brother would feel he is a failure;*
- *if I feel sexual pleasure, my partner would feel used;*
- *if I get intensely moved, I will lose control.*

The possible examples are endless. If we analyze each of the pathogenic beliefs used as examples, we will quickly grasp a constant characteristic: They all imply an anti-goal and all express a conflict between a desire and an anti-goal, or, in more general terms, a conflict between a goal and an anti-goal. In the premise the desire is often implicit, in the conclusion the anti-goal is expressed, i.e., the feared consequence that hinders the realization of the desire; when the first occurs, the second also occurs or risks occurring:

- *I intensely want to get engaged to that girl, but I don't want my mother to feel betrayed because of it;*
- *I intensely want to express my opinion, but I don't want to run the risk of being ignored;*
- *I intensely want to buy a nice car, but I don't want my brother to feel like a failure because of it;*
- *I intensely want to experience sexual pleasure, but I don't want my partner to feel used for it;*
- *I intensely want to feel intense emotions, but I don't want to lose control of myself in any way.*

In the patient's mind, the satisfaction of a desire involves the realization of an unintended scenario (of an anti-goal, precisely) and the prevention of anti-goal inhibits the satisfaction of desire. There is not much choice: One either tries to satisfy the desire by taking a risk to make the feared scenario possible, or one tries to prevent the feared scenario by giving up desire (Mancini 1996; Mancini and Giacomantonio 2018). This type of belief formulation is very similar to that used by control-mastery theory (Silberschatz 2017). However, even in control-mastery theory, as in standard CBT, the fundamental role played by anti-goals is not made explicit.

For the sake of clarity, it is not intended to say that beliefs formulated with rules such as "if...then..." should always propose a conflict between a desire and an anti-goal—in fact, in some cases the premise simply expresses the condition that makes the anti-goal come true (e.g., *if* I have anxiety, *then I* am weak; *if* my partner asks for more freedom, *then he does* not love me; *if I* lose my hair, *then* I will be disgusting; etc.). However, these beliefs still include an anti-goal, whereas the feared scenario is an anti-goal by virtue of its valuable correspondence with the terminal or hierarchically superior anti-goal (I don't want to have anxiety because having anxiety means being weak—and I don't want to be weak; I don't want my partner to ask for more freedom because if he does it means he doesn't love me—and I don't want him not to love me anymore; I don't want to lose my hair because if I lose it I will be disgusting—and I don't want to be disgusting).

Let us now consider the beliefs formulated with simple and apparently apodictic propositions ("I am stupid," "I am weak," "everyone hates me," "I am a burden for everyone," "I will be alone forever," and so on). Although these may appear as self-evident truths, they often do not express a conclusive conviction but rather the fear that the described scenario is true, mixed with the hope of discovering it is false. In other words, they also reveal an anti-goal of the patient perceived as more or less current, such as being judged or feeling stupid or fragile or hateful or a burden or selfish or evil or harmful or ugly or unworthy or insecure, or being left, scolded, deceived, disappointed, humiliated, and so on. As written above, the examples are endless. That is, everything he or she would ever want to come true.

Even when beliefs in the form of simple propositions emphasize a positive and desired quality of self (e.g., "I am good," "I am a balanced person," "I am a good professional," etc.), they could be pathogenic if they hide an overinvested anti-goal (and therefore, for example, the fear of "being judged bad," "losing mental balance," "disappointing expectations," and so on). Therefore, even beliefs expressed with a simple statement, which signal self-criticism or positive qualities, can suggest something the patient defends him- or herself against but, unlike the others (those of the "if... then..." type), they lack the condition that makes the anti-goal come true and do not enlighten on possible conflicts between goals that hinder the pursuit of his or her life plan.

In summary, beliefs, however they are formulated, always signal an anti-goal if they are pathogenic. This is true for those expressed through a simple statement and it is true for those expressed through a hypothetical period of "if... then... ." Among the latter, those that suggest a consequential relationship between the realization of a desire and an anti-goal coming true have a special value because they synthesize in a single sentence both the patient's plans and the reasons that hinder them.

We have a final note on overinvested anti-goals and their role in the genesis of suffering. If there is suffering, it means that some goals are threatened: As described above, the threatened goal is sometimes a desire, a need, mostly healthy and legitimate, different from the anti-goal and in conflict with it (e.g., the desire to have a fulfilling sex life is threatened because it conflicts with the fear—the anti-goal—of failure and feeling humiliated. To defend myself from the risk of humiliation I avoid sexual approaches and by avoiding sexual approaches I suffer because I give up the satisfaction of a desire); other times the overinvestment of the anti-goal causes suffering because it makes the anti-goal come true. In other words, the tenacious attempts to prevent the anti-goal end up having the opposite effect, in a totally unexpected and unintended way by the mind. For example, I live in the terror of not being a good father—anti-goal—and to ward off this fear I behave exaggeratedly scrupulously with my children; the excess of care transmits anxiety and insecurity to them, ending up confirming, despite myself, the fear of not being a good father.

Anti-goals and Their Implications for the Case Formulation Methodology

The idea of placing motivations, and in particular anti-goals, at the center of the structural factors that hinder the well-being of an individual goes beyond mere formal clarification. It has important consequences with respect to the method of case formulation and the principles of therapeutic strategy.

As far as the case formulation is concerned, it requires that the section dedicated to the internal profile of the disorder is not limited to the search for pathogenic beliefs, but starts precisely from the assessment of the patient's motivations and in particular from what he or she is most defensive. There is clearly no limit to the number of a person's anti-goals, but clinical observation suggests that those who play a decisive role in the suffering of patients are few and overinvested (in some cases it may even happen that a single anti-goal is enough to summarize an entire pathogenic life theme), so it is not advisable to include in the formulation long lists of goals, it is better to focus on those that better characterize the patient and more clearly related to the psychological problem of the patient. Anti-goals can consist of objective facts (e.g., being abandoned), behaviors (e.g., making a crucial mistake), personal qualities (e.g., being characterfully weak), or internal states (e.g., feeling boredom) that are unwanted, feared, and should be formulated as closely as possible to the patient's subjective representation.

Once the patient's anti-goals have been identified, it will be easy to formulate the beliefs related to them, avoiding lingering over those that are not relevant to the anti-goal and more generally to the patient's problem. As already suggested in the previous section, the beliefs that shed light on the conditions under which the anti-goal comes true are particularly useful, and, among these, those that establish a possible consequential relationship between a desirable and healthy goal and the feared realization of the anti-goal. Let us suppose that the anti-goal is *"to be considered an insignificant and rejected person"* and let us suppose that the patient suffers because he intensely wants to have an intimate relationship, friends, and a job in which he is able to affirm him-, but is far from having all this. Let us now suppose that the patient is convinced that trying to realize his desires, i.e., courting a possible partner or making friends or exposing him- and saying his opinion at work, exposes him to what he fears most: appearing insignificant and being rejected. It is clear that in order to defend him- from this painful scenario, the patient will have to give up trying to realize his desires or try to realize them in such a dysfunctional way that he will end up finding confirmation of his fears. The pathogenic belief could be formulated as follows: *"If I try to approach a possible partner, have close friends, and make myself more visible at work, they will find me insignificant and reject me."* As can be easily observed, here as in the previous examples, the belief is composed of two propositions, the first one contains the possibility of pursuing one's own plans (courting a possible partner and so on), while in the second, the consequence, the feared scenario, the catastrophe, the anti-goal (to be judged insignificant and to be rejected) comes true. To build this kind of belief, therefore, you always need two elements: what the patient wants and would do if he did not have an emotional problem and what prevents him from doing so, that is, the fear that the anti-goal comes true. For this reason, it is fundamental that a well formulated case always foresees not only the anti-goal, but also the healthy goals, the patient's desires, the therapeutic goals: Without the latter, one does not understand what the patient wants to achieve with the help of psychotherapy; without the former one does not understand what prevents the patient from achieving it on his own.

Finally, it is always useful to remember the methodological principles of consistency and economy to be applied when formulating the different points of the case: A common thread must link the problem of which the patient complains, his or her goals (i.e., how he would like his or her life to be), the beliefs and anti-goals that hinder the achievement of these goals, the processes that maintain the problem, the events that produced the clinical decompensation and the onset of the problem, and the early life experiences that have fostered the development of pathogenic beliefs and anti-goals. In a good formulation, everything must be consistent and interconnected and the elements that add nothing to the understanding of the case should be omitted. For example, the patient complains of a *problem* of social inhibition and depressed mood; he *aims* to improve his mood, cultivate social and sentimental relationships, and improve his working position. He has a problem because even if he wants to have a partner, close friends, and a better job, he cannot have any of that because he has overinvested the *anti-goal* of avoiding being judged insignificant and rejected and the *belief* that if he tries to court a possible partner, make friends, and make him- more visible among colleagues and superiors, others will find him insignificant and reject him. He has this fear and this belief because his *life story* has been dominated by a relationship with a depressed mother who showed boredom and disinterest when he spoke to her and a father who mocked him for his thoughts and moods. The *clinical decompensation* occurs at seventeen years after a brief love affair ended because the partner claims to find him not interesting. The *maintenance* of the problem is due to pervasive avoidant behaviors that systematically deprive the patient of the opportunity to lower his guard against his fears (anti-goals) and challenge dysfunctional beliefs.

Anti-goals and Their Implications for the Therapeutic Strategy

Let us consider the implications regarding the principles of therapeutic strategy due to the centrality of motivations, and in particular of anti-goals. One of the classic ways CBT produces therapeutic change involves correction of the dysfunctional belief. To simplify: I believe I am an insignificant person; if the therapist shows me through disputing and behavioral exercises that things are not as I believe, the belief will be challenged and reframed and I will feel better. Here the therapeutic strategy basically follows a *truth/falsity* criterion: I think I am an insignificant person when I talk to others, and thanks to the therapy, I discover that this belief *is not true*. But if we analyze the pathogenic belief (and its anti-goal), we discover that the therapeutic path can also be another one. Let us start again from the pathogenic belief: *"If I try to court a possible partner, have close friends, and make myself more visible at work (desires), others will find me insignificant and reject me (anti-goal)."* It is pathogenic not only because it is largely false and painful in itself, but also and above all because, by causing overinvestment in the prevention of anti-goal, it hinders or completely blocks the pursuit of one's desires. This scenario is a bit like a severe reaction of the immune system to a pathogen that inflames the patient's lungs so severely that it prevents him or her from breathing: The extent of the immune reaction is either reduced or the patient dies, killed by the attempt of his body to defend itself. In the same way, if it is true that the pathogenic power of the belief also originates from an excess of defense against the anti-goal, then it is necessary to divest from it in order to counteract its harmful effects and encourage the pursuit of healthy objectives (courting a possible partner, have friends, and so on).

In other words, The patient can also walk the road of reducing his defensive investment, i.e., to defend him- less from the feared scenario in order to devote him-more freely to his life plans. From this point of view, the therapeutic aim would not only be to falsify the belief, but also to favor the lowering of the guard against what is feared and to encourage the patient to *accept* the reasonable risk that the anti-goal will come true in order to dedicate him- to the realization of its plans. Specifically, the classic strategy of correcting the belief comprises demonstrating with logical arguments or empirical evidence (Ruggiero and Sassaroli 2013) that the link between the premise and the conclusion of the belief is false (i.e., it is not true that if you try to court a possible partner you will appear insignificant and will be rejected. It will be all right, the anti-goal will not come true) or, even more incisively, convey the idea that even if the scenario described in the belief (to be rejected, i.e., the anti-goal) were to come true, this would not affect the overall and intrinsic quality of the person (i.e., whatever happens, whatever they tell you, this does not make you an insignificant person).

In both forms, this strategy rests on a *truth/false* criterion, but the second one opens more interesting perspectives because distinguishing facts from the intrinsic value of the person allows you to accept and challenge even painful scenarios (e.g., possible rejections) to invest in the achievement of your goals. The limits of the strategies that aim at pure falsification are, however, at least three: (1) feared things can happen; the therapist works on the perception of probability of the worst scenario, usually unrealistically too high from the patient's view, but the therapist should also encourage the patient to be ready for the worst scenarios; (2) the strategy very often clashes with general beliefs about oneself that are apodictic and therefore not very permeable to attempts at falsification; and (3) even when they break the patient's belief system, his fear of the anti-goal is sometimes so high that he prefers cautious and complacent solutions with the pathogenic belief. In other words, the patient can agree that perhaps it is true that he is not an insignificant person, but it is better not to believe too much in this healthy belief in order not to feel too bad afterward in case the worst scenario comes true. This means that, the patient adopts a cognitive strategy known as *better safe than sorry* that maintains the dysfunctional belief (Mancini et al. 2007).

For all the reasons explained above, the strategies of *falsification*, while remaining fundamental throughout the course of therapy, must be accompanied by strategies of *acceptance* (Perdighe and Mancini 2012). The term acceptance should of course not be understood as resignation to pathogenic beliefs; on the contrary, it means disinvesting, at least partially, from a purpose that has become pathogenic (i.e., the anti-goal) in order to encourage the pursuit of healthy goals. Acceptance cannot be prescribed, but it can be encouraged. How? Human beings usually reduce investment in a purpose when they realize that it is *useless*, unproductive (pragmatic criterion; Ruggiero and Sassaroli 2013), when it is too *expensive*, inconvenient (economic criterion), when it is *legitimate or due to* reduce it—or illegitimate and not due to maintain it (moral criterion).

The therapist concretely encourages a process of acceptance in the patient if he succeeds in showing that continuing to invest in the pathogenic belief and in the relative anti-goal of being rejected: (1) does not completely eliminate the risk of being rejected and does not bring it closer to his objectives (pragmatic criterion); (2) involves enormous costs in psychological, practical, and relational terms (economic criterion); and (3) is neither right nor fair. In other words, to point out that the patient has the right (and the duty toward him-) not to deal with the belief (true or false) and the related anti-goal to freely dedicate him- to the pursuit of his psychological well-being.

To sum up, pathogenic beliefs are always evaluative with respect to a goal. Without desires, without motivations, without conflicts, beliefs are neutral, they lose any emotional color and any pathogenic power. They do not facilitate or hinder anything. For these reasons, it might be useful not to limit the formulation of the internal profile of the disorder to beliefs but to extend it to the formulation of anti-goals. In addition, the pathogenic goal is rarely such because it is in itself wrong or harmful; it becomes so if it chronically complicates the person's healthy plans. Indeed, in many cases it is the excessive investment of the anti-goal, the strenuous defense against it, that makes it pathogenic. To put it bluntly, always with the help of a few examples: There is clearly nothing wrong with the aim of preventing the unhappiness of a loved one, but if the fear of this goal systematically hinders the fulfillment of the legitimate desire for personal affirmation, then the aim of preventing the unhappiness of the other becomes pathogenic. Furthermore, if the abnormal investment in the purpose leads to self-feeding spirals that undermine the purpose itself (e.g., a doctor who worries a lot about the therapy to be prescribed in order to be sure not to harm his or her patient and ends up delaying the treatment too much is really damaging his or her patient), then the goal becomes pathogenic. From this perspective, it is fair to suggest that a good therapeutic strategy should always include how to encourage the patient both to withdraw the investment from his or her pathogenic anti-goal and to pursue his or her desires, rather than just trying to establish whether a belief is true or false.

The Five Components of the CASE Formulation

The core of the formulation is the hypothesis about the nature of the difficulties underlying the symptoms presented by the patient, i.e., the description of the factors that determine, regulate, and maintain the patient's suffering (Eells 2009; Eells et al. 1998; Persons 2008). Translated into cognitive terms, it is the reconstruction of the representations and mental processes that cause specific symptoms and that will be the guide in treatment planning. We present below a formulation scheme based on five points (Barcaccia 2010; Mancini and Barcaccia 2009; Mancini and Perdighe 2009).

Target Definition of the Intervention: Description of Symptoms and Problems

This first component of the formulation is the one in which the therapist strives to give a synthetic picture of the symptoms and problems that the patient brings and in which, therefore, the level of inference is at its lowest. This does not mean that the therapist simply records and reports the patient's answers to the question "why is he or she here?"; rather it is the description of the problems presented from the therapist's point of view and, if possible, his or her assessment in nosographic terms. The key questions are:

- *How and when do the symptoms occur? Under what circumstances? With what frequency, intensity, duration?*
- *How much do the symptoms interfere with the patient's overall functioning?*
- *Why is the patient asking me for help? Why now?*

How Do I Explain the Problem Presented: The Internal Profile

The heart of the formulation is the explanatory hypothesis on what generates and regulates the patient's behavioral, emotional, and somatic symptoms. The core question to answer is: What are the reasons that determine and regulate the patient's symptoms? From a cognitive point of view, the idea is to focus on what goals and beliefs regulate the symptomatology.

For example, in the case of a patient with obsessive symptoms, a well-constructed internal profile will be able to explain what goal regulates the entire symptomatology and make predictions about how the patient will react to possible stimulus situations, in order to confirm or reject the formulated hypothesis of functioning. For example, consider the patient Ms. F., who presents ruminations, avoidance, anxious activation, and request for reassurance; all her symptoms are regulated by the fear of ruining her life and her family due to her own negligence (anti-goal): F. believes that if she does not constantly and scrupulously prevent it, she risks becoming like her mother, ruining her life and the life of her children and her partner. The anti-goal is to do everything in her power to prevent this "ruin" and protect herself from this guilt. From this hypothesis, we can predict that any event that corresponds to an increase in responsibility toward the family or a risk of distraction from one's commitment will trigger more fear of feeling negligent and guilty and, consequently, will exacerbate symptoms, i.e., an increase in attempts to prevent the feared scenario.

The key questions that can help are:

- What are the independent variables that regulate the symptomatology?
- What are the states of mind, and in particular the goals and beliefs that underlie the problem?

What Prevents a Resolution of Suffering: Maintenance Factors

An important aspect of understanding a disorder or symptom is to answer the question: How is possible that the patient does not obtain a solution, even though he or she usually has the resources, information, and possibilities? Understanding why the patient cannot find or implement the solution means understanding that her/his solution attempts are often part of the problem.

Maintenance factors are all the processes and mechanisms—intra-psychic or interpersonal—that feed the credibility of dysfunctional beliefs and the investment in pathogenic goals; they are dynamic and interactive factors triggered by the activation of the patient's pathogenic structures (his or her overinvested anti-goal and dysfunctional beliefs described in the internal profile) that end up reinforcing the same structures in a vicious circle. For example, F., when a stimulus activates her fear of feeling guilty due to negligence, compulsively asks her partner for reassurance about the correctness of her conduct; the partner, after some unsuccessful attempt of reassurance, bursts out and accuses her of ruining everyone's life with her absurd demands, ending up reinforcing F.'s fear of being negligent and guilty and her need to protect herself from such an eventuality. In other words, F.'s attempts at a solution have, in spite of herself, triggered a self-feeding spiral that has exacerbated her fear of guilt.

The key questions that can help are:

- What prevents spontaneous remission of symptoms?
- Which processes or mechanisms (individual and/or interpersonal) prevent the resolution of the patient's problem and suffering? In what way? What goals/beliefs do they reinforce?
- How do any attempts to solve the problem fuel the problem? How do interpersonal reactions and cycles contribute to the stabilization of the disorder?

What Made the Patient's Functioning Fail: The Clinical Decompensation

One of the most interesting aspects of a clinician's work is to understand why a person at a certain point in his or her life goes into crisis and starts to function differently from what has happened up to that point. To reconstruct the clinical decompensation is, therefore, to investigate what happened in the patient's life before or at the beginning of the symptomatology, to analyze what significant events occurred before, and, above all, what meaning and cognitive-emotional impact they had on the patient's aims and beliefs. For example, a job promotion can be considered a positive event, but for a patient it can also be equivalent to a threat of some of his or her own relevant purpose—for example, the goal of protecting him- or herself from the possibility of revealing him- or herself to others as unsuitable—and, therefore, become a disruptive event.

The key questions are:

- What has happened in the life of the patient that has caused a crisis (or aggravated) the previous psychological functioning?
- What living conditions preceded and facilitated the onset of the problem (described in the profile)?
- What psychological variables have been altered by the decompensating events? In other words: What significance did these events have for the subject and how did they modify the psychological functioning of the patient?

How the Patient Has Built Up His or Her Psychological Functioning and What Aspects of His Current Life Stress His Weaknesses: Vulnerability

The reconstruction of vulnerability is always a point of great interest for the clinician. It involves what makes or has made the patient vulnerable to a certain theme, and can therefore concern two distinct aspects, one synchronic and another diachronic and biographical. The first has to do with the current living conditions that expose the patient to continuous stress capable of permanently affecting his or her structural fears, regardless of his or her actions. A chronic illness, a low socioeconomic status, a degraded social context, and a particularly competitive working environment are examples of current vulnerability factors that, mind you, will be mentioned in the formulation if—and only if—they contribute to the patient's subjective fragilities, and not because of objectively stressful conditions. Not all stressors take on the same meaning in the eyes of different people. For example, a very competitive environment for someone will be a cause of continuous distress of his or her fear of not being suited or adequate; for someone else it will be a stimulating condition and therefore a protective factor.

The second way of understanding vulnerability is the historical-biographic one and concerns the traumas of the past or more generally the early experiences that have sensitized the patient to certain issues and therefore contributed to the development of his or her overinvested anti-goal and related dysfunctional beliefs. That is, historical vulnerability gives an account of the remote causes of the patient's problem. Mr. E., for example, depressed and suffering from severe social inhibition, had developed the fear and belief that he was insignificant and rejected during childhood because of a mother who showed boredom when he spoke to her and a father who mocked him no matter what he said or did.

What is important is not the detailed description of the life story, but rather the elements plausibly associated with the development of the specific beliefs and purposes that govern the symptomatology presented. It is guided, therefore, by the hypothesis on the functioning of the patient.

The key questions that can help are:

- How did you build the goals, patterns, and beliefs that generated and maintain your problem?
- What elements of life history have fostered the development of psychological sensitivities that make him or her vulnerable to a given problem?
- What current and permanent conditions in his or her life contribute to making him or her vulnerable to a given issue?

Conclusions

The mind constructs representations of what it wants, needs, and desires, and also of what it fears and really does not want. In other words, it takes the structure of goals and anti-goals. The beliefs inform it of where it is in relation to them: If it is more or less close to reaching what it wants or to suffering what it does not want, it will experience anxiety or hope, joy or sadness.

The formulation of the case in cognitive psychotherapy has always given great importance to the dysfunctional beliefs of the patient, less to his or her pathogenic goals. Yet, clinical observation suggests that a dysfunctional belief is such because it always implies an anti-goal, threatened, or already currently undermined. In the absence of an anti-goal, the dysfunctional belief would simply not be one. For these reasons, it would always be appropriate, at the beginning of any psychotherapy, to first identify and formulate the patient's anti-goal. The formulation of his or her dysfunctional beliefs will then be necessary to establish the conditions under which the patient believes the most feared scenarios are fulfilled.

The centrality attributed to aims in the formulation of a case also determines a clear strategic perspective: The therapist's task is not limited to correcting false and irrational beliefs; rather, it aims to encourage disinvestment, at least partially, from certain goals and anti-goals.

Good case formulation should always include five key points:

1. the description of the problem presented by the patient in quantitative terms and if possible, on the basis of this, as a nosographic diagnosis;
2. the definition of the proximal psychological determinants that explain the presence of the problem (purposes and beliefs that cause the symptoms);
3. the factors that maintain the problem, i.e., the self-feeding circle processes that reinforce purposes, dysfunctional beliefs, and symptoms;
4. the clinical decompensating (or precipitating) events that determined the onset of the problem, i.e., justifying the passage from a pre-morbid state to a morbid outcome;
5. finally, vulnerability, understood in two distinct meanings, as a set of stable and current stressful conditions for the specific mental structure of the patient, and as the remote origin of his psychological problems.

References

Barcaccia, B. (2010). La formulazione del caso clinico [The formulation of the clinical case]. In C. Perdighe & F. Mancini (Eds.), *Elementi di psicoterapia cognitive [Elements of cognitive psychotherapy]* (pp. 23–32), Fioriti Editore, II ed.

Beck, A. T. (1976). *Cognitive therapy and the emotional disorders*. Madison, CT: International Universities Press.

Castelfranchi, C., & Miceli, M. (2004). Gli scopi e la loro famiglia: ruolo dei bisogni e dei bisogni "sentiti" [Goals and their family: the role of needs and of "felt" needs]. *Cognitivismo Clinico, 1*, 5–19.

Eells, T. D. (2009). Invited book review of Jacqueline Persons. the case formulation approach to cognitive-behavior therapy. *Psychotherapy: Theory, Research, Practice, Training, 46*, 400–401.

Eells, T. D., Kendjelic, E. M., & Lucas, C. P. (1998). What's in a case formulation? Development and use of a content coding manual. *Journal of Psychotherapy Practice and Research, 7*, 144–153.

Ellis, A. (1962). *Reason and emotion in psychotherapy*. New York, NY: Lyle Stuart.

Mancini, F. (1996). L'egodistonia [The Hegodistonia]. In B. Bara (Ed.), *Manuale di psicoterapia cognitive [Handbook of cognitive psychotherapy]* (pp. 131–174). Torino: Bollati Boringhieri.

Mancini, F., & Barcaccia, B. (2009). Come usa la diagnosi lo psicologo cognitivista? [How does the cognitivist psychologist use the diagnosis?]. In N. Dazzi, V. Lingiardi, & F. Gazzillo (Eds.), *La diagnosi in psicologia clinica: personalità e psicopatologia [Diagnosis in clinical psychology: personality and psychopathology]* (pp. 157–170). Milano: Cortina.

Mancini, F., Gangemi, A., & Johnson-Laird, P. N. (2007). Il ruolo del ragionamento nella psicopatologia secondo la Hyper Emotion Theory [The role of reasoning in psychopathology according to the Hyper Emotion Theory]. *Giornale italiano di psicologia, 4*, 763–794.

Mancini, F., & Giacomantonio, M. (2018). I conflitti intrapsichici [Intrapsychic conflicts]. *Quaderni di Psicoterapia Cognitiva, 42*, 41–64.

Mancini, F., & Perdighe, C. (2009). La formulazione del caso: schema per la presentazione dei casi clinici e per la supervision [The formulation of the case: scheme for the presentation of clinical cases and for supervision]. *Psicoterapeuti in formazione*. Retrieved from http://lnx.psicoterapeutiinformazione.it/wp-content/uploads/2009/11/Schema%20formulazione%20del%20caso%20per%20PiF.pdf

Miller, G. A., Galanter, E., & Pribram, K. H. (1960). *Plans and structure of behavior*. New York, NY: Holt, Rinehart & Winston.

Perdighe, C., & Mancini, F. (2012). Dall'investimento alla rinuncia: favorire l'accettazione in psicoterapia [From investment to renunciation: encouraging acceptance in psychotherapy]. *Cognitivismo Clinico, 9*, 116–134.

Persons, J. B. (2008). *The case formulation approach to cognitive-behavior therapy*. New York, NY: Guilford.

Ruggiero, G. M., & Sassaroli, S. (2013). *Il colloquio in psicoterapia cognitiva [The interview in cognitive psychotherapy]*. Milano: Cortina.

Silberschatz, G. (2017). Control-mastery theory. *Reference Module in Neuroscience and Biobehavioral Psychology, 2017*, 1–8.

Case Formulation in the Behavioral Tradition: Meyer, Turkat, Lane, Bruch, and Sturmey

Giovanni Maria Ruggiero, Gabriele Caselli, and Sandra Sassaroli

Contents

Case Formulation in Behavioral Therapies

The Cognitive Conceptualization Diagram (CCD, Beck 2011: p. 200) of Beck's cognitive therapy (CT) was not the first form of case formulation in the history of cognitive behavioral therapy (CBT). The case formulation procedure, although

G. M. Ruggiero (✉)
"Psicoterapia Cognitiva e Ricerca," Cognitive Psychotherapy School and Research Center, Milan, Italy

Sigmund Freud University, Milan, Italy

Sigmund Freud University, Vienna, Austria
e-mail: gm.ruggiero@milano-sfu.it

G. Caselli
Sigmund Freud University, Milan, Italy

Sigmund Freud University, Vienna, Austria

Department of Psychology, London South Bank University, London, UK

S. Sassaroli
Sigmund Freud University, Milan, Italy

Sigmund Freud University, Vienna, Austria

"Studi Cognitivi," Cognitive Psychotherapy School and Research Center, Milan, Italy

G. M. Ruggiero et al. (eds.), *CBT Case Formulation as Therapeutic Process*,
https://doi.org/10.1007/978-3-030-63587-9_6

increasingly used within various psychotherapeutic orientations, is primarily part of the clinical tradition of the behavioral psychotherapy and it was subsequently adopted in CBT. It is not a question of claiming the chronological primacy of clinical behaviorism but of being aware that the explicit and shared use of case formulation is specifically related to the theoretical principles of behavioral and then CBT approaches.

Behavioral therapies have historically been the first to use this construct, as reported by Bruch (2015), Eells (2007, 2009), Sturmey (2008, 2009). It is true that the term was only coined by the behavior therapist Turkat (1985) in the 1980s, but it is equally true that Turkat credited the original elaboration of this instrument to a previous series of behaviorist clinicians and scholars headed by Victor Meyer who, according to Turkat, was the spiritual father of the case formulation, having come forward with some publications in the 1960s. Meyer applied the principles of learning theory to clinical contexts with psychiatric patients. In so doing, he realized that behavioral intervention presupposes a hypothesis about the mental functioning of the patient and his or her underlying dysfunction. However, this formulation does not work by itself but, in order to clinically act on this functioning, it is essential to share the model and its implied rationale of the behavioral treatment with the patient.

Although Meyer actually used the term *behavioral formulation*, according to Turkat, he was the first to imbue that term with all the characteristics that made it a clinical operational tool one that could be employed with the patient to generate a hypothesis regarding his/her functioning. This conception allows the use of case formulation as a treatment rationale, i.e. a proposal for intervention that targets the dysfunction and therefore aims to ensure the maximum possible clinical effect, a real strategic bottleneck.

As discussed in chapter "Case Formulation in Standard Cognitive Therapy" (focusing on CT), the risk that accompanies case formulation is taking for granted that it is shared with the patient. The importance of the work of Meyer is that this risk was absent in his procedure of formulation; he always stressed that case formulation should be explicitly shared. Indeed, Meyer discusses this sharing in terms of both technique and theoretical assumptions. Michael Bruch (2015) drew general attention to this contribution of Meyer in his seminal book, *Beyond Diagnosis*, where he reported that Meyer recommended providing the patient the outline of the treatment procedures and the rationale behind them before each behavioral exercise. Specifically, "the patient is then given the formulation in simple terms, and the objective of treatment is discussed with him. The subject should give his consent concerning the goal of treatment" (Bruch 2015: p. 11). In addition, the therapist emphasizes the provisional nature of the concept that can be reformulated according to the patient's response (Bruch 2015: p. 12). It should be stressed again that Meyer shares a hypothesis about the emotional problem by connecting it to a rationale for the treatment he proposes to the patient. On this basis, he builds an alliance with that person in specific cognitive terms.

Meyer was certainly not the only one who went in this direction. The term "case formulation" was present in the work of other pioneers of behavioral approaches and then CBT: Shapiro (1957), Lazarus (1959, 1976), Wolpe (1964), Yates (1958), Kanfer and Saslow (1969), Sanavio (1991). Meyer's contribution, however, stands out because it introduces an element of alliance whereas case formulation for the other authors did not contain in itself any element of agreement or sharing with the patient (Meyer and Turkat 1979). For example, Shapiro, after collecting data, did not reformulate it for the patient, did not seek his or her consent and, finally, did not ask him or her to use the formulation as a touch point for collaborative work.

Shared Case Formulation, Functionalism and Free Choice

This technical difference is not merely operational but has a theoretical root. Sharing case formulation implies the assumption that the work on voluntary executive functions plays a significant role in the psychotherapeutic process. In other words, enhancing executive function means augmenting the patient's ability to make a voluntary choice in the here and now and detaching it from any factor that precedes it, including the same cognitive reasoning on beliefs and purposes that precedes a choice but does not decisively condition it. Executive function means that I can now decide to focus my attention on the choice of whether or not to go down to the cafeteria and have a coffee beyond any conscious Beckian belief about myself and the pleasure of drinking coffee or even any Freudian unconscious drive for oral pleasure. It's a higher metacognitive level in which voluntary attention and executive control do not depend on the elaboration of cognitive content but autonomously regulate it. This executive function can be used in therapy to proactively encourage change (Wells and Mathews 1994).

Before Meyer, in the behavioral paradigm, this emphasis on executive functionality was scarce if not absent. Effectively then, it could be argued, behaviorism presented a model of the mental process that emphasized unconscious states—in a manner not so far away from psychoanalysis. When Watson (1924, 1958) argued that the only way to achieve a truly scientific study of human behavior was to elude the theoretical construct of the mind and focus experimental research only on manifest behavior, he actually overlooked the role of executive conscious functions. After all, for the experimental science to which Watson's behaviorism referred, consciousness remained an ineffable object. Consciousness is immaterial, while science is borne from materialistic and mechanistic reductionism. The mind is not driven by causes. However, a mysterious agent dwells in the mind; it, by definition, completely escapes all determinism: it's free will, and therefore choice. The merit of CBT approaches, even before Meyer's behaviorism, was the rediscovery of the value of conscious willpower.

Meyer in Action: Behavioral Formulation

After collecting data on the patient's problematic situations, Meyer would share and discuss the case formulation with the patients in terms of background, behavioral responses, and consequences. The discussion was not a one-way transmission of information from the clinician to the patient; rather, it **was a dialogue between equals.** Thus, sharing information with the patient became **part of the behavioral modification** pursued by the clinician to achieve the therapeutic change. This modification, however, did not happen without the patient's knowledge: the patient and **his or her mental states are actively involved**. In this way, the therapist does not merely act externally on behavioral reactions but rather in a shared, allied, and relational way.

It was probably Meyer's strong clinical commitment that allowed him to understand the crucial role of talking to the patient as an allied experience. According to Meyer, therapists must develop hypotheses about the nature of the emotional problem and discuss and share them with the patient (Meyer 1975: p. 22). The promising aspect of the procedure of the shared case formulation is that it allowed Meyer to denominate the element of alliance in specific CBT terms. Drawing up an operational and specific terminology for the CBT area of the problems of the alliance and the therapeutic relationship without borrow terms from different psychotherapeutic traditions makes it possible to avoid theoretical confusion and technical eclecticism.

The Contribution of Turkat, Lane, and Bruch

In the case formulation approach described by Turkat (1985), the therapist uses the formulation to develop a hypothesis about the mechanisms that cause and maintain the patient's problems. Based on this hypothesis, he or she builds a rationale to justify the treatment plan. As the treatment progresses, the patient and the therapist monitor the progress of the therapy based on the variables used to formulate the case. Data that shows the patient is making good progress confirms the validity of the formulation. By contrast, if the data reveal poor progress, the therapist initiates a collaborative process of case reformulation that could lead to a different treatment plan and, ultimately, a better outcome.

Notably, Turkat was a colleague of Meyer, collaborating with him on some significant works. Indeed, in 1979 Meyer and Turkat together defined case formulation as "a hypothesis that (a) relates all the client's data to each other, (b) explains why the individual developed these difficulties, and (c) provides predictions about the patient's behavior given the triggering conditions" (pp. 261–262). Turkat then continued his reflections and, in 1985, he and Maisto defined case formulation as a "scientific approach to the clinical case," a definition in which the term "scientific approach" refers to the experimental method employing the generation and verification of hypotheses on the origin and change of the problematic behavior and the term "clinical case" indicates a method to modify the problematic behavior.

Lane (1990, p. 116) continued and further formalized Turkat's work in the field of CBT approaches. This work is summarized in the acronym DEFINE, which means:

1. *Define the problem or objective*;
2. *Explore the factors of influence*;
3. *Formulate an explanation of factors of influence*;
4. *INtervene using an action plan based on the formulation*;
5. *Evaluate the outcome of the plan based on the formulation.*

In the exploration phase, data are collected to determine the factors of the problem (framed within the principles of learning theory). In the formulation phase, the observations are evaluated and integrated to obtain an explanatory model and behavioral experiments are proposed to test the validity of the explanations. In the intervention phase, a strategy and a treatment plan are developed, based on the formulation and operationally specifying the modalities. Finally, in the evaluation phase, either standardized or *ad hoc* measures are used to assess improvements and deteriorations and to determine new objectives.

The case formulation procedure was finally brought to maturity by Michael Bruch in his model developed at University College London (UCL). UCL case formulation also represents an experimental procedure that is tailored to the patient, based on an explanatory model of dysfunctionality. Bruch's UCL model is similar to Beck's CT; yet, it is much freer and more flexible. In CT, some variables are predetermined, in particular all those concerning the cognitive mediator: automatic thoughts, beliefs about the self and the world, and intermediate beliefs. This increased rigidity of the CT model is not necessarily a disadvantage because it creates a language that facilitates communication among clinicians. At the same time, however, it undoubtedly rigidifies the process on set tracks.

For Meyer, Turkat, Lane, and Bruch, case formulation flexibly conceptualizes human behavior according to the goal of obtaining the satisfaction of a need and/or the avoidance of an adverse situation. The rationale of the behavioristic oriented formulation is shared, and therefore it is false that it treats the patient as a guinea pig to be trained. This aspect introduces an additional variable in which the internal mental function, capable of representation and choice, governs the behavior itself, representing the goal it wants to achieve, the context in which it acts, and choosing and imagining the functional behavior in advance. Therefore, it is not a question of training a system by means of negative or positive behavioral reinforcements that would act without the patient's consent. On the contrary, the task requires acting in concert with the conscious and volitional function of the patient and encouraging him or her to critically re-examine his dysfunctional reactions to the antecedents and the disadvantageous consequences of his behavior.

Behavioral Formulation: The Steps

Let us now examine the various steps of the method. Case formulation involves a functional analysis, which is the evaluation of how a patient manages his or her problem relative to his or her goals (Haynes and O'Brien 2000). In functional analysis, the dysfunctionality is signaled by the explicit declaration of a discrepancy between the patient's current state and the desired state. The statement:

I'm sick, I need your help

represents a variety of internal or external impediments that prevent or make it difficult for the patients to achieve their goals without the help of a therapist. The formulation based on functional analysis is therefore articulated in different points that include (1) the definition of the problem (i.e. outlining the reasons why a given situation is a problem and tends to be an obstacle to the satisfaction of a need) and specifying a series of goals instrumental to the satisfaction of the need; (2) the generation of behavioral alternatives by exploring a wide range of possible solutions; (3) the cost-benefit analysis of the various alternatives envisaged by assessing the potential positive and negative consequences; and (4) monitoring the effectiveness of the solution plan after its implementation.

In view of the shared formulation, it should be noted that problems and goals must be defined by the patient. The therapist invites the patient to define their problems and emotional distresses in their own words, which initially will be generic:

When I'm around other people, I worry about everything and want to feel better. I have a lot of problems in having good social relations.

Which can be translated into a formal diagnosis of social anxiety and related to specific goals such as:

Improving social relations;

Feeling less stupid in the midst of others.

Once the goal and formulation of the problem are shared, the therapist moves on to analyze the background, behaviors, and consequences on which it is possible to act. Notably, from a shared point of view, all this should be steadily carried out by informing the patient of the rationale of the therapeutic action by saying:

Now we formulate your problem by articulating it in three main groups of elements, that is (1) the situation in which your distress is present, (2) what you do during the distress, that is your behavior, and (3) the consequences of your behavior. The idea is that your problem consists of these elements and that once articulated in this way it will be easier for us to identify the points where you can effectively act.

This diagram can be displayed on a whiteboard or on paper during the session; this visual tool also provides a strong element of sharing:

Let's divide this whiteboard/sheet of paper into three columns that correspond to situations, behaviors, and consequences and let's assign the elements we will collect and examine to these three classes of elements.

The clinician then goes on to ascertain the relationship between the current state and the goals:

Furthermore, we should compare these elements with the goals, that is to say, with either the conditions of the environment or your behaviors that you would like to change or achieve. We could write them down here at the bottom of the whiteboard/sheet of paper.

And then moving on:

We could act on your behaviors by looking for the ones that can be more easily changed initially. Are there things you could do that you hasn't done so far? We could also reflect on elements of your environment such as the places you visit and where you might meet possible acquaintances or friendships and so on. The consequences of what you do or have done so far are also interesting, they help us to understand how what you do might have changed the situation and how this change might have influenced you.

All this work must ultimately only serve to introduce the sharing of the formulation:

Above all, however, I would like you to consider this formulation as the key to understanding your distress. I would like you to use this scheme to frame your problems, not just the one you brought me today. Dismantling a problem in its elements and seeking in it the point where to act is the core of this treatment, the explanation of how it works.

This operation must be incessantly implemented. Any reformulation of the case should provide an opportunity for an accurate and careful reconsideration. Above all, it should not be taken for granted that the patient has understood his or her active role. The patient could unfortunately adhere to a *naive* idea of psychotherapy as a place where people talk, feel welcome, and come out changed without personal commitment.

To achieve this agreement, the therapist frequently reviews the functional analysis by identifying those instrumental goals that are probably related to the final goals. This process involves exploring behavioral, affective, cognitive, social and cultural, and even biological variables. Relational agreement is found in this procedure and not before or outside it. Likewise, the generation of alternatives must once again be an active function of the patient:

Now that you have a picture of the situation, can you see alternatives? Maybe they came to your mind while we were making this picture. Compare the data collected with the targets we wrote. How can we cover the gap?

The therapist will of course contribute by using his or her scientific and clinical experience. In social anxiety, for example, it would be good to explore the patient's tendency to nervously monitor the judgment of others about his or her performance in any micro-social event and, instead, encourage the patient to think simply about what he or she should or would like to say or do in that context in a non-judgmental way.

Let us look at a case of behavioral exposure. As is widely known, some types of phobias are particularly well suited for this type of exercise. Examples include cases linked to the fear of transportation or the fear of eating in public. A classic behavioral intervention would comprise a simple invitation:

This thing you're afraid of, can we really try to do it?

When could you do that? Let's see how your week is organized. Let's seek the best opportunity.

The intervention is expected to work by exposure and habituation. In the shared case formulation, we instead work with the patient by sharing with him or her all the variables that hinder achievement of the objective, i.e. to increase his or her behavioral repertoire. The various elements include, as we stated above, thoughts about external and internal aspects and their consequences. Hence, what matters is not so much to recommend exposure directly but to analyze point by point with the patient how each aspect of the formulation would change as he or she implements the exposure exercise. How does the situation of driving on a motorway interact with a thought of danger that comes with it on the motorway? Further, how does the current consequence, no longer taking the motorway, end up reinforcing your anxieties and avoidances? This process then continues:

Let's look together at all the elements we found and transcribed on this whiteboard/sheet of paper. How would they change once you actually take the motorway this weekend? What would happen to the thought of being in danger?

Despite Meyer's use of the term "behavioral formulation," his emphasis on sharing included what we might consider a functionalistic principle of both emotional suffering and the therapeutic process. Specifically, emotional disorders emanate from cognitive dysfunctions that are relatively consciously activated through voluntary executive function at a metacognitive level. For these reasons, Meyer believed it was possible for the therapist to ascertain and treat these in a conscious collaboration with the patient, i.e. by activating those same voluntary functions already used by the patient to inflict to him- or herself the dysfunctional states—but this time to restructure the mental state in functional terms. However, in the CBT environment, we have not always been aware of this functionalistic principle, either in clinical research or in the actual applied clinic. It is only with the most recent turning point that this awareness has increased— as, for example, in the recent process-based reformulation of CBT by Hayes and Hofmann (2018).

Shared Case Formulation and Functionalism

From a theoretical point of view, Bruch proposes that there exists a close relationship between shared case formulation and so-called abductive logic. To reason abductively means to construct the best hypothesis on the most likely explanation in light of all the facts under examination. Evers and Wu (2006) call it inference at best explanation. Abduction is a provisional generalization that explains the empirical observed data better than any other alternative hypothesis. This type of reasoning is typical of case formulation, where information is often incomplete and highly contextual in nature. This last point is important because it is very unlikely that there is a single explanatory hypothesis that can explain all the facts about a person's life (Bruch 2015).

In summary, case formulation of the clinical tradition, ranging from Meyer to Bruch through Turkat and Lane, has a solid behavioral ground based on functional analysis. It offers to the patient an explanation of what supports his or her dysfunctional behavior by ascertaining the reinforcing factors and a rationale for creating alternative behaviors. The main merit of case formulation in this clinical tradition is that in it the shared nature of the formulation is not taken for granted but rather conceptualized as a factor of the quality of the therapeutic relationship, which becomes an outcome of sharing. As we have already written elsewhere, it is not so obvious that the formulation is shared. It is not true that the formulation, being both an explanation of the emotional disorders and a rationale of the treatment, by definition, is shared with the patient and understood by him or her if the therapist does not clearly share it. This concept also includes the therapeutic relationship: Explicit and unceasing sharing of the formulation with the patient encourages a therapeutic relationship in which the element of trust in the patient's collaboration is dominant and the therapeutic process is not considered to involve overcoming a series of resistances. This view implies that dysfunctions are not considered to be resistances or defenses; they are dysfunctions.

Peter Sturmey: The Meaning of Functionalism

In 1996 (Sturmey 1996) and in 2008 Peter Sturmey wrote two seminal books in which he described the basic concepts and methods that go from functional analysis into behavioral case formulation and intervention. He retrieved the explicit behavioral tradition which dated back to Skinner's work. However, in order to conceptualize an updated version of behaviorism, Sturmey stressed that thought and language are an important aspect of human behavior. Thought and language are nothing else than verbal behaviors, private and internal (thought) or public and external (verbalized language), respectively. However, this does not mean that this verbal behavior is structurally superior to other behaviors. It is no coincidence that Sturmey provides the ultimate definition of the difference between structuralist and functionalist approaches. In functionalist approaches, language does not have an underlying and structural meaning but only has effects, as with any other behavior. Consequently, language must be assessed not for its invariant essence, i.e. its meaning, but on the basis of its behavioral consequences, the effects. Sturmey rightly traces the concept of structural approach to Chomsky (1959) who thought that verbal behavior is a mere token of underlying grammatical structures, and the concept of verbal behavior to Skinner (1953, 1957), who offered an extensive account of thinking and feeling as internal and private verbal behaviors. Public and private language can be a key aspect of psychopathology and an integral part of case formulation and treatment for many behaviorists.

Sturmey also stresses the contribution of Wolpe (1964) to the development of case formulation. As in the aforementioned case of Victor Meyer, Wolpe not only recommended careful interviewing of the patient in order to identify potential conditioning experiences and stimuli, more importantly, he required clinicians to interrogate their client's situation using hypothesis-driven interviewing—in other words, case formulation. However, it is not clear whether, for Wolpe, confirmation of the hypotheses depended solely on the positive behavioral outcome of the intervention or, as well, on the verbal exchange shared with the patient (as seemed to be the case with Victor Meyer's approach). It is true that, while Wolpe's approach included clear tests of case formulation aimed at investigating the validity of the formulation itself: exposing the client to different kinds of stimuli to identify which were antecedents of the functional consequence (e.g., anxiety), ratings of the functional consequence to various stimuli, and psychophysiological measures of the functional consequence, by the time of Turkat and Bruch, testing formulations was no longer a requirement of the model. It was replaced by the verbal confirmations of the patient. This shift implied a larger importance of a verbally-shared formulation depending on the growing influence of the CBT models.

Regarding Skinner's contribution to the psychotherapeutic use of shared case formulation, Sturmey reports that Skinner advised that the therapist should not unilaterally deliver the formulation to the patient. Admittedly, this advice does not seem entirely compatible with the rule of sharing the case formulation recommended in this book. Summing up, Skinner provides a functionalist reason for his distrust of sharing the case formulation: Skinner correctly notes that sharing the formulation would contaminate the purity of the behavioral antecedent‘s action, preventing testing the hypothesis of the intervention's functioning. Skinner's objection must be accepted by turning it into a strength, i.e., accepting that sharing the case formulation must actually be considered a consciously inserted antecedent in the hypothesis of the intervention's functioning. On the other hand, we must take note that only Meyer offers a definitive transition to a formulation of the case verbally shared according to the mature CBT tradition, while Skinner was still tied to limits inherent in the purely behavioral approach.

However, it is fascinating to observe that Skinner has provided a genuinely metacognitive explanation in his recommendation to not deliver the formulation to the patient. In fact, Skinner notes that a shared case formulation itself changes the patient's behavior, becoming a component of the functional analysis. For this reason, Skinner prefers that patients make by themselves the discovery of the relationship between their own behavior and the environment. Therefore, it is confirmed that Skinner does not conceive the case formulation as a shared task of the patient and the therapist. However, his metacognitive conception of the effect of verbal awareness reached by the patient on his overall behavior is a prefiguration of the conception of the shared formulation of the case as an internal element of the therapeutic process (Sturmey 2008, p. 193). Further, the Skinnerian concept of self-management was a sort of functionalist version of metacognition: Verbal behavior is able to regulate other behaviors through representations not only of their antecedents and consequences but also of the effects of these representations themselves.

Case Formulation, Empathy, and Therapeutic Relationship

A possible criticism of this model is the risk of an overly managerial clinical style inherent within, which might result in a lack of empathy and a threat to patient fragility. We can find many examples of this crucial criticism in chapters "Schema Therapy, Contextual Schema Therapy and Case Formulation: Commentary on Chapter "Case Formulation in Process-Based Therapies"", "Commentary on the Presentation of the Metacognitive Interpersonal Therapy Model in Chapter "Strengths and Limitations of Case Formulation In Constructivist Cognitive Behavioral Therapies"", "The Case Formulation in the Post-Rationalist Constructivist Model. Commentary on Chapter "Strengths and Limitations of Case Formulation In Constructivist Cognitive Behavioral Therapies"", "Case Formulation and the Therapeutic Relationship from an Evolutionary Theory of Motivation. Commentary to Chapter 15," "Emotion, Motivation, Therapeutic Relationship and Cognition in Giovanni Liotti's Model: Commentary on Chapter 15" and "Case Formulation as an Outcome and Not an Opening Move in Relational and Psychodynamic Models" of this book. Bruch (2015) is very eager to respond; he writes that one cannot be empathetic if one fails to understand the specifics of a problem. For Bruch, the idea that a patient is "too fragile" to handle a direct investigation has little empirical support. On the contrary, Bruch believes that frankness and openness are highly appreciated by most patients.

Clearly, Bruch does not deny the benefits of a positive therapeutic relationship. He conceptualizes the therapeutic relationship as an integral part of the entire treatment process and does not treat this aspect in isolation. Undoubtedly, you must be able to empathize with the patient if you want to be able to formulate the case. In a careful formulation, the interviewer has the opportunity to show a higher level of empathy when investigating explanatory hypotheses in cooperation with the patient. For Bruch, there is a good relationship if the clinician has created an environment for the patient that allows him or her to receive the information necessary.

Summing up, it is not true that, in the CBT field, no importance has been assigned to the therapeutic relationship—we just need to understand how it is called, conceptualized and managed. The importance of the therapeutic relationship has been highlighted by distinguished clinicians who proposed a CBT approach (e.g. Beck et al. 1979; Brady 1980; Goldfried and Davison 1976; Kohlenberg and Tsai 1991; Linehan 1988; Meichenbaum 2006; Meyer and Gelder 1963; Wolpe and Lazarus 1966). Even earlier work has confirmed that behavioral therapists are at least as warm, empathetic, sincere, and caring as therapists within other orientations (e.g. Brunink and Schroeder 1979; Fischer et al. 1975; Sloan et al. 1975). In addition, AuBuchon and other CBT scholars have reflected on the role of the CBT therapist as a reassuring figure who models a positive relationship with the world (AuBuchon and Calhoun 1990; Bandura and Menlove 1968; Linehan 1988; Meyer 1957; Rachman 1983; Rosenfarb 1992; Wolpe 1980).

Peter AuBuchon (2015) is the scholar who perhaps has most understood how shared case formulation could be conceived as a specific way of managing the therapeutic relationship within the framework of CBT (AuBuchon and Malatesta 1998). He has followed a sort of reverse path compared to Bruch, i.e. from a therapeutic relationship to case formulation and not vice versa. In short, the therapeutic relationship in the model of AuBuchon and Malatesta (1998) is guided by case formulation. From this principle, AuBuchon has reviewed empirical data regarding the clinical effect of the shared approach to case formulation; this endeavor has proved to be empirically effective with a number of disorders, including schizophrenia (Adams et al. 1981), chronic pain (AuBuchon 1983), complex phobia (AuBuchon 1993), complex obsessive-compulsive disorder (OCD), personality disorders (AuBuchon and Malatesta 1998; Turkat and Carlson 1984), and tic disorders (Malatesta 1990).

AuBuchon and Malatesta (1998) also introduced and operationally defined their model of relational intervention, the "style of the therapist" that once again is a procedure of case management. In fact, AuBuchon and Malatesta do not define this style as proactive interpersonal behavior shown by the therapist, which is almost redundant. Rather, their definition is more operational, namely, as the therapist's formulation of the patient's difficulties, which is another component of a shared case formulation (p. 144). In conclusion, the therapeutic alliance reinforced by case formulation offers many additional benefits for CBT approach therapists. When the case formulation is shared, patients seem to trust their therapist more and report feeling well understood by their therapists.

References

Adams, H. E., Malatesta, V. J., Brantley, P. J., & Turkat, I. D. (1981). Modification of cognitive processes: A case study of schizophrenia. *Journal of Consulting and Clinical Psychology, 49*, 460–464.

AuBuchon, P. G. (1993). Formulation-based treatment of a complex phobia. *Journal of Behavior Therapy and Experimental Psychiatry, 24*, 63–71.

AuBuchon, P. G. (2015). Case formulation and the therapeutic relationship. In M. Bruch (Ed.), *Beyond diagnosis: Case formulation in cognitive behavioural therapy* (2nd ed., pp. 74–95). Chichester: John Wiley & Sons.

AuBuchon, P. G., & Calhoun, K. S. (1990). The effects of therapist presence and relaxation training on the efficacy and generalizability of in vivo exposure. *Behavioural Psychotherapy, 18*, 169–185.

AuBuchon, P. G., & Malatesta, V. J. (1998). Managing the therapeutic relationship in behavior therapy: The need for a case formulation. In M. Bruch & F. W. Bond (Eds.), *Beyond diagnosis: Case formulation approaches in CBT* (1st ed., pp. 141–165). Chichester, UK: John Wiley & Sons.

Bandura, A., & Menlove, F. L. (1968). Factors determining vicarious extinction of avoidance behavior through symbolic modeling. *Journal of Personality and Social Psychology, 8*, 99–108.

Beck, A. T., Rush, A. J., Shaw, B. F., & Emery, G. (1979). *Cognitive therapy of depression*. New York, NY: The Guilford Press.

Beck, J. S. (2011). Cognitive therapy: Basics and beyond (2nd ed.) London, UK; New York, NY: Guilford Press.

Brady, J. P, et al. (1980). Some views on effective principles of psychotherapy. *Cognitive Therapy and Research, 4*, 271–306.

Bruch, M. (2015). *Beyond diagnosis: Case formulation in cognitive behavioural therapy* (2nd ed.). Chicester: John Wiley & Sons.

Brunink, S. A., & Schroeder, H. E. (1979). Verbal therapeutic behavior of expert psychoanalytically oriented, gestalt, and behavior therapists. *Journal of Consulting and Clinical Psychology, 47*, 567–574.

Chomsky, N. (1959). A review of BF Skinner's verbal behavior. *Language, 35*, 25–68.

Eells, T. D. (2007). *Handbook of psychotherapy case formulation*. New York, NY: Guilford.

Eells, T. D. (2009). Contemporary themes in case formulation. In P. Sturmey (Ed.), *Clinical case formulation. Varieties of approaches* (pp. 293–316). Chichester: John Wiley & Sons.

Evers, C. W., & Wu, E. H. (2006). On generalising from single case studies: Epistemological reflections. *Journal of Philosophy of Education, 40*, 511–526.

Fischer, J., Paveza, G. J., Kickertz, N. S., Hubbard, L. J., & Grayson, S. B. (1975). The relationship between theoretical orientation and therapists' empathy, warmth, and genuineness. *Journal of Consulting Psychology, 22*, 399–403.

Goldfried, M. R., & Davison, G. C. (1976). *Clinical behavior therapy*. New York, NY: Holt, Rinehart, & Winston.

Hayes, S. C., & Hofman, S. G. (2018). *Process-based CBT: The science and core clinical competencies of cognitive behavioral therapy*. Oakland, CA: New Harbinger Publications.

Haynes, S. N., & O'Brien, W. H. (2000). *Principles and practice of behavioral assessment*. New York, NY: Kluwer.

Kanfer, F. H., & Saslow, G. (1969). Behavioral diagnosis. In C. M. Franks (Ed.), *Behavior therapy: Appraisal and status* (pp. 417–444). New York, NY: McGraw-Hill.

Kohlenberg, R. J., & Tsai, M. (1991). *Functional analytic psychotherapy: Creating intense and curative therapeutic relationships*. New York, NY: Plenum Press.

Lane, D. (1990). *The impossible child. Stoke on Trent*. London: Trentham.

Lazarus, A. A. (1959). The elimination of children's phobias by deconditioning. *Medical Proceedings, 6*, 261–265.

Lazarus, A. A. (1976). *Multimodal behavior therapy*. New York, NY: Springer.

Linehan, M. M. (1988). Perspectives on the interpersonal relationship in behavior therapy. *Journal of Integrative and Eclectic Psychotherapy, 7*, 278–290.

Malatesta, V. J. (1990). Behavioral case formulation: An experimental assessment study of transient tic disorder. *Journal of Psychopathology and Behavioral Assessment, 12*, 219–232.

Meichenbaum, D. (2006). Trauma and Suicide: A Constructive Narrative Perspective. In T. E. Ellis (Ed.), *Cognition and suicide: Theory, research, and therapy* (p. 333–353). Washington, DC, USA: American Psychological Association Books.

Meyer, V. (1957). The treatment of two phobic patients on the basis of learning principles. *Journal of Abnormal and Social Psychology, 55*, 261–266.

Meyer, V. (1975). The impact of research on the clinical application of behaviour therapy. In R. I. Thompson & W. S. Dockens (Eds.), *Applications of behaviour modification*. New York: Academic Press.

Meyer, V., & Gelder, M. G. (1963). Behaviour therapy and phobic disorders. *British Journal of Psychiatry, 109*, 19–28.

Meyer, V., & Turkat, I. D. (1979). Behavioural analysis of clinical cases. *Journal of Behavioural Assessment, 1*, 259–269.

Rachman, S. (1983). The modification of agoraphobic avoidance behavior: Some fresh possibilities. *Behaviour Research and Therapy, 21*, 567–574.

Rosenfarb, I. S. (1992). A behavior analytic interpretation of the therapeutic relationship. *The Psychological Record, 42*, 341–354.

Sanavio, E. (1991). *Psicoterapia cognitiva e comportamentale [Cognitive and behavioral psychotherapy]*. Roma: Carocci.

Shapiro, M. B. (1957). Experimental methods in the psychological description of the individual psychiatric patient. *International Journal of Social Psychiatry, 111*, 89–102.
Skinner, B. F. (1953). *Science and human behavior*. New York, NY: The Free Press.
Skinner, B. F. (1957). *Verbal behavior*. New York, NY: Appleton-Century-Crofts.
Sloan, R. B., Staples, F. R., Cristol, A. H., Yorkston, N. H., & Whipple, K. (1975). *Psychotherapy versus behavior therapy*. Cambridge, MA: Harvard University Press.
Sturmey, P. (1996). *Functional analysis in clinical psychology*. Chicester: John Wiley & Sons.
Sturmey, P. (2008). *Behavioral case formulation and intervention: A functional analytic approach*. Chicester: John Wiley & Sons.
Sturmey, P. (Ed.). (2009). *Clinical case formulation: Varieties of approaches*. Chicester: John Wiley & Sons.
Turkat, I. D. (1985). *Behavioural case formulation*. New York, NY: Plenum.
Turkat, I. D., & Carlson, C. R. (1984). Data-based versus symptomatic formulation of treatment: The case of a dependent personality. *Journal of Behavior Therapy and Experimental Psychiatry, 15*, 153–160.
Watson, J. B. (1924). *Behaviorism*. New York, NY: W. W. Norton & Company, Inc..
Watson, J. B. (1958). *Behaviorism (revised ed.)*. Chicago, IL: University of Chicago Press.
Wells, A., & Mathews, G. (1994). *Attention and emotion: A clinical perspective*. Hove, UK, Hillsdale, NJ: Erlbaum.
Wolpe, J. (1964). The systematic desensitization treatment of neuroses. In H. J. Eysenck (Ed.), *Behavior therapy and the neuroses* (pp. 21–40). New York, NY: The Macmillan Co..
Wolpe, J. (1980). Behavior therapy for psychosomatic disorders. *Psychosomatics, 21*, 379–385.
Wolpe, J., & Lazarus, A. A. (1966). *Behavior therapy techniques: A guide to the treatment of neuroses*. Elmsford, NY, US: Pergamon Press.
Yates, A. J. (1958). The application of learning theory to the treatment of tics. *Journal of Abnormal and Social Psychology, 56*, 175–182.

Some Thoughts on Chapter "Case Formulation in the Behavioral Tradition: Meyer, Turkat, Lane, Bruch, and Sturmey" by Giovanni Maria Ruggiero, Gabriele Caselli and Sandra Sassaroli

Peter Sturmey

Contents

Introduction

It is a pleasure to be asked to comments on the chapter, "Case formulation in the behavioral tradition: Meyer, Turkat, Lane, Bruch, and Sturmey" by Giovanni Maria Ruggiero, Gabriele Caselli and Sandra Sassaroli. This brief commentary addresses four points that arise from this chapter: (1) What is meant be "sharing a case formulation"; (2) the relationship between case formulation and therapeutic relationship; (3) the conception of cognition and meta-cognition in behavioral case formulation; and (4) The self-managed life.

What is Sharing a Case Formulation?

Early work on case formulation emphasized its utility for the clinician in guiding them toward the most effective idiographic treatment; indeed, therapist rather like their formulations and find them helpful (Pain et al. 2008). Research on the role of

P. Sturmey (✉)
The Graduate Center and Queens College, City University of New York, New York, NY, USA
e-mail: peter.sturmey@qc.cuny.edu

G. M. Ruggiero et al. (eds.), *CBT Case Formulation as Therapeutic Process*,
https://doi.org/10.1007/978-3-030-63587-9_7

sharing case formulation came after initial work on case formulation has already taken place but produced some mixed results: Although some clients liked their formulations and found them helpful, a significant minority disliked them or reported that the formulations were overwhelming and led them to be pessimistic about their own prognosis (Chadwick et al. 2003). These results may not apply to all versions of case formulation and perhaps there are better ways of doing it that client appreciate more. Thus, at first the reasons for sharing formulations with clients appear to be primarily to do with respect for clients' autonomy rather than evidence that this helps.

These mixed outcomes may partly reflect a lack of clarity regarding the process of "sharing a formulation" but, even more importantly, might also reflects a lack of analysis of what this term means and how it might affect relevant client behavior. Adaption of a Skinnerian perspective regarding case formulation clarifies this.

There are several approaches to sharing case formulations. One option is not to share the formulation. The client might be assigned activities based on the therapist's case formulation, such as learning relaxation or graded in vivo self-exposure. This might be quite helpful, but today many therapists would reject this as being disrespectful of the client's autonomy and seemingly arrogant or even authoritarian on the part of the therapist. At the very least there might be a missed opportunity to get more client buy-in to the therapy process, so perhaps even at a simple pragmatic level, this approach might be sub-optimal. So, what is sharing a formulation?

Sharing a formulation might refer to several different activities between therapists and clients. In the first version that therapist might state the formulation or hand a written or diagrammatic summary little or no request for input from the client but might offer the opportunity for client questions and answer them. This might be framed as a client educational activity by the didactic clinician, but many of us would reject this for reasons discussed in the preceding paragraph. What is interesting about this way to share the formulation is there is no direct opportunity for the client to respond before the formulation is made and little opportunity for the client to respond once it is delivered. If the material is unfamiliar, difficult to understand or elicits a negative client emotional response then the client may say or do little. Some clients may not know what to think and so have nothing much to say. Further, this situation may resemble other previous situations that have involved punishment for appearing ignorant or ungrateful. Perhaps some of the unhappiness that some clients expressed (Chadwick et al. 2003) when given their formulation is that it is too much, too unfamiliar, too overwhelming, too complex for them to respond to.

In a second version the therapist might teach the client in various ways how to make a formulation. The therapist might prompt the client to do so by presenting antecedents such as a shell of a standard formulation and prompt the client to elaborate and individualize it in various ways. The therapist modifies the client's behavior though antecedents ("Does any of this apply to you in some way?) and consequences ("That's a good point, I think you are on to something here" or "I am not quite sure you understand how the formulation translates to a treatment for you. Don't you think avoiding all criticism is impossible for all of us?" In so doing, the therapist might bring the verbal and other client behavior under the control of the therapist, written stimuli and perhaps the client's own verbal behavior. This is not necessarily a bad thing as the client may begin to discriminate many important environment-behavior relationships that might help resolve their problems and begin to change their own verbal behavior which might be a prelude to changing other clinically relevant behavior outside the therapy session.

The third version is based on Skinner's recommendations which are based on a behavior analytic understanding of psychopathology and the therapy process. As Ruggiero et al. noted, Skinner saw the job of the therapist as a kind of bridge who provides minimal but sufficient prompting to change the client's behavior by inducing them to discriminate the relationships between the environment and their problematic and adaptive behavior and them use this as the basis for self-managed client behavior change.

These three versions of sharing a case formulation identify several dimensions of therapist behavior: (1) The formulation may be developed sometime before the intervention or shared immediately before interventions; (2) the therapist may provide some or no opportunity for client input; (3) client input into the formulation might take place at different times; and (4) may provide different frequency and intrusiveness of prompts for clients to have input to the formulation. There may be other relevant dimensions to case formulations. These four dimensions could be used to derive multiple ways to develop and share case formulations with clients which future research could evaluate.

Case Formulation and Therapeutic Relationship

A good therapeutic relationship is important in all forms of psychotherapy including that based on behavioral case formulation. Thus, the work of AuBuchon and Malatesta on the therapeutic relationship in behavioral case formulation (AuBuchon 2015; AuBuchon and Malatesta 1998) is important in providing some guidance to clinicians. A behavioral case formulation might guide a therapeutic relationship in a number of idiographic ways. For example, a therapist might decide that when working with a client with a paranoid personality disorder who is socially very avoidant that initially the therapist should be particularly warm and unchallenging. Only later on after a good therapeutic relationship has been established, the therapist might then gradually increase the presentation of elements of the formulation, agreeing goals and evaluation of treatment outcome that might involve some implied criticism. For other clients a case formulation might suggest other strategies to manage the therapeutic relationship that reflect the function of the clients presenting problems.

There is, however, little empirical research on case formulation and the therapeutic relationship. At least three empirical studies of this topic have addressed this issue and all have found rather mixed results. Clients may respond either positively or negatively to the presentation of a case formulation, even if it has apparently been worked on collaboratively, whereas therapists tend to believe that it strengthens the therapeutic relationship (Chadwick et al. 2003; Evans and Parry 1996; Pain et al. 2008). Pain et al. (127) commented that the presentation of the case formulation, even after sharing information and shaping the formulation with the client's collaboration, might be an emotionally significant even to which some clients might react negatively. If we conceive of the presentation of the formulation as an antecedent stimulus which evokes problematic negative emotional behavior in some clients, then perhaps we can consider alternate strategies to manage this potentially problematic antecedent stimulus, such as presenting a formulation more frequently earlier on and in graded steps rather than all at once after a period of time.

Cognition and Meta-Cognition

In several places, Ruggiero et al. discuss cognition, meta-cognition and executive function. For example, they wrote "it is fascinating that Skinner has provided a genuinely metacognitive explanation …. The Skinnerian concept of self-management was a sort of functionalist version of meta-cognition."

Behavioral conception of private verbal behavior is a sticking point for many non-behaviorists. I think there are two distinct problems: Misunderstanding of behavioral approaches to cognition and a more fundamental disagreement on the nature of the causes of human behavior. I believe behaviorism and behavior analysis is often not taught to clinicians or poorly and inaccurately represented in much clinical training. To reach minimal professional levels of competency in behavior analysis practitioners require at least 1500 h of instruction and studying and a similar amount of supervised practicum experience (Board Analysis Certification Board 2012). Most clinical courses may provide a few tens of hours of lectures and may or may not provide any supervised practice. Hence, many mental health professionals do not learn the basics of behavior analysis and make common mistakes such as believing that behavior analysis is only about contingencies, behavior analysis does not believe that people think or do not recognize Acceptance and Commitment Therapy (Hayes 2004) as a behavior analytic treatment that addresses private behavior.

Behaviorism has never denied private verbal behavior. Skinner (1953) wrote extensively about thinking. He saw thinking as a covert behavior to be analyzed in behavioral terms. It can have motivational, stimulus control and consequential functions, for example, ruminating about having a panic attack might both be the beginning of a stimulus-repose behavior chain acting as a discriminative stimulus for the next member of the stimulus-response chain and might also be a motivational operation temporarily increasing the negative reinforcing value of escape. Like overt behavior, covert behavior can also be controlled in numerous ways, including behavioral self-management, as when we remove distractions and present ourselves with ambiguous stimuli "to be creative" to change how we think and write (Epstein 1991).

The Self-Managed Life

Although ultimate control of everyone's behavior lies in the environment rather than the mythical initiating self or initiating brain, we can all do much to behave in an apparently agentic manner that gives us the appearance and perhaps welcome illusion of autonomy (Skinner 1953). Ironically, it is the person who believes that are an initiating organism but who lack a repertoire of behavioral self-management who may be most vulnerable to undesirable and problematic control of their behavior resulting in many mental health issues.

Rather than be passive victims of our biology, personal history, diagnoses, and psychiatric illnesses, we can all design a better life for ourselves. We can all learn to behave (overtly and covertly) in ways that are more meaningful, less painful, happier, more productive by redesigning our social and physical environments to help us behave in the ways we wish to. We can apply these principles and this technology to behave better in even the most difficult of circumstances where may would give up and suffer; we can apply them to the end of life and even die better if we wish (Fantino 2007; Hopko et al. 2011).

Behavioral case formulation continues to be refined and applied and to a wide range of clinical problems (Sturmey 2020). Its evidence-base, dissemination, understanding and acceptance by the broader community of clinicians is a continuing project. We can anticipate that work in this area will continue for many decades to come.

References

AuBuchon, P. G. (2015). Case formulation and the therapeutic relationship. *Beyond Diagnosis: Case Formulation in Cognitive Behavioural Therapy, 110*, 74.

AuBuchon, P. G., & Malatesta, V. J. (1998). Managing the therapeutic relationship in behavior therapy: The need for a case formulation. *Beyond diagnosis: Case formulation approaches in CBT*, 141–166.

Board Analysis Certification Board (2012) *Coursework Requirements for BACB Credentials Fourth Edition Task List.* Retrieved August 2, 2020 from https://www.bacb.com/wp-content/uploads/2020/05/BACB_CourseContentAllocation.pdf

Chadwick, P., Williams, C., & Mackenzie, J. (2003). Impact of case formulation in cognitive behaviour therapy for psychosis. *Behaviour Research and Therapy, 41*(6), 671–680.

Epstein, R. (1991). Skinner, creativity, and the problem of spontaneous behavior. *Psychological Science, 2*(6), 362–370.

Evans, J., & Parry, G. (1996). The impact of reformulation in cognitive-analytic therapy with difficult-to-help clients. *Clinical Psychology & Psychotherapy: An International Journal of Theory and Practice, 3*(2), 109–117.

Fantino, E. (2007). *Behaving well: Strategies for celebrating life in the face of illness*. Atlanta, GA, US: Performance Management Publications.

Hayes, S. C. (2004). Acceptance and commitment therapy, relational frame theory, and the third wave of behavioral and cognitive therapies. *Behavior Therapy, 35*, 639–665.

Hopko, D. R., Armento, M. E., Robertson, S., Ryba, M. M., Carvalho, J. P., Colman, L. K., et al. (2011). Brief behavioral activation and problem-solving therapy for depressed breast cancer patients: Randomized trial. *Journal of Consulting and Clinical Psychology, 79*(6), 834.
Pain, C. M., Chadwick, P., & Abba, N. (2008). Clients' experience of case formulation in cognitive behaviour therapy for psychosis. *British Journal of Clinical Psychology, 47*, 127–138.
Skinner, B. F. (1953). Some contributions of an experimental analysis of behavior to psychology as a whole. *American Psychologist, 8*, 69–78.
Sturmey, P. (2020). *Functional analysis in clinical treatment* (2nd ed.). New York: Elsevier.

How B-C Connection, Negotiation of F and Rationale of D Allow the Design and Implementation of a Cooperative and Effective Disputing in Rational Emotive Behavior Therapy

Giovanni Maria Ruggiero, Diego Sarracino, Gabriele Caselli, and Sandra Sassaroli

Contents

G. M. Ruggiero (✉)
"Psicoterapia Cognitiva e Ricerca", Cognitive Psychotherapy School and Research Center, Milan, Italy

Sigmund Freud University, Milan, Italy

Sigmund Freud University, Vienna, Austria
e-mail: gm.ruggiero@milano-sfu.it

D. Sarracino
Department of Psychology, University of Milano Bicocca, Milan, Italy

G. Caselli
Sigmund Freud University, Milan, Italy

Sigmund Freud University, Vienna, Austria

Department of Psychology, London South Bank University, London, UK

S. Sassaroli
Sigmund Freud University, Milan, Italy

Sigmund Freud University, Vienna, Austria

"Studi Cognitivi," Cognitive Psychotherapy School and Research Center, Milan, Italy

G. M. Ruggiero et al. (eds.), *CBT Case Formulation as Therapeutic Process*,
https://doi.org/10.1007/978-3-030-63587-9_8

Two Key Moments in REBT: B-C Connection and Negotiation of F

Let us now consider the other great cognitive model, rational emotive behavior therapy (REBT; Ellis 1955, 1962; Ellis and Grieger 1986; Dryden 2008; DiGiuseppe et al. 2014). REBT declares itself to be a directive treatment; sometimes this aspect is used to define it as a therapy with little attention to the therapeutic relationship and alliance with the patient. However, from our viewpoint, the real dividing line is not between therapies that are careful about the relationship and those that are directive. This classification is based on a unilateral and limited dimension that simplifies the relationship and reduces it to its welcoming and caring side. This view almost suggests that non-directive therapies are flattened on the validation of the patient while directive ones lack a spontaneous alliance. This view is questionable. For example, Transference Focused Psychotherapy (Clarkin et al. 2006) is a non-directive therapy that manages the relationship in complex terms and is not reducible to the validation side. A different dividing line could lie in the way the case formulation is shared: explicitly and negotiated from the outset in a broad sense in the case of cognitive behavioral therapy (CBT) approaches, which include REBT, or instead as the result of a gradual discovery in other orientations.

The REBT therapist, as in other CBT approaches, proceeds quite quickly to illustrate and share with the patient the principles of action of the treatment. REBT focuses on ascertaining so-called unhealthy emotions in problematic situations, agreeing on the pursuit of healthy emotional states as a therapeutic goal, and conceptualizing the connection between these emotions and the so-called irrational beliefs or dysfunctional thoughts as the main psychopathological process. The patient is encouraged to think that he or she can act on these thoughts by disputing them. This action would allow the patient to think new thoughts that are at the ground of the healthy emotions that have been established as goals (Ellis and Grieger 1986; DiGiuseppe et al. 2014).

This procedure, called ABC DEF, is explicitly explained to the patient at every step, with the rationale always provided for each step. Hence, REBT works beyond the mere mechanical implementation of its procedure. It works above all because its steps and rationale are shared with the patient, who learns it as a tool of understanding and of active management of his or her functioning—a tool to be used autonomously. Once again, it is a matter of transmitting a skill to the patient rather than simply discovering and modifying dysfunctional mental contents.

The two key moments in which this phenomenon occurs are called the B-C connection (DiGiuseppe et al. 2014: pp. 57–58) and negotiation of F (DiGiuseppe et al. 2014: pp. 25–27; 59–63). They are the two pivots from which the REBT therapist shares the case formulation and builds a therapeutic alliance with the patient. Unlike CBT, in REBT we are faced with a formulation of the problem rather than a formulation of the case. Every single ABC DEF of REBT, unlike in CBT, does not tend to be articulated in a structure of core beliefs and coping strategies that is superordinate to individual problems. Irrational thinking and functional alternatives are specific to each single ABC DEF procedure, which is in turn specific to a given problematic situation. Further, in REBT there is no formalized larger structure, as with the Cognitive Conceptualization Diagram (CCD) of cognitive therapy (CT). REBT distrusts the big picture. It is up to the *good practice of* the REBT therapist to link the different DEF ABCs in a general formulation.

The REBT Procedure

The ABC Framework

REBT is a problem-oriented approach; this information should be communicated to the patient in order to continuously share the case formulation as well as the treatment rationale and, in particular, the rationale of the disputing, the D of the ABC DEF. As in the case of Beck's CT in chapter "Case Formulation in Standard Cognitive Therapy," we do not pretend to propose here the REBT official procedure but rather our clinical use of REBT, which pays great attention to the shared formulation. The therapist can first ask:

What problem would you like to talk about?

And so on at each subsequent session, always constantly reiterating the focus on single problems:

What problem do we want to work on today?

We have discussed this in the last session; how did you deal with these issues after that session?

These questions keep the focus on the problems and prevent the session from going off track. On the other hand, consider a vague question such as:

How did it go this week?

This question is incorrect because it invites the patient to get out of the REBT spirit and could lead him or her to a different conception of therapy as an explorative journey. For this reason, many REBT therapists try—from the very first session—to instruct the patient to use REBT-specific terminology: rational and irrational beliefs, healthy and unhealthy emotions, disputing, and so on. However, this approach represents only one possible style. REBT therapists have different styles, all of which can be equally effective in achieving agreement on the formulation of the problem and the rationale of the key interventions, in particular the disputing.

It is important to stress that this approach is always explicitly shared. When the therapist explains the principles of REBT therapy to the patient, he or she conveys the message that the therapist and patient are working together on something; that REBT is an efficient, emotion-focused, and problem-solving approach; that the procedure will be mostly active and directive; and, above all, that the patient must be fully aware of these principles and not just understand them from context. Consequently, activism and directivity from the REBT therapist should be declined by continuously explaining to the patient what is being done. It is not coincidental that the ABC DEF self-help scheme is on paper in the waiting room of the Albert Ellis Institute. These sheets of paper make the key points of REBT therapy available to anyone who is waiting.

Therefore, in order to really share the ABC DEF procedure, the REBT therapist could say something like this to the patient:

ABC is a structure that will help you deal with your problems in a fruitful way. The ABC is simply a sheet of paper divided into vertical columns, on which a problematic event is analyzed by articulating it into situations, emotions, and thoughts. In more detail in this sheet, we find these three columns:

A: the activating event or situation, in particular the disturbing aspect of the external reality or event of your internal world, such as a thought, a feeling, or a perception that triggers a negative reaction;

B: the beliefs or irrational thoughts you might have about an event or situation;

C: the unhealthy emotional and behavioral consequences, what you felt and what you did that didn't help you;

Negotiation of goals (F): Healthy and Unhealthy Emotions

Once the problematic situation (A) has been ascertained, the REBT therapist looks for the dysfunctional emotions and behaviors (C) that have not helped the patient to optimally manage the problem:

Therapist: *What did you feel at that moment that didn't help you?*

Of course, open questions are also allowed:

Therapist: *How did you feel at that moment?*

In addition, behaviors are also assessed in terms of dysfunctionality:

Therapist: *What did you do at that moment that didn't help you?*

What the patient has experienced and done in dysfunctional terms finds its full meaning in the REBT procedure only in relation to the functional goals which are also emotional and behavioral. In the REBT procedure, these goals go under the name of F. At this point, in the negotiation of the so-called F, we can say that both the actual REBT formulation and the construction of the REBT therapeutic contract begins. A characteristic theoretical principle of REBT is the distinction between healthy and functional negative emotions, that is, F, and pathological and dysfunctional negative emotions, that is, C. For example, if the patient suffers from anxiety, the emotional alternative F is introduced in this way:

Therapist: *How would you have preferred to feel in that situation instead of anxious?*

To understand this step, we must be aware that patients are often inclined to answer this question by stating that the optimal emotional condition would be tranquility or positivity:

Patient: *Instead of being anxious, I would like to feel calm...*

Which, of course, is an understandable desire and must be validated:

Therapist: *I can understand that you would like to feel calm rather than anxious. However, is this realistic? Can you stay totally calm in that situation? What could be a more realistic emotional alternative?*

In REBT, negative emotions are not *per se* pathological and should not be changed in quantitative terms, that is, by trying to dwarf them. According to REBT, negative emotions are not undesirable; on the contrary, they represent an essential part of our skills to adapt and cope with negative activating events. Emotions tell us that we have a problem that requires attention and response (Ellis and DiGiuseppe 1993; Dryden 2008). REBT pursues a qualitative change from a dysfunctional negative emotion that tends to be intolerable to a healthy and tolerable negative emotion that acts as a stimulus to action and not as an obstacle. To guide the patient to this proactive position, the REBT therapist could ask:

Therapist: *Do you think it is realistically possible to go from a paralyzing anxiety to perfect serenity?*

And then suggest:

Therapist: *How about if the goal of this therapy was to feel just a little concerned instead of heavily anxious?*

This functional emotional goal leads to a functional behavioral goal:

Therapist: *If you just felt concerned instead of anxious, don't you think it might be easier to act differently? For example, would it be easier to do something useful instead of running away?*

In this way, the REBT therapist suggests a functional behavioral goal: not to avoid but to expose oneself to anxiety-inducing situations. In summary, in REBT, negative pathological and dysfunctional emotions undermine the patients' ability to achieve their goals, react to problems, and face adversities. These emotions often lead to self-destructive behavior. While it is absolutely appropriate for a patient to feel sad and even very sad, a debilitating depression is a problem that requires therapeutic intervention. Maladaptive emotions tend to be experienced inwardly as painful and heartbreaking; they can lead to self-destructive behavior, can hinder problem-solving skills, and, above all, are fed by irrational thoughts.

However, what really matters in REBT is that this conception of healthy and unhealthy emotions is shared with the patient, not as a verbal trick but as a shared process of shared management of the specific REBT model of case formulation which is also, in turn, a therapeutic contract. The REBT therapeutic contract holds the principle of sharing the particular REBT conception of healthy and unhealthy emotions.

Sharing the B-C Connection

In REBT, the B-C connection is the theoretical assumption according to which irrational beliefs (B) contribute largely to pathological emotions (C). This principle is the REBT version of the Epictetus's quote: "It isn't the events themselves that disturb people, but only their judgements about them.", and represents the stoic foundation of the rational-emotive and cognitive model. Patients who continue believing that the triggering events (A) are the cause of their pathological state are instead still linked to an anti-therapeutic conception that is called the A-C connection. Once the patients have accepted the principle that the emotions they feel are influenced by their thoughts, the next task will be to show them that by changing these thoughts they can also influence their emotions. It should be stressed to patients that what we inwardly say to ourselves influences our reactions.

Therefore, REBT therapists share with patients the formulation of the problem in ABC DEF terms; this approach is potentially faster than in Beck's CT because the formulation can already be completed for a single problem without the need to build a general model that conceptualizes several problematic situations. This endeavor can be undertaken, usually after the patient has reported the first problem, by saying:

As we have seen in this first example, your problems can be explained in terms of unhealthy emotions that depend on thoughts that do not help you. We will learn to understand and manage these unhealthy emotions by connecting them to these thoughts that do not help you. I will point out some of your thinking styles and ask you to reconsider the way you evaluate situations by using certain thoughts that we call irrational so that you can access more helpful emotional states. It is essential that you take an active role in this therapy. I'll help you by giving you a direction, but you're the one doing the work.

The REBT therapist also encourages the patient to say when he or she disagrees with what is done or said during the session. The therapist provides hypotheses, but the patient confirms them and has the final word. Overall, the REBT therapist shares with the patient that we must distinguish between functional and dysfunctional unhealthy emotions and those irrational beliefs and not events influence unhealthy emotions.

It is well known in REBT that there are four irrational beliefs: awfulizing, demands (once called musts), frustration intolerance, and self-downing. REBT works by encouraging the patients to consider their unhealthy emotions as dependent on these four thoughts. Again, what really matters is that therapist and patient share this principle. This task is not automatically implemented without the cooperation of the patient. For example, in an REBT treatment of a dependent personality the target could be the belief that sentimental relationships should last forever or the patient would become desperate. The patient would share with the therapist that this idea is irrational and that the emotion that does not help the patient depends on this idea (B-C connection):

Do you agree that your anxiety depends on the idea that relationships "should" last forever?

The Rationale of D

From the B-C connection, it consequently follows that in order to manage the emotional discomfort, it may be useful to dispute and challenge (rationale of D) the irrational beliefs. In the example of the dependent patient, the therapist encourages the patient to dispute the idea that he or she would become desperate if the relationship ended. The D rationale has to be explicitly shared in order to prevent the D from becoming a personal bickering between therapist and patient. It is important to stress that sharing the negotiation of F and the B-C connection might not be sufficient. The rationale of D must be shared as well, for instance by saying:

And do you agree that if we challenge this idea, we might weaken this anxiety that doesn't help you?

The patient should be encouraged to use the D actively and not to passively receive it from the therapist. Otherwise, the risk of perceiving the D as a personal attack is high. The therapist might tell the patient:

I wish the two of us together would dispute this unhelpful idea and that it not become a quarrel between the two of us.

After the rationale of D is shared, we can start disputing:

This is why I say to you: is it really so?

Until the REBT *dictum*:

Or rather, where is it written?

We can prefer either "is it really so?" that is more cooperative and involving or "where is written?" that is undoubtedly a strong sentence. In any case, the D—if well prepared with a good negotiation of F and a good B-C connection—is of great help for patients, encouraging them to detach themselves from the dysfunctional beliefs in order to come up with more flexible and functional ideas. In the specific case of this patient:

So, let's see if it really is this way. Why should relationships last forever? Where is it written that relationships "must" last forever?

The Rationale of the ABC DEF Framework and the Philosophy of REBT

If at the end of the REBT disputing, the patients think that "in life, these things happen" or, in the orthodox REBT formulation, that "I would like sentimental relationships to last forever but nowhere is it written that they should," they will have a different emotional reaction, and the paralyzing anxiety mentioned earlier will be replaced by a different emotional reaction, namely the tolerable concern (F). In the first case, the patient might show an intolerable and catastrophic emotional reaction called "end of the world," while in the second, they would just be annoyed, a state of mind called, in the expressive terminology typical of Albert Ellis, "pain in the ass." The rationale of the treatment to be shared with the patient is that the second emotional reaction favors concrete problem solving while still being negative.

The idea is that by going from a catastrophic "end of world" negative assessment to a more tolerable one ("pain in the ass"), you will release mental energies that can be committed to solving the problem instead of just staying desperate.

Ellis' strong, humorous terminology is intended to detach the patients from their irrational beliefs and should be used if it has a good effect on the patient. Even this REBT spirit can be shared:

Let's learn to play down these thoughts that torment and do not help us. I use this humorous terminology for this very reason, so that you learn to take these thoughts less seriously. Try it yourself.

In an effort to fully share the rationale of each step, REBT encourages patients to move from the first to the second mode of reaction to adverse situations. The patient is not expected to be less anxious or less angry about what happened; rather, he or she should show a less awfulizing, demanding, intolerable, or self-downing mental state. According to REBT, we do not have to believe our own thoughts, and this passage can also be shared by the therapist:

We are crossed by thousands of thoughts every day, most of them negative. The healthy attitude is not to stay without negative thoughts but rather to tolerate them and not take seriously their demands and awfulizing aspects.

This REBT attitude is one that somehow anticipates metacognitive procedures, even if it does not gain the pure metacognitive principle of not giving importance to these thoughts: REBT disputes their content. The best way to reduce emotional pain is, therefore, to change irrational beliefs via active and persistent as well as cooperative work aimed at disputing and replacing them with rational beliefs.

I would like you to share with me the idea that the best way to reduce your emotional suffering is to recognize, dispute, and change the beliefs that do not help you.

It is this unceasing sharing of the rationale of the B-C connection, of the negotiation of F, and of the D that allows the REBT therapist to show empathy and respect toward the patient. When the REBT therapist disputes irrational beliefs, he or she never questions the patient as a person. Hence, the premise is:

Therapist: *You're fine, it's your thoughts I want to dispute, not you as a person. The disputing is not a struggle between me and you, but a struggle of us together against these thoughts that do not help you. I would like you to put these thoughts here on the desk between me and you and have you disputing them yourself.*

The philosophical ground of REBT is to accept ourselves as we are and that the value of a person is unconditional (Ellis 1962). In REBT, self-downing is not replaced by positive assessments and higher self-esteem; rather, "unconditional and functional self-acceptance," in which self-value is not related to performance and self-judgment but is recognized as an intrinsic attribute of human dignity, serves as the replacement (DiGiuseppe et al. 2014: pp. 50–54). This philosophical concept is related to the theoretical principle that in REBT, the belief about the self does not play the organizing key role, as we have seen in Beck's CT, and to the clinical tenet that in REBT, emotional disorders do not depend on biased core beliefs related to self-knowledge but on functionally maladaptive evaluations that are only partially related to self-knowledge. This phenomenon suggests that REBT is a precursor to "third wave" functionalism in the clinical cognitive paradigm. It also implies a very pragmatic and functional use of case formulation linked to the here and now of individual problems.

Even the classic REBT distinction between healthy and unhealthy emotions must be conceived in terms of an operational tool to be shared and a pragmatic principle rather than a theoretical tenet. The distinction between healthy and unhealthy emotion helps patients to normalize what they think about their emotions: They come to conceive that there is a healthy way to feel anxiety instead of thinking that normality is not having it. This intervention is actually a validation and can be introduced to the patient as follows:

These moods are neither wrong nor right but just make sense. However, you relate to them in a way that does not help you. We could reconsider this emotion not to change it but to formulate it in less destructive and paralyzing terms. How would you prefer to feel in order to deal with your problem?

References

Clarkin, J. F., Yeomans, F. E., & Kernberg, O. F. (2006). *Psychotherapy of borderline personality: Focusing on object relations*. Arlington, VA: American Psychiatric Publishing, Inc.

DiGiuseppe, R., Doyle, K. A., Dryden, W., & Backx, W. (2014). *A Practioner's guide to rational emotive behavior therapy*. New York, NY: Oxford University Press.

Dryden, W. (2008). *Distinctive features of rational emotive behavior therapy*. Hove: Brunner-Routledge.

Ellis, A. (1955). New approaches to psychotherapy techniques. *Journal of Clinical Psychology, 11*, 207–260.

Ellis, A. (1962). *Reason and emotion in psychotherapy*. New York, NY: Stuart.

Ellis, A., & DiGiuseppe, R. (1993). Are inappropriate of dysfunctional feelings in rational-emotive therapy qualitative or quantitative? *Cognitive Therapy and Research, 17*, 471–477.

Ellis, A., & Grieger, R. M. (Eds.). (1986). *Handbook of rational-emotive therapy* (Vol. 2). New York, NY: Springer.

Commentary on Chapter "How B-C Connection and Negotiation of F allow the Design and Implementation of a Cooperative and Effective Disputing in Rational Emotive Behavior Therapy": REBT's B-C Connection and Negotiation of F

Raymond DiGiuseppe and Kristene Doyle

Contents

Introduction

In the first chapter of this book, Ruggiero et al. identified several aspects of the case conceptual process that they think are critical to the effectiveness of different forms of CBT. In chapter "How B-C Connection and Negotiation of F allow the Design and Implementation of a Cooperative and Effective Disputing in Rational Emotive Behavior Therapy" they have applied the case conceptualization (CC) model to REBT. We address our remarks to the eight chapter and the issues raised in the first chapter. Ruggiero et al. (chapter 8 of this book)'s comments concerning the CC within REBT are divided into two sections; aspects of the CC that involve the teaching CBT and REBT principles to patients; and aspects of the CC process that address the understanding of the individual patient and the development of a specific treatment plan for that patient. They say that "Unlike the CBT model, it must be

R. DiGiuseppe (✉)
St. John University and The Albert Ellis Institute, New York, NY, USA
e-mail: digiuser@stjohns.edu

K. Doyle
The Albert Ellis Institute and St. John University, New York, NY, USA

G. M. Ruggiero et al. (eds.), *CBT Case Formulation as Therapeutic Process*,
https://doi.org/10.1007/978-3-030-63587-9_9

understood that in the REBT we are faced with a formulation of the problem rather than a formulation of the case."

Case Formulation of the Problem

The first set of issues involving the CC process comprises things that we share with patients that enhance the therapeutic alliance. Ruggiero et al. (chapter 8 of this book) identify three characteristics of the treatment process: (1) a formulation of the explanatory model of the patient's emotional suffering, (2) a rationale for the treatment strategy proposed to the patient, and (3) the monitoring of therapeutic progress, sharing this feedback with the patient to revise the CC, and the treatment strategy when necessary. We believe that Ruggiero et al. (chapter 8 of this book) adequately described the REBT model and how REBT therapists address these three issues in most, if not all, psychotherapy sessions.

These elements of the CC process are identical to the common factors model of effective psychotherapy espoused by Wampold and colleagues [see Wampold and Imel 2015 for a review of this model]. The common factors model maintains that all major psychotherapies are equally effective (a postulate with which we do not agree) and that set common factors or activities of psychotherapy that contribute to a significant amount of the variance in any psychotherapies' effectiveness. The common factors include (1) the development of the therapeutic alliance (Horvath and Luborsky 1993), which include agreement on the goals and tasks of therapy, (2) the patients' acceptance of an explanation of their problems offered by the psychotherapist, and (3) a rationale for the treatment that is consistent with the explanation of the client's problems (Wampold and Imel 2015). Saul Rosenzweig first proposed the idea that common factors, techniques, and procedures influenced the effectiveness of all psychotherapies in 1936. His work was followed by an influential book by Jerome and Julie Frank in (1961).

Ellis (1964) recognized that there might be some common factors that lead to effective psychotherapy. One of us (RD) recalls Ellis talking about the work of Rosenzweig and Frank and Frank in lectures and supervision sections. We propose that REBT, as devised by Ellis, includes all the aspects of the common factor model as defined by Frank and Frank (1962), and more recently, by Wampold and Imel (2015).

Let us examine the first aspect of the therapeutic alliance, the agreement on the goals of therapy. As Ruggiero et al. (chapter 8 of this book) noted, Ellis always began his therapy session by asking the client to identify the issue(s) they wanted to discuss in the present session. Doing so helps the client develop a problem-focused attitude for their therapy and facilitates a thoughtful process concerning what they want to work on in each session, thereby improving efficiency. Having listened to hundreds of Ellis' psychotherapy sessions during our training, we observed that Ellis routinely attained agreement on the long-term goals and the goals of the present session. He was not shy about suggesting to clients that they return to a topic that was not resolved or focus on a topic that a patient was avoiding. An issue that was not mentioned by Ruggiero et al. (chapter 8 of this book) is that Ellis identified emotional and behavioral goals. This trend continues in our present teaching and practice of REBT. Historically, REBT has focused on the emotional consequences of IBs, misleading some to think behaviors are not as significant as emotions. One aspect during our professional trainings in REBT that we have emphasized more in the recent years is acknowledgment and assessment of behavioral consequences of irrational beliefs. Specificity matters in identifying goals. Identifying vague goals prevents one from developing a specific CC, can lead to a vague treatment plan, and prevents the accurate monitoring of treatment progress. Vague As, Bs, and Cs, leads to a vague or inaccurate treatment plan. The identification of specific goals was revolutionary for his time, since the predominate models of psychotherapy, Psychodynamic and Rogerian therapies, at the dawning of REBT (Ellis 1962), were non-directive.

From its inception, REBT has provided patients with a rationale for their disturbance and for the treatment (Ellis 1962). REBT has always followed a psychoeducational model and taught patients the A-B-C model and explained the relationship between irrational beliefs and disturbing emotions and dysfunctional behaviors (Ellis 1962). This activity leads to developing agreement on the tasks of psychotherapy. Also, REBT always has involved assessing whether patients understand and accept these rationales, as well as elicit from the client any doubts or reservations of the model (or interventions during the course of therapy). This assessment can lead to different strategies to convince the patients a rationale for their disturbance and the treatment.

The research on the common factors model has demonstrated that there are significant therapist effects on psychotherapy outcomes. That is the person of the psychotherapist matters. Certain traits and behaviors of the psychotherapist can discriminate the most effective psychotherapists from other, less effective ones (Wampold 2007; Wampold 2016; Wampold and Imel 2015). REBT is consistent with the common factors model in this way as well. The common factor model identifies persuasiveness as a characteristic of effective psychotherapists (Wampold and Imel 2015). REBT has always stressed the importance of psychotherapist communicating in a convincing and persuasive manner with patients, particularly during the disputation phase of therapy (DiGiuseppe et al. 2014).

Ellis stressed some other therapist's characteristics that contributed to the effective psychotherapy that were mentioned by Wampold (Wampold 2007, 2016; Wampold and Imel 2015). These include verbal fluency, good interpersonal perception, affective modulation, and expressiveness, expressing warmth towards one's clients, unconditionally accepting one's patients, and empathy. Thus, the common factors model and REBT posit that accomplishing the goals of the CC process includes not only a cognitive model of the problem but the enactment of specific psychotherapist's behaviors.

REBT does an exceptional job of developing a case formulation in the manner that Ruggiero et al. (chapter 8 of this book) describe through teaching the model to patients. This strength of REBT rests on the strong emphasis on the elements that Rosenzweig (1936), Frank and Frank (1962), and Wampold and Imel (2015) see as common factors of psychotherapy. Perhaps Ellis consciously or unconsciously was influenced by the work of Rosenzweig and the Franks by infusing so many aspects of the common factors model into the core elements of REBT.

Case Formulation of the Patient

In their discussion of the CC with REBT, Ruggiero et al. (2020) commented that "Unlike the CBT model, it must be understood that in the REBT we are faced with a formulation of the problem rather than a formulation of the case."

Their discussion of the CC in REBT is limited to teaching clients the model and how it applies to specific problems and teaching patients about the A-B-C model and other aspects of REBT. Ruggiero et al. (chapter 8 of this book) are correct that the CC literature in REBT has focused more on clinical problems. Several good resources do exist that discuss REBT case formulation for specific clinical problems. Yankura and Dryden (1997) published the first book to provide information on a problem-focused approach to CC. Dryden and Bernard (2019) produced an invaluable book on implementing REBT with many clinical problems and diagnostic disorders in adults. Ellis and Bernard (2006) provide a similar compilation for the problems of children and adolescents (a revised version of this book is "in press" and edited by Bernard and Terjesen (in press)).

The fact that Ruggiero et al. (chapter 8 of this book) failed to discuss CC from the perspective of the individual patient forced us to reflect on why. Perhaps the clinical literature on REBT focuses more on the unique model of REBT and less on how to individualize that model to a patient.

To explore this issue, we conducted a search n *PsycINFO* by using "REBT" and "case conceptualization" as subject terms. We found three publications. Vernon and Doyle (2018) included a case study in a textbook on Cognitive Behavior Therapies, and the authors of each theoretical approach, including REBT, described how their respective theories would approach the CC of the case and developed a treatment plan. MacLaren (2002) described how the assessment of the behavior symptoms would influence the REBT treatment plan.

The most extensive discussion of developing CC using REBT was an unpublished doctoral dissertation by Barris (1996). Using the procedures of Persons (1993) with inpatient diagnosed with depression, Barris created an REBT CC that examined a patient's underlying cognitive mechanism that led to their depression. He hypothesized that patients receiving individualized case formulations, and REBT (treatment plans based upon those formulations), would display more significant improvement on post-treatment measures of irrational beliefs and depression than patients who received a standard REBT inpatient treatment program. The results demonstrated that both treatments showed significant improvement from pre to post-test. However, the case formulation treatment group did no better than the standard REBT.

The literature concerning CC commonly discussed in CBT (Persons 1993) with REBT is small. Shame on us for not writing such material, and this realization provides several good projects for REBT aficionados to do in the future. Thus, we thought it prudent to review what is involved in developing a CC and determine whether this type of activity occurs in REBT.

Persons and Hong (2016) proposed that a CC includes the following steps. First, the psychotherapist examines the intake assessment data to develop a CC. The CC represents an understanding or a mini theory concerning the psychological mechanisms (e.g., beliefs and attitudes, contingencies, skills deficits) that initiated and maintain the patient's problems. The CC identifies the stimuli or events that activate the psychological constructs or mechanisms that elicit the symptoms and problems. It also included features of the patient or his or her environment that can influence the treatment progress; these could include the patient's cultural and ethnic background, personality traits, motivation for change, and social support. Second, the psychotherapist uses the CC to select interventions and decisions about the treatment, such as whether to focus on increasing the patient's motivation to change, or which problems to focus on first. Third, the psychotherapist collects feedback and progress-monitoring data in each session to evaluate the patient's improvement and to test the formulation. If necessary, the psychotherapist uses the data to reformulate the CC and develops a new treatment plan to improve the patient's progress. The next questions are whether REBT practitioners collect the data needed to develop a CC, and do the practitioners use the data for such purposes? To answer these questions, we will examine how Ellis practiced and how psychotherapy is done now at the Albert Ellis Institute.

Assessment in REBT Practice and Supervision. Albert Ellis spent the first decade of his professional life working in psychological assessment (Hollon and DiGiuseppe 2010). Both of us co-lead groups with Ellis during our training and had plenty of opportunities to observe how he practiced. Ellis was very adept at assessing a person's personality, clinical problems, environmental stressors, and symptoms, and then making inferences and hypotheses about the cognitive mechanism (i.e., Beliefs) largely contributing to the patient's symptoms. From these ideas, Ellis identified the irrational beliefs that he would target and the behavioral excesses and deficits that lead to the patient's homework assignments. Similar processes occurred in supervision then and now.

The intake process for each new or returning patient at the Albert Ellis Institute includes many standardized assessment instruments that are discussed in supervision and used to develop a CC and a treatment plan. For adults, these instruments include the Millon Clinical Multiaxial Inventory 4th Edition (Millon et al. 2015), the Psychiatric Disorders Screening Questionnaire (Zimmerman 2002), the Attitudes and Beliefs Scale—Short Form (DiGiuseppe et al. 2020a, 2020b), the Outcomes Questionnaire (Lambert et al. 2013), and a four-page personal history survey. Clients who seek specialized services for anger problems, eating disorders, or obsessive-compulsive and related disorders complete assessment intake packets tailored to these problems. For children and adolescents, The Institute's intake packet includes the Millon Adolescent Clinical Inventory, Second Edition (Millon et al.

2020), both the self-report, parent and teacher version of the Comprehensive Behavior Rating Scale (Conners 2008), and a background information form to be a completed by the parents and a problem checklist that is completed by the child/adolescent. Thus, we spend considerable time examining and reviewing assessment material to develop a thorough understanding of the patient to develop the most effective treatment plan.

At the Albert Ellis Institute, we instruct trainees to prepare for supervision. Each trainee receives a form that instructs them on the information about their patients that the trainees should present at supervision. The most recent version of this form appears in Table 1.

Considerable thought goes into the case formulation process at this stage. However, REBT still recognizes that the assessment process and development of a case formulation is ongoing and progresses over time. A goal of the first couple of sessions is to provide the client with hope and re-moralization, which we accomplish by working on a problem that the patient wishes to discuss first. Thus, the interventions do not wait until the case formulation is complete. We recommend that psychotherapists start to treat the patients and develop a case formulation as the process unfolds and get more information about the patient. In other words, assessment and treatment often occur simultaneously.

Much of the discussion among REBT therapists concerns which irrational belief is most prominent in a particular client based on the information provided (Artiran and DiGiuseppe 2020). In designing a measure of irrational and rational beliefs, does the patient's problem result from endorsing Demandingness, Awfulizing, Frustration Intolerance, Self-Condemnation, or Other Condemnation? Our recent research on the nature of irrational beliefs has led to two conclusions that appear relevant to developing a CC and a treatment plan. First, the five irrational cognitive processes of Demandingness, Awfulizing, Frustration Intolerance, Self-Condemnation, or Other-Condemnation are highly correlated. Endorsing one type of irrational belief usually occurs with endorsing them all (DiGiuseppe et al. 2020a, 2020b). Thus, the discussion of which irrational beliefs the client endorses might not be that helpful to know. When researchers write items for irrational belief questionnaires, the item are worded to represent both a cognitive process and a content domain. For example, the item, I think it is awful for other people to reject me," represents endorsement of the beliefs about awfulizing within the context of social rejection or approval. Researchers exploring the assessment of irrational beliefs usually look for the items to group by the cognitive processes (i.e., demandingness, awfulizing, etc.). However, the results of exploratory factor analyses usually show that the items load along factors representing context (i.e., factors for affiliation, achievement, etc.). Thus, while professionals see the important dimension of the items as the cognitive processes, the research subjects see the items as varying across the contexts (David et al. 2019; DiGiuseppe et al. 2020a, b). Thus, the context appears more important than cognitive processes. This suggests that psychotherapists need to know what the irrational beliefs are about (success, failure, rejection, fairness, etc.), and less about whether the irrational belief is a demand, catastrophic thinking, or self/other-condemnation. The information about context is

Table 1 Instructions for presenting cases for supervision

When presenting cases for supervision, be prepared to describe the following information and your Cases Conceptualization:
1. Present identifying data: Client's first name, age, gender, relationship status, ethnicity, religion, and educational background.
2. Provide a brief overview of the client's social, family, and romantic relationships, past and present.
3. Present a brief description of the client's educational background and the client's current and past jobs.
4. Describe the presenting problems as the client sees them.
5. What are the client's goals?
6. Describe the goals in measurable behaviors.
7. Describe any behavioral excesses and behavioral inhibitions.
8. Describe the client's primary, dominant affective state (depressed, anxious, flat, manic, euphoric, normal range).
9. Do you and the client agree on the goals?
10. Describe the client's cognitions, attitudes, and beliefs that influence the problems;
(a) Negative automatic thoughts /cognitive distortions
(b) Problem-solving skills
(c) Irrational beliefs
11. Describe the client's major coping strategies (e.g., does the client cope by engaging in passive or hyperactive behavior, using drugs or alcohol, overeating, engaging in promiscuity, isolating themselves)?
12. Describe any positive or negative reinforcers of the client's inappropriate behavior or symptoms.
13. Describe the results of any objective psychological tests at intake or the results of Routine Progress Monitoring Instruments.
14. Present a description of any previous mental health treatment.
15. Describe any physical or medical problems (illness, disabilities, regular medications).
16. Describe any family history of severe psychological disturbance.
17. What is your purpose in presenting this segment of the tape?
18. What diagnoses would you apply to this client?
19. Describe any homework assignments that you gave the client, and whether the client completed it or did not. If not, what obstacles interfered with completion?
20. Are there any resistances to therapy that you can predict will occur?
21. Describe your case conceptualization based on the above information.
22. What are your treatment recommendations based on your case conceptualization?
23. What issues would you like to present in supervision?
24. What did you do in this session?
25. What did you do poorly in the session? What aspects of REBT did you struggle with?
26. What did you do well in this session?
27. What do you want to learn in supervision today?
28. If you are presenting a recording of a section of a psychotherapy session, describe what aspect of the session or questions about the session you want feedback.

more easily gleaned from personality measures and background information that reveals what is important to the client.

Routine Progress Monitoring. Similar to Wampold and Imel (2015), we believe that effective psychotherapists are flexible and can change their CC and treatment plans when patients are not progressing. Since the 1980s, the Albert Ellis Institute has continually used Routine Outcome Measures (ROMs: Progress monitoring,

2015) at each session to assess patients' progress (or lack thereof). Presently, most patients receive the Outcomes Question (Lambert et al. 2013) each week. Some patients receive other scales more relevant to their problem, or they complete multiple measures that are relevant to the individual case. Trainees are asked to present the ROMs for their cases each time they present a case for supervision. The computer program printout we use for the OQ scoring is color-coded to inform the psychotherapist if the client is on track for improvement compared to other patients, making better progress than other patients, or not progressing. The use of ROMS helps us spot our failures, which leads us to a reevaluation of the case, a new CC, and a new treatment plan. Research has demonstrated that clients who are not progressing often fail to do so for one of three reasons (Lambert 2007). First, the therapist has missed the diagnosis of a severe mental disorder. Second, the patient has low motivation for change; and third, the patient and psychotherapist have a weak therapeutic alliance. Thus, a patient's failure to attain the degree of change expected by statistical norms on a ROM triggers a reevaluation of the CC and the treatment plan and suggests three hypotheses concerning the lack of progress. A new CC can be formulated, and a new treatment plan devised.

Although the REBT literature has focused little on describing how we use CC, we have described now those who practice REBT use CCs.

References

Artiran, M., & DiGiuseppe, R. (2020). A Turkish Translation of a measure of irrational and rational beliefs: reliability, validity studies and confirmation of the four cognitive processes model. *Journal of Rational Emotive and Cognitive Behavior Therapies, 38*, 369–398. https://doi.org/10.1007/s10942-020-00340-9.

Barris, B. P. (1996). Developing reliable case formulations and individualized treatment plans for a depressed inpatient population [ProQuest Information & Learning]. *Dissertation Abstracts International: Section B: The Sciences and Engineering, 57*(6–B), 4021.

Bernard, M. E., & Terjesen, M. (in press). *Rational emotive and cognitive behavioral approaches to child and adolescent mental health.* New York: Springer-Nature.

Conners, C. K. (2008). *Conners comprehensive behavior rating scales.* Toronto, ON: Multi-Health System.

David, D., DiGiuseppe, R., Dobrean, A., Păsărelu, C. R., & Balazsi, R. (2019). The measurement of irrationality. In M. E. Bernard & W. Dryden (Eds.), *REBT: advances in theory, research and practice, promotion.* New York: Springer-Nature.

DiGiuseppe, R., Doyle, K. A., Dryden, W., & Backx, W. (2014). *A practitioner's guide to rational emotive behavior therapy* (3rd ed.). NY: Oxford University Press.

DiGiuseppe, R., Gorman, B., & Raptis, J. (2020a). The factor structure of the attitudes and beliefs scale 2: implications for rational emotive behavior therapy. *Journal of Rational emotive and Cognitive Behavior Therapies, 38*(2), 111–142. https://doi.org/10.1007/s10942-020-00349-0.

DiGiuseppe, R., Raptis, J., Gorman, B., Agiurgioaei Boie, A., Agiurgioaei, F., Leaf, R., & Robin, M. (2020b). The development of a short form of an irrational/rational beliefs inventory. Under review.

Dryden, W., & Bernard, M. E. (Eds.). (2019). *REBT: Best practice and applications.* New York: Springer/Nature.

Ellis, A. (1962). *Reason and emotion in psychotherapy.* New York, NY: Stuart.

Ellis, A. (1964). Thoughts on theory versus outcome in psychotherapy. *Psychotherapy: Theory, research & practice, 1*(2), 83–87. https://doi.org/10.1037/h0088576.

Ellis, A., & Bernard, M. E. (Eds.). (2006). *Rational emotive behavioral approaches to childhood disorders: Theory, practice, and research.* New York: Springer-Nature.

Frank, J. D., & Frank, J. B. (1962). *Persuasion and healing: A comprehensive study of psychotherapy.* Baltimore, MD: The Johns Hopkins University Press.

Hollon, S. D., & DiGiuseppe, R. (2010). Cognitive psychotherapies. In J. C. Norcross & G. VandenBos (Eds.), *History of psychotherapy: Continuity and change* (2nd ed.). Washington, DC: American Psychological Association.

Horvath, A. O., & Luborsky, L. (1993). The role of the therapeutic alliance in psychotherapy. *Journal of Consulting and Clinical Psychology, 61(4)*, 561–573. https://doi.org/10.1037/0022-006X.61.4.561.

Lambert, M. (2007). What we have learned from a decade of research aimed at improving psychotherapy outcome in routine care. *Psychotherapy Research, 17*, 1–14.

Lambert, M. J., Kahler, M., Harmon, C., Burlingame, G. M., Shimokawa, K., & White, M. M. (2013). *Administration and scoring manual: Outcome questionnaire OQ-45.2.* Salt Lake City, UT: OQ Measures.

MacLaren, C. (2002). The role of "B" in REBT. *Romanian Journal of Cognitive & Behavioral Psychotherapies, 2*(2), 141–146.

Millon, T., Grossman, S., & Millon, C. (2015). *Millon Clinical Multiaxial Inventory-IV.* San Antonio, TX: Pearson.

Millon, T., Tringone, R., Grossman, S., & Millon, C. (2020). *Millon adolescent clinical inventory-second edition (MACI-II).* San Antonio, TX: Pearson.

Persons, J. B. (1993). Case conceptualization in cognitive-behavior therapy. In K. T. Kuehlwein & H. Rosen (Eds.), *Cognitive therapies in action: Evolving innovative practice* (pp. 33–53). San Francisco, CA: Jossey-Bass.

Persons, J. B., & Hong, J. J. (2016). Case formulation and the outcome of cognitive behaviour therapy. In N. Tarrier & J. Johnson (Eds.), *Case formulation in cognitive behaviour therapy: The treatment of challenging and complex cases* (2nd ed., pp. 14–37). Routledge/Taylor & Francis Group, London: UK

Progress Monitoring and Feedback [Special issue]. (2015). *Psychotherapy, 52(4).*

Rosenzweig, S. (1936). Some implicit common factors in diverse methods of psychotherapy. *American Journal of Orthopsychiatry, 6(3)*, 412–415.

Vernon, A., & Doyle, K. A. (Eds.). (2018). The case of Marcos from each theoretical perspective. In *Cognitive behavior therapies: A guidebook for practitioners* (pp. *281–310*). American Counseling Association.

Wampold, B. (2007). Psychotherapy: The humanistic (and effective) treatment. *American Psychologist, 62*, 857–873.

Wampold, B. (2016). *Qualities and actions of effective therapists.* Washington, DC: American Psychological Association.

Wampold, B., & Imel, Z. (2015). *The great psychotherapy debate: The evidence for what makes psychotherapy work* (2nd ed.). New York: Routledge.

Yankura, J., & Dryden, W. (Eds.). (1997). *Using REBT with common psychological problems: A therapist's casebook.* New York: Springer Publishing Co..

Zimmerman, M. (2002). *The psychiatric diagnostic screening questionnaire.* Los Angeles, CA: Western Psychological Services.

Commentary on Chapter "How B-C Connection and Negotiation of F Allow the Design and Implementation of a Cooperative and Effective Disputing in Rational Emotive Behavior Therapy": REBT Provides a Firm Basis for Case Formulation by Employing an Ongoing, Implicit and Hypothetico-Deductive form of Data Collection in Critical Collaboration, Negotiation and an Equal Relationship with the Client

Wouter Backx

Contents

W. Backx (✉)
Nederlands Instituut voor RET en CGT, Haarlem, The Netherlands
e-mail: w.backx@ret-instituut.nl; http://www.ret-instituut.nl

G. M. Ruggiero et al. (eds.), *CBT Case Formulation as Therapeutic Process*,
https://doi.org/10.1007/978-3-030-63587-9_10

REBT Distinguishes Between Healthy and Unhealthy Emotions

One of the principles that makes REBT unique is the distinction between dysfunctional and functional ways of reacting emotionally to or anticipating negative events. An important general principle of Cognitive Behavioural Therapy (CBT) is that reacting (or anticipating) consists of feeling, behaving and thinking (and physical reactions) and that they strongly influence one another: one feels as one thinks as one behaves as one feels. In CBT one discriminates easily between dysfunctional and functional thoughts and behaviours. Unfortunately, this distinction is not made for feelings or emotions. Negative emotions are apparently viewed as being one dimensional (Wolpe used the term Subjective Units of Distress, SUDS; Wolpe 1961, 1990), while the two other components in the reaction (thoughts and behaviours) are two-dimensional. When a negative event occurs or when a critical event is about to happen, REBT distinguishes between healthy and unhealthy negative emotions as well. This is not only theoretically more elegant, but especially practical and useful because we only have to focus on the unhealthy part of the emotional reaction. In English and in many other languages, the emotional terminology we use does not make a clear distinction between healthy and unhealthy negative emotions. However, there is one exception where there is a very clear dividing line between the two. When someone experiences a great loss (of a partner or a child), no one is surprised if the person feels very sad. We view this as a healthy or functional emotional reaction. Even very strong sadness can be viewed as functional. The corresponding dysfunctional emotion, however, is denoted by the word 'depressed'. Any level of depression can be viewed as dysfunctional. Thus, we have two components that differ qualitatively from each other (Backx 2012; DiGiuseppe et al. 2014). Both healthy and unhealthy emotions are almost always present in the mixture that we experience. This also holds for sadness and depression. When we separate the two, we can focus on the dysfunctional emotional part, that is on the depression. According to the CBT principle, different thoughts are connected to these different emotions. It follows that dysfunctional negative emotions are connected to irrational beliefs and functional ones to rational beliefs. Disputing rational beliefs is not advocated by the CBT approaches, but when we do not separate healthy from unhealthy emotions and work on the mixture of the two, we are forced to change unhealthy emotions and at the same time healthy emotions as well.

F-Negotiation

The editors in chapter "How B-C Connection and Negotiation of F Allow the Design and Implementation of a Cooperative and Effective Disputing in Rational Emotive Behavior Therapy" use the term F-negotiation, meaning that REBT therapists discuss with their clients, after having assessed the unhealthy feelings and behaviours that bother them, what the client wants to feel or do instead. Most clients want to feel some kind of a positive feeling besides choosing a more constructive behaviour. In that case, the REBT therapist has to explain that it is not realistic to experience no negative feelings at all as a reaction to (or in anticipation of) a negative event. Referring to the discrimination between healthy and unhealthy negative emotions, a healthy counterpart of the unhealthy feelings can be looked for and agreed upon. This is not a very common REBT procedure and has not been described in the Practitioner's Guide (DiGiuseppe et al. 2014). The F-negotiation is just one way of doing it. Another (more common) way is to ask the client to imagine how he or she would feel if he or she said the Effective New Belief (EB) very convincingly. Often the client will experience some kind of relief and the unhealthy negative emotion will become weaker. For some clients it even vanishes.

According to the editors, F-negotiation implies that the therapist will negotiate the feelings and behaviours a client would like to experience as a result of the therapeutic interventions. According to Ellis and Grieger (1986, p 20), the F (Feelings and Behaviours) will be experienced by the client after arriving at his or her Effective Rational Beliefs. This occurs as a result of saying the Effective Rational Beliefs or EBs and not as a result of the negotiation. Theoretically, this makes sense because clients almost always experience a mixture of unhealthy and healthy negative feelings. Most likely both the healthy and the unhealthy feelings have been discussed during the inventory of the C and have already been separated, which means that the client often knows the healthy counterpart. Suppressing the unhealthy part makes the healthy part comparatively stronger and thereby the client will feel relieved of the emotional problems.

Case Formulation Outside of Disputation and F-Negotiation

Case formulation also takes place outside of the disputation, F-negotiation, and B-to-C connection check. For example, CF also takes place during the search for the accurate Irrational Belief (IB) and the search for the exact or critical A (Activating Event or Adversity, as defined by Dryden 1995). In order to find the accurate B, typically there will be a process of negotiation between the client and the therapist: either the client brings in thoughts that are not considered to be irrational (not demanding or human-worth rating in character), e.g. 'I will not pass my exam' or the client comes up with preferences which are the goals, but do not in themselves produce the unhealthy reactions, e.g. 'I want very much to pass my exam'. The irrational belief could be here: 'I must pass the exam!' More specific negotiation takes place when the therapist and client do not find an IB that fully accounts for the dysfunctional way the client reacts to the adversity. During this search, it is rather common that the critical A (adversity) will change too.

What exactly do you feel so anxious about, if it is not failing the exam?

I think that my parents would find out!

Is it in fact that you aren't thinking 'I must not fail the exam', but 'my parents must not find out'?

Exactly!

The accuracy of the IB will be measured by the B-to-C connection check: how much does this IB explain or cause the client's unproductive reaction?

When you say to yourself about the eventuality of not passing the exam 'My parents absolutely must not find out that I did not pass my exam', does that create your anxiety?

Yes!

Even more negotiation can be expected at the formulation of the EB (Effective New Belief). The EB is an essential part of the REBT schedule. Especially while formulating the EB, one may find another irrational belief (IB) at work apart from the one the therapist and client are trying to counteract at that moment.

Formulating the Effective New Belief (EB)

A neglected aspect of REBT theory and practice is the letter E in the A B C D E schedule. It stands for Effective New Belief (DiGiuseppe et al. 2014) and refers to the new belief that is meant to replace and contradict the irrational belief (IB) that is causing the problem(s) i.e. the counterproductive feelings and behaviours. The EB does two things: (1) it will oppose as strongly as possible the IB and (2) it will provide an alternative way of thinking (in terms of preferring instead of demanding and without any form of human-worth rating) about the same adversity (A). The (ideal) effect on the client is that he or she only experiences healthy feelings resulting in constructive behaviours. Formulating this EB together with the client offers the therapist a very decisive moment in case negotiation.

Although the EB can be constructed according to certain rules (DiGiuseppe et al. 2014, pp. 217–218), it will happen at this point that the client might feel some friction with his/her own view and understanding of the problems. When the client and psychotherapist agree on the content of the EB, the therapist will ask the client to say the EB out loud and very convincingly. Here the client might feel resistance against what she actually says. Either the client realizes that the IB in fact is slightly different or he/she has difficulties giving up the familiar IB. It is important for the therapist to know which feeling the client experiences as a result of indoctrinating himself/herself with this EB. This is the ultimate check if the IB is accurate or not, because contradicting it will make it weaker and, because the IB causes the (unhealthy) C, we expect the unhealthy reaction to diminish. It holds: IB causes unhealthy reactions (C) and EB causes healthy reactions (C).

REBT Uses Case Formulation in a Different Way than Most Other Therapies

CF is not made explicit in REBT as it is in other therapies because CF forms an essential part of the whole therapeutic approach. It is an ongoing process that will be present in almost every session and often even more than once in the same session.

In other forms of CBT, the therapist commences with a CF by collecting a lot of data, and then, having completed the CF, uses it without many revisions during the therapy as a framework and guide for the course of the therapy. In contrast, in REBT one starts relatively quickly with one of the problems and looks for the relevant information concerning the issue at stake. As the editors argue, REBT does not formulate the case but rather the problem.

Hence, many steps during the process leading to interventions are tentative and are subject to negotiation. The therapist can and often does explicitly invite the client at the beginning of the course of the sessions to follow the process of therapy critically and to give comments on the interventions the therapist does. This is especially important if the client feels that the direction the therapist has chosen does not fit. Not all of the therapist's appropriate interventions feel good for the client. Therefore, sometimes the client and therapist have to negotiate at such a moment about the differences.

One of the theoretical underpinnings of REBT's explanation for psychopathology is the fact that humans have a strong tendency to use a dysfunctional (demanding and human-worth rating) attitude besides a clearly functional (preferring and accepting) approach when confronted with adversities. This demanding attitude can be seen as an ineffective strategy for reaching one's goal. Unfortunately, to some extent the client believes that it is a productive one because he/she is biased by the desire for short-term gratification. Showing the unproductivity of the strategy is one of the therapist's tasks.

Because REBT does not view an individual's psychological condition as being more or less fixed, but rather as a dynamic process, REBT practitioners rarely classify people. Instead they focus on the separate incidents the client brings in. Although different clients tend to use different strategies when confronted with adversities or obstacles in their way, that does not mean that people always use the same strategy for the same type of adversities or obstacles. Classifying people according to the use of strategies certainly has advantages, but it certainly has even more disadvantages. For example, clients might feel they are being unfairly or incorrectly labelled by the therapist.

The Hypothetico-Deductive Method of Assessment

Concerning the assessment of the problems, REBT uses a hypothetico-deductive model rather than an inductive model. REBT uses the falsification principle of Karl Popper (1959), which means that one comes up with a hypothesis, for example regarding which Irrational Belief is responsible for a certain unhealthy reaction or anticipation (C). Either the therapist or (preferably) the client thinks of a possible belief. Then the therapist and client check for the B-to-C connection, i.e. does this IB actually cause this C? That proves or disproves whether the irrational belief accounts for the disturbed feeling and/or behaviour. The inductive approach on the other hand requires first an inventory of many circumstances that might have contributed to the problem(s) for which the client is seeking help. From that information it might be possible, of course, to come to the same conclusion but at least the deductive method is quicker and still involves negotiation and information gathering. In order to be able to formulate any hypothesis about the aetiology of the problems, it is necessary to have some minimal amount of information about the context. However, the amount of information a regular case formulation requires is certainly not necessary. Much of the information collected during the inductive procedure turns out to be not useful for the course of the therapy and thus the procedure does not seem particularly goal oriented to the client. In fact, clients do not really feel they are being helped when they are asked for information that they cannot connect to their problems. Of course, the therapist has some credibility and the therapeutic alliance will not come under pressure immediately, but looking for information that is directly connected to the problems does strengthen this alliance. The deductive method might also improve the therapeutic relationship because it closely follows the way the client presents his or her problems and thereby makes the client a co-leader. This equality between client and therapist is also characteristic of the REBT approach.

The REBT therapist will let the client know right from the start that there may be moments in which there will be a difference in opinion about what is the explanation (often the irrational belief under discussion) for certain problematic behaviours and/or feelings. The therapist will then follow the client's point of view as long as the client is not convinced of the therapist's different view. The client may later come back and embrace the same idea. Or the therapist may say something to the extent of: Most people would have this kind of thought, but that does not mean that you must have it too. We therefore adopt your idea as long as we do not find any evidence that we should not.

Information as an Overall Structure or as Pieces Collected from Individual Problems

As the editors maintain, "REBT, unlike CBT, does not tend to be articulated in a structure of core beliefs and coping strategies that is superordinate to individual problems.". It seems that the editors recognise that most approaches and regular CBT tend to rely on structure, fixed patterns and (over)generalizations. The desire to classify human personalities and mental syndromes easily leads to overgeneralizations and prejudices as might be experienced by the client. It can alienate the client from the therapist because the former might feel they are being judged by the latter. Though many clients accept the therapist's generalized view because they view him or her as an authority, that is not the ideal form of negotiating and sharing information. The conclusions might be very true (or not true at all) and therefore useful (or not) for the course of therapy, but the context in which they are drawn is far from ideal.

On the other hand, when a client only brings in symptoms for which he or she seeks help, there is no guarantee that the therapist will find the underlying structures that cause the symptoms. But at least the therapist follows the client in the original request for help and that might help the client feel that he/she is being taken seriously.

Hypothetico-Deductive Versus Hypothetico-Inductive Method

Many clinical psychologists, researchers and theoreticians dismiss any approach where the psychotherapist starts from the symptoms for which the patient seeks help, without using a defined case formulation of that client to create a comprehensive treatment plan. They feel that one must have "a careful clinical history and concise summary of the social, psychological, and biological factors that may have contributed to developing a given mental disorder" (DSM-5, fifth edition 2013). Furthermore, the DSM-5 continues, "It requires clinical training to recognize when the combination of predisposing, precipitating, perpetuating, and protective factors has resulted in a psychopathological condition in which physical signs and symptoms exceed normal ranges." (Ibid.). This contrast in how psychotherapists make use of case formulations is the essential difference between the hypothetico-deductive and the hypothetico-inductive method (Popper 1959), with the latter being advocated by the DSM-5 manual.

There are some practical differences between the two as far as psychotherapy is concerned. The inductive method consists of collecting a sufficient amount of information from which one tries to form hypotheses by generalizing, drawing conclusions from and interpreting the data. The way psychotherapists do this is not very well researched and sometimes leads to overgeneralizations or too simple conclusions (e.g. I have difficulties being alone because I come from a big family) which does not improve the efficiency and the effect of the therapy. Then there is a serious risk that the client will not fully agree with the hypothesis presented. For various reasons clients will not always utter their disagreement, but experience nevertheless the friction, which will not contribute to the therapeutic relationship either.

References

Backx, W. (2012). The distinction between quantitative and qualitative dimensions of emotions: Clinical implications. *Journal of Rational Emotive and Cognitive Behavior Therapy, 30*, 25–37. https://doi.org/10.1007/s10942-010-0122-0.

DiGiuseppe, R. A., Doyle, K. A., Dryden, W., & Backx, W. (2014). *A practitioner's guide to rational emotive behavior therapy* (3rd ed.). New York, NY: Oxford University Press.

Dryden, W. (1995). *Preparing for client change*. London: Whurr.

DSM-5, fifth edition. (2013). *Diagnostical and statistical manual of mental disorders*. Washington, DC/London: American Psychiatric Publishing.

Ellis, A., & Grieger, R. M. (Eds.). (1986). *Handbook of rational-emotive therapy* (Vol. 2, p. 20). New York, NY: Springer.

Popper, K. (1959). *The logic of scientific discovery*. New York, NY: Basic Books.

Wolpe, J. (1961). The prognosis in unpsychoanalysed recovery from neurosis. *American Journal of Psychiatry, 118*, 35–39.

Wolpe, J. (1990). *The practice of behavior therapy*. Needham Heights, MA: Allyn & Bacon.

Case Formulation in Process-Based Therapies

Giovanni Maria Ruggiero, Gabriele Caselli, Andrea Bassanini, and Sandra Sassaroli

Contents

The Third Wave: Process Models

Since the end of the 1990s, there has been a turning point in the field of cognitive psychotherapies with the emergence of the so-called "third wave" or process models, namely *acceptance and commitment therapy* (ACT; Hayes and Strosahl 2004),

G. M. Ruggiero (✉)
"Psicoterapia Cognitiva e Ricerca," Cognitive Psychotherapy School and Research Center, Milan, Italy

Sigmund Freud University, Milan, Italy

Sigmund Freud University, Vienna, Austria
e-mail: gm.ruggiero@milano-sfu.it

G. Caselli
Sigmund Freud University, Milan, Italy

Sigmund Freud University, Vienna, Austria

Department of Psychology, London South Bank University, London, UK

A. Bassanini
MeP—Mindfulness e Psicoterapia, Milan, Italy

Società di Psicoterapia Cognitivo Comportamentale CBT-Italia, Milan, Italy

S. Sassaroli
Sigmund Freud University, Milan, Italy

Sigmund Freud University, Vienna, Austria

"Studi Cognitivi," Cognitive Psychotherapy School and Research Center, Milan, Italy

G. M. Ruggiero et al. (eds.), *CBT Case Formulation as Therapeutic Process*,
https://doi.org/10.1007/978-3-030-63587-9_11

behavioral activation (BA; Kanter et al. 2009; Martell et al. 2001), the *cognitive behavioral analysis system of psychotherapy* (CBASP; McCullough and Goldfried 1999), *dialectical behavior therapy* (DBT; Linehan 1993), *functional analysis psychotherapy* (FAP; Kohlenberg and Tsai 1991), and *integrative behavioral couples therapy* (IBCT; Christensen et al. 1995; Doss et al. 2002).

Third wave cognitive psychotherapy process models suggest that emotional disorders do not depend on biased mental representations of the self (i.e., self-knowledge and self-beliefs) as Beck (1976) thought. Rather, they rely on the dysfunctional interaction between voluntary and regulatory processes—for example, attention and executive control—and emotionally charged, automatic associative processes (Kahneman and Frederick 2002; Martin and Sloman 2013; Sloman 2002; Stanovich and West 2002; Wells and Mathews 1994).

What is the function of case formulation in these new approaches? To understand this question, we must remember that these models have maintained a strong relationship with the behavioral tradition and represent a return to contextual and functional analysis (Jacobson et al. 2001). The emphasis on functional analysis suggests that in these methods there is a different relationship to case formulation compared to how it is used in Beck's standard *cognitive therapy* (CT; Beck 2011). Indeed, in CT, case formulation is primarily a function of ascertaining and thus preparing for treatment. Through case formulation, the therapist may explore the *core beliefs* and *coping strategies* on which the *questioning*, which is the heart of CT treatment, focuses. Case formulation also serves to establish the therapeutic alliance by sharing the rules of the CT game through the so-called socialization phase, a name that is not far from the term alliance. This conception of case formulation in Beck's CT is in line with the proposal of this book, that shared case formulation not only establishes the sharing of rules but serves to manage the therapeutic relationship in specifically cognitive terms.

Although case formulation had already been important and present in CT, the emphasis and structural centrality of the core schemes on the self in CT's therapeutic process in part did not help to understand the key role that explicit and unceasing sharing of the case formulation plays in the therapeutic process of CT and *cognitive behavioral therapy* (CBT) approaches in a broad sense. Process therapies are therefore a turning point in the theoretical conception of mental functioning as well as the clinical conception of the therapeutic process in which case formulation can definitively assume a key role in either procedural or theoretical terms. Third wave process CBT approaches can be interpreted as a paradigm shift from a concept of psychotherapy as discovery of the self to a model focused on sharing a representation of mental functioning with the patient in order to plan a treatment. These approaches accomplish this goal by encouraging the development of mental flexibility in the management of adverse situations and the promotion of a broader behavioral repertoire in daily life (Hayes and Strosahl 2004; Wells 2008).

In addition, while traditional-CBT-approach therapies have focused on change, third wave process approaches recommend flexibility in balancing acceptance and change. Consequently, with regard to the clinical practice of case formulation in process therapies, flexibility, acceptance, and commitment to change have replaced the role that core beliefs play in CT. The basic principle of case formulation in process therapies is that the goal is not to ascertain the structural basis of the emotional disorder in terms of whether, for example, a negative belief underlies and fuels anxiety. Rather, it is to examine the function of the symptom and share it with the patient. In short, what matters is to share with the patient how he or she organizes his or her life around anxiety. Anxiety and its cognitive correlates for the ACT therapist perform a function and are not a mistake, except that they cannot be flexibly applied. This function is presumably to protect against more or less realistic risks and, in a broader sense, to define one's life in terms of safety and prudence as general goals.

Case Formulation in Acceptance and Commitment Therapy

Among process approaches, ACT seems to be the most popular. Its main therapeutic goal is to achieve a state of mind of acceptance, develop flexibility toward personal values, and promote commitment in the patient to change (Hayes et al. 2013). In addition, ACT often shows a sophisticated experiential component that is reminiscent of an updated form of behavioral extinction. However, this concept includes a more extended degree of metacognitive awareness and executive mastery (Hayes et al. 2013). The theoretical background of ACT is the relational frame theory, whose therapeutic principle is that it is not a priority to intervene directly on the contents of dysfunctional thoughts but that it is more convenient to act on how the individual relates to his or her own thoughts. To achieve this goal, ACT therapists do not limit themselves to a question as emblematic of pragmatic CBT questioning as:

What do you need this for?

Instead, they carefully examine the patient's behavior in life situations through a detailed functional analysis that is articulated in various ways in different approaches. For example, ACT is organized in six behavioral repertoires:

Acceptance/experiential avoidance;
Cognitive defusion/fusion;
Contact with the present moment/conceptualized past and feared future;
Self as context/attachment to conceptualized self;
Values/lack of values clarity;
Committed action/inaction, impulsivity, or avoidance.

Let us now discuss them in detail. *Experiential avoidance* comprises the set of strategies we put in place in order to control and/or alter our internal experiences (thoughts, emotions, feelings, or memories), even when this endeavor causes behavioral damage. **The flexible alternative to experiential avoidance is acceptance. When it comes to acceptance,** the therapist uses sentences of more or less the same type with the patient (the following interventions are an adaptation from ACT training in which one of the authors has participated):

What should we accept? The painful emotions, the harmful thoughts that every day our mind proposes to us, the sad impulses and memories.

Cognitive fusion refers to the tendency of human beings to be captured by the contents of their own thoughts. According to the process, CBT updates the cognitive principle: **It is not what we think about that creates problems (standard CBT formulation) and pain but the way we relate to what we think (process CBT formulation).** According to ACT, *the alternative to cognitive fusion is simply defusion. To obtain it,* ACT *promotes the ability to:*

Learn to observe one's own thoughts, images, or memories, recognizing them for what they are, i.e., products of the mind and not absolute realities.

Look at one's experience from above and in a decentralized way, an endeavor that promotes awareness of one's own mental experience.

Conceptualized past and the feared future comprises the difficulty of directing and maintaining attention to the present moment and changing the focus of attention between the various dimensions of one's life. Some useful questions to identify how the conceptualized past influences the way we describe and label ourselves in the present can be formulated as follows:

What rules do you carry around from your past?

When you were a kid, what were the "right" and "wrong" emotions you could and could not feel?

As a child, what did your significant ones tell you about how to deal with your emotions, especially unpleasant ones?

In your family, how did adults handle their negative/unpleasant emotions?

In your family, how did adults react to your unpleasant/negative emotions?

To this dysfunctional process, which increases psychological lack of flexibility, ACT opposes the promotion of contact with the present moment, which involves *being psychologically available to what happens by disengaging the autopilot, using the experience of the five senses (hearing, touch, etc.), and the possibility of cultivating awareness in order to stay tuned with what happens from moment to moment. Our actions are often managed according to an automatism that, although useful and functional on many occasions, in other cases is harmful and dysfunctional.* By living automatically, we limit the quality of our experience and are unaware of what is happening to us during the present moment. By living the experiences according to preconceptions learned in the past or to rigid expectations about the future, the patient faces them with an anxiety-inducing emotional burden. Getting in touch with the present moment means encouraging patients to consciously choose to bring their attention to what is happening inside them and in the outside world at that moment. There are many signs to be assessed of the patient's possible tendency to be out of touch with his present moment. For example:

Can the patient maintain eye contact or is he or she lost in his or her own thoughts?

Is repetitive thinking present?

Does he or she get distracted often and easily?

When asked to change the subject or address a specific aspect, does he or she succeed?

Once established as signs of a poor ability to stay in the present moment, the signs should be shared with the patient so that they become part of the shared formulation. The difficulty of being in the present moment should be shared precisely by pointing out to the patient some of his or her attitudes that might suggest difficulty in pursuing this goal.

Conceptualized self is the set of definitions that our mind tells itself. When this process is present, we strongly identify ourselves with the contents of our mind by wearing the mask that our life story has built for us. ACT suggests as a virtuous counterpart the conceptualized self as a context or a perspective. In other words, ACT provides a new point of view, sometimes never experienced before, in which we learn to observe our internal and external experience from a privileged point of view, that is a participating, kind, compassionate, and curious observation of our own experience. We could call this a "participating witness." ACT promotes the observation of experiences as they happen, through a careful, conscious, and metacognitive self-reflection of one's own experience as it happens.

The next process is called the *lack of clarity of values*, the difficulties of identifying what is important and makes our life meaningful and rich. It can manifest in various forms and ways, but the central point is the confusion and vacuity of goals. It is necessary to specify that the term *values* in ACT means something other than concrete objectives, aspirations, and moral values. ACT defines values as a desired long-term quality of life, the factor that motivates people to change and to face difficult times (Hayes and Strosahl 2004).

In addition, the intervention on values does not take the form of a mentalistic conversation about what is or is not important for the individual, despite the verbal construction of the values. Knowing the person's world of values implies the ability to notice what moves the person him- or herself, what produces a change in physical sensations, what allows the emergence of emotions in the concrete aspect of activating the body and behaviors. In this way, it is possible to move in the area of values beyond and with words. The ACT therapist who works with the patient's value repertoire is careful to grasp the internal and external movements that some themes activate. In other words, one could understand the value as a discriminatory stimulus for the emission of productive behavior during that very moment of the session. A more technical definition of value is given by Wilson and Dufrene (2009): They are consequences, verbally built, of continuous, dynamic, evolving, and freely chosen activity patterns, which establish predominant reinforcements for that activity which are intrinsic to the implementation of the same behavioral pattern.

In formulating this problem in a way that is shared with the patient, we may meet many clinical scenarios. A frequent case is the utterance of a feeling of strong confusion, with respect to what the person considers important and significant for him- or herself, which can be expressed in sentences such as follows:

I just don't know what I want, what matters to me right now...

A second scenario emerges when the individual shows an apparent lack of significant areas of life interests, such as work, self-care, family, and social relationships, among others. In a third situation, all or almost all areas are considered to be of great importance for the individual but at the same time there is no real investment. Here, we can find patients blocked by an ideal of exceeding perfectionism that causes a lack of commitment:

I'm never happy anyway, so I don't even get into it.

According to ACT, important work to do with these patients is to reflect on the values—not only how to achieve them but also to become aware of the importance of being committed to values, considering the difficulties that could be encountered in the short term.

The last process of the ACT model is *inaction, impulsivity, or avoidance*, which means that the patient, even if aware of his dysfunctional processes, still has a significant step to face: to commit to action and pursue his or her own values. The ACT alternative is called *committed action*, that is:

Continuously choosing to engage in actions in the direction of your personal values, despite the painful emotions you may encounter along the way;

To maintain this commitment, keeping in mind the obstacles and difficulties, e.g., fear of making mistakes, painful memories, guilt, shame, and so on.

What is striking in ACT is how case formulation and therapeutic intervention are closely interwoven with each other. While in Beck's CT we can distinguish the assessment of *core beliefs* and *coping strategies* from the *questioning* and behavioral exposure intervention, in ACT, the six-point formulation is so interconnected with the intervention that it is indistinguishable in clinical practice. A second characteristic element of ACT case formulation is that its eminently qualitative nature perhaps hinders implementation of quantitative monitoring of clinical gains as happens in CT; this specific feature entails pros and cons. In general, ACT's reduced focus on the formalization of interventions in terms of protocols is a feature that perhaps also stems from the already mentioned close interconnection between intervention and case formulation. This aspect may be either a strength or a weakness of this approach.

Process-Based Cognitive Behavioral Therapy as an Approach to Case Conceptualization

Although process-based CBT models have opposed standard CT and repudiated its structuralist approach, with a focus on self-beliefs, it cannot be denied that they still belong to the CBT domain and that there are important lines of continuity with Beck's CT. Many process-based aspects of ACT were somehow already present in CT in a clinical form, although conceptualized differently from a theoretical viewpoint. For example, CT's *questioning* is a form of defusion from thoughts and behavioral exposure is a form of commitment to action. For these reasons, Hayes and Hofmann (2018) have committed themselves to an integration effort between standard CT and process-based CBT approaches, calling it *process-based CBT* (PB-CBT). PB-CBT, like ACT, departs from CT's protocol approach targeted toward psychiatric diagnoses and focuses on how best to address and modify key biopsychosocial processes in specific situations with specific clients for specific clinical purposes. PB-CBT, however, also recommends beginning treatment by adopting a standardized CT protocol for the most important problem; a standardized protocol provides a reference point that can be profitably used to evaluate results and offer heuristics that usefully simplify complex situations, although admittedly the evidence is not strong enough to treat protocols as algorithms.

On the other hand, when the therapist has to go beyond established protocols because a standard one is not available or does not assure the expected results, PB-CBT encourages therapists to use explicit case formulation to tailor interventions, assuming that they will exceed the limits of the standardized protocols. Hayes and Hofmann believe that case formulation specifies the hypothesis based on the variables that influence the disorder and on which the therapy acts (according to the rationale of the treatment). Although there is currently no clear evidence to suggest that tailor-made interventions based on case formulations are superior (Kuyken 2006), the idea is that the case formulation, if used systematically, can serve as a method for applying the scientific method to clinical work (Persons 2008).

Notably, PB-CBT does not yet seem to have developed its own specific method of case formulation. Currently, Hayes and Hofmann (2018) have merely suggested that the available guidelines, e.g., those of Persons (2008) or Kuyken et al. (2011), should be followed. This deficit is probably temporary because PB-CBT is recent, and partly understandable because PB-CBT does not present itself as an independent explanatory model, but rather as an integration between various CBT approaches, either core-belief-centered or process-based models. Moreover, the original contribution of Hayes and Hofmann's PB-CBT is the review of various CBT interventions (see Table 1). This effort reformulates the rationale of action of each of them in terms of functional processes and not core cognitive contents.

This task is not easy because functionalist and content approaches in psychology are situated at two distinct levels of explanation (De Houwer 2011; Hughes et al. 2016). Admittedly, functional psychology focuses on explanations of behavior in terms of dynamic interaction with the environment, while cognitive structuralism aims to explain environment–behavioral relationships in terms of contents, for example, core beliefs.

The conciliation encouraged by PB-CBT is that the two approaches are not in opposition with each other. Instead, they are two philosophically different levels of talking about similar events. Once this fact has been fully recognized, professionals and researchers from both traditions can begin to have a meaningful and hopefully mutually beneficial dialogue about human cognition and how it can be encouraged to change. PB-CBT also looks to suggest that the relationship between the two different levels of analysis, instead of ending in a theoretical incompatibility, can have a fruitful clinical outcome because it would help psychotherapists to identify the moments in which an analysis is more appropriate at either the cognitive or the environmental and behavioral level.

Overall, it appears that the PB-CBT solution adheres more to the analytical functional approach than the core content approach because it tends to interpret cognitive contents and beliefs in terms of functions. This factor is admittedly its true innovation. At the present moment, the two levels of PB-CBT analysis for different clinical situations constitute an extended functionalistic model that attempts to

Table 1 Repertoire of the process-based cognitive behavioral therapy approach

Behavioral activation
Cognitive defusion
Cognitive reappraisal
Contingency management
Coping and emotion regulation
Cultivating psychological acceptance
Enhancing motivation
Exposure strategies
Interpersonal skills
Mindfulness practice
Modifying core beliefs
Problem solving
Self-management
Shaping
Stimulus control
Values choice and clarification

preserve the results of content-based CBT approaches, first of all Beck's CT. Therefore, the provisional conclusions of PB-CBT seem to suggest that we are not dealing with two different levels of analysis but with two different points of view that describe the same phenomenon by using different languages.

However, this provisional solution, while useful, risks underestimating the paradigmatic difference between the functionalism of processes and the structuralism of self-beliefs. Flexibility, acceptance, and commitment to change in processualism should not be confused—despite possible similarities—with any concept of self-knowledge. Behaviors related to action and governed by rules do not represent internal knowledge of the self (Cordova 2001; Hayes and Strosahl 2004; Hayes et al. 2013). When PB-CBT really comes to identify specific indicators for the appropriate use of two different levels of analysis, it will also provide a clinically useful integration and a theoretical synthesis of the available literature on what is known about the function of the interventions in order to be able to evaluate the specific rationale for the various types of dysfunction and provide the indicators to the therapist for the choice of the interventions to be applied.

Currently, integration of PB-CBT has achieved a less ambitious purpose of helping clinicians who use different languages to communicate with each other. These indicators, being presented as heuristics to relate appropriate interventions to specific dysfunctions, can be suitable for case formulations to be shared with the patient and, therefore, essential tools for the management of the therapeutic alliance in functionalistic terms. In this way, the therapist would really get to customize the treatment in operational terms (Carlbring et al. 2010). As written above, provisionally the really original contribution of Hayes and Hofmann's PB-CBT is the capacity to reformulate the rationale of action of each CBT intervention in terms of functional processes.

Case Formulation in Schema Therapy

Schema therapy (ST; Arntz and van Genderen 2009; Young et al. 2003) is a model that has developed from the clinical and theoretical background of Beck's CT. In this modality, case formulation absorbs process-based elements while simultaneously maintaining a strong interest in self-centered schemes. As its name implies, ST conceptualizes emotional disorders in terms of self-schemata and self-beliefs. These constructs are not only purely cognitive as in Beck's CT; they also show a strong emotional and interpersonal aspect rooted in the personal development of the patient. These interpersonal characteristics are represented in so-called "modes," which are stereotypical and inflexible interpersonal patterns. Moreover, these "modes" have a significant metacognitive and functional component because their dysfunctional rigidity depends on a state of cognitive fusion between patients and these "modes" (Arntz and van Genderen 2009). Therefore, the clinical procedure of ST includes interventions aimed at regulating emotional and cognitive processes through experiential exposure and re-education, guided imagination, or role-playing (Bell et al. 2015; Hackmann et al. 2011) and cognitive and metacognitive interventions aimed at acting at the declarative level of verbal re-attribution (Wells and Mathews 1994; Williams et al. 1988).

In ST, the dysfunctionality depends on a functional deficit because the emotional pain seems to be contingent on traumatic experiences that leave the primary emotional needs of the child unsatisfied. As a result, early maladaptive patterns are generated that attribute a distorted meaning to the vision of self and the world. The aim of ST is to modify these patterns through cognitive and emotional–experiential techniques as well as the therapeutic relationship oriented to balance the unsatisfied needs of the patient's childhood. From this approach emerges: (1) a structuralist vision of the self that is similar to Beck's CT; (2) a theory of deficit that explains the impairment of functions; and (3) a vision of the therapeutic alliance as a relational compensation for missed needs.

From a clinical and therapeutic point of view, ST integrates metacognitive, developmental, experiential, and relational interventions. In particular, *guided imagery* and *self-disclosure* interventions seem to seek an **interpersonal experience of strong emotional sharing** that fosters **cognitive restructuring**. In ST, we explicitly speak of corrective emotional experience in which the painful events that serve as the basis of psychological dysfunctionality are relived in a non-traumatic, compensatory manner and are followed by a verbal re-elaboration that allows the definitive detachment from the dysfunctional modalities (Young et al. 2003). Notably, in ST we are not dealing with a generic and non-specific relational aspect that is already present in every psychotherapy and can be integrated in every paradigm. Instead, this technique uses a defined procedure consistent with the theory of the ST model. ST can show strong efficacy data in its favor (Bamelis et al. 2014).

ST uses case formulation that is oriented on interpersonal, emotional, and cognitive self-patterns as well as procedural modes. To understand the role of case formulation in ST, it is necessary to appreciate where ST places the strategic bottleneck of the therapeutic change, the decisive target of the treatment process. In fact, case formulation depends on the most significant process: Is the bottleneck located in the metacognitive awareness of modes or in the corrective emotional experience obtained by means of imaginative and relational interventions? Among these interventions are:

1. Relational intervention;
2. Shared cognitive formulation of self-patterns;
3. Shared metacognitive formulation of modes;
4. Imaginative intervention.

The question is which of the above is the key intervention that allows the implementation of others?

If the shared formulation of either the cognitive or metacognitive elements precedes the other interventions, then ST places itself among the approaches that consider the cognitive and metacognitive intervention as resolutive. Consequently, their shared formulation must always precede—at least ideally—the others. In this scenario, shared case formulation is an intervention that should be implemented at the beginning of ST. By contrast, in the second scenario, shared case formulation follows temporally—and above all ideally—relational and imaginative interventions because the corrective experience that occurs both in the management of the therapeutic relationship and during the imaginative exercises creates the ideal emotional conditions that promote metacognitive awareness of the "modes."

At this point, let us remember that the thesis of this book is to distinguish therapeutic approaches into two models. One proposes that shared case formulation is possible from the beginning of the treatment as an opening move of the therapeutic process. By contrast, the other model believes that the formulation is an outcome to be achieved during the course of the therapeutic process, basically emotional and neither cognitive nor metacognitive.

If we examine the role that case formulation plays in the ST process (Roediger et al. 2008), we see that it is immediately claimed that when working with clients with personality disorders, their maladaptive behavior will soon affect the therapeutic relationship. This phenomenon seems to support a scenario where initial sharing is difficult. However, it is also said that by quickly implementing and sharing a case formulation at the beginning of the treatment, both client and therapist are provided with a joint reference point outside of any turbulence in their relationship. In other words, in ST the case conceptualization allows the therapist and the patient to orient themselves toward a mutual understanding of what is happening and helps them to find common ground in case of alliance ruptures. This second scenario seems to favor an early shared formulation.

ST usually bases case formulation on what the patients report—questionnaires, evaluation scales, therapist's observations, third party stories (spouses, parents, or others)—as well as on a significant work called imaginative diagnostics. This technique utilizes videos that clarify the "modes" to the patient in a vivid way. This design suggests that in ST the imaginative interventions are preceded and supplemented by interventions that clarify for the patient the rationale of the intervention.

Hence, this procedure somehow always presupposes a high level of sharing of the case formulation at the beginning of the treatment.

This conclusion is confirmed by continuing the analysis of other steps of the ST procedure, such as the suggested usefulness of providing the client with texts on ST to support the intervention on "modes" (Jacob and Arntz 2013) and schemes (Young et al. 2003). Other cases in which the conclusion favors early and full sharing of the case formulation are confirmed by the use of a genogram, which serves to share with the patient the idea that both patterns and maladaptive modes feature an adaptive basis that is subsequently stiffened. Dysfunctional modes had previously been the best way to deal with our problems, but when applied mechanically they become mismatched. The developmental and evolutionary basis of this hypothesis, which is also shared with constructivist models, as we will see in chapter "Strengths and Limitations of Case Formulation in Constructivist Cognitive Behavioral Therapies" of this book, is found in the model of Cannon (1915, 1936). Healthy adult modalities, learned in therapy, can help people find more adaptive solutions.

In conclusion, ST seems to be placed among the therapies that share the case formulation from the beginning of the therapeutic path. In ST, shared case formulation plays a key role for management of the assessment and implementation of the interventions. Furthermore, the therapeutic alliance is definitively confirmed by the formalization effort pursued by the working group of the International Society of Schema Therapy, which is developing a training procedure for case formulation in ST.

Case Formulation in Metacognitive Therapy

In the clinical procedure of *metacognitive therapy* (MCT; Wells 2008, 2013), early implementation of sharing the case formulation is extremely important. In the theoretical model of the mental functioning of MCT, the executive and voluntary function of free choice plays a key role. This function can become dysfunctional due to metacognitive biases that lead the patient to misjudge the usefulness or controllability of so-called repetitive negative thinking (RNT), i.e., worry, rumination, anger rumination, desire thinking, brooding, and so on. Case formulation in MCT aims to share with the patient how these metacognitive biases work. Consequently, in the MCT clinical procedure, the case formulation is shared quickly and early with the client.

In detail, MCT assesses the dysfunctional processes that are activated when the person reacts to a triggering distress—turning it into an emotional disorder—by activating cycles of the abovementioned RNT that thrive on three main processes (Mathews and Wells 1999, 2004; Segerstrom et al. 2003; Wells 2008, 2013; Wells and Mathews 1994; Williams et al. 1988):

1. RNT can be erroneously conceived as a functional plan to deal with reality and its problems;

2. RNT is considered an uncontrollable state that is stronger than executive personal will;
3. RNT is considered harmful and dangerous and therefore fuel other worries.

From a clinical point of view, MCT has developed its case formulation implementation by adapting the procedures derived from Beck's CT socialization. However, the voluntary executive function of choice and attention play a different role in the two models. In Beck's CT model, voluntary attention and executive control depend on the elaboration of cognitive content related to self-beliefs. The model assumes that the therapeutic process works by the exploration and modification of these cognitive evaluations. Once the cognitive contents have been explored, voluntary attention will spontaneously adopt a more functional attitude and stop obsessively monitoring possible threats (Wells and Mathews 1994, p. 2).

In MCT, case formulation focuses on metacognition, i.e., beliefs about cognitive processes and beliefs. Therefore, MCT interventions mainly target a second-order metacognitive level in which mental states are regulated by attention, but are not completely controlled by rational reasoning. This theoretical difference helps us understand the difference between MCT and CT in the implementation of case formulation. Indeed, it is true that the importance of metacognitive components in normal and psychopathological functioning had already been intuited in previous CBT approaches, e.g., by Beck himself when he described the vicious cycles of fear of fear (Beck et al. 1985), by Ellis with his concept of secondary ABC (DiGiuseppe et al. 2014, pp. 64–65), or in Leahy's *emotional schema therapy* (EST; 2015), a CT-derived therapeutic model that focuses entirely on meta-emotional patterns, i.e., beliefs about emotions. However, only the MCT model places metacognition at the center of the psychopathological process and firmly states that metacognitive beliefs about mental states are psychopathological biases among many others and are the fundamental explicative principle of emotional disorders (Mathews and Wells 1999, 2004; Wells and Mathews 1994; Wells 2008, 2013).

MCT attributes a key role to the functions of attention and executive will and choice. This approach makes case formulation and therapeutic intervention in MCT even more closely interwoven with each other than in ACT. In Beck's CT, there is an ambiguity that makes the questioning intervention apparently able to function without its rationale being shared between therapist and patient. By contrast, in MCT, implementation of explicit sharing of the rationale, which is admittedly the case formulation—before the execution of the changing techniques of MCT, first of all detached mindfulness—is ineludible. Therefore, MCT more than any other psychotherapy places sharing the case formulation at the heart of the therapeutic process.

The way the case formulation is shared in MCT comprises a few simple questions and statements. As in the previous cases of CT and *rational emotive behavioral therapy* (REBT), we do not intend to display the whole procedure but only to comment on some steps as happens in our clinical practice. The MCT therapist encourage patients to recognize that the emotional problem depends on the fact that they focus their attention too much on threats by worrying and thinking too much:

How do you think you would be if you didn't think about it? if you didn't notice it? if you didn't pay so much attention to the problem?

The assessment of metacognitions occurs through equally simple questions:

Why do you think so much? What makes you worry?

After the initial assessment, the therapist works out an MCT case formulation in terms of trigger, level of rumination and reasons for rumination as already written, utility, and uncontrollability and shares it with the patient:

In summary, I would suggest that your emotional problem depends on a level of excessive worrying and attention to the problems that seems justified to you because it looks useful but also because you seem unable to stop it. The idea that I propose is that worrying over the problems is less useful than you thought and it is not at all true that you cannot stop it. You can control your worry more than you think.

References

Arntz, A., & van Genderen, H. (2009). *Schema therapy for borderline personality disorder*. Chichester: John Wiley & Sons Ltd.

Bamelis, L. L., Evers, S. M., Spinhoven, P., & Arntz, A. (2014). Results of a multicenter randomized controlled trial of the clinical effectiveness of schema therapy for personality disorders. *American Journal of Psychiatry, 171*, 305–322.

Beck, A. T. (1976). *Cognitive therapy and the emotional disorders*. New York, NY: International Universities Press.

Beck, A. T., Emery, G., & Greenberg, R. L. (1985). *Anxiety disorders and phobias: A cognitive perspective*. New York, NY: Basic Books.

Beck, J. S. (2011). *Cognitive therapy: Basics and beyond* (2nd ed.). London/New York, NY: Guilford Press.

Bell, T., Mackie, L., & Bennett-Levy, J. (2015). 'Venturing towards the dark side': The use of imagery interventions by recently qualified cognitive–behavioural therapists. *Clinical psychology & psychotherapy, 22*, 591–603.

Cannon, W. B. (1915). *Bodily changes in pain, hunger, fear and rage*. New York, NY: D. Appleton & Company.

Cannon, W. B. (1936). The role of emotions in disease. *Annals of Internal Medicine, 9*, 1453–1465.

Carlbring, P., Maurin, L., Törngren, C., Linna, E., Eriksson, T., Sparthan, E., et al. (2010). Individually-tailored, Internet-based treatment for anxiety disorders: A randomized controlled trial. *Behaviour Research and Therapy, 49*, 18–24.

Christensen, A., Jacobson, N. S., & Babcock, J. C. (1995). Integrative behavioral couples therapy. In N. S. Jacobson & A. S. Gurman (Eds.), *Clinical handbook for couples therapy* (pp. 31–64). New York: Guildford.

Cordova, J. V. (2001). Acceptance in behavior therapy: Understanding the process of change. *Behavior Analyst, 24*, 213–226.

De Houwer, J. (2011). Why the cognitive approach in psychology would profit from a functional approach and vice versa. *Perspectives on Psychological Science, 6*, 202–209.

DiGiuseppe, R., Doyle, K. A., Dryden, W., & Backx, W. (2014). *A practioner's guide to rational emotive behavior therapy*. New York, NY: Oxford University Press.

Doss, B. D., Jones, J. T., & Christensen, A. (2002). *Integrative behavioral couples therapy*. In F. W. Kaslow (Ed.), *Comprehensive handbook of psychotherapy: Integrative/eclectic* (Vol. 4, pp. 387–410). John Wiley & Sons Inc..

Hackmann, A., Bennett-Levy, J., & Holmes, E. A. (2011). *Oxford guide to imagery in cognitive therapy*. Oxford: Oxford University Press.

Hayes, S. C., & Hofmann, S. G. (2018). *Process-based CBT. The science and core clinical competencies of cognitive behavioral therapy*. Oakland, CA: Context Press, New Harbinger.

Hayes, S. C., Levin, M. E., Plumb-Vilardaga, J., Villatte, J. L., & Pistorello, J. (2013). Acceptance and commitment therapy and contextual behavioral science: Examining the progress of a distinctive model of behavioral and cognitive therapy. *Behavior therapy, 44*, 180–198.

Hayes, S. C., & Strosahl, K. D. (2004). *A practical guide to acceptance and commitment therapy*. New York, NY: Guildford Press.

Hughes, S., De Houwer, J., & Perugini, M. (2016). The functional-cognitive framework for psychological research: Controversies and resolutions. *International Journal of Psychology, 51*, 4–14.

Jacob, G. A., & Arntz, A. (2013). Schema therapy for personality disorders—A review. *International Journal of Cognitive Therapy, 6*, 171–185.

Jacobson, N. S., Martell, C. R., & Dimidjian, S. (2001). Behavioral Activation for depression: Returning to contextual roots. *Clinical Psychology: Science and Practice, 8*, 255–270.

Kahneman, D., & Frederick, S. (2002). Representativeness revisited: Attribute substitution in intuitive judgment. In T. Gilovich, D. Griffin, & D. Kahneman (Eds.), *Heuristics and biases* (pp. 49–81). New York, NY: Cambridge University Press.

Kanter, J. W., Bush, A. M., & Rush, L. C. (2009). *Behavioral activation*. New York, NY: Routledge.

Kohlenberg, R. J., & Tsai, M. (1991). *Functional analytic psychotherapy: Creating intense and curative therapeutic relationships*. New York, NY: Plenum Press.

Kuyken, W. (2006). Evidence-based case formulation: Is the emperor clothed? In N. Tarrier (Ed.), *Case formulation in cognitive behaviour therapy. The treatment of challenging and complex cases* (pp. 28–51). Hove/New York, NY: Routledge.

Kuyken, W., Padesky, C. A., & Dudley, R. (2011). *Collaborative case conceptualization: Working effectively with clients in cognitive-behavioral therapy*. New York, NY: Guilford.

Leahy, R. L. (2015). *Emotional schema therapy*. New York, NY: Guilford Press.

Linehan, M. M. (1993). *Cognitive-behavioral treatment of borderline personality disorder*. New York, NY: Guilford Press.

Martell, C. R., Addis, M. E., & Jacobson, N. S. (2001). *Depression in context: Strategies for guided action*. New York, NY: Norton.

Martin, J. W., & Sloman, S. A. (2013). Refining the dual-system theory of choice. *Journal of Consumer Psychology, 23*, 552–555.

Mathews, G., & Wells, A. (1999). The cognitive science of attention and emotion. In T. Dalgleish & M. Power (Eds.), *Handbook of cognition and emotion* (pp. 171–192). New York, NY: Wiley.

Mathews, G., & Wells, A. (2004). Rumination, depression, and metacognition: The S-REF model. In C. Papageorgiou & A. Wells (Eds.), *Rumination: Nature, theory, and treatment* (pp. 125–151). Chichester: Wiley.

McCullough, J. P., Jr., & Goldfried, M. R. (1999). *Treatment for chronic depression: Cognitive behavioral analysis system of psychotherapy*. New York, NY: Guilford Press.

Persons, J. B. (2008). *The case formulation approach to cognitive-behavior therapy (guides to individualized evidence-based treatment)*. New York, NY: Guilford.

Roediger, E., Stevens, B. A., & Brockman, R. (2008). *Contextual schema therapy: An integrative approach to personality disorders, emotional dysregulation & interpersonal functioning*. Oakland, CA: New Harbinger Pub.

Segerstrom, S. C., Stanton, A. L., Alden, L. E., & Shortridge, B. E. (2003). Multidimensional structure for repetitive thought: What's on your mind, and how, and how much? *Journal of Personality and Social Psychology, 85*, 909–921.

Sloman, S. A. (2002). Two systems of reasoning. In T. Gilovich, D. Griffin, & D. Kahneman (Eds.), *Heuristics and biases* (pp. 379–396). Cambridge: Cambridge University Press.

Stanovich, K. E., & West, R. F. (2002). Individual differences in reasoning: Implications for the rationality debate. In T. Gilovich, D. Griffin, & D. Kahneman (Eds.), *Heuristics and biases* (pp. 421–440). Cambridge: Cambridge University Press.

Wells, A. (2008). *Metacognitive therapy for anxiety and depression*. London: Guilford Press.
Wells, A. (2013). Advances in metacognitive therapy. *International Journal of Cognitive Therapy, 6*, 186–201.
Wells, A., & Mathews, G. (1994). *Attention and emotion: A clinical perspective*. Hove/Hillsdale, NJ: Erlbaum.
Williams, J. M. G., Watts, F. N., MacLeod, G., & Mathews, A. (1988). *Cognitive psychology and emotional disorders*. Chichester: John Wiley.
Wilson, K. G., & Dufrene, T. (2009). *Mindfulness for two: An acceptance and commitment therapy approach to mindfulness in psychotherapy*. Oakland, CA: New Harbinger.
Young, J. E., Klosko, J. S., & Weishaar, M. (2003). *Schema therapy: A practitioner's guide*. New York, NY: Guilford.

Commentary on Chapter "Case Formulation in Process-Based Therapies": Process Based CBT as an Approach to Case Conceptualization

Avigal Snir and Stefan Hofmann

Contents

The Innovation of Process-Based Cognitive Behavioral Therapy

The chapter "Case Formulation in Process-Based Therapies" describing case formulation in Process-Based Cognitive Behavioral Therapy (PB-CBT) (Hayes and Hofmann 2018; Hofmann and Hayes 2019), focused mainly on the contribution of PB-CBT to reformulation traditional CBT interventions using functional processes terminology. The editors also discuss the integration of various treatment approaches under a broad theoretical umbrella, which allows clinicians to communicate with their colleagues, who use different therapeutic languages, and to be more flexible navigating psychotherapy. Whereas these aspects are definitely present in PB-CBT, and might benefit fruitful clinical outcome, we would like to argue that these are merely by-products of the broader innovation that PB-CBT offers. This would be the idiographic, dynamic, multifunctional and scientific approach toward case conceptualization and formulation in psychotherapy.

PB-CBT in its core is based on idiographic assessment and analysis, aimed to form and test hypotheses on how to best treat the individual based on his or her unique biopsychosocial characteristics, goals, and needs. In a different terminology,

A. Snir · S. Hofmann (✉)
Department of Psychological and Brain Sciences, Boston University, Boston, MA, USA
e-mail: asnir@bu.edu; shofmann@bu.edu

G. M. Ruggiero et al. (eds.), *CBT Case Formulation as Therapeutic Process*,
https://doi.org/10.1007/978-3-030-63587-9_12

this is indeed the complex, shared and dynamic process of case formulation. Meeting a new client, conducting the idiographic assessment, the main question to explore is:

Given this client and his or her individual needs, what core biopsychosocial processes should be addressed and what is the most efficient and effective means of doing so?

We believe that most competent, experienced and ethical clinicians would attest that they take this question under consideration with each client. However, the question remains open regarding what evidence clinicians are using for making treatment recommendations and for engaging in therapy. Recent developments in PB-CBT indeed offer clinicians with guidelines as well as structured models to guide the assessment and case formulation process. In this Commentary, we would like to share the advanced framework PB-CBT already offers for clinicians, review main data collection and analysis techniques, and present clinical examples. These are not strict guidelines or templates for case formulation, but a broad theoretical analytic framework that guide clinician as they navigate the complex, multi-dimensional progressive process of case formulation.

The Framework of Process-Based Cognitive Behavioral Therapy

Case formulation in PB-CBT differs from traditional approaches in its core, as it moves far from diagnostic categories, treatment structured protocols and interventions. Latent disease models were, and still are widely prevalent in research and clinical contexts. Initially, following the assessment process people are grouped in diagnostic de-individualized categories (Greenhalgh et al. 2014). Accordingly, specific sets of information, theories and interventions are applied, and expected to encompass and benefit the entire conceptual group. These labels are in the core of traditional CBT manuals starting with the case formulation procedure. The latent disease model tends to blind treatment developers to the key role of normal psychological processes in behavioral outcomes, and to the centrality of pragmatic outcomes desired by clients such as social effectiveness or quality of life, instead prioritizing the referred list of signs and symptoms. Most of all, it tends to reduce human suffering to brain abnormalities and biological dysfunctions and de-emphasize the importance of the biopsychosocial context of the individual (Greenhalgh et al. 2014).

While the application of CBT approaches to specific disorders is decreasing with the emergence of a process-based approach (Hayes and Hofmann 2018), narrow attention to the patient's specific symptoms or presented problems remains a main feature of CBT case formulation and treatment delivery. To demonstrate these ideas, consider a client, named Sam:

Sam is a 30-year-old man, who reached out for a clinician to get help with his intrusive obsessive thoughts. Sam, is seeing a CBT trained clinician. Luckily, the clinician is experienced enough to go beyond diagnosis and a structured manual. Treatment main goal is set for reduction in obsessions, and more specifically ability to manage the distress and interference caused by the intrusive thoughts. Sam is receiving psychoeducation about obsessions and is learning various cognitive and behaviors skills to cope and manage his thoughts in an effective way. Treatment success is then defined as reduction in interference and distress caused by the obsessions. When achieved, treatment is terminated. The question than arises, is this an excellent and satisfying outcome for the client?

PB-CBT suggests that focusing solely on the DSM or ICD-defined symptoms and on the presenting problems will lead to non-satisfactory, short-term outcomes of treatment. In PB-CBT, we will work under the assumption that a specific symptom is always a part of a network, the symptom is maintained and is also maintaining a network that is maladaptive and in the same time, resilient for change. In fact, the term *symptom* is misleading because it implies the existence of a latent disease. Instead, the term *problem* might me more appropriate. Going back to Sam:

Further exploring the presenting problem through contextual idiographic assessment, leads us to reveal that the obsessions are mainly interpersonally focused, and are maintained by past poor social experience with a woman that Sam dated 5 years ago. In the interaction, Sam felt humiliated and de-evaluated. He felt that he was misled by this woman, after giving her his trust. Further exploration reveals that current interactions in romantic contexts, are linked with negative thoughts about the future and the self, and diminished self-efficacy. Additionally, Sam tends to spend long hours watching videos at and tend withdrawal from social activities and gatherings. In these times, at home alone, Sam finds himself constantly bothered by obsessive intrusive thoughts about his past mistakes which are causing sadness and hopelessness (See Fig. 1 for a schematic representation of Sam's dynamic network model).

In the model, note that the node containing Sam's history has round edges to differentiate this node as a moderator. Whereas the squared nodes represent mediators. Additionally, thicker arrow heads represent stronger influence. For example, the strong bidirectional influence of negative emotions (i.e., sadness and anxiety) on behavioral avoidance and isolation is represented in thick arrow heads. Intrusive thoughts are highlighted as the presenting problem and the main reason to reach out for therapy.

Having this network as a map, changes the focus of treatment, from finding the best interventions to fight obsessions. Alternatively, clinician might shift to finding the best way to reduce social withdrawal and promote accurate cognitive appraisals in a client who developed emotional and behavioral avoidance strategies and obsessive thinking style following a very negative experience with women in romantic setting.

The goal of treatment is now more ambitious, rather than just reduction in symptoms, PB-CBT aims to help the client replace a maladaptive network with an adaptive one, to strengthen processes that promote well-being and experiences that goes in line with the clients' values and ambitions. For this purpose, traditional case formulation must advance.

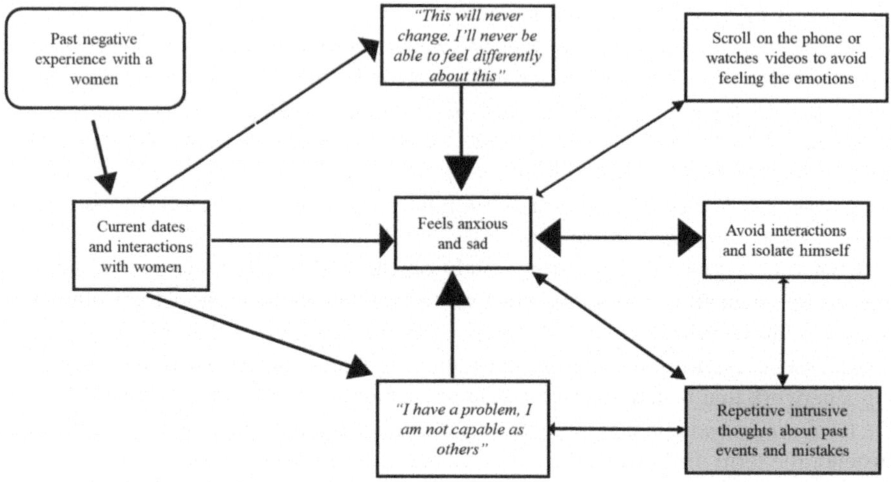

Fig. 1 Dynamic network model for Sam

Persons' (2008) case-formulation approach to CBT was an important step toward the translation of general principles to individual applications. Whereas, case formulation in its cognitive therapy traditional form, could be experienced as a didactical and mechanically directive process. Subsequently, this might lead to undermining the therapeutic alliance (Guidano 1993), lacking validation for the patient full experience and to poor or mediocre treatment outcomes. However, Persons (2008) acknowledged that most patients' presenting problems are not successfully resolved by the simple application of a single CBT protocol to a single disorder, and therefore emphasized the importance of individual differences in assessment, case formulation, and treatment planning. There have been attempts to evaluate this approach empirically (e.g., Persons et al. 2013), but further progress required theoretical, methodological and statistical innovations that Persons didn't have at that time. Today, as we describe below, there is a solid model, strong methodological and statistical tools and sufficient evidence to take this approach.

Case Formulation in Process-Based Cognitive Behavioral Therapy

Treatment starts with a contextual *idiographic assessment*. This assessment is intended to be a collaborative process in which both client and therapist examine a particular context or situation and use the clients' unique knowledge of themselves and therapists' unique knowledge of psychology to formulate a shared understanding of the process occurring in that particular context and to identify targets for intervention. Questions to facilitate this understanding might be:

"What was going through your mind during the situation?" or *"What were you thinking about when X happened?"* and *what happened then? How did you feel when this happened? What was going through your mind? Did anything else happen before this occur?*

The assessment builds-up toward a functional analysis. Whereas functional analysis has its roots in the early days of psychology, applying principles to individual patterns of behavior was more an art than a science, making replicable assessment difficult (Hayes and Follette 1992). Traditional functional analysis was neglected from psychology literature for decades, probably because it didn't show effectivity encompassing the complex multilevel human experience and suffering. Haynes and O'Brien (1990) explained functional analysis as the identification of relevant, causal and controllable functional relations to an individual's specific behaviors. In recent decades, functional contextualism is emphasized in the newer forms of CBT (Hayes 2016) and in relational frame theory (RFT; Hayes et al. 2001). Additionally, interventions based on a functional analytic assessment have demonstrated utility in improving clinical outcomes of some conditions (Ghaderi 2006; Hurl et al. 2016; Miller and Lee 2013). Important components of modern functional contextualism include focusing on an event as a whole, having sensitivity for context, emphasizing pragmatic truth criterion, having specific goals against which to apply that criterion, prediction, and influence. In its broader sophisticated version, modern functional analysis is being increasingly popular now in clinical and research setting.

One way to facilitate and guide contextual idiographic assessment and functional analysis is by using a functional-analytic network based on the Extended Evolutionary Meta-Model (EEMM; Hayes et al. 2019). Generally speaking, PB-CBT considers psychological disorders as reflections of maladaptive networks. In evolutionary terms, maladaptations are caused by problems in variation, selection, and/or retention of specific biopsychosocial dimensions in a given context. EEMM is a tool for researchers and clinicians to identify, study, categorize and target the processes involved in their psychopathology. Clinicians can use core change processes to determine the ways in which selection, retention, variation, and context interact to form maladaptive networks of thoughts, emotions, and behaviors. Therapeutic changes can also be seen as clients use these same evolutionary dimensions to form adaptive responses through treatment (for a more detailed review, see Barthel et al. 2020). See Fig. 2 for a scheme of EEMM.

Problems can be described as having one or more of the following facets or existing on one or more of the following dimensions: affective, cognitive, attentional, behavioral, motivational and self-related dimensions. For each of these dimensions, problems can involve variation, selection, retention and context issues. As most clients are reporting more than one problem when attending therapy, a treatment target hierarchy can help therapists identify which problems their client identifies as most important, and thus which problem areas to target in what order.

This process of generating a shared understanding of the situation and choosing a target for intervention is always collaborative. Many times, the process also includes drawing a schematic of the relevant processes. This contextual model captures the joint understanding of client and therapist and it is important that clients

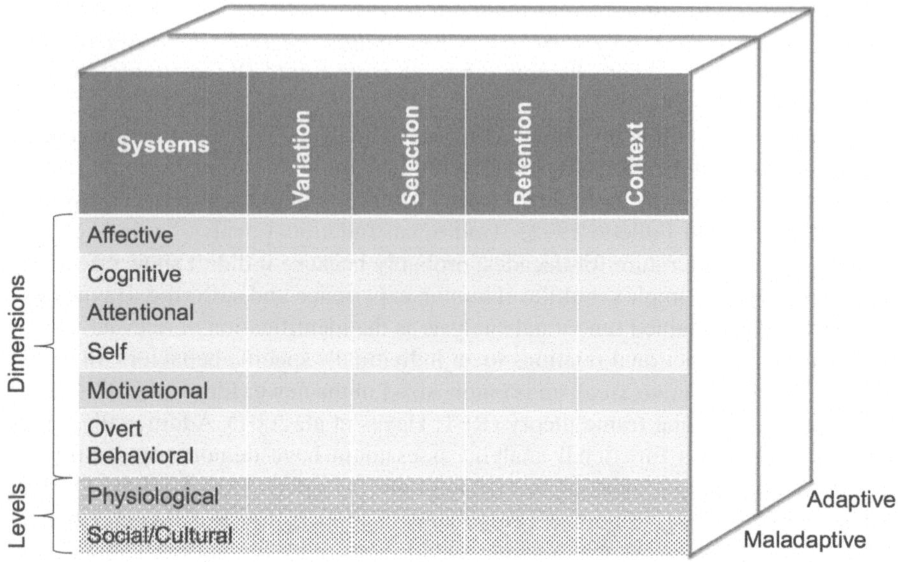

Fig. 2 The extended evolutionary meta-model (EEMM) for organizing target problems and identifying appropriate interventions (© Steven C. Hayes and Stefan G. Hofmann. Used by permission)

feel that the model is a good representation of their experience. Consider the example of Sam:

Idiographic assessment already revealed that Sam's obsessions are linked with his poor romantic past experiences. Network analysis also revealed negative biased cognitions toward the self and the future, behavioral/social withdrawal and affective avoidance. EEMM analysis might help in conceptualizing the problem on the different dimensions:

- *Cognitively, involving low variation (i.e., the client is unable to think flexibly about the situation),and is holding negative core believes regarding his competancy and self value. Additionally, Sam presents with low selection (i.e., even in the presence of alternative realistic thoughts he tends to ruminate).*
- *Affectively, involving low variation (i.e., Sam is unable to come in touch with his intense emotions in a flexible manner and use obsessions as an avoidance strategy).*
- *Behaviorally, involving low variation and selection (i.e., Sam tends to choose avoidance as main strategy and is struggling with selecting other approached type actions such as communicating his thoughts with others, facing the fears and initiating interactions to achieve better experiences).*
- *On the self dimension, Sam is holding limiting beliefs about his ability to overcome his fears and to create change in his life.*
- *From a motivational point of view, Sam seems to escape to a passive mode, were he is able to express his long-term goals and wishes, but is struggling with*

actively and consistently put effort toward promoting important life goals. Mainly, finding a partner for a committed long term relationship.

- *Potential interventions could target variation (e.g., developing alternative thoughts, engaging in exposures) and facilitate selection of appropriate and helpful strategies in the different dimensions.*
- *Lastly, applying the interventions in a way that maximizes retention (i.e., applying them with easy safer targets at first, reaching the end targets in a gradual manner).*

Case Formulation as a Progressive and Cyclic Process in Process-Based Cognitive Behavioral Therapy

Beyond explorative, context grounded questions, leading the idiographic assessment, it is necessary to implement advanced data collection strategies as integral part assessment and treatment. Thus, frequent assessments of change processes are needed to increase the intensity of the analytic focus at the level of the individual. Examples of some available methods that can be taken in clinical settings are frequent measures of processes taken in session and between sessions, and measures of social, psychological, and physical context (Hayes et al. 2019). In research setting, statistics involved in PB-CBT seek to understand meaningful changes at the individual level, in consideration of context, non-linear progress that builds across time, and cyclical symptom relations. Examples of statistical approaches used for process-based research include ecological momentary assessment (EMA), complex network analysis, time-series analysis, and examination of critical slowing down and tipping points that can shift symptom trajectory (for review, see Barthel, Hofmann and Hayes, in press). Frequent, broader, and more contextually focused assessment, set up the stage for the creation of comprehensive, functional analytic working model with each of our clients.

The idiographic assessment and the functional network model analysis form the first stages of PB-CBT, and set the stage for implementing evidence-based interventions to target the identified problems dimensions. However, in PB-CBT case formulation continues as long as treatment is still ongoing. Following an intervention, the client's experiences are discussed. Receiving the client's feedback on the intervention is essential in order to decide whether to adapt or change the intervention and conduct it again (e.g., if something went wrong, was misunderstood, was not properly planned), whether to choose a different intervention for the same target, or whether to move on to a different context, or therapeutic target. Thus, eliciting feedback provides essential information that can inform the next cycle beginning with idiographic assessment (i.e., the second cycle of idiographic assessment will include information about the client's experiences and processing of the first intervention). Case formulation in PB-CBT is a progressive process that goes on throughout the entire treatment and hopefully, will continue to evolve in the client's mind, enhance self-knowledge and self-efficacy long after treatment is over.

It is inevitable that assessments and case formulations will become more complex in order to match the complexity of each individual. However, we now have the theoretical models supported with methodological tools and expertise (data collection, network analysis and more) to offer clients with a complex, evidence guided, dynamic individualized assessment and treatments. As the editors and authors of chapter "Case Formulation in Process-Based Therapies" rightfully noticed, the interventions used in PB-CBT and the arguments in which its theory supports are not novel. However, as we briefly reviewed in this Commentary—asking individualized, context related questions through the idiographic assessment, using advanced tools for data collection and analysis, organizing the data in a comprehensive working model (such as the EEMM), and working in a cyclic manner throughout the therapeutic process, are indeed a new way in which case formulation and evidence-based clinical practice can now be delivered to our clients.

References

Barthel, A. L., Hofmann, S. G., & Hayes, S. C. (2020). Process-based therapy (PBT): An integrative approach to clinical treatment and research via idiographic methodology. Procognitive (Cognitive Therapy Update Program). Unissued manuscript.

Ghaderi, A. (2006). Does individualization matter? A randomized trial of standardized (focused) versus individualized (broad) cognitive behavior therapy for bulimia nervosa. *Behaviour Research and Therapy, 44*, 273–288.

Greenhalgh, T., Howick, J., & Maskrey, N. (2014). Evidence based medicine: A movement in crisis? *BMJ, 348*, g3725. https://doi.org/10.1136/bmj.g3725.

Guidano, V. F. (1993). A constructivist outline of human knowing processes. In M. Mahoney (Ed.), *Cognitive and constructive psychotherapies: theory, research and practice* (pp. 89–102). New York, NY: Springer.

Hayes, S. C. (2016). Acceptance and commitment therapy, relational frame theory, and the third wave of behavioral and cognitive therapies- Republished article. *Behavior Therapy, 47*, 869–885.

Hayes, S. C., Barnes-Holmes, D., & Roche, B. (Eds.). (2001). *Relational frame theory: A post Skinnerian account of human language and cognition*. New York: Kluwer Academic/Plenum Publishers.

Hayes, S. C., & Follette, W. C. (1992). Can functional analysis provide a substitute for syndromal classification? *Behavioral Assessment, 14*, 345–365.

Hayes, S. C., & Hofmann, S. G. (2018). *Process-based CBT: The science and core clinical competencies of cognitive behavioral therapy*. Oakland, CA: New Harbinger Publications.

Hayes, S. C., Hofmann, S. G., Stanton, C. E., Carpenter, J. K., Sanford, B. T., Curtiss, J. E., & Ciarrochi, J. (2019). The role of the individual in the coming era of process-based therapy. *Behaviour Research and Therapy, 117*, 40–53. https://doi.org/10.1016/j.brat.2018.10.005.

Haynes, S. N., & O'Brien, W. H. (1990). Functional analysis in behavior therapy. *Clinical Psychology Review, 10*, 649–668. https://doi.org/10.1016/0272-7358(90)90074-K.

Hofmann, S. G., & Hayes, S. C. (2019). The future of intervention science: Process-based therapy. *Clinical Psychological Science, 7*, 37–50. https://doi.org/10.1177/2167702618772296.

Hurl, K., Wightman, J., Haynes, S. N., & Virues-Ortega, J. (2016). Does a pre-intervention functional assessment increase intervention effectiveness? A meta-analysis of within-subject interrupted time-series studies. *Clinical Psychology Review, 47*, 71–84.

Miller, F. G., & Lee, D. L. (2013). Do functional behavioral assessments improve intervention effectiveness for students diagnosed with ADHD? A single-subject meta-analysis. *Journal of Behavioral Education, 22*, 253–282.

Persons, J. B. (2008). *The case formulation approach to cognitive-behavior therapy*. New York, NY: Guilford.

Persons, J. B., Beckner, V. L., & Tompkins, M. A. (2013). Testing case formulation hypotheses in psychotherapy: Two case examples. *Cognitive and Behavioral Practice, 20*, 399–409. https://doi.org/10.1016/j.cbpra.2013.03.004.

Clinical Behavior Analysis, ACT and Case Formulation. A Commentary on Chapter "Case Formulation in Process-Based Therapies"

Paolo Moderato and Kelly G. Wilson

Contents

Behavior Analysis and Psychological Flexibility

Acceptance and Commitment Therapy (ACT) is deeply rooted in Behavior Analysis (Anchisi, Moderato and Pergolizzi 2017), though ACT therapists are not necessarily knowledgeable about behavior analytical principles or even aware of what those principles might be. There are some basic points of Behavior Analysis on that are worth highlighting.

The core of ACT is psychological flexibility. Twentieth-century psychologists coined the term "construct" to provide substance and consistency to the incorporeality of human behavior in order to measure it. Even the best constructs, like the Big Five Personality Model have problems, however: they work pretty well explaining and predicting behavior, but fail to offer a framework to influence it. By definition, these constructs are stable and reliable, and not readily modifiable, if at all. Prediction and influence are basic tenets of clinical Behavior Analysis (and should be of any psychotherapy).

P. Moderato (✉)
IULM University, Milano, Italy
e-mail: paolo.moderato@iescum.org

K. G. Wilson
The University of Mississippi, Oxford, MS, USA
e-mail: kwilson@olemiss.edu

G. M. Ruggiero et al. (eds.), *CBT Case Formulation as Therapeutic Process*,
https://doi.org/10.1007/978-3-030-63587-9_13

Psychological flexibility is not a construct in the usual sense. It is an overarching (high order) repertoire. In the contextual behavioral tradition, we talk about repertoires of skills rather than constructs. The term repertoire makes the dynamics that characterize our lives clearer. If we look at the repertoire of a famous concert performer, for example a pianist, we can see that in it there are rather stable nuclei of compositions that he or she presents to the audience in rotation: for example, Beethoven's, Rachmaninoff's, and some of Mozart's concertos. Then there are the pieces for piano solo, and here the list is endless (but not infinite, here too there is stability). Then, for some, there is curiosity, openness, and moves into experimental, innovative repertoires. In any case, if you follow an artist over the years you can see the consistency that characterizes his or her repertoire: those who have specialized in Chopin and Schumann etudes are unlikely to perform Bach's Well-Tempered Clavier or his Goldberg Variations, or vice versa. In short, the repertoire is a pattern that can be modified with learning and practice—new pieces come in, old pieces get out—and, nevertheless, some stability remains.

Psychological flexibility is a complex repertoire of skills that allow clients to better live their lives, to improve their state of living, without trying to escape what they cannot escape. It is the ability to be willing to feel and think, to open themselves, with awareness, to the experience of the present moment and to direct their lives in ways that are important to them (Wilson and Dufrene 2008).

There is no need to teach or explain to clients how thinking, feeling and acting interconnect functionally. They do need to make experiential contact with the relevant contingencies, but being able to describe those contingencies may not be necessary at all. We do think that some agreement needs to be made at the outset of therapy, but it is not a technical agreement. They do not need to become behaviorists. Rather, it is a practical agreement: This is going to hurt. But we will only do things that hurt with your permission, at your pace, and for the pursuit of directions that matter to you.

Behavior Analysis and Mentalism

Another basic aspect of Behavior Analysis is its non-mentalistic assumption. We live in a mentalist world. It is so difficult to break the habit of mentalism. Thus, when talking about the six behavioral repertoires that ACT is organized into (*Acceptance/experiential avoidance; Cognitive defusion/fusion; Contact with the present moment/conceptualized past and feared future; Self as context/attachment to conceptualized self; Values/lack of values clarity; Committed action/inaction, impulsivity, or avoidance*) it is worth clarifying that commitment is not in any sense **in** the patient. All ACT processes are behavioral patterns in context and should not be cognitivized. Patients do not possess commitment or contain commitment, rather they bring behavior into alignment with values. That is, they **do** commitment, rather than feeling commitment or "having" a commitment. The same is true with acceptance. As ACT therapists, we do not worry much about thoughts or feelings of acceptance and commitment. We focus on the behavioral patterns inherent in acceptance and commitment.

In chapter "Case Formulation in Process-Based Therapies," the editors write that basic principle of case formulation in process therapies is that the goal is not to ascertain the structural basis of the emotional disorder in terms of whether, for example, a negative belief underlies and fuels anxiety. Rather, it is to examine the function of the symptom and share it with the patient. Here again, the suggestion seems to be that teaching **about** contingencies is somehow central. It is simply not true that one must know about contingencies in order for them to have an impact. Consciously knowing the contingencies might be useful, but is not necessarily so. It is just as possible that a person would weaponize that knowledge against themselves: "I know how this works and I keep doing it! I must be an idiot!" Knowing about contingencies might be persuasive, but there are lots of methods of persuasion that do not require us to turn our clients into behavioral engineers or even to sell them on that idea.

Case Formulation and Functional Analysis

Another aspect that has a strong impact on case formulation is functional analysis. The term analysis is one of the pillars of science. Analysis means breaking a complex thing down into simpler units. The natural world is too complex to be studied as a whole, it must be reduced, both in the material physical world and in the immaterial psychological one. Reductionism is an old issue in psychology, mostly in behavioristic psychology. The main question is: where should we stop on the endless road of reduction? In other words, which is the right level of analysis? Behavior analysis has its own history of arguments between molar and molecular accounts of behavior. The answers for ACT are the same as the answers in Behavior Analysis. We analyze context in a molecular way as is necessary to allow for the influence of behavior.

The "right" level of analysis can be only defined pragmatically: does the analysis work? The pragmatic criterion to establish at which level analysis works comes from the case formulation. Case formulation and therapeutic intervention are closely interwoven with each other: the six-point formulation is so interconnected with the intervention that it is indistinguishable in clinical practice, the editors suggest. Actually, the six-point formulation is a six + six, because every repertoire of skills lacking in the hexaflex has its positive, and vice versa.

The six-point case formulation is a mid-level analysis. A more molecular level can be helpful (or necessary) to better understand the process. For example, the process of experiential avoidance can be analyzed more in depth with a more molecular functional analysis. It is important to keep in mind that in ACT (and Contextualistic Clinical Behavior Analysis), the term "behavior" includes any and all of the activities of a whole organism. If an organism can do it, it is behavior. Behavior can only be defined by referring to the organism that is behaving. Thus, actions such as walking and talking are behaviors, but so is wishing, wanting, imagining, thinking, dreaming, loving, grieving, fearing, hating, despairing and finding meaning, and on. These are all things we humans can do in and with a context and are all the proper dependent variables of ACT (Presti and Moderato 2019).

The same is true for working on the lack of contact with the present moment, which involves turning off the autopilot, using the experience of the five senses, and staying tuned with what happens from moment to moment. Much cognitive experimental research (Tversky and Kahneman 1974; Kahneman 2011) has shown that many of our daily actions are in form of routines and automatic behaviors that were useful and functional on many occasions in our ontogenetic and or phylogenetic history, and therefore are maintained by strong contingencies of reinforcement, but that unfortunately can be very harmful and dysfunctional in different contexts. Functional analysis could be very helpful to assess the patient's patterns of behavior that are out of touch with his present moment.

In other words, functional analysis plays, in behavioral psychology, the same role that cell analysis plays in medicine in understanding and diagnosing the pathological process, which is a different way to define case formulation. In addition to sometimes being quite automatic, behavior is often determined in a complex manner. That is, it often does not have a single function. And, at times, formally similar behavior might have different functions at different moments. Consider, for example, a very capable graduate student who feels a bit of imposter in class discussions. Such a student might become disengaged. The functional analysis might be quite simple and result in the student becoming more generally engaged in discussions. But more analysis might be needed. They might raise a hand to answer at times in order to advance the class conversation. And, other times, that same raising of the hand might function as a way of avoiding looking stupid. One function of hand-raising is the pursuit of better intellectual understanding, the other is functionally related to fitting in socially. A careful, more molecular, moment-by-moment examination of such interactions may help the student to read their own behavior and to make choices about what sort of student they want to be.

Values

There is another critical point that should be discussed—the definition of value. In ACT, the term *values* refers to patterns of activities that give our lives meaning. Values are not goals. Goals can be accomplished. Instead, values are like a compass, they help us to make choices based on the directions in which we want our lives to go but have no endpoint. Values are very individual and define who we want to be, even if/when we face difficult or painful experiences. Values are not consequences, but they establish predominant reinforcements for those activities that are intrinsic to the implementation of the same behavioral pattern: it is important that values should not be confused with consequences. Rather, they make patterns of action consequential.

Process-Based Therapy

Finally, a few words about Process-Based Therapy (PBT, Hayes and Hofmann 2018). We would argue that all, or very nearly all, therapies began as process models. Consider Beck's book *Cognitive Therapy and the Emotional Disorders*. That book is a strategy document and Beck says that explicitly: "Before starting to evaluate the psychotherapies, we should distinguish between a system of psychotherapy and a simple cluster of techniques. A system of psychotherapy provides both a format for understanding the psychological disorders it purports to treat and a clear blueprint of the general principles and specific procedures of treatment." (Beck 1976, p. 278).

The behavioral folks were always process-based—beginning with operant and respondent interactions. Likewise, the psychodynamic folks were always process-based. The humanistic, existential and family systems folks all proposed processes that they conceived as responsible for suffering and thriving.

The shift to a focus on procedures and outcomes was, in our view, an artifact of the era of Randomized Clinical Trials (RCT) within which relatively fixed protocols were tested against diagnostic syndromes. Creating a fixed protocol allowed researchers to mimic pharmaceutical trials, with the DSM diagnosis playing the part of the disease and the protocol playing the part of the stable molecule to be tested. The therapies that thrived in that funding environment were the ones who could best fit their treatments into the procrustean bed of rigid manuals. RCTs were focused on outcomes and the top scientists of the time would say things like "First we should figure out **IF** something works before we waste time figuring out how it works" (i.e., validating processes). PBT, as an idea, returns us to our original focus — what processes produce change and stability.

ACT has always been a process-based therapy. However, the rise of PBT brings new and heightened focus on process as the central issue for research and training. Hayes and Hofmann (2019) have recently suggested that "PBT is not a new form of therapy—rather, it's a more Contextual Behavior Science (CBS) coherent vision of what we even mean by 'evidence-based intervention.'" Really this is a new version of the functional analytic dreams of early behavior therapists, but now integrated within multi-level, multi-dimensional evolutionary science, and with new analytical tools that can stand on top of the mountain of evidence we have accumulated as a field (and as a CBS community) on processes of change.

References

Anchisi, R., Moderato, P., & Pergolizzi, F. (2017). *Roots and Leaves*. In *Radici e sviluppi contestualisti in psicoterapia comportamentale e cognitiva [Contextualist roots and developments in behavioral and cognitive psychotherapy]*. Milano: FrancoAngeli.

Beck, A. T. (1976). *Cognitive therapy and the emotional disorders*. New York, NY: Penguin.

Hayes, S. C., & Hofmann, S. G. (2018). *Process-based CBT. The science and core clinical competencies of cognitive behavioral therapy*. Oakland, CA: Context Press, New Harbinger.
Hayes, S. C., & Hofmann, S.G. (2019). CBT, ACT, and the coming era of process-based therapy. Workshop held in DCU Helix, Dublin City University. Retrieved June 25–26, 20149, from https://contextualscience.org/cbt_act_and_the_coming_era_of_processbased_therapy
Kahneman, D. (2011). *Thinking fast and slow*. New York, NY: Farrar, Straus and Giroux.
Presti, G., & Moderato, P. (2019). *Pensieri, parole, emozioni [Thoughts, words, emotions]*. Milano: FrancoAngeli.
Tversky, A., & Kahneman, D. (1974). Judgment under uncertainty: Heuristics and biases. *Science, 185*, 1124–1131.
Wilson, K. G., & DuFrene, T. (2008). *Mindfulness for two: An acceptance and commitment therapy approach to mindfulness in psychotherapy*. Oakland, CA: New Harbinger.

Schema Therapy, Contextual Schema Therapy and Case Formulation: Commentary on Chapter "Case Formulation in Process-Based Therapies"

Eckhard Roediger, Gabriele Melli, and Nicola Marsigli

Contents

Cognitive Formulation

The section on *Schema Therapy* of chapter "Case Formulation in Process-Based Therapies" hits the nail: Schema Therapy is a kind of hybrid in dealing with the case formulation. The founder – Jeffrey Young - was a disciple of Aaron Beck and his thinking is entrenched by cognitive theory. Nevertheless, his approach is also influenced by constructivistic ideas (Guidano and Liotti 1983), attachment theory (Bowlby 1969) and Kelly's personal construct model (Kelly 1955). Giving the client an introduction into the impact of early childhood need frustrations leading to schemas and how our current mental processes are to a large extend impacted by them at the beginning of therapy is crucial to convey an understanding how to deal with these schema activations in the present. In the next step, the therapist tailors this theoretical framework to the client by collecting examples of need frustration from the client's history, observing the in-session behaviorur or using inventories to access schemas and the resulting modes. Putting all this together in an initially cognitive case formulation serves the purpose to show the client that the universal model matters to him or her too and to invite them to buy into the therapy. These

E. Roediger (✉)
Institut für Schematherapie, Frankfurt, Germany
e-mail: kontakt@eroediger.de

G. Melli · N. Marsigli
Institute for Behavioral and Cognitive Psychology and Psychotherapy (IPSICO), Florence, Italy

G. M. Ruggiero et al. (eds.), *CBT Case Formulation as Therapeutic Process*, https://doi.org/10.1007/978-3-030-63587-9_14

steps are still content based and in line with conventional cognitive behavorial therapy (CBT) approaches. However, the focus on aversive early childhood experiences and resulting schemas broadens the scope of conventional CBT-Case formulations into the very early childhood years, like the results of attachment research incline us to do.

The aim of the therapist is now to precisely connect present dysfunctional behavior with patterns of early childhood experiences based on structural similarities between the present and the past relationships in order to reveal how schemas are still impacting the client's life today. In fact, schemata act like glasses we are wearing, tainting our perceptions, judgement and impulses while we are not aware that we are wearing them. We strongly believe that the world is (still) the way we see it. Bringing these glasses into the client's awareness is an important goal to achieve.

Experiential Interventions

In the next step, the key experiential interventions used in Schema therapy, such as Imagery Rescripting and Chair Dialogues add "*emotional flesh*" to the bones of the initial cognitive framework, by bringing the clients vividly in touch with significant childhood experiences again. In a so-called Child mode they re-experience the former childhood scenes again and the therapist actively supports them to "rescript" these scenes by bringing them to a good end. The pivotal part is that the clients experience themselves in a kind of "therapeutic dissociation": first in the Child-mode and later in their so-called Healthy Adult-mode. If necessary, in a *limited reparenting relationship*, the therapist acts as role model of a good caretaker. Later in therapy, the clients internalize this behavior as the Healthy Adult mode, to deal with schema activations in a self-compassionate way themselves.

The goal of Imagery Rescripting as well as the Chair Dialogues is to confront and "impeach" dysfunctional caretakers (in imagery) or dysfunctional internalized beliefs (in chair dialogues) and care for the child in the image (or the Child mode feelings in the Chair Dialogues) like good parents do. This makes use of the resources the clients possess today and applies them to their own "frozen", schema-based states. In fact, many clients are pretty well able to care e.g. for their physical children, but still neglect themselves. In a metaphorical way, we ask them to "adopt" their internal Child Mode state and care for it for the rest of their life. The key target of these interventions is not to "*change memory, but change meaning*" (Arntz 2012). This wording already contains a spark of process-oriented thinking in terms that it is not about the content of the memory itself, but how we relate to it today.

Contextual Schema Therapy Approach

New developments in Schema therapy, such as the Contextual Schema Therapy approach (Roediger et al. 2018) try to turn this spark into a flame by using the 6 *Acceptance and Commitment Therapy* (ACT) processes to describe in detail, how the clients in their Healthy Adult modes relate to schema activations and the resulting modes. I.e., are they open to face their emotional states (Child modes)? Do they get aware of interfering thoughts (so called critic modes)? Are they able to distance from them by putting them on a separate chair? Do they manage to re-focus their attention to their emotional core needs and their values? Can they recognize automatic pilot impulses (in terms of coping modes), anticipated the (dysfunctional) outcome and let them go instead of acting them out rigidly? At this point, we finally leave the initial case formulation. In-session, we continuously track how the clients deal with their given mode states in terms of a co-constructed and shared adaptive case formulation. It creates a joint perspective and a reference point in terms of a "road map" to relate to whenever the going gets tough along the way of therapy. This is why Schema therapy is a hybrid in dealing with case formulations.

Like in other process-based approaches, the content of the schemas themselves doesn't matter anymore. The cutting edge point is the functional analysis from a (mindful and centered) observer perspective following 3 steps: (1) Get aware of the full content of your mind in an open, accepting way, (2) stay centered and get aware of your needs and values and understand, which of the emotions, thoughts and impulses are in line with your needs and values, (3) let dysfunctional thoughts, feelings and impulses go or stay without allowing them to bother you too much and do what fulfils your needs and values in a committed way.

How to apply this on a practical level? If a schema activation occurs in the therapy relationship during the session, the therapist stops the interaction, asks the client to stand up together side by side and look down on the interaction on the chairs below. Using third person language the therapist and the client relate this interaction to the case formulation. Instead of evaluating the content, they look at the interactional pattern and the interpersonal effects: Are the client's needs and values met? This experiential evaluation includes that the clients in their child modes experience and accept the suffering resulting from their ongoing maladaptive coping behavior. If the clients realize, that they are acting out a schema-based interaction pattern, the motivation to look out for a more functional new behavior and carry it out between the sessions grows. Moreover, this entire procedure is also helpful to strengthen the bond between client and therapist.

At this point in therapy understanding the mechanisms of schema activation only serves the purpose to realize that the deriving emotions, thoughts and impulses are "ghosts from the past" we better get rid of for the sake of a better life quality. Nevertheless, a deep emotionally entrenched understanding of the nature of schema driven experience based on the experiential techniques makes it much easier for the client to "check out" and distance from the induced modes. Finally, it is about what to do best NOW. Once our clients (re-)gained the ability to step back from the current schema-based activations, shift into an observer stance (Mode **A**wareness) and connect with their needs and values (Mode **B**alance), they are free to choose a more adaptive and functional behavior (Mode **C**hoice) and carry it out in a committed and self-compassionate way. This is when Schema therapy finally becomes a contextual or process-based therapy.

References

Arntz, A. (2012). Imagery rescripting as a therapeutic technique: Review of clinical trials, basic studies, and research agenda. *Journal of Experimental Psychopathology, 3*, 189–208.

Bowlby, J. (1969). *Attachment. Attachment and loss: Vol. 1. Loss*. New York, NY: Basic Books.

Guidano, V. F., & Liotti, G. (1983). *Cognitive processes and emotional disorder: A structural approach to psychotherapy*. New York, NY: Guilford Press.

Kelly, G. A. (1955). *The psychology of personal constructs*. New York, NY: Norton.

Roediger, E., Stevens, B., & Brockman, R. (2018). *Contextual schema therapy: An integrative approach to personality disorders, emotional dysregulation, and interpersonal functioning*. Oakland, CA: New Harbinger.

Strengths and Limitations of Case Formulation in Constructivist Cognitive Behavioral Therapies

Giovanni Maria Ruggiero, Gabriele Caselli, and Sandra Sassaroli

Contents

G. M. Ruggiero (✉)
"Psicoterapia Cognitiva e Ricerca," Cognitive Psychotherapy School and Research Center, Milan, Italy

Sigmund Freud University, Milan, Italy

Sigmund Freud University, Vienna, Austria
e-mail: gm.ruggiero@milano-sfu.it

G. Caselli
Sigmund Freud University, Milan, Italy

Sigmund Freud University, Vienna, Austria

Department of Psychology, London South Bank University, London, UK

S. Sassaroli
Sigmund Freud University, Milan, Italy

Sigmund Freud University, Vienna, Austria

"Studi Cognitivi," Cognitive Psychotherapy School and Research Center, Milan, Italy

G. M. Ruggiero et al. (eds.), *CBT Case Formulation as Therapeutic Process*,
https://doi.org/10.1007/978-3-030-63587-9_15

Constructivism and Rationalism

As it is widely known—although memory fades—after the strictly early behavioristic phase of the development of *cognitive behavioral therapy* (CBT) approaches, the classic cognitive phase emerged. However, this development was not unitary. In the tale handed down by Michael Mahoney (1995a), the cognitive phase admittedly forked into a rationalist approach—including both Beck's *cognitive therapy* (CT) and Ellis' *rational emotive behavioral therapy* (REBT) that conceived cognition as a conscious computational knowledge—and a constructivist approach that considers cognition as a hermeneutical, emotionally charged, and tacit knowledge derived from human relations (Mahoney 1995a, 1995b; Guidano and Liotti 1983). Beck's CT model became standard based on its clinical efficacy in controlled trials (Clark et al. 1999; Hollon et al. 2006; Otte 2011; Rush et al. 1977). Later, while the rationalist approach became the official standard CBT, the constructivist one had the naughty glory of the maverick, with all the pros and cons of this condition. Nowadays, however, the importance of constructivist models in their heyday moment of greatest popularity is underestimated.

In truth, in the 1970s the constructivist approach was not a kinky alternative to the standard CT/CBT model; rather, it contributed to the unitary institutional success of the CBT approach that was not yet officially standard. For example, one of the greatest theorists of the constructivist movement, Michael Mahoney, was also an exponent who fostered the general acceptance of the term "cognitive" by establishing in 1977 the eponymous newspaper *Cognitive Therapy and Research*, with himself as its inaugural editor (Dobson and Dozois 2010). In addition, up to the 1980s, theoretical sophistication gave a temporary prevalence to the constructivist branch, given that even Beck and Ellis proclaimed themselves constructive therapists for a while—up to the mid-1990s (Mahoney 1995b).

Michael Mahoney was actually the scholar who, dissatisfied with the limitations of behavioral techniques, felt the need for a more mentalistic model of smental suffering, recognizing the role played by conscious thought (Lazarus 1977; Mahoney 1991). He decided it was necessary to introduce a cognitive mediator into the behavioral model on which the therapist could verbally intervene through a conscious channel. In fact, psychoanalysis as well as behaviorism conceived mental suffering as a dysfunctional state learned in a state of unconsciousness (Liotti and Reda 1981). As a constructive therapist and theorist, Mahoney developed a CBT clinical model comparable to those of Ellis and Beck (Dobson and Dozois 2010); he also possessed behavioral training, unlike Beck and Ellis, both of whom had been trained in the psychodynamic model.

Mahoney's major contribution to the success of the initial unitary CBT model was that he reassessed consciousness in relation to the behavioral unconscious as well as Beck did in relation to the psychodynamic unconscious. However, the similarities between Mahoney and Beck end there. In fact, Mahoney's theoretical development toward radical constructivism (Mahoney 1974, 1991, 1995a, b, 2003) had been encouraged by his encounter with other constructivist theorists, such as Vittorio

Guidano (1987, 1991) and other authors in Europe (Feixas and Mirò 1993; Guidano and Liotti 1983; Lorenzini and Sassaroli 1995; Winter and Viney 2005) and America (Balbi 2004; Guidano and Quiñones 2001; Neimeyer 2009; Neimeyer and Mahoney, 1995).

As written above, while for Beck the symptoms came from a biased interpretation of reality, in the constructivist approach the symptoms are not the product of a cognitive mistake: They always have a meaningful function in the constellation of subjective meanings of the person (Botella and Feixas 1998; Guidano 1987, 1991; Guidano and Liotti 1983; Mahoney 1995b). Second, Mahoney believed that cognitive processes cannot be reduced to their conscious representations in terms of internal dialogue—as Beck believed. Mahoney considered this development to be an oversimplification and posed the need for a more sophisticated definition of cognition; he suggested the distinction between rationalist and constructivist approaches (Mahoney 1995b, p. 7). The rationalist approach considers cognition as a direct evaluation of reality immediately accessible to consciousness. The constructivist approach conceives cognition as a hermeneutical and proactive activity that develops in conscious and tacit knowledge terms (Guidano 1987, 1991; Guidano and Liotti 1983; Mahoney 1995b). As a result, Guidano (1991), Mahoney (2003), Neimeyer (2009), and other constructive thinkers and clinicians have considered the Beckian style of verbal evaluation and re-attribution of beliefs to be simplistic. From a clinical point of view, constructive therapists prefer interventions focused on personal meanings, including the reconstruction of patients' life stories and the treatment of recursive vicious circles of emotional distress and fear (Sassaroli et al. 2005).

Clinical Constructivism and Case Formulation

From these premises, one could expect the constructivist movement to have contributed significantly to the clinical reflection on the importance of case formulation. However, the relationship between clinical constructivism and case formulation is an uneven story, conditioned by the fact that in some phases of its development constructivism indulged in highly speculative clinical thinking that tended not to meet the empirical challenge. Further, this approach—under the influence of Maturana and Varela (1980) and von Glaserfeld (1995)—became highly hermeneutical and radical; it sometimes rejected the task to develop replicable treatment protocols and case formulation procedures based on psychiatric diagnoses, similar to Beck's CT, judging this effort as illusory, artificial, and far from clinical reality.

However, and despite their propensity for abstract speculation, constructive therapists have promoted the initial development of the practice of case formulation. Indeed, they introduced the concept of personal meanings, namely Bruner (1973), and personal constructs, specifically Kelly (1955). After this initial push, the speculative interests of constructivism did not favor the development of replicable procedures for case formulation. Nevertheless, it is also true that one of the most fascinating developments in constructivism includes a case formulation procedure: *dilemma-focused therapy* (DFT; Feixas and Compañ 2016; Feixas and Saúl 2004). DFT proposes an intriguing case formulation procedure based on a dilemmatic conception of constructs that are mainly focused on the self and derives from Kelly's (1955) personal construct psychology as developed by his epigones (Neimeyer and Mahoney 1995; Neimeyer 2009; Winter and Viney 2005).

The contribution of the constructivist approach to case formulation comprises the concept of subjective meaning that people attribute to themselves, to others, and to events they experience, including symptoms, problems, and even therapeutic interventions. Constructivist therapy involves conducting a systematic and careful exploration of the subject's interpretations of their own experience. From a constructivist perspective, the symptoms are not the result of a violation of the laws of rational behavior; instead, they are embodied in people's personal meanings. When a person's expectations are invalidated by reality, negative emotions emerge that can stiffen into symptoms because the psychological system tends to preserve its coherence and identity. A too abrupt flexibilization would entail the abandonment of a structure of central meaning that in the constructive approach is essential to make sense of oneself and the world (Bannister and Fransella 1986, 2019; Guidano 1987, 1991; Guidano and Liotti 1983; Mahoney 1995b). According to Kelly: "even an obviously invalid part of a construction system might be preferable to the vacuum of anxiety that might be caused by its elimination altogether" (Kelly 1955, p. 831).

Self-Knowledge in Constructivism and Standard Cognitive Therapy

Although there are prominent theoretical differences between the rationalist and constructivist CBT approaches, constructivist therapies also conceive self-knowledge as a superordinate structure that explains both healthy and psychopathological states. For example, in the works of Judith Beck (2011, p. 233) we can observe the emergence of a classification table of personal beliefs that resembles the constructivist architecture of personality organizations outlined by Guidano and Liotti (1983) and Mahoney (Mahoney, 2003; Mahoney et al. 1995). Table 1 compares self-knowledge in Beck's CT self-beliefs and constructive personality organizations.

This attention of either CT or constructivist models to self-knowledge is not accidental. For many authors, the self provides consistency, continuity, and identity and is the guarantee of good psychological functioning. This idea applies to cognitivist authors, including Bandura (1977), Markus (1977), and Neisser (1967), as well as to those who follow the psychodynamic orientation, such as Erikson (1950), Hermans (1996a, 1996b, 2002), and Kohut (1977), or humanistic authors like Rogers (1959, 1977).

Table 1 Self-knowledge in constructive and cognitive therapy approaches

Beck's cognitive therapy self-beliefs (adapted from Beck 2011, p. 233)	Constructive personality organizations (Guidano and Liotti 1983, pp. 171–306; Mahoney 2003; Mahoney et al. 1995)
Helpless self Defective; Failed; Helpless; Incompetent; Ineffective; Loser; Needy; Not good enough; Out of control; Powerless; Trapped; Victim; Vulnerable; Weak **Unlovable self** Bad; Bound to be abandoned; Bound to be alone; Bound to be rejected; Defective; Different; Unattractive; Uncared for; Undesirable; Unlikeable; Unlovable; Unwanted **Worthless self** A waste; Dangerous; Do not deserve to live; Evil; Immoral; Toxic; Unacceptable; Worthless	**Phobic personality organization** Being despised; Being ridiculed; Needing protection; Not amiable; Not in control; Unable to cope; Weak **Depressed personality organization** Abandoned; Being wrong; Disappointed; Failed; Helpless; Isolated; Missing significant ones (loss); Needing approval; Not loved; Rejected; Separated; Worthless **Obsessive personality organization** Controlled; Detached; Doubtful; Guilty; Judgmental; Looking for certainty; Moral; Perfectionistic; Responsible; Restrained; Unemotional **Eating disordered personality organization** Adhering to others' judgment; Craving emotional contact; Dependent; Self-criticizing; Self-deprecating; Undefined

Of course, constructivist theory prefers to speak of personal meanings, for example, Bruner (1973), or personal constructs, such as Kelly (1955). Unlike CT's beliefs about the self, personal meanings and constructs would be more closely related to the patient's life history and subjective emotional experiences. Personal meanings are not a single set of beliefs about the self in a situation; rather, they are an ampler vision of oneself in the world (Mahoney 1995b, pp. 11–13). Moreover, in Kelly's *personal construct psychology* (PCP) model (1955), case formulation is organized around a set of bipolar personal constructs. For Kelly, an emotional disturbance depends on dispositions of particular constructs that lead to contradictions in actions or dispositions. For example, the "shy–confident" construct can be linked to the "unpopular–popular" and "polite–arrogant" constructs; thus, a socially anxious patient's motivation to overcome his or her shyness could be undermined by the fear of becoming arrogant (Winter and Viney 2005).

Therefore, the use of self-knowledge in case formulation of constructive approaches is very different from its use in Beck's CT. The CT setting focuses on the symptoms and implies a fairly quick assessment of the patient's self-beliefs and coping strategies as part of the case formulation in order to share the rationale of an effective CT intervention, i.e. basically questioning. By contrast, the constructivist approach accentuates the character of gradual discovery and progressive construction of the self as more flexible; the final outcome of the therapy substantially extends the exploration phase to the entire therapeutic process. In constructivism, one can say that therapy comprises this incessant exploration of the self only at the end, at which time there is a real, exhaustive formulation to be shared. Sharing the case formulation is therefore the ideal outcome and not the therapy management tool. It follows that in constructivist therapies, each initial episode of shared formulation of the therapy plan is only a provisional formulation, a stopover station. That the formulation is provisional is in fact also true in CT, but in a different manner: The provisional nature of each CT formulation does not prevent it from being a treatment management tool and not a long-term goal as in constructivist approaches.

The Role of the Therapeutic Relationship

There is another difference between the constructivist approach and Beck's CT model: the role of the relationship in the therapeutic process. In constructivist approaches, the growing emphasis on the effort of self-discovery has developed in parallel with a growing attention toward interpersonal relationships and, consequently, to the therapeutic relationship between the patient and therapist. Indeed, it is considered the key of the therapeutic change. This evolution can be observed in the late works of Guidano (1987, 1991) and Mahoney (2003), and especially in the work of Liotti (1994, 2001; Liotti and Farina 2011; Liotti and Monticelli 2014).

This attention to the therapeutic relationship is also partly present in the standard CT (Aspland et al. 2008; Beck 2011, pp. 17–20; Hofmann et al. 2013; Leahy 2008, 2015) but set according to a different approach. In fact, in the standard CT framework, the care for the relationship is not the key intervention of the entire therapeutic process. It is instead limited to the management of the possible patient's relational troubles, which could undermine the therapy without conceiving them as the most significant manifestation of the patient's psychopathology and as the clinical aspect where therapeutic action is most effective. On the other hand, the CT therapist seeks a solution for the relational troubles in an accurate analysis of the distorted beliefs of an interpersonal type (Beck et al. 2015) and can consider the therapeutic relationship as a good (but not unique) opportunity to come into direct contact during the session with the relational difficulties of the patient that are at the basis of both his or her emotional problems and the therapeutic difficulties (Leahy 2012, pp. 239–287).

The Role of Trauma

The crucial role played by interpersonal intervention in constructive approaches interested in the clinical use of the therapeutic relationship is also connected to a conception of emotional problems in terms of traumatic deficit. Liotti and Farina (2011) proposed a psychopathological model that—at least in certain populations of patients—establishes that emotional suffering is influenced by traumatic experiences that contribute to undermine psychic structures. These experiences shape a deficit that subjectively manifests itself in the form of dissociative experiences. In these models, trauma is defined as a complex experience that includes many aversive situations and not only a life threatening episode, as proposed by Courtois and

Ford (2009), who argue that the inability of borderline personality disorder sufferers to emotionally regulate themselves is associated with stories of neglect and traumatizing interpersonal insufficiencies in primary care relationships (Courtois and Ford, 2009, pp. 17–18). These experiences of relational and careless *neglect* are at the heart of the concept of complex trauma (van der Kolk 2005) and are much more common in the population than previously thought, as demonstrated by the Kaiser Permanente Adverse Childhood Experiences study by Felitti et al. (1999). As a result of the trauma, the patient would not, at least initially, have the relational skills to establish a satisfactory therapeutic alliance, not to mention the ability to share his or her functioning in a CBT-style case formulation. It is therefore a relational failure based on a structural inadequacy that acts by compromising the executive and explicit ability to manage emotions and impulses.

This condition of traumatic *neglect* would prevent the subject from learning, in an affectively intense relationship, the cognitive and emotional modalities necessary to relate with the world in a cooperative and healthy way. In the psychodynamic model of Winnicot (1965), the traumatized person would be induced to use styles of interaction with other people that are defensive and therefore a substantially fabricated if not false self, in which the most authentic feelings of the individual remain hidden from oneself and others. The suffering subject fears that sharing these needs would expose him or her not to the satisfaction of the relational need but to further neglect. The protected relationship of the therapeutic setting would instead allow the sufferer to expose his or her authentic self and to finally put aside the fabricated defensive false self.

It is interesting to note that this conception of the false self in Winnicot, albeit not present in the work of Liotti, reflects the clinical recommendation of a certain phase of the development of Liotti's clinical model. He, at least in the early 1990s, believed that clinical work should consist in promoting a therapeutic relationship whose main quality was authenticity, that is, the possibility that the patient felt sufficiently protected and able to show his or her true self (Onofri and Tombolini 1997).

In this sense, the therapeutic relationship cannot merely be an intellectual process; it must be an emotional and affective experience, as stressed by Ruberti and Visini in chapter "Emotion, Motivation, Therapeutic Relationship and Cognition in Giovanni Liotti's Model: Commentary on Chapter "Strengths and Limitations of Case Formulation in Constructivist Cognitive Behavioral Therapies"" of this book. Consequently, the therapeutic work would comprise managing the patient's insufficiencies by setting an emotional compensation that would meet and satisfy the basic relational deficiencies suffered by the patient, as happens in the psychoanalytic model of Mitchell and Aron (1999) or, in terms more integrable with CBT approaches, in the model of ruptures and repairs of Safran and Muran (2000).

The analogies between the authentic relationship and Winnicot's concept of holding are clear. Liotti later turned to more operational concepts such as that of ruptures and repairs (Safran and Muran 2000) or co-therapy (Liotti et al. 2008), as reported by Farina in chapter "The Role of Trauma in Psychotherapeutic Complications and the Worth of Giovanni Liotti's Cognitive-Evolutionist Perspective (CEP): Commentary on Chapter "Strengths and Limitations of Case Formulation in

Constructivist Cognitive Behavioral Therapies"" of this book. From our viewpoint, in either case the therapist would use the relationship as an unique opportunity to explore in vivo the interpersonal functioning of the patient and share it as an outcome to be conquered and gradually erected rather than as a tool to be shared at first. The psychotherapeutic work passes through channels of elaboration that are not immediately subject to executive control and explicit, pondered, and rational elaboration. Rather, they are revealed through an experiential, emotional, relational, and even perceptive and embodied elaboration.

The Model of Gianni Liotti: Therapeutic Use of the Relationship

Compared to standard CT, in the constructivist sphere the idea of considering the relationship as the center of emotional suffering and the field par excellence of exploration and elaboration of the patient's emotional difficulties is more pronounced, especially in the model developed by Gianni Liotti and his collaborators (Liotti 1994, 2001; Liotti and Farina 2011; Liotti and Monticelli 2014). In the first part of Liotti's scientific career, he was Vittorio Guidano's main collaborator, before Guidano's hermeneutical turning point toward radical constructivism. While hermeneutics led Guidano to a monadic vision of the self as an autopoietic entity whose organization is autonomously created and whose main purpose is the maintenance of internal identity coherence, Liotti instead went in the opposite direction. He proposed that the self exists only in the relationship with other people. This model of the relational mind—i.e., the mind as an entity that comes to life only in social and interpersonal interactions—is a view that is supported by the neuroscientific and evolutionary studies of Gazzaniga (1985), Siegel (1999), and Tomasello and Call (1997).

Liotti's innovation comprises bringing these ideas from neuroscience and the neo-Darwinist evolutionary field to the clinic: If there is no mind outside the relationship, in the same way there is no therapy outside the relationship, it is necessary to find the factors of change and the techniques of intervention, a bit like in Mitchell and Aron's (1999) relational psychoanalysis within the psychodynamic paradigm. In the model proposed by Liotti, the relational intervention essentially involves promoting a cooperative attitude and in the accurate monitoring and response to episodes of relational crisis. From an operational viewpoint, Liotti and Monticelli (2014) seem to refer to the procedures of Safran and Muran (2000) in terms of ruptures and repairs.

The Safran and Muran (2000) model manages the therapeutic process in the elaboration of the crisis of the relationship between therapist and patient. This model shares with Liotti the principle that only in the relationship can the normal mind develop and mature. Further, disturbing relationships place the premises of emotional disorders and relational ruptures and repairs that happen during the sessions. According to this model, these ruptures represent fruitful opportunities for a significant psychotherapeutic intervention (Safran 1990a, 1990b, 1998; Safran and Segal 1990).

We could say that case formulation for Safran and Muran (2000) and Liotti and Monticelli (2014) is the result of the management of these episodes of rupture and repair. The rupture is managed by the therapist through an intervention called self-involving, in which the therapist reports and shares with the patient his or her emotional reactions to the moment of crisis (Henretty and Levitt 2010). For example, a typical rupture can be announced by a declaration of dissatisfaction by the patient when faced with a proposed therapeutic intervention. As in previous cases, we do not intend to display the whole procedure, a task much better implemented by Safran and Muran themselves (2000, pp. 150–174), but only to comment on some similar steps as experienced in our clinical practice.

Patient: And how would this would help me?

After an exchange in which mutual irritation grows, the therapist responds with an intervention called disembedding, a disengagement from the relational trap, through the above mentioned self-involving, in which the therapist honestly exposes the patient to his or her own discomfort:

Therapist: I am sorry that you are disappointed with the results and with my proposals. However, I must tell you that in turn I feel as if nothing I say satisfies you, I feel confused and pressured.

The rationale of this technique is to encourage the patient to move from a state of personal dissatisfaction to a state of sharing of relational dynamics in which the patient is made aware of the consequences of his or her mental states. The therapist uses this sharing of the state of mind to propose a hypothesis to the patient, which more or less sounds like:

If I react like this it is because you act and talk in a certain way and this could be a good example of your emotional problems.

In the specific case, the goal is to compose a model for how the patient's state of dissatisfaction functions. A good hypothesis could be that the dissatisfaction arises from aggressive dysfunctional behavior that the patient uses to manage his or her internal discomfort. Once the hypothesis is proposed, the therapist encourages him or her to look for alternatives:

Therapist: It's as if you have strategies to get what you want that give you a momentary relief but in the long run don't work. For example, you express dissatisfaction during our joint efforts. It seems to me that similar things happen when you tell me about your relational troubles. I don't know what the alternative to this strategy is, but I want to work with you to find one.

From our viewpoint, the outcome is not unlike a cognitive intervention of a reformulation of the case because the exchange ends with what Safran and Muran call an exploration of construal (2000, pp. 150–174). The difference between a rupture and repair intervention and a cognitive intervention lies in the key role played by the interpersonal analysis of what happens between the therapist and the patient: Safran and Muran explore it in detail, while a standard CT therapist would probably first both encourage the patient and validate the reasons of his or her discouragement and then reformulate the case in a manner not different from Safran and Muran (2000, pp. 165–166), when they would say something like:

Therapist: It seems to me that similar things happen when you tell me about your relational troubles.

but without necessarily referring to the current relationship difficulties between the therapist and patient. This difference is deep-seated. If the real therapeutic bottleneck is the rupture and repair episode and its analysis—i.e., the state of relational crisis followed by an understanding that is not only abstractly cognitive but intensely emotional and relational—it follows that each initial episode of shared formulation and negotiation of the therapeutic plan and its rationale is only a trigger and not a real explicit therapeutic contract, as in the standard CT. It is only a trigger because it has not yet been subjected to the decisive test, which is the relational rupture and its analysis, an indispensable condition for real change.

The clinical and operational consequences of this hypothesis are that in Safran and Muran's procedure, the initial shared case formulation is not the decisive and resolutive aspect of the therapeutic process because it is no longer the contractual premise—as it happens in standard CT. Rather, the outcome of the real key event of the therapeutic process is the relational crisis of rupture and repair. In addition, initially sharing the case formulation is not the major management tool of the therapeutic intervention or the relationship itself.

The theoretical and clinical correlate of such a model is that of an uneven compatibility with the possibility of an early shared case formulation. It would seem that in Safran and Muran's approach for managing ruptures and repairs (and in Liotti's relational model when it adopts Safran and Muran's procedures), the therapist's core task is to overcome the patient's relational trap and not to be conditioned by the patient's more or less conscious attempt to break the relationship. In this model, the eventual explicit cognitive intervention is just a sort of final stabilizer, a "save" command that stops the videogame until the next session. By contrast, in the CBT approaches not focused on the therapeutic use of the relationship, the explicit exploration and shared formulation of the patient's dysfunctional interpersonal cycles can be implemented outside the in vivo relational episodes that happen during the sessions.

The Metacognitive Interpersonal Therapy Model

Another model that has combined a constructivist root and an interest in the relational aspects is the *metacognitive and interpersonal therapy* (MIT; Semerari et al. 1999, 2007, 2014). However, MIT has also developed a significant metacognitive component, although in different terms compared to Wells' metacognitive therapy (MCT, Wells, 2008). In the MIT model, emotional problems depend on metacognitive insufficiencies in the ability to identify emotions, interpret mental states, distinguish them from those of others, and finally master them with functional behaviors (Semerari et al. 1999, 2007, 2014). MIT is a complex model that includes metacognitive interventions aimed at promoting the patients' awareness in their own functioning and relational interventions that either encourage a classic CBT explorative procedure of biased mental states or seems to accept Liotti's idea that relational intervention precedes any conscious emotional regulation, which would only come later to consolidate the skills learned through the relationship into a new cognitive routine.

In the MIT model, case formulation seems to be shared with the client at either the beginning, similar to Beck's standard CT, or at the end of the process, consistent with the constructive relational models as a final outcome, since the therapeutic process seems to depend both on the metacognitive promotion of the functioning and on the sharing of so called corrective relational experiences in which new regulatory skills are learned. The therapeutic relationship is conceived as an *in vivo* opportunity to experience this kind of complex thinking after which MIT stimulates the development of higher metacognitive functions. In summary, MIT combines interpersonal and metacognitive concepts and seems to aim to integrate both a CBT conception of case formulation with a relational conception that focuses on interpersonal experience. However, MIT never attempts to conceive the corrective experience as an intense revelation of authentic states as sometimes happens with Liotti, at least as reported by Ruberti and Visini in chapter "Emotion, Motivation, Therapeutic Relationship and Cognition in Giovanni Liotti's Model: Commentary on Chapter "Strengths and Limitations of Case Formulation in Constructivist Cognitive Behavioral Therapies"" of this book.

Moreover, in MIT, sharing the case formulation seems to be closely related to management of the therapeutic relationship with the so-called difficult patient, i.e. patients who have problems accepting the therapeutic contract and understanding the rationale of the proposed treatment (Perris and McGorry 1998). The tenet that the relationship is the resolutive element is theoretically justified by the hypothesis that poor collaboration in therapy of these patients would depend on a relational-based metacognitive insufficiency that should be understood (but perhaps not emotionally compensated) by working in the interpersonal relationship with the therapist (Semerari et al. 1999, 2007, 2014). At the same time, however, Semerari and colleagues seem to believe that these relational difficulties are also managed through the proposal of a strong explicit therapeutic contract that in turn implies clear sharing of the case formulation. For Semerari, the contract represents the initial negotiation of the therapeutic alliance in which the patient and therapist try to define an explicit agreement on the purposes of the treatment, mutual tasks and factors, and behaviors that can compromise the common work (Semerari et al. 2014). These aspects are all part of the shared case formulation.

The MIT setting shows this double loyalty. On the one hand, it tends to maintain the cognitive principle of the influence on emotional states by cognitive processing. Indeed, in the MIT model the concept of cognitive and conscious mastery remains central: Cognitive control is indicated as the highest (and even noblest) degree of mastery. On the other hand, in MIT, the concept of a difficult patient who is unable to respect and assimilate the rules of the therapeutic alliance is significant. It seems to influence the clinical vision to the point of suggesting that the turning point of therapeutic change is—along with the cognitive sharing of knowledge of patient's functioning—the corrective emotional experience that occurs in the relationship and that allows the patient to access those *mastery* skills that are currently precluded from him or her. From this viewpoint, it is not coincidental that some MIT developments have shown a preference for more experiential, imaginative, and body-focused interventions, such as guided imagery, or for very intense relational interventions, *self-disclosure* (Dimaggio et al. 2019).

This double position of MIT, whereby sharing the case formulation now appears to be both the inevitable starting condition on which to build the therapeutic relationship and also the outcome of a significant relational intervention that paves the way to the shared formulation, is partly contradictory, because it also considers a starting point as a goal to achieve at the end of the therapeutic work. Liotti's model, on the other hand, does not seem to run this risk: It more consistently assumes the position of dependence of the therapeutic contract on the construction of the relationship. However, the ambiguity of MIT could also be a *felix culpa*, a way to preserve what is—from our viewpoint—a distinctive feature of the CBT approach, i.e., sharing of the case as the initial move of the therapeutic process.

The Relational Model in Constructivism

A marked accentuation of the role of intersubjectivity in the patient–therapist relationship is the crucial element of a successful psychotherapy in Bruno Bara's relational cognitive model (Bara 2018). The focus is on the here and now of the therapeutic relationship to assess what happens between the two subjects of the therapeutic dyad during the session.

Drawing on the results of evolutionary theory, neuroscience on the social brain, and shared mental states, Bara explains and treats the therapeutic relationship as a complex intersubjective process linked to the experience that a therapist and patient live together. He considers shared awareness as the main therapeutic factor because it allows the patient to show pathological interpersonal patterns that, if properly managed by the therapist, can be replaced by new, more functional modes of interaction.

In order to understand the spirit of this cognitive relational approach, it is crucial to understand that Bara specifies it is not possible to manualize such a subjective experience that involves two people as the therapeutic relationship. As Bara himself warns:

It is not possible to detail a specific sequence to live the synchronic experience, it would immediately become so abstract as to block the immediacy of the here and now. I will still try to describe the ideal passages, but without forcing them into a formal protocol. The demand for an always applicable technique, such as the fear of being able to do something wrong, derive from the idea of having to achieve a certain goal. From a synchronic point of view there is nothing to be achieved but an increase in patient awareness. (Bara 2018, p. 87)

Bara prefers to outline a path in which the shared and synchronic cognitive, emotional, and perceptively embodied experience of the patient with the therapist is encouraged by the expertise of the therapist him- or herself, who in a mindful, non-judgmental and accepting attitude that pays attention to either verbal or non-verbal communication, acts in order to increase the degrees of freedom from the pathological mode of interaction of the patient.

Admittedly, the crucial moment is not just a vague relationship but the enactment of the patient's pathological patterns with the therapist.

The experience of enactment allows one to become physically, emotionally and cognitively aware of the relational games the patient puts into action, underlining how much depends on him or her more than on others and putting the patient in a position to attempt significant changes. (Bara 2018, p. 120)

This attention to the patient's enactments brings Bara's relational constructivist model to that of Safran and Muran's ruptures and repairs, in a manner similar to what happened for Liotti's model. After the shared experience of enactment has surfaced, the therapist encourages the patient to stay within the relational scheme and observe it in order to make the patient aware of what happens. It is a shared re-reading that allows one to create an alternative, leaving the patient with the choice of new modes of interaction.

What distinguishes this approach from other relational models such as Liotti's (Liotti and Monticelli 2014) is that the technique does not aim to replace a pathological relational scheme with a healthy cooperative one. Rather, it aims to increase the degrees of freedom from the patient's painful patterns. More adaptive interpersonal patterns will have to be built by the patient when living his or her life. This mode of interaction goes beyond the cooperative intersubjective plan between patient and therapist because the therapeutic plan is the conscious sharing of emotional and cognitive states and not necessarily the replacement of one dysfunctional mode of interaction with another more adaptive one encouraged by the therapist. From a more standard CBT viewpoint, a critical aspect that should be noted is that the skill of the patient to change his or her dysfunctional behaviors is assumed to be grounded only in the awareness of the pathological interpersonal pattern gained in the relational here and now.

In summary, it seems to us that the theoretical and clinical correlates of Bara's cognitive and relational model is, as in the previous cases, unevenly compatible with the possibility of early shared case formulation, as happens in other CBT approaches that are not mainly focused on the relational aspect. In Bara's relational cognitive model, the shared formulation is an outcome at the end of a fascinating path of growth and discovery but not a move that sets the rules in the field of play.

A Historical Note: Victor Meyer and Italian Constructivism

In this historical review of the various forms of case formulation in psychotherapy, it is interesting to note how the Italian constructivist authors we have mentioned—Vittorio Guidano, Giovanni Liotti, and Bruno Bara—all came into contact with one of the founding fathers of case formulation, namely Victor Meyer. Relations between Guidano, Liotti, and Meyer date back to the summer of 1972, when Meyer was invited to the University of Rome to give a lecture on behavioral therapy. From that moment, he became, for some years, a reference point for behavioral therapy training and in general for the newborn CBT movement in Italy. Bruno Bara, in turn, was a direct pupil of Meyer in London during those same years or shortly afterward. A debate on this topic took place in 2000 between Bara and Liotti; it is available online (Liotti and Bara 2018). Bara and Liotti both refer to themselves as direct pupils of Victor Meyer, and both of them reflect on the technical and relational aspects in Mayer's practice, including case formulation. Both Liotti and Bara were very impressed with the clinical aspects of Meyer's practice that can never really be fully expressed with operational clarity in verbal instructions:

Liotti: Have you ever tried to edit a VCR in words, following the instruction manual? You don't understand anything. If you read it, you say, 'How do I do it?' It is not easy to imagine what the instructions you read correspond to if you do not have in front of you the concrete device with all its cables and connections still to be established. (Liotti and Bara 2018, p. 11)

This aspect that Liotti talks about can be called learning by mimesis; it cannot actually be reproduced in an instruction manual. However, Liotti does not call this ineffable aspect "learning by mimesis." He prefers to call it either relationship or empathy, attributing it—to a significant extent—to Victor Meyer. For example:

Liotti: What did Victor Meyer teach us? He metaphorically embraced the patients: he taught it to Bruno (i.e., Bara), he taught it to me, he taught it to Salkovskis, who in his theories speaks explicitly of empathy. (Liotti and Bara 2018, p. 11)

Salkovskis is the originator of the CBT protocol for obsessive compulsive disorders. Mentioning him is not coincidental: Liotti suggests that Salkovskis owes Meyer his relational skills that supposedly make his CBT protocol work. Bara further accentuates this relational aspect by eliminating the learning by mimesis aspect altogether and underlining how the relationship encompasses everything. In fact, he begins by saying:

Bara: The starting point of my speech today is that there are no techniques outside the relationship. (Liotti and Bara 2018, p. 6)

According to Bara, and there is no reason not to believe him, Meyer's CBT techniques only worked within the patients' relationship with Meyer, i.e. when he was present:

Bara: I remember with great precision that if, from Monday to Friday, when he [Meyer] was present, there was a marked improvement in patient performance with a significant decrease in obsessive coercion, on Friday, when I come or whoever for me, the patient got worse and only on Monday morning he went back to the symptomatology levels of the previous week. (Liotti and Bara 2018, p. 6)

Bara therefore establishes that in the implementation of the techniques there is an ineffable element that he defines in terms of pure relational warmth, including physical contact:

Bara: Observing him [Meyer] in action I could see that when he met patients, mostly Indians who had immigrated to England with an experience of cold detachment, and being he Polish and having experienced how hard it could be to be accepted in England, he immediately established a very physical contact: he hugged the Indian lady, he touched the Indian, in short he had a very physical interaction, he went into direct contact with the patient. (Liotti and Bara 2018, p. 6)

Liotti, however, maintains an appreciation for the operational component of Meyer's CBT techniques, when he says:

Liotti: And I still say thank you, thank you Vic, thank you for teaching me and for telling me 'you may not use them, just use the principles'. How many times having a technique has given me the answer for the patient, having it in the drawer, knowing how to implement it. (Liotti and Bara 2018, p. 6)

It is undeniable that learning techniques cannot be reduced to their verbal instruction; it also has an operational component that can be defined as learning by gestural mimesis. Moreover, this mimetic learning necessarily occurs within a relationship. However, we can make some remarks. First, we must avoid the risk of reducing this relational component to an aspect of trivial friendly welcome. We all have this risk in mind, but then it is sometimes easy to fall for it. For example, this phenomenon happens at least in some points of Liotti and Bara's writing: The relational component is reduced to human warmth and acceptance, with a technical aspect that can be traced back to Rogers' validation. It happens when Bara speaks of Meyer's human warmth when he demonstrated his ability to welcome immigrants in a friendly manner, being himself an immigrant.

Instead, it is true that Liotti has a more sophisticated vision whereas he does not reduce the relationship to validation when he reports an interesting clinical case in which a Kohutian-trained analyst—therefore particularly inclined to validating interventions—risked breaking the therapeutic alliance with a phobic patient by validating her avoidance instead of encouraging her to face it. Hence, the therapist preferred to send the patient to Liotti for a behavioral exposure that restored the alliance (Liotti and Bara 2018, p. 5). In truth, Bara himself realizes the risk he runs in reducing Meyer's contribution to the empathic acceptance of Indian immigrants when he says that if this were the case:

Bara: We would have to abandon all training activities, we would have to give up trying to explain to the new therapists how to do it and if so much is all the same in the end Carl Rogers would have for better or for worse captured the essence of the therapeutic work. (Liotti and Bara 2018, p. 7)

There is the risk that a care-giving drift of the therapeutic relationship, expelled from the theory, comes back in a *naïve* way in the clinical examples—for example, by reducing Meyer's contribution to the above-mentioned embrace, albeit metaphorical. An embrace is not a good metaphor because it reduces the therapeutic relationship to its moment of human warmth, ending up adhering to the concept of empathy of Carl Rogers we were talking about earlier.

The second problem is that once we have defined the relationship as everything that cannot be expressed either operationally or verbally, we need to be careful in our search for alternatives that may turn out to be just as verbal and, on closer inspection, not very relational. For example, describing the evolutionary roots of the relationship in Darwin's evolutionist theories, a tendency to which Liotti sometimes indulges, can be an operation just as abstract and clinically sterile as consulting a CBT approach instruction manual. Likewise, theorizing the theoretical cognitive science aspects of the relationship is equally irrelevant to a clinician. Bara is surely correct when he says that:

Bara: While with Wolpe it was the therapist who built the desensitization scale, in a constructivist vision the patient builds it together with the therapist. (Liotti and Bara 2018, p. 8)

However, the risk is to reduce this cooperative building to an exhortation. It is necessary to add a reasonably operational aspect. In recent years, the level of operational prowess has risen by adding to instruction manuals of CBT approaches more attention to concrete training, which has now become a continuous training composed of supervisions and practical demonstrations that help learning by mimesis, as explained by Layard and Clark (2014). This more concrete, mimetic, and relational learning can also comprise reflections and insights on shared case formulation that, according to Bruch (2015), are some of the main teachings of Victor Meyer to be added to his metaphorical embraces and the warm welcome that he was able to implement. They can also be traced back to Carl Rogers' welcoming and validating empathy, which Bara rightly says cannot explain everything. Meyer's contribution is more than this, as explained in chapter "Case Formulation in the Behavioral Tradition: Meyer, Turkat, Lane, Bruch, and Sturmey" of this book.

Another problem is how to include within either the relationship or shared case formulation the management of the most conflicting and sabotaging aspects. This issue may indeed be outside of a shared formulation of a CBT approach. However, this aspect does not seem to be very manageable even in terms of constructivism, a movement that in turn has remained substantially within a cooperative vision of the therapeutic relationship that is not unlike Beck's collaborative empiricism. Admittedly, the management of these aspects has deepened, especially in models of psychodynamic derivation such as that of the ruptures and repairs model of Safran and Muran (2000) that we have already dealt with in this chapter and that we will discuss again in chapter "Case Formulation as an Outcome and Not an Opening Move in Relational and Psychodynamic Models" of this book.

References

Aspland, H., Llewelyn, S., Hardy, G. E., Barkham, M., & Stiles, W. (2008). Alliance ruptures and rupture resolution in cognitive-behavior therapy: A preliminary task analysis. *Psychotherapy Research, 18*, 699–710.

Balbi, J. (2004). *La Mente Narrativa [The Narrative Mind]*. Buenos Aires, Argentina: Paidós.

Bandura, A. (1977). Self-efficacy: Toward a unifying theory of behavioral change. *Psychological Review, 84*, 191–215.

Bandura, A. (1988). Self-efficacy conception of anxiety. *Anxiety Research, 1*, 77–98.

Bannister, D., & Fransella, F. (1986). *Inquiring man: The psychology of personal constructs*. London: Croom Helm.

Bannister, D., & Fransella, F. (2019). *Inquiring man: The psychology of personal constructs* (3rd ed.). London: Routledge.

Bara, B. G. (2018). *Il terapeuta relazionale: tecnica dell'atto terapeutico [The relational therapist: technique of the therapeutic act]*. Torino: Bollati Boringhieri.

Beck, A. T., Davis, D. D., & Freeman, A. (Eds.). (2015). *Cognitive therapy of personality disorders*. New York, NY: Guilford.

Beck, J. S. (2011). In U. K. London (Ed.), *Cognitive therapy: Basics and beyond* (2nd ed.). New York, NY: Guilford Press.

Botella, L., & Feixas, G. (1998). *Teoría de los constructos personales: Aplicaciones a la práctica psicológica [Theory of personal constructs: Applications to psychological practice.]*. Barcelona, Spain: Laertes.

Bruch, M. (2015). *Beyond diagnosis: Case formulation in cognitive behavioural therapy* (2nd ed.). Chicester: John Wiley & Sons.

Bruner, J. (1973). *Going beyond the information given*. New York, NY: Norton.

Clark, D. A., Beck, A. T., & Alford, B. A. (1999). *Scientific foundations of cognitive theory and therapy of depression*. New York, NY: Wiley & Sons.

Courtois, C. A., & Ford, J. D. (Eds.). (2009). *Treating complex traumatic stress disorder: An evidence-based guide*. New York, NY: Guilford Press.

Dimaggio, G., Ottavi, P., & Popolo, R. (2019). *Corpo, immaginazione e cambiamento: Terapia metacognitiva interpersonale [Body, Imagination, and change: Metacognitive interpersonal therapy]*. Milano: Cortina.

Dobson, K. S., & Dozois, D. J. A. (2010). Historical and philosophical bases of the cognitive-behavioral therapies. In K. S. Dobson (Ed.), *Handbook of cognitive-behavioral therapies* (pp. 3–38). New York, NY: Guilford Press.

Erikson, E. (1950). *Childhood and Society*. New York, NY: Norton and Company.

Feixas, G., & Miró, M. (1993). *Aproximaciones ala Psicoterapia. Una Introducción a los Tratamientos Psicológicos [Approaches to Psychotherapy. An Introduction to Psychological Treatments]*. Barcelona: Paidós.

Feixas, G., & Compañ, V. (2016). Dilemma-focused intervention for unipolar depression: A treatment manual. *BMC Psychiatry, 16*, 235. https://doi.org/10.1186/s12888-016-0947-x.

Feixas, G., & Saúl, L. Á. (2004). The Multi-Center Dilemma Project: An investigation on the role of cognitive conflicts in health. *The Spanish Journal of Psychology, 7*, 69–78.

Felitti, V., Anda, R., & Nordenberg, D. (1999). Relationship of childhood abuse and household dysfunction to many of the leading causes of death in adults: The adverse childhood experiences (ACE) study. *Year Book of Psychiatry and Applied Mental Health, 1999*, 44–45.

Gazzaniga, M. S. (1985). *The social brain*. New York, NY: Basic Books.

Glaserfeld, E. von (1995). *Radical constructivism*. London: The Falmer Press.

Guidano, V. F. (1987). *Complexity of the Self*. New York, NY: Guilford Press.

Guidano, V. F. (1991). *The Self in process: Toward a post-rationalist cognitive therapy*. New York, NY: Guilford Press.

Guidano, V. F., & Liotti, G. (1983). *Cognitive processes and emotional disorders: A structural approach to psychotherapy*. New York, NY: Guilford Press.

Guidano, V. F., & Quiñones, A. T. (2001). *El Mode lo Cognitivo Postracionalista: Hacia una Reconceptualización Teórica y Crítica [The Postrationalist Cognitive Mode: Towards a Theoretical and Critical Reconceptualization]*. Bilbao: Desclée de Brouwer.

Henretty, J. R., & Levitt, H. M. (2010). The role of therapist self-disclosure in psychotherapy: A qualitative review. *Clinical Psychology Review, 30*, 63–77.

Hermans. (1996a). Opposites in a dialogical self: constructs as characters. *Journal of Constructivist Psychology, 9*, 1–26.

Hermans, H. J. M. (1996b). Voicing the self: From information processing to dialogical interchange. *Psychological Bulletin, 119*, 31–50.

Hermans, H. J. M. (2002). The dialogical self as society of mind: Introduction. *Theory & Psychology, 12*, 147–160.

Hofmann, S. G., Asmundson, G. J., & Beck, A. T. (2013). The science of cognitive therapy. *Behavior Therapy, 44*, 199–212.

Hollon, S. D., Stewart, M. O., & Strunk, D. (2006). Enduring effects for cognitive behavior therapy in the treatment of depression and anxiety. *Annual Review of Psychology, 57*, 285–315.

Kelly, G. A. (1955). *The psychology of personal constructs: Vol 1 and 2*. New York, NY: Norton.

Kohut, H. (1977). *The restoration of the self*. New York, NY: International Universities Press.

Layard, R., & Clark, D. M. (2014). *Thrive: the power of evidence-based psychological therapies*. London: Penguin.

Lazarus, A. (1977). Has behavior therapy outlived its usefulness? *American Psychologist, 32*, 550–554.

Leahy, R. L. (2008). The therapeutic relationship in cognitive-behavioral therapy. *Behavioural and Cognitive Psychotherapy, 36*, 769–777.

Leahy, R. L. (2012). *Overcoming resistance in cognitive therapy*. New York, NY: Guilford.

Leahy, R. L. (2015). *Emotional schema therapy*. New York, NY: Guilford.

Liotti, G. (1994). *La dimensione interpersonale della coscienza [The interpersonal dimension of consciouness]*. Roma: NIS.

Liotti, G. (2001). *Le opere della coscienza [The works of consciousness]*. Milano: Cortina.

Liotti, G. & Bara, B. G. (2018). Dibattito di Gianni Liotti e Bruno G. Bara. In F. Moser & A. Genovese (Eds.), *La dimensione relazione in psicoterapia cognitiva, incontri di aggiornamento e formazione clinica, 13*. Retrieved from http://centroterapiacognitiva.it/wordpress/wp-content/uploads/2018/09/Bara-Liotti-Appunti-N%C2%B0-13-20184.pdf. Accessed 7 July 2020.

Liotti, G., & Farina, B. (2011). *Sviluppi traumatici [Traumatic developments]*. Milano: Cortina.

Liotti, G., & Monticelli, F. (2014). *Teoria e clinica dell'alleanza terapeutica. Una prospettiva cognitivo-evoluzionista [Theory and clinic of the therapeutic alliance. A cognitive-evolutionary perspective]*. Milano: Cortina.

Liotti, G., & Reda, M. (1981). Some epistemological remarks on behavior therapy, cognitive therapy and psychoanalysis. *Cognitive Therapy and Research, 5*, 231–236.

Liotti, G., Cortina, M., & Farina, B. (2008). Attachment theory and the multiple integrated treatments of borderline patients. *Journal of the American Academy of Pyschoanalysis, 36*, 295–315.

Lorenzini, R., & Sassaroli, S. (1995). *Attaccamento, Conoscenza e Disturbi di Personalità [Attachment, Knowledge and Personality Disorders]*. Milano: Raffaello Cortina Editore.

Mahoney, M. J. (1995a). *Human change processes: The scientific foundations of psychotherapy*. New York, NY: Basic Books.

Mahoney, M. J. (1995b). Theoretical developments in the cognitive and constructive psychotherapies. In M. J. Mahoney (Ed.), *Cognitive and constructive psychotherapies. Theory, research, and practice* (pp. 103–120). New York, NY/Washington, DC: Springer Publishing Company, Inc./American Psychological Association.

Mahoney, M. J. (2003). *Constructive psychotherapy: A practical guide*. New York, NY: Guilford.

Mahoney, M. J. (1974). *Cognition and behavior modification*. Cambridge, MA: Ballinger.

Mahoney, M. J. (1991). *Human change process*. New York, NY: Basic Books.

Markus, H. (1977). Self-schemata and processing information about the self. *Journal of Personality and Social Psychology, 35*, 63–78.

Maturana, H. R., & Varela, F. J. (1980). *Autopoiesis and cognition*. Boston, MA: Reidel.

Mitchell, S. A., & Aron, L. E. (1999). *Relational psychoanalysis: The emergence of a tradition*. Hillsdale, NJ: Analytic Press.

Neimeyer, R. A. (2009). *Constructivist psychotherapy. Distinctive features*. London: Routledge.

Neimeyer, R. A., & Mahoney, M. J. (Eds.). (1995). *Constructivism in psychotherapy*. Washington, DC: APA Press.

Onofri, A., & Tombolini, L. (1997). Il se autopoietico e il se-con-l'altro [The autopoietic self and the self-with-the-other]. *Psicobiettivo, 17*, 35–51.

Otte, C. (2011). Cognitive behavioral therapy in anxiety disorders: current state of the evidence. *Dialogues in Clinical Neurosciences, 13*, 413–421.

Perris, C., & McGorry, P. D. (Eds.). (1998). *Cognitive psychotherapy of psychotic and personality disorders: Handbook of theory and practice*. New York, NY: John Wiley.

Rogers, C. (1959). A theory of therapy, personality and interpersonal relationships as developed in the client-centered framework. In S. Koch (Ed.), *Psychology: A study of a science. Vol. 3: Formulations of the person and the social context* (pp. 184–256). New York, NY: McGraw Hill.

Rogers, C. (1977). *On personal power: Inner strength and its revolutionary impact*. London: Constable & Company Limited.

Rush, A. J., Beck, A. T., Kovacs, M., & Hollon, S. D. (1977). Comparative efficacy of cognitive therapy and pharmacotherapy in the treatment of depressed outpatients. *Cognitive Therapy and Research, 1*, 7–37.

Safran, J. D. (1990a). Towards a refinement of cognitive therapy in light of interpersonal theory: II. *Theory. Clinical Psychology Review, 10*, 87–105.

Safran, J. D. (1990b). Towards a refinement of cognitive therapy in light of interpersonal theory: II. *Practice. Clinical Psychology Review, 10*, 107–121.

Safran, J. D. (1998). *Widening the scope of cognitive therapy: The therapeutic relationship, emotion, and the process of change*. Northvale, NJ: Jason Aronson, Inc..

Safran, J. D., & Muran, J. C. (2000). *Negotiating the therapeutic alliance: A relational treatment guide*. New York, NY: Guilford.

Safran, J. D., & Segal, Z. V. (1990). *Interpersonal process in cognitive therapy*. New York, NY: Basic Books.

Sassaroli, S., Lorenzini, R., & Ruggiero, G. M. (2005). Kellian invalidation, attachment and the construct of 'control'. In D. A. Winter & L. L. Viney (Eds.), *Personal construct psychotherapy. Advances in theory, practice and research* (pp. 34–42). London, UK: Whurr Publishers.

Semerari, A. (1999). *Psicoterapia cognitiva del paziente grave. Metacognizione e relazione terapeutica [Cognitive psychotherapy of severe patient. metacognition and therapeutic relationship]*. Milano: Raffaello Cortina.

Semerari, A., Carcione, A., Dimaggio, G., Nicolò, G., & Procacci, M. (2007). Understanding minds: Different functions and different disorders? The contribution of psychotherapy research. *Psychotherapy Research, 17*, 106–119.

Semerari, A., Colle, L., Pellecchia, G., Buccione, I., Carcione, A., Dimaggio, G., et al. (2014). Metacognitive dysfunctions in personality disorders: Correlations with disorder severity and personality styles. *Journal of Personality Disorders, 28*, 751–766.

Siegel, D. J. (1999). *The developing mind* (Vol. 296). New York, NY: Guilford Press.

Tomasello, M., & Call, J. (1997). *Primate cognition*. Oxford: Oxford University Press.

van der Kolk, B. A. (2005). Developmental trauma disorder: Toward a rational diagnosis for children with complex trauma histories. *Psychiatric Annals, 35*, 401–408.

Wells, A. (2008). *Metacognitive therapy for anxiety and depression*. London: Guilford.

Winnicot, D. W. (1965). Ego distortion in terms of true and false self. In D. W. Winnicot (Ed.), *The maturational process and the facilitating environment: Studies in the theory of emotional development* (pp. 140–152). New, NY: International UP Inc..

Winter, D. A., & Viney, L. L. (Eds.). (2005). *Personal construct psychotherapy. Advances in theory, practice and research*. London: Whurr Publishers.

A Constructivist Pioneer of Formulation: A Commentary on Chapter "Strengths and Limitations of Case Formulation in Constructivist Cognitive Behavioral Therapies"

David A. Winter and Guillem Feixas

Contents

Personal Construct Psychotherapy and Cognitive-Behavioral Therapy

As the authors of the chapter "Strengths and limitations of case formulation in constructivist cognitive behavioral therapies" rightly indicate, constructivist trends have been increasingly apparent for some years in cognitive-behavioral therapy, as indeed has been the case in all of the major models of therapy (Procter and Winter 2020). Therefore, although research in the 1990s indicated clear differences in the therapeutic process between rationalist cognitive therapies and a major form of constructivist therapy, personal construct psychotherapy (Winter and Watson 1999), it is probably less likely that this would be the case if personal construct psychotherapy were compared with at least some of the contemporary forms of cognitive-behavioral therapy. Most personal construct psychotherapists would nevertheless still share George Kelly's resistance to viewing their approach as a constructivist

D. A. Winter (✉)
University of Hertfordshire, Hertfordshire, UK
e-mail: d.winter@herts.ac.uk

G. Feixas
Institut de Neurociències, Universitat de Barcelona, Barcelona, Spain

Institut d'Estudis Catalans, Barcelona, Spain
e-mail: gfeixas@ub.edu

G. M. Ruggiero et al. (eds.), *CBT Case Formulation as Therapeutic Process*,
https://doi.org/10.1007/978-3-030-63587-9_16

variant of cognitive-behavioral therapy, which is how it appears to be seen in this chapter.

The Personal Construct Approach to Formulation

Also noted by the editors of this book is that 'constructivist therapists have significantly contributed to the development of the practice of case formulation'. In fact, one can probably go further than this as, although the cognitive-behavioral tradition is generally credited with introducing the notion of formulation (Bruch 1998), its first use was probably by George Kelly (1955), who devised personal construct psychology and its associated form of psychotherapy. In discussing formulation, he distinguished between *structuralization* and *construction.* In the former, the clinical information on a client is roughly structured; while in the latter, the client's personal constructs (the bipolar distinctions by which they make sense of and anticipate their world) are inferred and then 'subsumed' by the use of a set of 'professional, diagnostic constructs'. This is an example of what Kelly termed *sociality*, in which one person (in this case, the clinician) attempts to construe the construction processes of another (in this case, the client). As Winter and Procter (2014) indicate, the diagnostic constructs of personal construct theory may be divided into various types. Some concern *covert construing*, that which is at a low level of cognitive awareness. This may involve *preverbal constructs*, which lack consistent verbal symbols; *submergence*, where one pole of a construct is relatively inaccessible; or *suspension*, where a construction is held in abeyance. Other diagnostic constructs concern the *structure of construing*, for example whether a construct is in a *superordinate* or *subordinate* position in the person's construct hierarchy or has a *core* or *peripheral* role in their identity. A further set of diagnostic constructs concerns the *strategies* that the person uses, for example to avoid invalidation of their construing. These include *constriction* and *dilation*, which respectively involve the delimiting or extension of the person's perceptual field; and *tight* and *loose* construing, which respectively involve precision and vagueness in the person's constructions. Diagnostic constructs concerning *control* consider the person's decision-making as involving a process in which the person engages in *circumspection*, considering all of the constructs involved in a decision; *pre-emption*, selecting the most important of these; and *control,* applying one pole of this construct to a situation. Emotions are viewed in terms of another set of diagnostic constructs which regard these as involving awareness of transitions in construing. Some of the most clinically relevant of these are *threat*, in which there is awareness of an imminent comprehensive change in core structures; *anxiety*, in which events seem unconstruable; *guilt*, when one is dislodged from one's core role, one's characteristic way of interacting with others; and *hostility*, when rather than revising one's constructions in the face of invalidation, one tries to change the world to fit with these constructions.

Kelly (1955) defined a psychological disorder as 'any personal construction which is used repeatedly in spite of consistent invalidation' (p. 831). This may involve imbalance in the use of strategies to avoid invalidation (Walker and Winter 2005; Winter 2003): for example, the persistently loose construing that, in his classic research, Bannister (1960, 1962) found to characterize people diagnosed with schizophrenic thought disorder; or the persistently tight construing that may characterize those diagnosed with disorders involving anxiety or depression (Winter 1992). While a personal construct formulation of a client's problems is likely to involve such aspects of the structure and process of the person's construing, which are the primary concern of Kelly's diagnostic constructs, it will not ignore the content of construing since this will determine the pathways and choices available to the client. As indicated by the editors of this book, of particular relevance may be *implicative dilemmas,* in which the preferred pole of one construct is associated with the non-preferred pole of another (Feixas and Saúl 2004). For example, a client might want to change from the pole "sad" (where the "self now" is located) to the opposite pole "happy" ("ideal self") of his construct. However, he tends to construe people who are "happy" also as "selfish" and "careless" while for him being "generous" and "sensitive" (the opposite poles of these constructs) are core values, part of his identity. Because of this connection between these constructs in the client's construct system, a change in the direction of being more "happy", although desired, might also be experienced as a threat to self-identity. Such dilemmas may explain a client's resistance to change and, once identified, can be the subject of a *dilemma-focused intervention* (Feixas and Compañ 2016). This intervention is proposed to the client whenever it is possible to reframe their problem as a dilemma and the client accepts to focus on solving it. Therefore, it involves a reformulation which is shared with the client after the application of repertory grid technique (Feixas et al. 2009) and a process of meaning exploration involving prototypical figures, laddering, and other techniques. In further sessions, episodes involving the dilemma are explored in detail, along with the historical reconstruction of the dilemma, the exploration of the role of significant others, and other methods to resolve the dilemma as a way to relieve symptoms and facilitate personal development.

Kelly's original approach to formulation, and his diagnostic constructs, have been elaborated and supplemented by later constructivists, who, consistent with the more general trends in constructivist approaches described in this book, have given somewhat greater attention to the relational and developmental aspects of disorders. Thus, in *experiential construct psychotherapy* (Leitner et al. 2000), there is a particular focus on sociality, and a triaxial diagnostic system is used in which the first axis concerns 'developmental/structural arrests' that may occur in the construing of self and others due to childhood traumas; the second concerns interpersonal styles; and the third concerns limitations and strengths in the construing of others' construction processes. In *narrative hermeneutic constructivist psychotherapy* (Chiari and Nuzzo 2010), there is a particular concern with dependency paths, categorized into those channelized by aggression, threat, guilt, and anxiety; and with types of intersubjective recognition which impact upon the development of identity in childhood (Chiari 2017; Chiari et al. 1994). In *personal and relational construct psychotherapy* (Procter and Winter 2020), Kelly's diagnostic constructs are applied not only to the personal construct systems of individuals but also to the shared construct systems of families and other social groups. There is also a concern with *relationality*, the construing not just of another person's construing but of relationships.

Principal Features of Personal Construct Formulation

Four principal features of the personal construct approach, and some other constructivist approaches, to formulation are worthy of note, and some of these have been indicated by the editors of this book. One is that the diagnostic constructs used refer to processes that 'in themselves are neither good nor bad, healthy nor unhealthy, adaptive nor maladaptive' (Kelly 1955, p. 453). Their use leads to a *transitive diagnosis* that indicates the pathways of movement open to a person rather than, as in traditional psychiatric systems, the placement of the individual in a fixed diagnostic category. They are applicable to every individual, not just to clients, and concern the processes and structures of construing that each of us uses to give meaning to our world and to deal with possible invalidation of our construing. Therefore, although there are some exceptions, personal construct psychologists and psychotherapists would generally not consider there to be a clear mapping of features of construing and 'constructive personality organizations' in terms of psychiatric nosological categories as in Table 1 in the chapter "Case Formulation in the Behavioral Tradition: Meyer, Turkat, Lane, Bruch, and Sturmey" or in the work of Ugazio (2013) on semantic polarities.

A second major feature of a personal construct formulation is that transitive diagnosis is viewed as 'the planning stage of therapy' (Kelly 1955, p. 203) and 'is not complete until a plan for management and treatment has been formulated' (p. 810). Even in clients who are presenting with what may appear to be similar problems, that may attract the same psychiatric diagnoses, this plan for treatment may be very different depending upon how these clients' predicaments are viewed in terms of diagnostic constructs focusing on the clients' construing. For example, considering people who attempt suicide, one of Kelly's (1961) distinctions was between those where this is *deterministic*, in that 'the course of events is so obvious that there is no point in waiting around for the outcome' and those where it is *chaotic*, in that 'the only definite thing one can do is abandon the scene altogether' (p. 260). From a personal construct perspective, the tight construing that is likely to characterize the former types of case will require a form of intervention that is in marked contrast to that required for the loose construing that is likely to characterize the latter (Winter 2005).

Thirdly, the personal construct formulation process is a collaborative affair rather than involving expert pronouncements by the clinician. The clinician adopts a *credulous attitude*, taking the client's own views about their predicament seriously. Consistent with this attitude, both therapist and client can be regarded as experts (Feixas 1995). While clients are the best experts in the content of their lives, therapists are experts in human functioning, as governed by meaning-making processes, in the way relationships work and, in particular, in the therapeutic setting and process. Thus, in the structuralization phase, a particular concern will be the client's construction of their complaint since 'the manner in which it is formulated throws important light upon the complainant's basic framework of ideas' (Kelly 1955, p. 788) and 'the statement of the client is, by definition, a true formulation of the problem' although it 'may not be the most fruitful one' (pp. 797–798). As the clinician gradually subsumes the client's construing with the aid of professional constructs, he or she will share, test out, and refine the resulting hypotheses with the client. The clinician's formulations are therefore fluid and responsive to feedback from the client throughout the course of therapy. As Kelly (1955) put it, 'Within an hour's psychotherapeutic interview the clinical psychologist may have successively formulated and accepted approximate answers to dozens of items....the clinical psychologist is in the process of developing hypotheses as he goes along, and...the emphasis of the method is on formulating appropriate questions whose answers may have relevance to the client's difficulty, rather than on extracting definitive answers to irrelevant questions' (pp. 192–193). Or, in the words of the authors of the chapter, "therapy comprises this incessant exploration of the self only at the end of which there is a real, exhaustive formulation to be shared....It follows that in constructivist therapies, each initial episode of shared formulation of the therapy plan is only a provisional formulation, a stopover station". The process is therefore one of formulation and constant *reformulation*.

Finally, although the therapeutic relationship is a collaborative one, the clinician, consistent with Kelly's (1955) metaphor of the relationship between a research supervisor and their student, will have expertise in various tools that may aid the formulation and testing of hypotheses. A personal construct formulation may therefore draw upon the results of various constructivist assessment techniques (Caputi et al. 2012) to elucidate both the content and structure of the client's construing. As we have seen, of particular value, for example in identifying implicative dilemmas, may be repertory grid technique (Fransella et al. 2004).

Conclusions

In their consideration of limitations of constructivist approaches, the editors of this book note that at times these 'have indulged in a highly speculative clinical thinking that tended not to meet the empirical challenge.... rejected the task to develop replicable treatment protocols and case formulation procedures based on psychiatric diagnoses' and have shown a 'propensity for abstract speculation'. In this commentary, we have sought to indicate that one such approach, personal construct psychology, in fact pioneered case formulation procedures, albeit not 'based on psychiatric diagnoses'. The personal construct view of the latter would be to accept that they provide an alternative set of diagnostic constructs, not necessarily better or worse than any other (Raskin and Lewandowski 2000), but we would agree with Johnstone (2014) that the combined use of psychological formulation and psychiatric diagnosis can lead to 'damaging contradictions' (p. 465), for example in relation to the personal meaning of the client's complaints.

Personal construct psychology also provides an illustration that at least one constructivist approach has certainly not shied away from the empirical challenge in investigating the features of construing associated with psychological complaints and in evaluating personal construct methods for the treatment of these (Metcalfe et al. 2007; Winter 1992). Furthermore, it offers not just a theoretical system but also practical methods of assessment of construing; and it is not inconsistent with the provision of treatment protocols (e.g., Feixas and Compañ 2016; Winter and Metcalfe 2005).

References

Bannister, D. (1960). Conceptual structure in thought-disordered schizophrenics. *Journal of Mental Science, 106*, 1230–1249.

Bannister, D. (1962). The nature and measurement of schizophrenic thought disorder. *Journal of Mental Science, 108*, 825–842.

Bruch, M. (1998). The development of case formulation approaches. In M. Bruch & F. W. Bond (Eds.), *Beyond diagnosis: Case formulation approaches in cognitive-behavioural therapy*. Chichester: Wiley.

Caputi, P., Viney, L. L., Walker, B. M., & Crittenden, N. (Eds.). (2012). *Personal construct methodology*. Chichester: Wiley-Blackwell.

Chiari, G. (2017). Highlighting intersubjectivity and recognition in Kelly's sketchy view of personal identity. In D. A. Winter, P. Cummins, H. Procter, & N. Reed (Eds.), *Personal construct psychology at 60: Papers from the 21st International Congress* (pp. 54–67). Newcastle upon Tyne: Cambridge Scholars Publishing.

Chiari, G., & Nuzzo, M. L. (2010). *Constructivist psychotherapy: A narrative hermeneutic approach*. London: Routledge.

Chiari, G., Nuzzo, M. L., Alfano, V., Brogna, P., D'Andrea, T., Di Battista, G., et al. (1994). Personal paths of dependency. *Journal of Constructivist Psychology, 7*, 17–34.

Feixas, G. (1995). Personal constructs in systemic practice. In R. A. Neimeyer & M. J. Mahoney (Eds.), *Constructivism in psychotherapy* (pp. 305–337). Washington, DC: American Psychological Association. Retrieved from http://hdl.handle.net/2445/48706.

Feixas, G., & Compañ, V. (2016). Dilemma-focused intervention for unipolar depression: A treatment manual. *BMC Psychiatry, 16*, 1–28.

Feixas, G., & Saúl, L. A. (2004). The Multi-Center Dilemma Project: An investigation on the role of cognitive conflicts in health. *Spanish Journal of Psychology, 7*, 69–78.

Feixas, G., Saúl, L. A., & Ávila-Espada, A. (2009). Viewing cognitive conflicts as dilemmas: Implications for mental health. *Journal of Constructivist Psychology, 22*, 141–169.

Fransella, F., Bell, R., & Bannister, D. (2004). *A manual for repertory grid technique*. Chichester: Wiley.

Johnstone, L. (2014). Controversies and debates about formulation. In L. Johnstone & R. Dallos (Eds.), *Formulation in psychology and psychotherapy* (2nd ed.). London: Routledge.

Kelly, G. A. (1955). *The psychology of personal constructs* (Vol. I, II). New York: Norton. (2nd printing 1991): London: Routledge).

Kelly, G. A. (1961). Theory and therapy in suicide: The personal construct point of view. In M. Farberow & E. Shneidman (Eds.), *The cry for help* (pp. 255–280). New York: McGraw-Hill.

Leitner, L. M., Faidley, A. J., & Celentana, M. A. (2000). Diagnosing human meaning-making: An experiential constructivist approach. In R. A. Neimeyer & J. D. Raskin (Eds.), *Construction of disorders: Meaning making frameworks for psychotherapy* (pp. 175–203). Washington, DC: American Psychological Association.

Metcalfe, C., Winter, D. A., & Viney, L. L. (2007). The effectiveness of personal construct psychotherapy in clinical practice: A systematic review and meta-analysis. *Psychotherapy Research, 17*, 431–442.

Procter, H., & Winter, D. A. (2020). *Personal and relational construct psychotherapy*. London: Palgrave.

Raskin, J. D., & Lewandowski, A. M. (2000). The construction of disorder as human enterprise. In R. A. Neimeyer & J. D. Raskin (Eds.), *Constructions of disorder: Meaning-making frameworks for psychotherapy* (pp. 15–40). Washington, DC: American Psychological Association.

Ugazio, V. (2013). *Semantic polarities and psychopathologies in the family: Permitted and forbidden stories*. New York: Routledge.

Walker, B., & Winter, D. (2005). Psychological disorder and reconstruction. In D. A. Winter & L. L. Viney (Eds.), *Personal construct psychotherapy: Advances in theory, practice and research* (pp. 21–33). London: Whurr.

Winter, D., & Procter, H. G. (2014). Formulation in personal and relational construct psychology: Seeing the world through clients' eyes. In L. Johnstone & R. Dallos (Eds.), *Formulation in psychology and psychotherapy* (2nd ed., pp. 145–172). London: Routledge.

Winter, D. A. (1992). *Personal construct psychology in clinical practice: Theory, research and applications*. London: Routledge.

Winter, D. A. (2003). Psychological disorder as imbalance. In F. Fransella (Ed.), *International handbook of personal construct psychology* (pp. 201–209). London: Wiley.

Winter, D. A. (2005). Self harm and reconstruction. In D. A. Winter & L. L. Viney (Eds.), *Personal construct psychotherapy: Advances in theory, practice and research* (pp. 127–135). London: Whurr.

Winter, D. A., & Metcalfe, C. (2005). From constriction to experimentation: A personal construct approach to agoraphobia. In D. A. Winter & L. L. Viney (Eds.), *Personal construct psychotherapy: Advances in theory, practice and research* (pp. 148–164). London: Whurr.

Winter, D. A., & Watson, S. (1999). Personal construct psychotherapy and the cognitive therapies: Different in theory but can they be differentiated in practice? *Journal of Constructivist Psychology, 12*, 1–22.

Commentary on the Presentation of the Metacognitive Interpersonal Therapy Model in Chapter "Strengths and Limitations of Case Formulation in Constructivist Cognitive Behavioral Therapies"

Antonino Carcione and Antonio Semerari

Contents

Significant Features of the Metacognitive Interpersonal Therapy Model

Chapter "Strengths and Limitations of Case Formulation in Constructivist Cognitive Behavioral Therapies" of this book is an effective effort to present and discuss the concepts of Metacognitive Interpersonal Therapy (MIT; Dimaggio et al. 2007, Carcione et al. 2016, 2019), within the limitations due to space. This allows us to focus our commentary on a few observations. It is profitable to reiterate, albeit already reported in Chapter "Strengths and Limitations of Case Formulation in Constructivist Cognitive Behavioral Therapies", that MIT is a treatment specific to relatively difficult patients with either complex personality disorders (PDs) or psychotic disorders. Section III of the DSM 5 itself (APA 2013) reports the alternative model for personality disorders (AMPD) that arranges the formulation of the diagnosis in terms of the functioning of: (a) Self, which implies a good ability to reflect on one's mental states (self-reflectivity and self-awareness); (b) Interpersonal

A. Carcione · A. Semerari (✉)
"Terzo Centro di Psicoterapia Cognitiva" Third Centre of Cognitive Psychotherapy, Rome, Italy

Scuole di Psicoterapia Cognitiva, Rome, Italy
e-mail: carcione@terzocentro.it; semerari@terzocentro.it

G. M. Ruggiero et al. (eds.), *CBT Case Formulation as Therapeutic Process*,
https://doi.org/10.1007/978-3-030-63587-9_17

relationships, which includes good skills of understanding other people's mental states, empathy and the capacity to build intimate relationships. The diagnosis also includes the assessment of the relational skill to recognize one's own role in determining the reactions of others. Owing to their relational difficulties, these patients can activate problematic interpersonal cycles during treatment, in which the therapist is involved. The MIT intervention aims to describe the most frequent interpersonal cycles and suggests procedures to use for therapy. Therefore, the interventions described in MIT and its management of the therapeutic relationship have been designed to address the specific difficulties of these patients. The comparison with modalities designed for the treatment of other types of patients remains still interesting, as long as we keep in mind the obvious differences between the relational contexts that are created with different forms of psychopathology. For this reason, if the assessment leading to the case formulation does not show metacognitive dysfunctions, the therapy can develop according to what is described by other cognitive behavioral therapy (CBT) interventions already proven to be effective. Once this point has been clarified, we aim to discuss some, albeit venial, inaccuracies reported in Chapter "Strengths and Limitations of Case Formulation in Constructivist Cognitive Behavioral Therapies".

The statement that, in the MIT model, emotional problems depend on metacognitive impairments could lead to the misunderstanding that a disorder in metacognition can be considered the direct cause of emotional suffering. Our view is that poor metacognition leads to problems in self-regulation, self-directedness, and the ability to establish and maintain interpersonal relationships. Difficulties which, in turn, can be the cause of emotional problems, but not always and not necessarily. Rather, with low levels of effective metacognitive functions, the individual would remain exposed to emotional problems. In other words, metacognitive functions are considered a sort of resilience factor, in the absence of which any psychological problem tends to occur as severe (Semerari et al. 2007).

Of course, we can also wonder whether it is possible that the cause–effect relationship is reversed. In other words, is it possible that, instead of being the low level of metacognition that influences emotional problems, it is the intensity of emotional suffering that would decrease the level of metacognitive functioning? We have attempted to answer this question in a study (Semerari et al. 2014) that compared two clinical samples—198 patients with a PD and 108 anxious and depressed patients without a PD, respectively. Given that patients with PDs requiring treatment showed not only lower levels of metacognition but also higher levels of symptomatology than anxious and depressed patients, we wondered whether the lower level of metacognitive functioning could depend on the greater severity of the symptoms, instead of being the cause. We therefore controlled for the effect of symptoms on these differences and the result was that, although there was a slight reduction, the difference in metacognition between the two groups remained largely significant. From our viewpoint, the result suggested that the difference in metacognition is only minimally dependent on the severity of symptoms.

Moreover, we stress that some PD can feature a low level of subjective emotional suffering. As an instance, we often observe the lack of depression and guilt in patients with narcissistic PD (Bilotta et al. 2018) or the lack of anxiety in some patients with borderline PD. For this reason, we suggest that it is better to refer more than to emotional suffering, to psychological problems in PDs. The key concept is that when a psychic problem occurs, metacognitive dysfunctions prevent us from dealing with it adequately and, moreover, usually exacerbate the problem and create new problems owing to dysfunctional attempts to manage it. The consequences of these processes are the highly frequent comorbidities that suggest the simultaneous presence of manifold psychopathological problems. A good metaphor that helps us to understand metacognitive difficulties is to compare them to an immune system disorder. If an infection finds no obstacles, it exposes us to new infections. Of course, the primary cause of an infection is a virus, but without the immune system disorder the disease would not assume that particular form.

Case Formulation, Therapeutic Relationship and Emotional Corrective Experience in the MIT Model

Correctly, the authors recall the importance that is assigned in MIT treatment to the initial case formulation, the contract, and the final case formulation. It should be stressed that the formulation is repeated several times during the treatment, both as a metacognitive "technique" to help the patient to acquire an integrated vision of his/her mental processes, and as a tool to modulate, if necessary, the therapeutic alliance (Carcione et al. 2016).

In Chapter "Strengths and Limitations of Case Formulation in Constructivist Cognitive Behavioral Therapies" it is reported that the MIT never views conceiving the corrective experience as an intense revelation of authentic states, as sometimes is affirmed by Liotti. This statement does not coincide with what is described by the MIT protocol, which emphasizes the importance of interventions aimed at an emotional and relational sharing in order to regulate the emotional tone of the session, to promote its recall and, above all, to manage a possible crisis in the alliance. The regulation of the emotional tone aims to put the patient in a metacognitive attitude, i.e., in the condition to think about his or her internal states, as well as to live them. If the emotional tone is too high or too low, the patient is unable to reflect and, in particular, is unable to reflect on him or herself. Regulation of the emotional tone does not necessarily mean that it has to switch from negative to positive; rather, it has to gain and maintain an intensity compatible with self-reflection. Moreover, regulation does not, therefore, have the purpose of acting as a corrective experience. Of course, there is nothing to prevent this from happening, but we do not believe that this can be a voluntary goal unless we manipulate the relationship by assuming a pre-established role, as Alexander (Alexander and French 1946; Alexander 1950) had suggested.

Regarding the management of moments of impasse or rupture of alliance, in agreement with Safran (Safran and Segal 1990; Safran and Muran 2000), the recourse to self-disclosure interventions is recommended (Carcione et al. 2016; Carcione and Semerari 2019). We would like to point out that self-disclosure does not present a particular value in itself, but is one of the interventions aimed at promoting a relational climate of perceived sharing, like the so-called "universal we" and others (Semerari 1999; Dimaggio et al. 2006, 2007; Carcione et al. 2016; Carcione and Semerari 2019). The importance of such sharing climate is confirmed not only in the scientific literature, but also from our analysis of session transcripts, where we have noticed that frequently it is accompanied by an increase in metacognitive skills. If the sharing between therapist and patient is in some way similar to the activation of the cooperative motivational system, we have also noticed that its activation is associated with a higher level of metacognitive skills, while the activation of the agonistic (as sometimes happens in moments of rupture of alliance) is associated with a lower level of them (Monticelli et al. 2018).

In Chapter "Strengths and Limitations of Case Formulation in Constructivist Cognitive Behavioral Therapies" it is recognized that from the MIT viewpoint the conscious (meta-)cognitive regulation is considered the highest degree of mastery. However, the authors note an inconsistency between the shared formulation of the case as an initial condition to build the therapeutic relationship and the fact that the sharing, in other moments of the therapy, is described as the outcome of significant relational interventions. From our viewpoint, this inconsistency rather is a fruitful circuit in the treatment of complex disorders, in which the initial alliance can be continuously challenged by recurring relational crises.

Summing up, we find the presentation and discussion of the MIT reported in Chapter "Strengths and Limitations of Case Formulation in Constructivist Cognitive Behavioral Therapies" to be legitimate, according to the central perspective of this book: the shared formulation of the case and its impact in the therapeutic relationship. We think it is right to respect this choice and not to pretend a more complete description that would be peripheral to the aims of the text. We hope that the added clarifications are a contribution to the achievement of these aims.

References

Alexander, F. (1950). Analysis of the therapeutic factors in psychoanalytic treatment. *The Psychoanalytic Quarterly, 19*, 482–500.

Alexander, F. G., & French, T. M. (1946). *Psychoanalytic therapy: Principles and applications*. New York, NY: Ronald Press.

American Psychiatric Association [APA]. (2013). *Diagnostic and statistical manual of mental disorders* (5th ed.). Washington, DC: American Psychiatric Publishing. https://doi.org/10.1176/appi.books.9780890425596.

Bilotta, E., Carcione, A., Fera, T., Moroni, F., Nicolò, G., Pedone, R., Pellecchia, G., Semerari, A., & Colle, L. (2018). Symptom severity and mindreading in narcissistic personality disorder. *PLoS One, 13*(8), 216. https://doi.org/10.1371/journal.pone.0201216.

Carcione, A., Nicolò, G., & Semerari, A. (2016). *Curare i casi complessi: la terapia metacognitiva interpersonale dei disturbi di personalità [Treating complex cases: Metacognitive interpersonal therapy of personality disorders]*. Bari: Gius. Laterza & Figli Spa.

Carcione, A., Riccardi, I., Bilotta, E., Leone, L., Pedone, R., Conti, L., Colle, L., Fiore, D., Nicolò, G., Pellecchia, G., Procacci, M., & Semerari, A. (2019). Metacognition as a predictor of improvements in personality disorders. *Frontiers in Psychology, 10*, 170. https://doi.org/10.3389/fpsyg.2019.00170.

Carcione, A., & Semerari, A. (2019). I cicli interpersonali problematici nei disturbi di personalità [The problematic interpersonal cycles in personality disorders]. *Quaderni di Psicoterapia Cognitiva, 45*. https://doi.org/10.3280/qpcoa.v0i45.8988.g531.

Dimaggio, G., Semerari, A., Carcione, A., Nicolo, G., & Procacci, M. (2007). *Psychotherapy of personality disorders: Metacognition, states of mind, and interpersonal cycles*. London: Routledge. https://doi.org/10.4324/9780203939536.

Dimaggio, G., Semerari, A., Carcione, A., Procacci, M., & Nicolo, G. (2006). Toward a model of self pathology underlying personality disorders: Narratives, metacognition, interpersonal cycles and decision-making processes. *Journal of Personality Disorders, 20*, 597–617.

Monticelli, F., Imperatori, C., Carcione, A., Pedone, R., & Farina, B. (2018). Cooperation in psychotherapy increases metacognitive abilities: A single-case study. *Rivista di Psichiatria, 53*, 336–340.

Safran, J. D., & Muran, J. C. (2000). *Negotiating the therapeutic alliance: A relational treatment guide*. New York, NY: Guilford Press.

Safran, J. D., & Segal, Z. V. (1990). *Interpersonal process in cognitive therapy*. New York, NY: Basic Books.

Semerari, A. (1999). *Psicoterapia cognitiva del paziente grave. Metacognizione e relazione terapeutica [Cognitive psychotherapy of severe patient. Metacognition and therapeutic relationship]*. Milano: Raffaello Cortina.

Semerari, A., Carcione, A., Dimaggio, G., Nicolò, G., & Procacci, M. (2007). Understanding minds: Different functions and different disorders? The contribution of psychotherapy research. *Psychotherapy Research, 17*, 106–119.

Semerari, A., Colle, L., Pellecchia, G., Buccione, I., Carcione, A., Dimaggio, G., et al. (2014). Metacognitive dysfunctions in personality disorders: Correlations with disorder severity and personality styles. *Journal of Personality Disorders, 28*, 751–766.

The Role of Trauma in Psychotherapeutic Complications and the Worth of Giovanni Liotti's Cognitive-Evolutionist Perspective (CEP): Commentary on Chapter "Strengths and Limitations of Case Formulation in Constructivist Cognitive Behavioral Therapies"

Benedetto Farina

Contents

Aims of the Commentary

In order to appreciate the clinical worth of Giovanni Liotti's work, which he himself has explicitly outlined as a Cognitive Evolutionary Perspective (CEP) (Liotti and Monticelli 2014), it is necessary to briefly examine its development, define its essential theoretical elements and understand its aims, especially in comparison with the theoretical and practical bases of standard cognitive behavioral therapy (standard CBT) described in this volume. Ruggiero, Caselli and Sassaroli (from now on the Editors) should be acknowledged for their valuable effort in extensively describing the central role of case formulation in standard CBT and to have sought a comparison with other models of clinical cognitivism. However, the value of this comparison, at least with respect to CEP and other aspects of Liotti's work, is partially compromised by their incomplete and sometimes inaccurate description. I

B. Farina (✉)
Università Europea di Roma, Rome, Italy

"Centro Clinico Janet" Cognitive Psychotherapy Center, Rome, Italy

G. M. Ruggiero et al. (eds.), *CBT Case Formulation as Therapeutic Process*,
https://doi.org/10.1007/978-3-030-63587-9_18

therefore thank the Editors for having given me the opportunity to clarify these issues in order to retrieve the meaning of the theoretical and pragmatic comparison between their work with standard CBT and that of Liotti and his collaborators. In this regard, it is right to warn the reader that even though I have personally worked closely with Liotti for approximately 20 years, and even if I want to faithfully respect the description of the CEP as described in his publications, this paper is only my personal reconstruction of Liotti's perspective.

Why a Cognitive-Evolutionist Perspective?

CEP is a theoretical psychotherapeutic perspective that has emerged from the principles of clinical cognitivism and has focused on the treatment of psychopathology resulting from abusive and, more specifically, neglectful family and interpersonal contexts. It is based on the principles of evolutionism, applied both to anthropology (the origin and evolution of man, his mind, and mental functions) and to scientific epistemology (the evolution of scientific knowledge). A basic principle derives from this foundation: psychotherapeutic theories and techniques are doomed to an incessant evolution in order to be defined as scientific, changing with the progress of knowledge and through empirical investigation; on the contrary, theories and practices that do not evolve and do not change are doomed to configure orthodoxies that tend to be ideological. The comparison with the natural and social sciences, with the neuroscientific plausibility of the theoretical premises and with the data of the empirical verifications, is therefore a bond for the CEP which should obviously concern any psychotherapeutic theory or practice that neither intends to place itself outside the scientific dimension nor wishes to run the risk of exercising its clinical activity in an ideological and non-scientific manner.

Another element of the CEP is that the study of the theoretical principles of psychotherapy and its technical and practical applications are not aimed at confirming the effectiveness of a specific psychotherapeutic model but rather at researching the methods and components of psychotherapy that are most effectively adapted to the treatment of each disorder, psychopathological alteration or individual patient. For this reason, Liotti in his latest writings has preferred to redefine his contribution to the study of psychotherapy as a "perspective" (we could say a meta-model) inspired by the aforementioned principles and developed to circumvent the obstacles to the treatment of specific patients.

In this sense, therefore, CEP was born with opposing aims to those of this volume, which has as its explicit goal the definition of what can be defined within the CBT and CT (cognitive therapy) labels. In fact, the Editors aim to propose and adopt an operationally CBT specific terminology for the concepts of alliance and therapeutic relationship such as "***shared case formulation***" without borrowing words from approaches that obey different principles, allowing one to remain focused on the historical proposal of CBT. The Editors also aim to show how the ***shared case formulation*** is increasingly becoming the hallmark of standard CBT approaches because it is in line with its basic principles, i.e. full confidence in the conscious agreement between therapists and patients, transparent cooperation, and an explicit commitment to the CBT model of clinical change, as reported in chapter "The Shared Case Formulation as the Main Therapeutic Process in Cognitive Behavioral Therapies" of this book.

Liotti, although he was among the founders of the Italian Society of Behavioral and Cognitive Therapy, was not as interested in understanding which features a cognitive psychotherapy model should have to be defined as such. On the contrary, he has always explored all the therapeutic orientations without ideological prejudices and with the sole aim of identifying useful and proven effective elements to comprehensively treat the clinical problems in which he specialized, ceaselessly seeking their theoretical integration. Liotti thought that the transdisciplinary nature of cognitive psychology and evolutionary anthropology compared to the different schools of psychotherapy allows us to hope that the understanding of the therapeutic relationship and of the therapeutic alliance based on the CEP perspective can be an opportunity for dialogue and comparison between different psychotherapies (Liotti and Monticelli 2014).

For this reason, Liotti came into contact with scholars and models that differed from standard CBT, not caring to defend the orthodoxy of his approach (Liotti and Gilbert 2011; Migone and Liotti 2018; Liotti and Monticelli 2014). This is verified by the authoritative words of John Bowlby who, discussing the relationship between psychoanalysis and cognitive therapy, wrote: "I think these labels are quite misleading because in reality the cognitive psychotherapy that Liotti represents and the psychoanalytic therapy that I represent converge" (Bowlby 2011, p. 167).

How and Why Was the Cognitive-Evolutionist Perspective Born and Developed?

In the 1980s, Liotti together with Guidano, like many other cognitive therapists, was partly dissatisfied with standard CBT, complaining about the lack of an adequate general psychological theory able to explain how the mind works and why and how it develops and the little consideration given both to the cognitive value of emotions and to unconscious mental processes, i.e. the structures, processes and contents of tacit and preverbal knowledge (Guidano and Liotti 1983; Farina and Liotti 2018). Thanks to Vittorio Guidano's omnivorous readings, Liotti discovered an essential reference in Bowlby's Attachment Theory (AT) which, according to Liotti and Guidano, was able to endow cognitive psychotherapy with a theory of development and a theory of structure able to give reason for how the contents of knowledge (beliefs, expectations and constructs), which were the object of clinical analysis and interventions of cognitive psychotherapy, originated and were organized (Liotti 2009).

As previously described in other parts of this volume, while Guidano radicalized his constructivism by formulating a theory of the Self understood as an autopoietic process in the continuous search for internal consistency, Liotti instead remained tied to the ethological and evolutionist bases of AT, following two distinct but strongly and consistently intertwined paths that form the framework of the CEP (Farina and Liotti 2018). The first starts from the clinical consequences of the disorganized attachment and arrives at the attempts to solve the problems and obstacles that developmental trauma generates on a relational, cognitive, and metacognitive level in psychotherapy (Liotti and Farina 2011). The other, that is the study of the innate social motivations active in psychotherapy, was born as an attempt to provide a general psychological theory that can broaden the focus beyond attachment, with the ultimate aim of providing theoretical and practical solutions to the relational difficulties of psychotherapy, in particular in the therapeutic alliance of which the shared formulation of the case comprises only one element (Liotti and Monticelli 2014).

Clearly, both trajectories start from the AT (a decidedly cognitivist theory because it is based on the principles of goals and beliefs) and reach an attempt to formalize therapeutic intervention strategies for specific clinical problems. I will individually deal with these two study trajectories in subsequent paragraphs, but it is crucial to stress that Liotti's program has never stood in opposition to the general principles and practices of CBT but has instead represented an attempt to overcome the limitations highlighted by controlled empirical studies when it is applied to patients with personal histories of abuse in primary care relationships (Liotti and Farina 2011).

Developmental Trauma Prevents Standard CBT from Working at the Optimum Level

An extensive and authoritative scientific literature provides convincing and repeated evidence of the poor effectiveness of standard treatments in patients with a history of maltreatment and abuse in childhood, regardless of diagnosis (Farina et al. 2019). McCrory and colleagues report that psychiatric disorders in individuals who have experienced maltreatment are likely to develop earlier, with more severe symptomatology and are more likely to be persistent and recurrent and less likely to respond to standard treatment approaches (McCrory et al. 2017). Among the standard treatments made ineffective by experiences of child maltreatment and abuse is CBT, the subject of this volume (Liotti and Farina 2013; Farina et al. 2019; Kameoka et al. 2015; Michelson et al. 1998; Nemeroff et al. 2003; Rufer et al. 2006; Semiz et al. 2014; Waller et al. 2001).

We can therefore consider CEP as an evolution of standard CBT, developed to overcome the therapeutic obstacles caused by maltreatment and abusive experiences that, according to the U.S. Department of Health, affect roughly one in seven children and that the most authoritative scientific literature indicates as a major risk factor in one third of adult patients (Green et al. 2010), representing the single biggest determinant of psychiatric illness, greater even than genetics (Targum and Nemeroff 2019).

In the 1980s, Liotti experienced several limitations of the standard approach of cognitive psychotherapy, noting its limited effectiveness in patients who, while seeking help for common anxiety or mood disorders, had traumatic childhood histories and dissociative states. Thanks to his interest in AT research, he was able to observe children's behaviors classified as disorganized attachment by developmental psychopathologists (Main and Hesse 1990). He derived the hypothesis that the disorganization of early attachment reported in many studies (Lyons-Ruth et al. 2006; Main and Hesse 1990; Schore 2009) could be assimilated to conditions of childhood relational trauma, as the child was exposed to the psychological condition of a 'no escape' threat (Liotti 1992).

In addition, Liotti hypothesized that the difficulties of applying the principles of standard CBT in patients with histories of maltreatment and abuse were likely due to the presence of the typical alterations of children with early disorganized attachment and childhood trauma, i.e. cognitive and metacognitive alterations generated by contingent states of mental disorganization, difficulties in relying on care relationships, and the emergence of implicit relational memories during therapy that prevented the patient from taking advantage of standard CBT techniques and undermined the optimal therapeutic alliance to proceed to collaborative empiricism, as described in the first chapter of this volume (Semerari 1999; Liotti and Farina 2011; Farina and Liotti 2018).

In the first chapter of this book, it is in fact explicitly stated that in order to proceed with the method proposed by the Editors, the patient must have intact cognitive abilities, to be able to optimally use their metacognitive functions, have confidence in their own abilities and in the therapist and build a collaborative plan with him or her. In fact, in many chapters of this book, the Editors write that the therapeutic change occurs in a type of collaboration and alliance between therapist and patient in which the shared formulation of the case is from the beginning a metacognitive process from an operational point of awareness.

The problem, however, is that a significant percentage of patients - regardless of the diagnosis or the reasons for approaching psychotherapy - show difficulties in building and maintaining the collaborative plan and the therapeutic alliance, showing sudden losses of confidence in the therapist and their method that can lead to real phobias for treatments, have temporary inflexions of metacognitive and cognitive abilities; they can also undergo contingent inflexions of executive functions (e.g. regulation of emotions and behavior), a fragmentation of the patient's structures of meaning and can suffer from subtle or more marked altered states of consciousness. Such alterations will prevent them from benefiting from the work indicated in the first chapter of this book.

The complexity of the psychopathological processes triggered by the trauma of development described in the scientific literature of the last 30 years and summarized in the work of Liotti and Farina (2011); Farina et al. (2019) differs in part, and appears much more articulated than the deficit that subjectively manifests itself in the form of dissociative experiences that the Authors attribute to the results of our studies in chapters "Strengths and Limitations of Case Formulation in Constructivist Cognitive Behavioral Therapies" and "Case Formulation as an Outcome and Not an Opening Move in Relational and Psychodynamic Models" of this volume. It is therefore necessary to complete their synthesis with some clarifications.

Pathogenetic Mechanisms of Child Abuse

The clinical and neuroscientific research of the last 30 years unquestionably demonstrates that child maltreatment and abuse generate simultaneously, and in a circular way, two main pathogenetic mechanisms. A first order of psychopathogenetic processes linked to developmental trauma generate a loss of the mind's higher integrative abilities at different levels, which, as mentioned before, prevents the functioning of standard CBT techniques and which can manifest themselves in different ways depending on the mental functions affected: from temporary alterations of the attentive abilities to the impairment of autobiographical memory, from the loss of the continuity of the experience of the self to the fragmentation of meaning structures, up until the flexion of executive functions and the optimal exercise of metacognitive functions (Carlson et al. 2009; Meares 2012; Farina et al. 2019). It therefore appears reductive and misleading to indicate that as a result of the experiences of child maltreatment there exists a psychopathological phenomenology which, as the Editors write, subjectively manifests itself in the form of dissociative experiences.

In an article published in 2016, Martin Teicher and his collaborators reviewed more than 180 neuroscientific studies on the neurobiological effects of maltreatment, abuse, and neglect experiences during development: it is clear that such traumatic experiences alter the neurophysiological basis of higher integrative structures and functions (Teicher and Samson 2016). This makes sense of the effect of disorganization apparent on the higher mental functions necessary to apply standard CBT techniques in an optimal and continuous way, including the shared formulation of the case. It is also vital to add that this demonstrated vulnerability to the mental disintegration of patients with a history of child maltreatment and the appearance of the associated complex psychopathology does not show itself to the clinician as a deficit, i.e. a stable trait that can be recognized immediately, but on the contrary it generally emerges either from the clinical history or after the start of therapy, when the formation of the care link between patient and therapist activates the implicit cognitive patterns related to attachment, the so-called Internal Operational Models conceptualized by Bowlby (1988). In order to better understand this passage and the conceptualization of the intervention according to CEP, it is necessary to face a second order of psychopathological processes that come into play in the developmental trauma; those that compromise the application of the therapeutic strategies of standard CBT due to the activation of relational memories implicit in the therapeutic relationship.

In the 1990s, Liotti began to hypothesize that the disorganization of early attachment and subsequent trajectories of psychopathological development such as the controlling strategies then identified by Lyons-Ruth et al. (2006) could be assimilated to conditions of relational childhood trauma as the continuous loss of vital contact with the caregiver, even only in terms of a lack of attentive and cognitive tuning (Carlson et al. 2009; Schore 2009). This relational childhood trauma constitutes for a mammal a condition of threat without escape, that is the condition that in psychopathology is indicated as psychic trauma (Liotti and Farina 2011, 2013, 2016). This explains why emotional neglect alone accounts for about 80% of all forms of child maltreatment (Farina et al. 2019). Needless to say, this condition is even more serious if the caregiver is actively maltreating or abusing. As indicated by a vast scientific literature, both in the case of neglect and in the case of active maltreatment the child experiences his or her caregiver simultaneously as a source of both security and threat (Liotti et al. 2008; Liotti and Farina 2016). This leads the child to experience two opposing drives: approaching and moving away from the caregiver, which testifies to the simultaneous activation of the attachment system and the archaic defense systems of attack and detachment. This contradictory and simultaneous activation causes a cascade of psychopathological events that lead to mental disorganization and the formation of chaotic, contradictory and emotionally charged fear and threat, which in turn seem to lead to the formation of a "phobia of attachment", as theorized by many authors (Schore 2009; Carlson et al. 2009; van der Hart et al. 2006; Liotti and Farina 2016).

The mental states characterized by the loss of higher integrative abilities would be, according to Liotti and many others, activated by the emergence of implicit relational memories related to the experiences of neglect and abuse suffered during early childhood within the relationships with parents and other significant figures (Liotti 2009; Liotti and Farina 2016; Meares 2012; van der Hart et al. 2006). The reactivation of these implicit disorganized cognitive patterns can provide alternative explanations to the relational, cognitive and metacognitive problems of adult patients with a childhood history of neglect, maltreatment and/or abuse, thus also explaining the difficulties that such patients have in relying on the therapist (sometimes even feeling threatened) and the tendency to alternate contradictory, chaotic and disorganized mental states during the course of the therapeutic relationship (Liotti and Farina 2011). Liotti's psychopathological hypotheses have found empirical confirmation in longitudinal studies conducted by the group of developmental psychopathologists led by Alan Sroufe and Elizabeth Carlson (Ogawa et al. 1997) and have had a wide influence on many scholars (Carlson et al. 2009; Dutra et al. 2009; Lyons-Ruth et al. 2006; Meares 2012; Schore 2009; van der Hart et al. 2006).

It should be manifest that the psychopathological model described so far - and widely shared with almost the entire international community of clinicians and researchers dealing with this issue - has nothing to do with what has been attributed to the work of Liotti and myself by the Editors when they write that the most authentic feelings of the individual remain hidden from others, because the sharing of these needs is intensely feared by the suffering subject (chapter "Strengths and Limitations of Case Formulation in Constructivist Cognitive Behavioral Therapies" of this book). This is a vision that would seem to refer rather to a model of the mind and psychopathology similar to the Freudian intrapsychic defense centered psychopathology, the farthest model from the CEP (Liotti and Farina 2013). It is highly interesting to note that the Authors seem once again to refer to Freudian metapsychology when they oppose the linearity of the relational processes of standard CBT to the difficulties with patients in building and maintaining the therapeutic alliance attributed by the Editors to a continuous and devious sabotage or a more or less unconscious sterile opposition.

On the contrary, it is particularly difficult to understand the Editors' statement that—in the model of Liotti—the difficult and traumatized patient uses, during the therapeutic relationship, substantially artificial if not fictitious styles of interaction. My limited knowledge has not allowed me to discover in any of the sources of psychopathological literature descriptions and explanations of fictitious and artificial relational styles, but I think I can say that these terms (whatever they mean) have never been used in Liotti's scientific production or inspired by him.

The Relational Nature of the CEP Inspired Intervention and the Specific Modes Thereof

According to the CEP model, the reactivation of implicitly traumatic relational memories in the therapeutic relationship can cause difficulties or prevent the use of, at least in the first phase of treatment, the techniques and operating methods described in this volume, for example the shared formulation of the case. These therapeutic difficulties are widely documented in the scientific literature and make it necessary to use additional (and I stress additional, not necessarily alternative) strategies for the management of relational aspects of therapy such as the use of specific interpersonal interventions implicit in the therapeutic relationship and sometimes the splitting of the therapeutic relationship into a double setting (Liotti et al. 2008; Liotti and Farina 2016). In order to avoid the undermining of misunderstandings and naive beliefs, it is necessary to repeat again that the specificity of the implicit and explicit relational interventions envisaged by the CEP does not imply the relinquishment of other effective tools originating from standard CBT or other approaches with empirical validation, as for example the *eye movement desensitization and reprocessing* (EMDR, Shapiro 2001) or body-centered approaches (Farina and Liotti 2018).

CEP has therefore developed as a response to therapeutic difficulties with patients with a history of early relational trauma presenting reduced interpersonal skills and a tendency to mental disorganization. Moreover, it has - to a higher extent than other approaches of clinical cognitivism - among its primary principles the need to address and overcome the clinical problems at the relational level (Liotti 1994; Liotti and Farina 2011).

Thus, what is the relational nature of CEP intervention? Not in what the Editors attribute to it when they say that the protected relationship of the therapeutic setting would allow the patient to expose his or her authentic self (Liotti and Monticelli 2014) and to finally put aside their defensive self. It is a conception that has significant analogies with that previously theorized by Winnicott (1960, 1989). In this case, the therapeutic work would consist of managing the patient's deficiencies by setting up emotional compensation that meets and satisfies the basic relational deficiencies suffered by the patient, as in the psychoanalytic model of Mitchell and Aron (1999). However, these vague interpersonal attitudes attributed by the Editors to the psychoanalytical traditions do not appear, at least in these descriptions, to even be psychotherapeutic interventions, and if misinterpreted they could even devalue the general sense of psychotherapy itself; they certainly have nothing to do with the technical complexity of the practice suggested by CEP.

On the other hand, the elements outlined in the previous paragraphs can instead help us to understand the rationale of the specific interventions of CEP (Liotti and Monticelli 2014; Liotti and Farina 2016). The first of these is precisely the opposite of the emotional compensation that one encounters and satisfies the basic relational deficiencies suffered by the patient attributed by the Editors to Liotti. On the contrary, having a caring attitude with a patient who has not been properly cared for is in fact a therapeutic error, at risk of promoting the activation of the attachment system, that leads to the activation of cognitive patterns and relational memories implicitly avoidant or, worse, disorganized and charged with emotional states dominated by fear and distrust (Liotti and Farina 2016).

Scientific literature also suggests that in all individuals the activation of attachment crushes the metacognitive abilities necessary for the functioning of the therapy, while the promotion of the cooperative system promotes them (Fonagy and Target 2009; Liotti and Gilbert 2011). Our ongoing research, conducted on approximately 70 psychotherapy sessions, offers an empirical confirmation of the relationship between metacognition and interpersonal structure in psychotherapy; the results illustrate that when the patient activates the attachment system it significantly reduces his or her metacognitive functions, while when the patient is coordinated with the therapist on an equal and cooperative level he or she promotes them in an optimal way (Farina et al. 2019).

Moreover, CEP points out the iatrogenic potential of caregiving attitudes in therapy, since they have the potential to reactivate the relational and implicitly traumatic memories in the therapeutic relationship by triggering the aforementioned pathogenetic processes. On the one hand, temporary mental disorganization makes the patient resistant to interventions that presuppose the exercise of refined cognitive and metacognitive functions: i.e., resistant to both standard CBT interventions described in this volume or in other manuals (Van der Kolk 1996; Liotti and Farina 2011) and to those of psychoanalysis, such as transference interpretation (Bateman and Fonagy 2004) or interventions based on mentalization (Bromberg 1998, 2006). On the other hand, the fear and distrust towards the therapist, which, we repeat, is not a more or less conscious attempt of the patient to break the relationship nor a devious sabotage or a more or less unconscious sterile opposition described by the

Editors by Freudianly attributing an unconscious drive to the patient, but rather the effect of the emergence of traumatic memories.

The CEP specific therapeutic procedures are consistently derived from the aforementioned psychopathological models and are aimed at recognizing and defusing the pathogenic effects of the reactivation of implicitly traumatic relational memories in the therapeutic relationship. The implicit or unconscious (in the cognitive and not Freudian sense of the term) nature of traumatic psychopathological processes and the consequent neurovegetative, cognitive and metacognitive dysregulation therefore require both the use of implicit relational strategies not immediately shared with the patient and so-called bottom-up strategies (La Rosa and Onofri 2017). These strategies are aimed at restoring the neurovegetative balance, executive functions and, more generally, higher integrative capacities that can, once restored, facilitate the explicit sharing of the treatment plan and the use of other therapeutic strategies, including those of standard CBT (Farina and Simoncini 2015).

Moreover, the therapeutic relationship can - in its deepest tacit components - constitute a corrective relational emotional experience capable of modifying the patient's profound cognitive patterns but also of overcoming or bypassing cognitive and metacognitive alterations; in this sense, relational work in cognitive therapy can be considered a specific and necessary therapeutic tool to work with difficult patients (Saliani 2008; Liotti and Farina 2011; Liotti and Monticelli 2014; Semerari et al. 2016). Finally, it is worth mentioning the contribution of CEP in the development and improvement of integrated multi-setting treatments (IMST), which provide the simultaneous use of different treatments in the same patient by different therapists in separate settings but in coordination with each other, in order to counteract the activation of the implicit relational memories of disorganized attachment (Liotti et al. 2005). The effectiveness of IMST in difficult patients has been confirmed and the general consensus on their use for patients with a history of early relational trauma is such as to have determined a substantial agreement among clinicians of different theoretical inspirations on the general principles and specific modalities that should regulate such therapeutic strategies (Liotti et al. 2008; Farina and Liotti 2018). For the sake of brevity, please refer to the more complete discussion of the CEP operating procedures and detailed clinical examples in the monographs written and edited by Liotti and his collaborators and reported in the bibliography (Liotti et al. 2005; Liotti and Farina 2011; Liotti and Monticelli 2014).

References

Bateman, A. W., & Fonagy, P. (2004). Mentalization-based treatment of BPD. *Journal of Personality Disorders, 18*(1), 36–51.

Bowlby, J. (1988). *A secure base: Parent-child attachment and healthy human development.* New York, NY: Basic Books.

Bowlby, J. (2011). John Bowlby, MD: Interview by Leonardo Tondo. *Clinical Neuropsychiatry, 8*(159–171), 2011.

Bromberg, P. M. (1998). *Standing in the spaces: Essays on clinical process, trauma, and dissociation*. Hillsdale, NJ: Analytic Press.

Bromberg, P. M. (2006). *Awakening the dreamer: Clinical journeys*. Hillsdale, NJ: Analytic Press.

Carlson, E. A., Yates, T. M., & Sroufe, L. A. (2009). Dissociation and the development of the self. In P. Dell & J. A. O'Neil (Eds.), *Dissociation and dissociative disorders: DSM-V and beyond* (pp. 39–52). New York, NY: Routledge.

Dutra, L., Bureau, J. F., Holmes, B., Lyubchik, A., & Lyons-Ruth, K. (2009). Quality of early care and childhood trauma: A prospective study of developmental pathways to dissociation. *Journal of Nervous and Mental Disease, 197*, 383–390.

Farina, B., & Liotti, G. (2018). La svolta relazionale in psicoterapia cognitiva: Origini e prospettive della psicoterapia cognitivo-evoluzionista [The relational turn in cognitive psychotherapy: Origins and perspectives of cognitive-evolutionsit psychotherapy]. *Cognitivismo clinico, 15*, 6–21.

Farina, B., & Simoncini. (2015). Il ruolo della guerra nella storia del trauma psichico. In F. R. Lenzi (Ed.), *Features of war. Identità e volti del mutamento sociale nel primo conflitto mondiale* (pp. 77–90). Morolo: If Press.

Farina, B., Liotti, M., & Imperatori, C. (2019). The role of attachment trauma and disintegrative pathogenic processes in the traumatic-dissociative dimension. *Frontiers in Psychology, 10*, 933.

Fonagy, P., & Target, M. (2009). Attachment, trauma and psychoanalysis. In E. L. Jurist, A. Slade, & S. Bergner (Eds.), *Mind to mind: Infant research, neuroscience and psychoanalysis* (pp. 15–49). New York, NY: Other Press.

Green, E. J., Crenshaw, D. A., & Kolos, A. C. (2010). Counseling children with preverbal trauma. International Journal of Play Therapy, *19*(2), 95–105.

Guidano, V. F., & Liotti, G. (1983). *Cognitive processes and emotional disorders: A structural approach to psychotherapy*. New York, NY: Guilford Press.

Kameoka, S., Yagi, J., Arai, Y., Nosaka, S., Saito, A., Miyake, W., et al. (2015). Feasibility of trauma-focused cognitive behavioral therapy for traumatized children in Japan: A pilot study. *International Journal of Mental Health Systems, 9*, 1–5.

La Rosa, C., & Onofri, A. (2017). *DAL BASSO IN ALTO (e ritorno...): Nuovi approcci bottom up: psicoterapia cognitiva, corpo, EMDR [FROM BOTTOM UP (and back ...): New bottom up approaches: Cognitive psychotherapy, body, EMDR]*. Roma: Edizioni Apertamenteweb.

Liotti, G. (1992). Disorganized attachment in the etiology of the dissociative disorders. *Dissociation, 5*, 196–204.

Liotti, G. (1994). *La dimensione interpersonale della coscienza [The interpersonal dimension of consciousness]*. Roma: Carocci.

Liotti, G. (2009). Attachment and dissociation. In P. Dell & J. A. O'Neil (Eds.), *Dissociation and dissociative disorders: DSM-V and beyond* (pp. 53–65). New York, NY: Routledge.

Liotti, G., & Farina, B. (2011). *Sviluppi Traumatici: etiopatogenesi, clinica e terapia della dimensione dissociative [Traumatic developments: ethiopathogenesis, clinical and dissociative dimension therapy]*. Milano: Cortina.

Liotti, G., & Farina, B. (2013). Un'esplorazione neuroscientifica della dissociazione post-traumatica e la sua rilevanza per l'etica della psicoterapia [a neuroscientific exploration of post-traumatic dissociation and its relevance to the ethics of psychotherapy]. *Rivista Internazionale di Filosofia e Psicologia, 3*, 325–337.

Liotti, G., & Farina, B. (2016). Painful incoherence: The self in borderline personality disorder. In M. Kyrios, R. Moulding, N. Nedeljkovic, S. S. Bhar, G. Doron, & M. Mikulincer (Eds.), *The self in understanding and treating psychological disorders* (pp. 169–178). Cambridge: Cambridge University Press.

Liotti, G., & Gilbert, P. (2011). Mentalizing, motivation, and social mentalities: Theoretical considerations and implications for psychotherapy. *Psychology and Psychotherapy: Theory, Research and Practice, 84*, 9–25.

Liotti, G., & Monticelli, F. (2014). *Teoria e Clinica dell'Alleanza Terapeutica. Una prospettiva cognitivo-evoluzionista [Therapeutic alliance theory and clinic. A cognitive-evolutionist perspective]*. Milano: Raffaello Cortina Editore.

Liotti, G., Farina, B., & Rainone, A. (2005). *Due terapeuti per un paziente [two therapists for a patient]*. Bari: Laterza.

Liotti, G., Cortina, M., & Farina, B. (2008). Attachment theory and the multiple integrated treatments of borderline patients. *Journal of the American Academy of Pyschoanalysis, 36*, 295–315.

Lyons-Ruth, K., Dutra, L., Schuder, M. R., & Bianchi, I. (2006). From infant attachment disorganization to adult dissociation: Relational adaptations or traumatic experiences? *Psychiatric Clinics of North America, 29*, 63–68.

Main, M., & Hesse, E. (1990). Parents' unresolved traumatic experiences are related to infant disorganized attachment status: Is frightened/frightening parental behavior the linking mechanism? In M. Greenberg, D. Cichetti, & M. Cummings (Eds.), *Attachment in the preschool years* (pp. 121–160). Chicago, IL: University of Chicago Press.

McCrory, E. J., Gerin, M. I., & Viding, E. (2017). Annual research review: Childhood maltreatment, latent vulnerability and the shift to preventative psychiatry - the contribution of functional brain imaging. *Journal of Child Psychology and Psychiatry, 58*, 338–357.

Meares, R. (2012). *A dissociation model of borderline personality disorder*. New York, NY: Norton.

Michelson, L., June, K., Vives, A., Testa, S., & Marchione, N. (1998). The role of trauma and dissociation in cognitive-behavioral psychotherapy outcome and maintenance for panic disorder with agoraphobia. *Behaviour Research and Therapy, 36*, 1011–1050.

Migone, P., & Liotti, G. (2018). Psicoanalisi e psicoterapia cognitivo evoluzionista. Un tentativo di integrazione [psychoanalysis and cognitive evolutionist psychotherapy. An attempt at an integration]. *Psicoterapia e Scienze Umane, 2*, 249–290.

Mitchell, S. A., & Aron, L. E. (1999). *Relational psychoanalysis: The emergence of a tradition*. Hillsdale, NJ: Analytic Press.

Nemeroff, C. B., Heim, C. M., Thase, M. E., Klein, D. N., Rush, A. J., Schatzberg, A. F., et al. (2003). Differential responses to psychotherapy versus pharmacotherapy in patients with chronic forms of major depression and childhood trauma. *Proceedings of the National Academy of Sciences, 100*, 14293–14296.

Ogawa, J. R., Sroufe, L. A., Weinfield, N. S., Carlson, E. A., & Egeland, B. (1997). Development and the fragmented self: Longitudinal study of dissociative symptomatology in a non clinical sample. *Development and Psychopathology, 9*, 855–879.

Rufer, M., Held, D., Cremer, J., Fricke, S., Moritz, S., Peter, H., & Hand, I. (2006). Dissociation as a predictor of cognitive behavior therapy outcome in patients with obsessive-compulsive disorder. *Psychotherapy and Psychosomatics, 75*, 40–46.

Saliani, A. M. (2008). Teoria e pratica della relazione terapeutica. In C. Perdighe & F. Mancini (Eds.), *Elementi di psicoterapia cognitiva [Elements of cognitive psychotherapy]* (pp. 69–89). Roma: Giovanni Fioriti.

Schore, A. N. (2009). Attachment trauma and the developing of right brain: Origin of pathological dissociation. In P. Dell & J. A. O'Neil (Eds.), *Dissociation and dissociative disorders: DSM-5 and beyond* (pp. 107–141). New York, NY: Routledge.

Semerari, A. (1999). La relazione terapeutica nella tecnica nel colloquio. In A. Semerari (Ed.), *Psicoterapia cognitiva del paziente grave [Cognitive psychotherapy of severe patient]* (pp. 71–112). Milano: Raffaello Cortina.

Semerari, A., Pellecchia, G., & Carcione, A. (2016). La relazione terapeutica (2016). In A. Carcione, G. Nicolò, & A. Semerari (Eds.), *Curare i casi complessi [Treating complex cases]* (pp. 114–151). Bari: Laterza.

Semiz, U. B., Inanc, L., & Bezgin, C. H. (2014). Are trauma and dissociation related to treatment resistance in patients with obsessive–compulsive disorder? *Social Psychiatry and Psychiatric Epidemiology, 49*, 1287–1296.

Shapiro, F. (2001). *Eye movement desensitization and reprocessing: Basic principles, protocols and procedures*. New York, NY: Guilford Press.

Targum, S. D., & Nemeroff, C. B. (2019). The effect of early life stress on adult psychiatric disorders. *Innovations in Clinical Neuroscience, 16*(1–2), 35.

Teicher, M. H., & Samson, J. A. (2016). Annual research review: Enduring neurobiological effects of childhood abuse and neglect. *Journal of Child Psychology and Psychiatry, 57*, 241–266.

Van der Hart, O., Steel, K., & Nijenhuis, E. (2006). *The haunted self: Structural dissociation and treatment of chronic traumatization*. New York, NY: Norton.

Van der Kolk, B. A. (1996). *The body keeps score: Approaches to the psychobiology of posttraumatic stress disorder*. London: Penguin Books.

Waller, G., Hamilton, K., Elliott, P., Lewendon, J., Stopa, L., Waters, A., et al. (2001). Somatoform dissociation, psychological dissociation, and specific forms of trauma. *Journal of Trauma & Dissociation, 1*, 81–98.

Winnicott, D. W. (1960). The theory of the parent-infant relationship. *The International Journal of Psycho-Analysis, 41*, 585.

Winnicott, D. W. (1989). *Psycho-analytic explorations*. Cambridge, MA: Harvard University Press.

The Case Formulation in the Post-Rationalist Constructivist Model: Commentary on Chapter "Strengths and Limitations of Case Formulation in Constructivist Cognitive Behavioral Therapies"

Maurizio Dodet

Contents

Rationalist and Constructivist Cognitivism

I have never considered rationalist and constructivist cognitivism to be in opposition to each other. The former represents the attempt to formulate explanatory hypotheses regarding the elemental aspects of psychological functioning while the latter presents hypotheses on personality functioning and a vision of the individual—man and woman—as a whole, searching for the dynamics that lead a person to experience a feeling of continuity and uniqueness.

The gap between the two models occurred, in my opinion, during the writing of *Cognitive Processes and Emotional Disorders* by Guidano and Liotti (1983). In that volume the divide between the two approaches appeared just in the inconsistency between the first theoretical part, in which the authors treated extensively the self and identity processes, and the second clinical part, in which an updated approach to standard CBT prevailed, paying more attention to the thought processes than to the process of signification, a process that is beyond just giving meaning to events.

M. Dodet (✉)
"Laboratorio di Psicologia Cognitiva Post-razionalista", Cognitive Psychotherapy Center, Rome, Italy

G. M. Ruggiero et al. (eds.), *CBT Case Formulation as Therapeutic Process*,
https://doi.org/10.1007/978-3-030-63587-9_19

The first part voiced Guidano's point of view while the second part uttered the vision of Liotti.

Not coincidentally, that book was the last act of their cooperation. Since then, Liotti has developed the study of attachment processes up until their extreme consequences, dealt with trauma and never abandoned a vision that paid attention to thought processes and functional analysis of the symptom and no longer spoke of identity processes. I believe that the subsequent work of Liotti's study group (Liotti and Farina 2011; Liotti and Monticelli 2014) and Antonio Semerari's group on the model of metacognitive intersonal therapy (Semerari et al. 2014) should be either included in the standard CBT framework in its most intellectualized evolution or at least distinguished from radical constructivism as approaches belonging to a moderated version of constructivism.

On the other hand, Vittorio Guidano, fascinated by the bursting contributions of radical constructivism (Guidano 1985, 1987, 1991, 1996–1999; Guidano and Dodet 1993; Quiñones 2000; Quiñones and Guidano 2001; Reda 1986) and of Second-Order Cybernetics of Maturana and Varela (1980, 1984), through the vision of the individual as an autonomous complex system builder of meanings, and in close collaboration with Michael Mahoney (1995, 2003), established the premises of an approach that appeared to be in contrast with the standard CBT but actually completed it. The name that he gave to this approach was "post-rationalist cognitivism" (Guidano 1991) when he aimed to clearly distinguish it from the standard CBT, but actually he preferred to call it "systemic process cognitivism" (Guidano 1996–1999; Guidano and Dodet 1993) whenever he aimed to underline the roots of the model, i.e. a constructivist epistemology in its most radical meaning, and focused on the complexity of the intrapsychic and relational processes (Damiano 2009).

Case Formulation in Post-Rationalist Cognitivism

In post-rationalist cognitivism the attention to case formulation has never been put in the background and neither has the interest in empirical research. The definition of the specific clinical interventions of post-rationalist cognitivism as implemented *in vivo* by Guidano himself in transcribed sessions is the object of study (Bercelli and Lenzi 1999). In this model, no specific protocols are proposed with respect to pathologies defined according to a classical descriptive psychopathology. This happens because in an explicative constructivist psychopathology each single diagnostic entity can be supported by different cores of meaning and by the resulting organization of personality. A method is proposed that indicates those operations that allow a problem to be faced without looking for a solution but trying to build its meaning in respect of its complexity (Dodet 2010). The reference to the work of Edgard Morin (1977, 1990, 2005) is clear.

This Method, rather than being an operational succession of acts, represents the guideline in the construction of a relationship respectful of the subjectivity of the other—a mode, therefore, that allows the therapist to guide the patient in the discovery of his own tacit functioning and that facilitates a process of articulation of his/her own specific way of being. The symptoms or discomfort are seen as a desperate attempt to maintain an internal consistency with respect to the patient's own specific meaning.

The concept of *personal meaning* represents the most complex assumption of post-rationalist constructivist cognitivism; today we can refer to Tronik (2011) who, starting from studies on subjects of a few months of age, has developed a research on the creation and experience of the signification processes in preverbal age. *Meaning*, therefore, is not giving a meaning to an event at the level of language, but is a complex structure through which a subject gives meaning first of all to him- or herself, generating a feeling of continuity and unity central to the maintenance of a stable identity (Lewis 1995, 1997).

Tronik (2011) has explored these meaning processes and underlines that it is biopsychological: it is made up of polymorphic systems operating at multiple levels. This is a hypothesis akin to those posited by Guidano and by my study group (Dodet 1999, 2002, 2003; Dodet and Merigliano 2001a, 2001b, 2009; Dodet 2010; Merigliano 1998, 2019; Nardi 2001, 2007). A psychological discomfort or a symptom either in the neurotic or psychotic sphere represents an attempt to maintain this feeling of continuity and unity of identity and therefore is a gateway to subjectivity. This method therefore represents a plot that allows the unfolding of a relationship that never redefines the patient's internal world and is never prescriptive. In the proposed scheme we can define specific phases.

Steps of the Post-Rationalist Case Formulation

The first step is the *presentation of the problem* in which the therapist helps the patient to describe his or her emotional suffering or symptoms and situate them over time in his or her personal life development. It takes the form of an *oriented anamnesis* in which the information is collected according to a specific thread that allows the therapist and the patient to connect clinical symptoms, emotional activations and specific relational contexts.

As regard the current crisis of the patient, there is a *reconstruction of the dynamics of decompensation* in which the precipitating events are described in a specific context through first-person narratives. The *first-person story* differs from the chronicle story in the emotional activation that takes place in the re-enactment of the event. The purpose of these reconstructions is to capture the emotional redundancies that characterize the individual. Identifying a personal meaning occurs through assessing, underlining and construing in their complexity those primarily emotional elements that are at the basis of the feeling of unity and continuity of identity, which had their origin in the relationships of attachment and that represent the pivotal points of subjectivity and of the relational modalities of the individual (Bennett et al. 1988; Bowlby 1969, 1973, 1980; Crittenden and Landini 2011). The next step is *contextualizing an event*, which is aimed at guiding an individual in the difficult *process of internalization*, that is, of discovery of his or her own verbally tacit core that is the ground of the personal emotional regulation (Fonagy and Target 1997).

In the construction of the *oriented anamnesis* the therapist encourages the patient to reconstruct moments of life that assume a particular meaning. Among these moments, emotional oscillations, feelings of self and behaviors are identified. They appear to be the expression of the *organization of personal meaning (OPS)* in various areas of life, which is the most controversial and most widely discussed post-rationalist concept from a standard CBT viewpoint. OPS is the emergence of an organizing process expressed by the primeval emotional core and the creation of a personological structure in which each element is related to all the others in the creation of that structural unity that generates the basic feelings characterizing a personal identity. Understanding OPS is not enough for the treatment process and represents only the starting point. The therapist is the catalyst of a process of articulation of the basic primeval core and encourages the development of higher levels of flexibility and generativity in the individual.

Attachment, Relationship and Trauma in Post-Rationalist Case Formulation

For example, we can consider a core of meaning that originates from an avoidant attachment and generates a redundant emotional oscillation between sadness/despair and anger with a centrality of abandonment and loss. This structure leads the individual to organize him- or herself through relational experiences characterized by anxiety of loss with distancing behaviors when an involvement with increased intimacy is perceived. Such distancing behaviors represent a test of the other to probe his or her reliability and thus to allow the increase of intimacy. These behaviors in descriptive terms may appear to be a misfit for the individual but are in fact an extreme attempt by patients to defend themselves from basic anxiety and to be able to get in touch with the other. The awareness of such mechanisms allows patients to live them as belonging to the self and to recognize the aspects of generativity. It is a bit like saying that anger or despair can be identified with conscious recognition of the needs that sustain them and therefore can be channeled and regulated by creating a change in meaningful relationships. In the analysis of the *cores of meaning* and their *personological organization* patients can discover the consistency of their emotions and therefore the emergence of the resilience of their way of being.

The work on and through the relationship is a cornerstone of the post-rationalist intervention and clearly differentiates it from how Gianni Liotti interprets the intersubjectivity as underlined in chapter "Strengths and Limitations of Case Formulation in Constructivist Cognitive Behavioral Therapies" the editors of this book when they notice that the therapeutic interaction goes beyond the cooperative intersubjective plan between patient and therapist, since the therapeutic plan is the conscious sharing of emotional and cognitive states and not necessarily the replacement of a dysfunctional mode of interaction with a more adaptive one encouraged by the therapist. In the post-rationalist intervention the relationship is understood as the creation of an emotional reciprocity between patient and therapist and seems to be an instrument of great incisiveness. The therapist uses the analysis of the flow of motive in therapy as an object of observation and in turn positions him- or herself as an object of observation. The relationship is also, above all, immediacy: two reciprocal immediate events with the possibility of being able to metacommunicate on the nature of the relationship itself.

Finally, a hint at the subject of *trauma*. Vittorio Guidano, now more than 25 years ago in a conversation with Mario Reda, talked about the theme of trauma and said that we must relate it to an upsetting event, assess its precipitants, its experience and its consequences and, last but not least, stress how the therapeutic approach to a traumatic experience cannot disregard the identity structure of the individual and the ongoing relationships. In the *post-rationalist constructivist model*, complex relational traumas are considered in individual history those events that give shape to an identity and therefore also those experiences that will give rise to the emergence of the specific resilience of the subject.

Where regarding to the case formulation procedure, I refer to a sheet that we use in the supervision groups.

Model of Post-Rationalist Clinical Case Formulation (Ver. 1/2017, Maurizio Dodet)

The model presents the process of case formulation in post-rationalist therapy, as described in the work of Vittorio Guidano. The goal is to identify the *self meaning* (*core of meaning*), which underlies the feeling of identity through the analysis of life episodes in order to assess emotional, cognitive and self-feeling redundancies. The course of therapy is described in its phases having as a thread the progressive articulation of the core of self meaning, in particular through the narration of the dynamics in significant relationships.

A. **Description of the Problem Presented:**

   (a) *Description of the therapeutic referral and the context of the session*
   (b) *Description of the form of the expressed emotional discomfort*
   (c) *Beginning, timing, current status*
   (d) *Diagnosis (DSM V)*

B. **Debut: Reconstruction of the Dynamics of Decompensation (Contextualization):**

   (a) *When: events that appear in relation to the crisis by synchronicity*
   (b) *How: the specifically precipitating event of the crisis*

(c) *With whom and in relation to whom: relational context*
(d) *Emotional oscillation/thought content/PREVALENT feelings of self*

C. **Critical Events in Life History:**

(a) *When: events that appear in relation to the crisis by synchronicity*
(b) *How: the specifically precipitating event of the crisis*
(c) *With whom and in relation to whom: relational context*
(d) *Emotional oscillation/thought content/PREVALENT feelings of self*
(e) *Resilience: what has enabled the crisis to be overcome, and how*

D. **Relevant Events with Significant Figures:**
Events that can allow *an analysis of the dynamics of child attachment*

E. **Hypothesis of Reformulation of the Problem (Internalization):**

1. *Situational redundancies*
2. *Emotional redundancies*
3. *Thought redundancies*
4. *Redundancy of self sense*

F. **Socialization/Redefinition of the Presented Problem:**

1. *Therapeutic project: What we will have to work on and to achieve what*
2. *Therapeutic contract: What we explain to the patient about the therapeutic project*
3. *Notes for integration (psycho/pharmaceutical therapy)*
   (a) *What I want to achieve with pharmacotherapy*
   (b) *What I want to achieve with psychotherapy*
4. *Progress of the therapeutic process:*
   (a) *Phases of therapy*
   (b) *Symptomatic indicators*
   (c) *Narrative indicators*
   (d) *Self-reading*
   (e) *Reading the other one*
   (f) *Ability to contextualize*
   (g) *Sequencing capability*
   (h) *Ability to read experience*

G. **End of Therapy:**

Point E *seems* to be the most tantalizing and elusive. By *reformulation of the presented problem* we mean bringing to a level of awareness the emotional oscillations and the dominant self feeling that are expressed in the critical event and therefore in specific situations in significant relationships—hence the therapeutic contract that will never be based on the concrete achievement of a goal but always on the explanation of the mechanisms that will be the object of exploration.

Table of Concepts in Post-Rationalist Therapy 1) Emotional redundancies

   a) Dominant self-feeling
   b) Prevailing emotion (search of contact)
   c) Prevalent emotion (in distancing)
   d) Basic anguish

2) Cognitive redundancies

   a) Dominant theme

      i) Self-attribution
      ii) Attribution prevalent to the other by itself

3) Presentation of the problem

   a) Anamnesis oriented

      i) Dynamic reconstruction of reward (current crisis)
      ii) Dynamic reconstruction of other rewards
      iii) History report

         (1) Crisis training
         (2) Turning point

      iv) Individual history
      v) Relationship with parents
      vi) Relationship between parents
      vii) Work/friends

4) Contextualization

   a) Internalization
   b) Self meaning
   c) Reciprocity

References

Bennett, L. A., Wolin, S. J., & McAwity, K. J. (1988). Family identity, ritual and myth: A cultural perspective on life cycle transitions. In C. J. Falicov (Ed.), *Family transitions: Continuity and change over the life cycle* (pp. 211–234). New York, NY: The Guilford Press.

Bercelli, F., & Lenzi, S. (1999). Riascoltando una seduta [Listening again to a session]. *Quaderni di Psicoterapia, 4*, 42–60.

Bowlby, J. (1969). *Attachement and loss* (Vol. 1). New York, NY: Basic Books.

Bowlby, J. (1973). *Attachement and loss* (Vol. 2). New York, NY: Basic Books.

Bowlby, J. (1980). *Attachement and loss* (Vol. 3). New York, NY: Basic Books.

Crittenden, P. M., & Landini, A. (2011). *Assessing adult attachment: A dynamic-maturational approach to discourse analysis*. New York, NY: Norton.

Damiano, L. (2009). *Unità in dialogo [Unity in dialogue]*. Milano: Mondadori.
Dodet, M. (1999). Coherence Individuelle, Reciprocite Emotionelle et Intimite: pour une Approche Post-Rationaliste des Relations de Couple [Individual coherence, emotional reciprocity and intimacy: For a post-rationalist approach to couple relations]. *Revue Francophone de Clinique Comportementale et Cognitive, IV*(3), 42–46.
Dodet, M. (2002). El cambio posible: un caso clinico: el Hombre de la barca [The possible change: A clinical case: The man of the boat]. *Revista de Psicoterapia, 13*(50/51), 87–98.
Dodet, M. (2003). L'intervento clinico sulla reciprocità di coppia [The clinical intervention on couple reciprocity]. In F. Lambruschi (Ed.), *Psicoterapia dell'età evolutiva. Procedure di assessment e strategie psicoterapeutiche [Developmental psychotherapy. Assessment procedures and psychotherapeutic strategies]* (pp. 280–308). Torino: Bollati Boringhieri.
Dodet, M. (2010). Self meaning e tema di vita. Una proposta cognitivo-costruttivista [Self meaning and life theme: A cognitive constructivist proposal]. In A. Pacciolla & F. Mancini (Eds.), *Cognitivismo esistenziale. Dal significato del sintomo al significato della vita [Existential cognitivism. From the meaning of the symptom to the meaning of life]*. Milano: Franco Angeli.
Dodet, M., & Merigliano, D. (2001a). La moviola [slow motion]. In S. Borgo, G. della Giusta, & L. Sibilia (Eds.), *Dizionario di psicoterapia cognitivo–comportamentale [Dictionary of cognitive-behavioral psychotherapy]* (pp. 177–178). Milano: Mc Graw-Hill.
Dodet, M., & Merigliano, D. (2001b). Narratività [Narrativity]. In S. Borgo, G. della Giusta, & L. Sibilia (Eds.), *Dizionario di psicoterapia cognitivo–comportamentale [Dictionary of cognitive-behavioral psychotherapy]* (pp. 181–182). Milano: Mc Graw-Hill.
Dodet, M., & Merigliano, D. (2009). Organizaciones de significado y personal y trastornos de personalidad: una propuesta constructivista [Organizations of personal meaning and personality disorders: A constructivist proposal]. *Revista de Psicoterapia, 19*(74/75), 73–88.
Fonagy, P., & Target, M. (1997). Attachment and reflective function: Their role in self-organization. *Development and Psychopathology, 9*(4), 679–700.
Guidano, V. F. (1985). A constructivistic foundation for cognitive therapy. In M. J. Mahoney & A. Freeman (Eds.), *Cognition and psychotherapy* (pp. 101–142). New York, NY: Plenum Press.
Guidano, V. F. (1987). *Complexity of the self*. New York, NY: Guilford Press.
Guidano, V. F. (1991). *The self in process: Toward a post-rationalist cognitive therapy*. New York, NY: Guilford Press.
Guidano, V. F. (1996–1999). *Psychotherapy training lectures. Unissued manuscripts*. Roma: Associazione di Psicologia Cognitiva.
Guidano, V. F., & Dodet, M. (1993). Terapia Cognitiva Sistemico-Processuale della Coppia [Systemic-process cognitive therapy of the couple]. *Psicobiettivo, 13*, 29–41.
Guidano, V. F., & Liotti, G. (1983). *Cognitive processes and emotional disorders: A structural approach to psychotherapy*. New York, NY: Guilford Press.
Lewis, M. (1995). *Shame: The exposed self*. New York, NY: Simon and Schuster.
Lewis, M. (1997). *Altering fate: Why the past does not predict the future*. New York, NY: Guilford.
Liotti, G., & Farina, B. (2011). *Sviluppi traumatici [Traumatic developments]*. Milano: Cortina.
Liotti, G., & Monticelli, F. (2014). *Teoria e clinica dell'alleanza terapeutica. Una prospettiva cognitivo-evoluzionista [Theory and clinic of the therapeutic alliance. A cognitive-evolutionary perspective]*. Milano: Cortina.
Mahoney, M. J. (1995). *Human change processes: The scientific foundations of psychotherapy*. New York, NY: Basic Books.
Mahoney, M. J. (2003). *Constructive psychotherapy: A practical guide*. New York: Guilford.
Maturana, H. R., & Varela, F. J. (1980). *Autopoiesis and cognition. The realization of the living*. Boston, MA: Reidel.
Maturana, H. R., & Varela, F. J. (1984). *The tree of knowledge. Biological basis of human understanding*. Boston, MA: Shambhala.
Merigliano, D. (1998). Trame narrative nella costruzione del Sé [Narrative plots in the construction of the self]. *Psicobiettivo, 1*, 95–98.

Merigliano, D. (Ed.). (2019). *La psicoterapia postrazionalista. Casi clinici, metodi di intervento e aspetti applicative [Postrationalist psychotherapy. Clinical cases, intervention methods and application aspects]*. Roma: FrancoAngeli.

Morin, E. (1977). *La Méthode [The method]*. Paris: Le Seuil.

Morin, E. (1990). *Introduction à la pensée complexe [Introduction to complex thinking]*. Paris: ESF.

Morin, E. (2005). *Introduction à la pensée complexe [Introduction to complex thinking]* (2nd ed.). Paris: Le Seuil.

Nardi, B. (2001). *Processi psichici e psicopatologia nell'approccio cognitivo [Psychic processes and psychopathology in the cognitive approach]*. Milano: FrancoAngeli.

Nardi, B. (2007). *CostruirSi. Sviluppo e adattamento del Sé nella normalità e nella patologia [Building ourselves. Development and adaptation of the self in normality and pathology]*. Milano: FrancoAngeli.

Quiñones, A. T. (2000). Organizaciòn de significado personal: una estructura hermenèutica global [Organizations of personal meaning: A hermeneutic global structure]. *Revista de Psicoterapia, 41*, 11–33.

Quiñones, A. T., & Guidano, V. F. (Eds.). (2001). *El modelo cognitivo postracionalista [The cognitive post-rationalist model]*. Bilbao: Desclée de Brouwer.

Reda, M. A. (1986). *Sistemi Cognitivi Complessi e Psicoterapia [Cognitive complex systems and psychotherapy]*. Roma: La Nuova Italia Scientifica.

Semerari, A., Colle, L., Pellecchia, G., Buccione, I., Carcione, A., Dimaggio, G., et al. (2014). Metacognitive dysfunctions in personality disorders: Correlations with disorder severity and personality styles. *Journal of Personality Disorders, 28*, 751–766.

Tronik, E. (2011). Multilevel meaning making and dyadic expansion of consciousness: The emotional and polymorphic polysemic flow of meaning. In D. Fosha, D. J. Siegel, & M. F. Solomon (Eds.), *The healing power of emotion: Affective neuroscience, development & clinical practice* (pp. 86–111). New York, NY: Norton.

Case Formulation and the Therapeutic Relationship from an Evolutionary Theory of Motivation: Commentary to Chapter "Strengths and Limitations of Case Formulation in Constructivist Cognitive Behavioral Therapies"

Fabio Monticelli

Contents

Topics of the Commentary

I thank the editors of this book for the invitation and their effort to integrate different perspectives that animate the current cognitive–behavioral approach. While I share some substantial views with the authors, I would like to briefly clarify two points. On the one hand, I would like to describe briefly some fundamental principles that guide therapeutic choices from an *evolutionary theory of motivation* (ETM; Liotti et al. 2017) perspective; this clarification is important to escape the suspicion that the so called "self-involving" interventions (Henretty and Levitt 2010) represent the only tools available to the therapist with the exclusive objective to encourage the patient to move from a state of personal dissatisfaction to a state of sharing relational dynamics. On the other hand, I would like to explain the reasons for my disagreement with the patient's presumed motivation to break the relationship in a more or less conscious way.

F. Monticelli (✉)
"Centro Clinico De Sanctis", Cognitive Psychotherapy Center, Rome, Italy

G. M. Ruggiero et al. (eds.), *CBT Case Formulation as Therapeutic Process*,
https://doi.org/10.1007/978-3-030-63587-9_20

Shared Positions

The editors assume that if, in the relational models including ETM, the real therapeutic bottleneck is the episode of rupture and reparation and its analysis—i.e., the state of relational crisis followed by an abstract, cognitive, and intensely emotional and relational understanding—it follows that each initial episode of shared formulation and negotiation of the therapeutic plan and of its rationale is only a trigger that activates the therapeutic process and not a real explicit therapeutic contract, as in the standard *cognitive behavioral therapy* (CBT). It is only a trigger because it has not yet been subjected to the decisive test, which is the relational rupture and its analysis, an indispensable condition for a real change.

The editors point out a substantial difference between an ETM approach and standard CBT regarding the way to conceptualize the case formulation; from what has been written, it can be assumed that standard CBT conceives case formulation as a static tool that is formulated at the beginning of the therapy, understood in a mainly abstract way, and assessed on a strictly narrative level. From an ETM perspective (Liotti et al. 2017), case formulation is instead conceived as a dynamic, concrete, and intensely emotional and relational element. In addition, from an ETM point of view, the case is formulated and shared with the patient at the beginning of the therapy but, as the editors point out, it is subject to continuous verification, especially during relational events (not only, therefore, during the alliance ruptures). Relational events present themselves, at times, as ruptures of the therapeutic alliance, and at other times as phases of impasse; others are characterized by a direct involvement of the therapist without configuring an ongoing rupture.

The emergence of a relational event (impasse, rupture, or in general relational events) induces the therapist to carefully monitor the *interpersonal motivational systems* (IMSs) in place in the relationship (Gilbert 1989; Liotti 1994, 2005; Liotti and Monticelli 2008, 2014; Monticelli et al. 2018) that attempts to identify the patient's expectations and needs. In order to do so, the therapist will analyze his or her mental states that, according to the theory of emotional contagion, allow him or her to perceive the mental states of the patient (Hatfield et al. 1994). In parallel, the therapist will be able to use the methodological criteria formalized in the AIMIT (*Analisi degli Indicatori della Motivazione Interpersonale nei Trascritti* [*analysis of the indicators of interpersonal motivation in the transcripts*]) method to identify the IMSs in progress in the report (Liotti and Monticelli 2008; Liotti et al. 2017; Monticelli et al. 2018). For example, if the patient presses the therapist with the intent to make him or her feel uncomfortable, to test his or her authority as a therapist, or to gain control of the relationship, this attitude would reveal activation of the antagonism system, configuring a rupture of the alliance. In light of new and unpredictable elements that emerge from the motivational analysis, the therapist will have the opportunity to correct the case formulation, which will be enriched with elements that have emerged from the relationship and that can be examined without filters and corrected in a "hot" modality (i.e., emotional and not abstract and cognitive) through intense work on the therapeutic relationship.

In a nutshell, the understanding of the motivational structure of the relationship allows a therapist (a) to correct the case formulation; (b) to improve the interpersonal tuning with the patient (which favors a subsequent increase in the patient's metacognitive skills and reduces the risk of dropout); and (c) to observe and correct in vivo the dysfunctional interpersonal patterns (DIPs) and problematic interpersonal cycles (PICs) that originate and reveal themselves, in real time, in the interaction between the therapist and the patient.

Clarifications on the General Principles of Therapeutic Theory in an Evolutionary Theory of Motivation Perspective

According to an ETM approach, therapeutic interventions represent the final step of an articulated and complex process that recognizes a central role in the motivational monitoring of the relationship. Continuous monitoring of the relationship and the therapeutic alliance significantly improves the outcome (Lambert and Kenichi 2011; Norcross and Wampold 2011). In an ETM reading, the outcome improves thanks to monitoring IMSs; this endeavor facilitates interpersonal tuning and, in particular, (a) the ongoing recognition of therapeutic alliance crises (impasses and ruptures); (b) the identification of who, between patient and therapist, is in charge of the ongoing rupture; (c) the assessment of the various types of ruptures; and (d) the formulation of the clinical intervention (to restore interpersonal tuning) and the verification of intervention outcomes.

Recognizing the Rupture

Patient.: And how will that help me?

In the example reported by the editors, they interpret this patient's sentence as a critical and provocative act, regulated by the antagonism system, from which originates a state of mutual irritation triggered by the patient that configures a rupture of the alliance. However, the sentence itself does not necessarily indicate a critical or agonistic attitude toward the therapist, as interpreted by the editors. Instead, it indicates the presence of a relational event and the therapist's need to understand the change in the motivational structure of the dyad. The therapist, in order to recognize the possible rupture in progress, must carefully monitor the motivational structure and exclude other options: For example, the therapist must exclude the possibility that the patient seeks reassurance (antagonism system) or that he or she needs further information in order to understand the task and to cooperate at his or her best (cooperative system). In order to be sure of the ongoing rupture, the therapist will take care to monitor the established IMSs as the clinical exchange progresses to understand the reasons and meaning of the alleged rupture and to carefully assess the appropriateness of the patient's criticism. For example, if the patient distrusts the techniques used by a therapist who is really too prone to silence, passivity, and an interpretative stance, the therapist should consider his or her criticism appropriate; in this case, he or she should plan—from a cooperative perspective—some technical changes to his or her work because the patient's attitude remains substantially critical. In this case, the cooperative intervention of the patient is not a rupture of the alliance because it is aimed at correcting the techniques used by the therapist to achieve the therapeutic objectives during the course of the work.

Who Originates the Rupture of the Alliance?

Let us assume that the sentence:

Patient: And how will that help me?

is a badly expressed request to the therapist to reassure the patient about the usefulness of the technique in order to overcome symptoms. If a therapist who is perhaps susceptible to the subject of shame (and does not monitor it carefully) misinterprets the patient's request as an expression of a distrustful attitude toward him or her, he or she could probably feel hostility toward the patient, causing a risk of conflict. In this case, it would be the therapist's dysfunctional interpersonal patterns that would be activated by representing the patient as a humiliating person. This appraisal would lead to an exchange in which mutual irritation grows.

If, on the other hand, the therapist observes—by monitoring IMSs—that the patient's intentions are really polemical and motivated by distrust toward him or her and the proposed techniques, it is plausible that a real rupture of the alliance is in progress. In this case, the rupture of the alliance represents the epiphenomenon of the patient's DIPs and PICs. For example, if the patient is at odds with the therapist, who is guilty of never having telephoned him or her during summer vacation, the therapist should consider the patient's connection inappropriate, perceiving his or her dysfunctional need for proximity and protection. This consideration does not mean that the therapist has to deal with the patient's demands; rather, he or she will have to be vigilant because the crisis may lead to a probable interpersonal disconnection.

The subsequent exchange between therapist and patient described by the editors—in which mutual irritation grows and the therapist responds with an intervention called *disembedding*—shows a growing interpersonal disconnection that does not help to solve the ongoing rupture of the therapeutic alliance. According to the editors, the disconnection originates from the patient's sudden shift from the original cooperative stance shared with the therapist to the antagonism system. In the phase of the rupture of the alliance, the therapist will have the opportunity—very tantalizing because of the risk of dropout—to observe the unfolding of the patient's DIPs and PICs, a process that favors an understanding of his or her interpersonal difficulties (Safran and Muran 2000). In light of this new knowledge, the therapist will be able to modify and refine the case formulation, a change that will allow in vivo intervention on the patient's DIPs and PICs in order to start an alliance repair phase and restore satisfactory interpersonal tuning.

Assessing the Type of Rupture

In the subsequent phase of disengagement from the patient's PICs, the therapist should refrain from making reckless interventions, reserving the possibility to do so after achieving full awareness of his or her mental states and of the active IMSs in the relationship. This awareness is necessary in order to choose and plan the most effective strategies.

In the disengagement phase, analysis of IMSs in the relationship is used to ascertain the reasons for the distrust of the patient toward the therapist, to understand the expectations underlying the patient's provocative attitude, and to assess the type of rupture (Monticelli 2017a; Monticelli and Liotti in press; Farina et al. 2019). This analysis adds additional information to the distinction proposed by Safran and Muran (2000) between contrasting ruptures and withdrawal ruptures.

To assess the different types of rupture, the therapist has to understand whether the patient is ill-disposed and resentful because he or she feels (a) be forced to apply techniques that in the patient's opinion are ineffective (this attitude activates an anger regulated by the antagonism system); (b) neglected and poorly accepted (this attitude activates a protest regulated by the attachment system); (c) sentimentally rejected (this attitude activates a feeling of rejection regulated by the sexual system); or (d) poorly supported in terms of collaboration, if the patient feels that he or she is not respecting the therapeutic contract (this attitude is activated by the cooperation system). Understanding the patient's active IMSs allows the therapist to distinguish the different types of ruptures in progress (i.e., antagonism, attachment, sexual, or cooperative) and to start a process to improve interpersonal tuning, attempting to activate the cooperation system and to correct the patient's DIPs and PICs.

Interpersonal tuning on a cooperative framework is of fundamental importance to maintain optimal metacognitive functioning (Fonagy and Target 2009; Liotti and Gilbert 2011; Monticelli et al. 2018). In fact, our research conducted on 70 sessions has shown a significant correlation between patient cooperation and metacognitive functioning (Semerari et al. 2003) and a significant inverse correlation between the latter and the activation of the attachment system (Farina et al. in progress).

Given that (a) metacognitive improvement represents a significant psychotherapeutic goal and a shared tool to reach the goal; (b) the therapeutic alliance involves sharing goals—and the tools to reach them—and by a bond based on trust (Bordin 1979), it is plausible that the loss of the patient's cooperation—which involves the decrease of the metacognitive functioning—also indicates a reduction in the therapeutic alliance. This is a significant aspect because weak alliances are correlated with the patient's dropout (Samstag et al. 1998, 2008) and probably also with a worsened quality of psychotherapy.

For example, if a therapist just supports the patient without attempting to establish a dialogue accompanied by cooperative goals (e.g., without trying to explore with the patient his or her problematic experiences in order to give him or her an emotional meaning), in the long run there may be a considerable risk of an impasse in the alliance related to a clear reduction in metacognitive functions (Farina et al. 2019; Fonagy and Target 2009; Liotti and Gilbert 2011; Monticelli et al. 2018).

Formulation of the Intervention and Monitoring Effects

In an ETM approach, the therapist's intervention corresponds to the last act of a sequence of operations necessary to formulate an appropriate clinical intervention in full harmony with the active IMSs in the patient. It is plausible that each intervention makes sense if it is both preceded and followed by monitoring the motivational condition of the therapeutic dyad, in order to evaluate the appropriateness and the outcome of the intervention itself respectively (Monticelli 2017b).

Only after having tuned in to the motivational system of the patient will the therapist be able to start a process aimed at repairing the alliance and to formulate interventions based on in vivo recognition and the change of interpersonal patterns. Safran and Muran (2000) and Kiesler (1988) favor a repairing process based on metacommunicative interventions that aims to make explicit the implicit communication of the patient during the rupture phase. Among the metaco-communicative interventions, self-involving interventions are particularly valuable, effective, and appreciated by patients (Hill et al. 1989; McCarthy and Betz 1978). Henretty and Levitt (2010) have reviewed this topic in detail. A self-involving intervention comprises a deliberate intervention aimed at encouraging a joint reflection on the patient's mental states that emerge during the session; to this end, the therapist shares with the patient his or her emotional states or some considerations regarding his or her representations or behaviors that emerged during a specific and concrete episode during the session. Self-involving intervention is very effective, but it is only one of the many available tactics in an ETM approach; for example, if direct modalities are unwelcome or too intimate or ineffective, the therapist can approach the patient through indirect modalities. These modalities focus the attention on the same dynamics that emerged during the ruptures but in contexts outside the therapy, a factor that frees the therapist from a direct and personal involvement.

The Implicit Goals of the Patient

The editors also state that in Liotti's relational model, and in Safran and Muran's (2000) procedure for the management of ruptures and repairs, the therapist's main task is to overcome the patient's relational traps and not be conditioned by the patient's more or less conscious attempt to break the relationship. In this way, the editors depict a therapist who is substantially relieved of any responsibility in the current relationship, because it is the patient who resists more or less consciously and tries to oppose the path of knowledge, growth, and change. From this rappresentation emerges a theme of fundamental importance relative to the patient's presumed implicit goals that, from this perspective, would painstakingly begin a therapeutic path only in order to sabotage it in a more or less conscious way.

This description, in my opinion, is limited and limiting. Limited because it focuses only on the patient's inner world; if the therapist excludes the hypothesis that the therapeutic relationship emerges from the interaction between patient and therapist, he or she will exclude a priori any possible involvement in the ongoing dynamic. For example, it often happens that the therapist makes mistakes, but, in a "one-mind" logic, the patient cannot show disagreement without risking being perceived as sabotaging and resistant to the path of growth, confirming his or her, often present, pathogenic beliefs of inadequacy. Limiting because this stigmatization can easily lead to a reduction of expectations and commitment in the mind of the therapist, who may feel himself or herself not responsible for the patient's preconceived resistance that would cause the rupture.

However, this "one-mind" perspective has been overcome, because the idea of a relational dimension has become increasingly significant in order to understand individual functioning. Since the 1970s, there has been an increasing convergence on this concept of a relational dimension where the patient and the therapist build the reality together, influencing each other in a process of dialectical integration (Liotti and Monticelli 2014). The relational turning point in the psychoanalytic field (Lingiardi et al. 2011) has, in fact, enabled a different way to interpret the therapeutic relationship and to conceive empirical research on the therapeutic process as a nuclear element to identify the elements that effectively contribute to the success or failure of psychotherapy (Smith and Glass 1977). It is due to the relational turning point of those years that the principles of research on the therapeutic alliance have been created. This phenomenon has proven to be very fruitful due to the considerable clinical implications that have originated.

Moreover, we often observe that, after several dropouts, many patients are finally able to benefit from psychotherapy (Monticelli et al. 2018). If we do not want to merely explain this data as a spontaneous evolution of the disorder—which generally occurs with the adult age of the patient—it is plausible that the final success is also attributable to other factors. One of these factors could be played by a therapeutic relationship that, unlike the previous ones, can find and maintain a good interpersonal tuning fundamental for good therapeutic efficacy. Therefore, it is plausible that the patient does not want, more or less consciously, to break the therapeutic relationship but, rather, he or she also uses the same DIPs and PICs with the therapist that compromise interpersonal relationships. The possibility of continuously monitoring the therapeutic relationship allows the therapist to identify the patient's mental states and to tune in to his or her expectations. This endeavor favors an improvement in metacognitive functions.

References

Bordin, E. S. (1979). The generalizability of the psychoanalytic concept of the working alliance. *Psychotherapy: Theory, Research & Practice, 16*, 252–260.

Farina, B., Onofri, A., Monticelli, F., Cotugno, A., Talia, A., & Liotti, M. (2019). Giovanni Liotti (1945–2018): the Pied Noir of research in attachment and psychotherapy. *Attachment & Human Development, 22*, 582–591. https://doi.org/10.1080/14616734.2019.1640258. Retrieved online: 15 Jul 2019.

Farina, B., Monticelli, F., Tombolini, L., Mallozzi, P., Gasparini, E., Russo, M., Simoncini Malucelli, G., & Imperatori, C. (in progress). Effects of attachment and cooperation on metacognition during psychotherapeutic sessions. Manuscript in progress

Fonagy, P., & Target, M. (2009). Attachment, trauma and psychoanalysis. In E. L. Jurist, A. Slade, & S. Bergner (Eds.), *Mind to mind: Infant research, neuroscience and psychoanalysis* (pp. 15–49). New York, NY: Other Press.

Gilbert, P. (1989). *Human nature and suffering*. London: LEA.

Hatfield, E., Cacioppo, J. T., & Rapson, R. L. (1994). *Emotional contagion*. Cambridge: Cambridge University Press.

Henretty, J. R., & Levitt, H. M. (2010). The role of therapist self-disclosure in psychotherapy: A qualitative review. *Clinical Psychology Review, 30*, 63–77.

Hill, C. E., Mahalik, J., & Thompson, B. (1989). Therapist self-disclosure. *Psychotherapy: Theory, Research, Practice, Training, 26*, 290–295.

Kiesler, D. J. (1988). *Therapeutic metacommunication: Therapist impact disclosure as feedback in psychotherapy*. Palo Alto, CA: Consulting Psychologists Press.

Lambert, M. J., & Kenichi, S. (2011). Collecting client feedback. *Psychotherapy, 48*, 72–79.

Lingiardi, V., Amadei, G., Caviglia, G., & De Bei, F. (2011). *La svolta relazionale [The relational turning point]*. Milano: Cortina.

Liotti, G. (1994). *La dimensione interpersonale della coscienza [The interpersonal dimension of consciousness]*. Roma: Carocci.

Liotti, G. (2005). *La dimensione interpersonale della coscienza, seconda edizione [The interpersonal dimension of consciousness]* (2nd ed.). Roma: Carocci.

Liotti, G., & Gilbert, P. (2011). Mentalizing, motivation, and social mentalities: Theoretical considerations and implications for psychotherapy. *Psychology and Psychotherapy: Theory, Research and Practice, 84*, 9–25.

Liotti, G., & Monticelli, F. (Eds.). (2008). *I sistemi motivazionali nel dialogo clinico. il manuale AIMIT [Motivational systems in the clinical dialogue. the AIMIT manual]*. Milano: Raffaello Cortina Editore.

Liotti, G., & Monticelli, F. (2014). *Teoria e Clinica dell'Alleanza Terapeutica. Una prospettiva cognitivo-evoluzionista [Therapeutic alliance theory and clinic. A cognitive-evolutionist perspective]*. Milano: Raffaello Cortina Editore.

Liotti, G., Fassone, G., & Monticelli, F. (Eds.). (2017). *L'evoluzione delle emozioni e dei sistemi motivazionali: Teoria, ricerca, clinica [The evolution of emotions and motivational systems: Theory, research, clinic]*. Milano: Raffaello Cortina Editore.

Mccarthy, P. R., & Betz, N. E. (1978). Differential effects of self-disclosing versus self-involving counselor statements. *Journal of Counseling Psychology, 25*, 251–256.

Monticelli, F. (2017a). L'alleanza terapeutica e la teoria evoluzionistica della motivazione [The therapeutic alliance and the evolutionary theory of motivation]. In G. Liotti, G. Fassone, & F. Monticelli (Eds.), *L'evoluzione delle emozioni e dei sistemi motivazionali: Teoria, ricerca, clinica [The evolution of emotions and motivational systems: Theory, research, clinic]* (pp. 179–198). Milano: Raffaello Cortina Editore.

Monticelli, F. (2017b). Rottura e riparazione dell'alleanza terapeutica: esempi clinici nella prospettiva della TEM [Rupture and repair in the therapeutic alliance: Clinical examples from the perspective of ETM]. In G. Liotti, G. Fassone, & F. Monticelli (Eds.), *L'evoluzione delle emozioni e dei sistemi motivazionali: Teoria, ricerca, clinica [The evolution of emotions and motivational systems: Theory, research, clinic]* (pp. 199–220). Milano: Raffaello Cortina Editore.

Monticelli, F., & Liotti, M. (in press). Motivational monitoring: How to identify ruptures and impasses and enhance interpersonal attunement. Journal of Contemporary Psychotherapy. In press.

Monticelli, F., Imperatori, C. A., Pedone, R., & Farina, B. (2018). Cooperation in psychotherapy increases metacognitive abilities: A single-case study. *Rivista di Psichiatria, 53*, 336–340.

Norcross, J. C., & Wampold, B. E. (2011). Evidence-based therapy relationships: Research conclusions and clinical practices. *Psychotherapy, 48*, 98–102.

Safran, J. D., & Muran, J. C. (2000). *Negotiating the therapeutic alliance: A relational treatment guide*. New York, NY: Guilford.

Samstag, L. W., Batchelder, S., Muran, J. C., Safran, J. D., & Winston, A. (1998). Early identification of treatment failures in short-term psychotherapy: An assessment of therapeutic alliance and interpersonal behavior. *Journal of Psychotherapy Practice and Research, 7*, 126–143.

Samstag, L. W., Muran, J. C., Wachtel, P. L., Slade, A., Safran, J. D., & Winston, A. (2008). Evaluating negative process: A comparison of working alliance, interpersonal behaviour, and narrative coherency among three psychotherapy outcome conditions. *American Journal of Psychotherapy, 62*, 165–194.

Semerari, A., Carcione, A., Dimaggio, G., Falcone, M., Nicolò, G., Procacci, M., & Alleva, G. (2003). How to evaluate metacognitive functioning in psychotherapy? The metacognition assessment scale and its applications. *Clinical Psychology & Psychotherapy, 10*, 238–261. https://doi.org/10.1002/cpp.362.

Smith, M. L., & Glass, G. V. (1977). Meta-analysis of psychotherapy outcome studies. *American Psychologist, 32*, 752–760.

Emotion, Motivation, Therapeutic Relationship and Cognition in Giovanni Liotti's Model: Commentary on Chapter "Strengths and Limitations of Case Formulation in Constructivist Cognitive Behavioral Therapies"

Raffaella Visini and Saverio Ruberti

Contents

The Relational Dimension and the Emotional Change

Chapter "Strengths and Limitations of Case Formulation in Constructivist Cognitive Behavioral Therapies" of this book on which we are commenting is so dense on the historical and conceptual levels, as well as with respect to the part dedicated to Giovanni Liotti's cognitive evolutionary model, that many points deserve reflection and the possibility of in-depth comparison. For understandable reasons of room, we dwell only on some of them.

Liotti's contribution participated in the constructivist development of cognitivism, and it highlights the importance of the therapeutic relationship in his own psychotherapeutic model. His interest in the relational dimension arose in the early 1980s from the encounter between his clinical and theoretical perspectives, then elaborated and formulated in collaboration with Vittorio Guidano, and John Bowlby's attachment theory (Guidano and Liotti 1983). The meeting was made possible by the rigorous scientific framework shared by the two perspectives, which enhanced basic research and empirical validation of clinical hypotheses. Liotti was constantly faithful to that framework, and on this basis, he revised the way that cognitive clinical theory had seen the relationship between cognition and emotion

R. Visini · S. Ruberti (✉)
Società italiana di Terapia Comportamentale e Cognitiva (SITCC), Rome, Italy

G. M. Ruggiero et al. (eds.), *CBT Case Formulation as Therapeutic Process*,
https://doi.org/10.1007/978-3-030-63587-9_21

until then, going so far as to argue that strictly cognitive processes (such as thoughts and beliefs) can play a role in the regulation of emotions, but they are not the first and only ones responsible for their genesis. Following this path, he questioned the hypothesis that a cognitive change (such as the modification of certain beliefs) is sufficient to produce an emotional change and to determine a therapeutic process. The complexity of the therapeutic process for Liotti could not be limited to operations in which patient and therapist interact exclusively on a cognitive, explicit and declarative level.

Therefore, Liotti promoted an intersubjective perspective in cognitive psychotherapy which, through attention to the dynamics of the therapeutic relationship in its emotional components also, would include an intervention in the affective and tacit aspects of the patients' interpersonal style, of their representation of themselves with others and of his expectations, and observation of these elements while they manifest themselves during the therapeutic relationship with the therapist. His work examined patients' emotional experience in therapy, generated mainly by how they felt welcomed, listened to and treated with regard to their problems, thoughts and moods. Of course, the therapist's ability to offer this relational context cannot be reduced to a vague willingness to listen, nor to the assumption of a caring attitude that would risk being childish and passive towards the patient. Instead, it requires the acquisition—during training and clinical work—of professional knowledge and skills related to the ability to carry out technical interventions with an adequate level of empathy and mentalization (Liotti and Monticelli 2014).

From this point of view, although the shared formulation of the case can be extremely useful for the construction of an agreement between therapist and patient on the goals and methods of treatment, its transformative power is not so much in the patient's adherence to the explanation that the therapist gives him or her—more or less directly—regarding the principles of the therapy and the reasons for his or her suffering. It would be even less transformative if the therapist invited the patient to recognize certain concerns and beliefs as being at the root of his or her problems by defining them as biases or cognitive errors, which, among other things, would risk triggering abstract discussions on values or encouraging the patient to represent himself or herself as a "bad" person. From an intersubjective perspective, the shared formulation of the case is a useful intervention starting from the fact that it brings the patients to talk about themselves and their suffering in a framework of acceptance, security and relational consonance.

Actually, the act of telling about his or her disorders makes the patient meet with the difficulty of showing himself or herself to the other as a person in difficulty, manifesting one's insecurities. Let's think of how embarrassed the patient may feel when talking about his or her own symptoms, how afraid he or she is of being judged, how much effort it takes to trust the therapist, how many doubts he or she has about the real usefulness of the therapy, how difficult it is to communicate all these experiences to the therapist, and so on. In this way the experience of communicating in therapy involves coming into direct contact with one's own insecurities and problematic relational patterns just when they emerge in the collaboration with the therapist, and it also allows one to verify the effect they have on each other.

Through the sharing of one's own worries and emotional difficulties, favored by an adequate therapeutic strategy, the patient can start not only focusing on his or her own intersubjective experience, but also on accepting, integrating and managing emotional difficulties as part of a person.

The shared formulation of the case, however, represents a refined kind of clinical work on symptomatology. Liotti did not neglect the intervention on symptoms. On the contrary, he suggested that psychotherapy should begin right from the first interview by exploring the symptoms, and he appreciated the use of effective techniques in order to reduce them when they were included in a more comprehensive strategy. However, he considered the work on symptomatology as one of the aspects of therapy, whose importance is largely created by allowing access to the patient's cognitive and affective internal world, and not the decisive and resolutive passage of the therapeutic process, as the editors of this book so define it.

Giovanni Liotti and His Evolutionary Constructivism

Chapter "Strengths and Limitations of Case Formulation in Constructivist Cognitive Behavioral Therapies" also mentions the large distance that arose between the positions of Giovanni Liotti and Vittorio Guidano after their period of collaboration, dwelling above all on the radical constructivist stance adopted by Guidano. In this regard, it is profitable to explore the way in which Liotti considered the constructivist orientation: This aspect is part of the epistemological foundations of his thought. Liotti loved to define his position as *naive* constructivism, emphasizing in this expression the mental, subjective and personal process by which each of us gives meaning to our own experience (Liotti 2001). However, he also aimed to include universal constraints, including evolutionary biological constraints, which cannot be ignored in the understanding of emotional experiences and human relational behavior. In this framework, Liotti has based much of his elaboration on the construct of the interpersonal motivational system (IMS), using it as a privileged tool for the identification and exploration of universal rules based on innate and phylogenetically grounded principles which guide and orient intersubjective dynamics (Liotti et al. 2017). In chapter "Strengths and Limitations of Case Formulation in Constructivist Cognitive Behavioral Therapies" explicit reference is made to the IMSs and their value in the therapeutic relationship.

Given the importance of IMSs to the cognitive evolutionary perspective, some clarification of their role may be useful. In Liotti's model, no IMS is in itself more functional or better than the other IMSs in general terms (or more "healthy" as is repeated several times in chapter "Strengths and Limitations of Case Formulation in Constructivist Cognitive Behavioral Therapies"): the usefulness and adequacy of each IMS depends on the relational context in which it is activated, and is related to its suitability in achieving the interpersonal goal of that specific interaction in progress. For example, when a person aims to obtain protection and care, the activation of the IMS of attachment is more advantageous, while when a person aims to assert himself or herself in a confrontation, the activation of the agonistic IMS is appropriate. In the context of the therapeutic relationship, the goal of activating as much as possible the cooperative IMS is not so much linked to a presumed superiority of this IMS in absolute terms. On the contrary, it is due to the fact that the cooperative dimension, with the particular type of security that accompanies it, is the one that favors in the patient the best metacognitive and self-reflective functioning, promoting in him or her precisely that type of exploration and self-knowledge that constitutes the essence of the cognitivist therapeutic process.

The emphasis on motivational aspects and cooperation in the therapeutic process and the centrality of the work on the patient's interpersonal operational models are elements that distinguish Liotti's position from other approaches which also underline the importance of the therapeutic relationship, such as that of Safran and Muran (2000), widely cited in the pages on which we are commenting. In chapter "Strengths and Limitations of Case Formulation in Constructivist Cognitive Behavioral Therapies", the two clinical perspectives are correctly compared by virtue of their strong reciprocal compatibility that Liotti himself has often recognized and emphasized. The cognitive evolutionary orientation, in fact, attributes a high importance to the intervention of understanding and repairing ruptures and therapeutic impasses as suggested by Safran and Muran, considering it to be of great utility in fostering cooperative interaction and accessing an exploration of the patient's internal operative model.

However, in the cognitive evolutionary approach, this type of intervention is considered neither the only nor the main tool in the construction of an effective therapeutic process, while chapter "Strengths and Limitations of Case Formulation in Constructivist Cognitive Behavioral Therapies" states that in Liotti's clinical perspective the real key event of the therapeutic process is the relational crisis of rupture and repair. It is simplistic to consider the two approaches to the point of overlapping them in a way that makes them difficult to distinguish from each other. In the cognitive evolutionary paradigm, the cognitive specificity is never lost, constituted by the importance of the work on representations, expectations, memory processes and integrative processes of consciousness (Liotti 1994). The scientific and clinical richness of this elaboration has allowed Liotti to explore the possibilities of treatment even for the most severe psychopathological frameworks, such as personality and dissociative disorders, and for theorizing and formalizing some principles of intervention for these conditions.

Therapeutic Strategies in the Cognitive Evolutionary Model

Of course, from a cognitive evolutionary viewpoint, therapeutic strategies are specific to the types of psychopathological disorders, their severity and the characteristics of the patients. For example, when a good level of consciousness integration and metacognitive skills are present, even though it is still necessary to pay attention to the quality of the relationship and of the therapeutic alliance, the intervention can give room to the treatment of the patient's beliefs and personal meanings. On the other hand, in cases where significant dissociative disorders and problems related to integrative abilities are present, which are usually marked by severe relational difficulties and a high level of distrust on the part of the patient in both the therapy and the therapist, the work on the relationship and the maintenance of the therapeutic alliance is the mainstay of the entire therapeutic process. In the treatment of complex patients, among other things, it is often necessary to tailor the intervention, which is not always compatible with standardized processes. In these cases, Liotti preferred to explore and discuss the principles that govern the intervention by referring to flexible guidelines rather than to rigid protocols (Liotti and Monticelli 2014).

All these aspects must be taken into account in order to understand what role the shared formulation of the case may have in the cognitive evolutionary perspective. In chapter "Strengths and Limitations of Case Formulation in Constructivist Cognitive Behavioral Therapies", the shared formulation of the case is given such a strong, absolute and general value that this operation, as it is described, cannot be easily integrated with the complexity and the different technical consequences of Liotti's model. The intervention is in fact defined as the "main operative tool" with which the therapist manages the psychotherapeutic process and as an "incessantly shared procedure" between patient and therapist, from the beginning to the end of the treatment, without any particular specification on the disorders and the phases of therapy in which it is advisable, distinguishing them from those in which it is presumably ineffective or even inadvisable.

In conclusion, we can agree with the opinion of the editors of the book when they state that, in the cognitive evolutionary orientation, the shared formulation of the case does not in itself constitute the main instrument of therapeutic intervention and the therapeutic relationship. Rather, in this model it can be considered one of the effective interventions to be used with clinical intelligence with those patients and in those moments of therapy in which this strategy appears appropriate.

References

Guidano, V. F., & Liotti, G. (1983). *Cognitive processes and emotional disorders: A structural approach to psychotherapy*. New York, NY: Guilford.

Liotti, G. (1994). *La dimensione interpersonale della coscienza [The interpersonal dimension of consciousness]*. Roma: Carocci.

Liotti, G. (2001). *Le opere della coscienza [The works of consciousness]*. Milano: Cortina.

Liotti, G., & Monticelli, F. (2014). *Teoria e Clinica dell'Alleanza Terapeutica—Una prospettiva cognitivo-evoluzionista [Therapeutic alliance theory and clinic—a cognitive-evolutionary perspective]*. Milano: Cortina.

Liotti, G., Fassone, G., & Monticelli, F. (2017). *L'evoluzione delle emozioni e dei sistemi motivazionali [The evolution of emotions and of interpersonal motivational systems]*. Milano: Cortina.

Safran, J. D., & Muran, J. C. (2000). *Negotiating the therapeutic Alliance: A relational treatment guide*. New York, NY: Guilford.

Case Formulation as an Outcome and Not an Opening Move in Relational and Psychodynamic Models

Giovanni Maria Ruggiero, Gabriele Caselli, and Sandra Sassaroli

Contents

G. M. Ruggiero (✉)
"Psicoterapia Cognitiva e Ricerca," Cognitive Psychotherapy School and Research Center, Milan, Italy

Sigmund Freud University, Milan, Italy

Sigmund Freud University, Vienna, Austria
e-mail: gm.ruggiero@milano-sfu.it

G. Caselli
Sigmund Freud University, Wien, Austria

Department of Psychology, London South Bank University, London, UK

S. Sassaroli
Sigmund Freud University, Wien, Austria

Sigmund Freud University, Vienna, Austria

"Studi Cognitivi", Cognitive Psychotherapy School and Research Center, Milan, Italy

G. M. Ruggiero et al. (eds.), *CBT Case Formulation as Therapeutic Process*,
https://doi.org/10.1007/978-3-030-63587-9_22

Case Formulation in Psychodynamic Models

So far, we have dealt with case formulation in cognitive behavioral therapy (CBT) approaches. In this chapter, we consider models related to the psychodynamic model, i.e. the control mastery theory (CMT) model (Weiss et al. 1986; Silberschatz 2005) and the ruptures and repairs model of Safran and Muran (2000). Before examining these models, we will present several reflections on the relationship between psychodynamic paradigm and case formulation and then some considerations on how the development of case formulation is revealed in Eells (2007, 2009, 2011, 2015), a scholar who has exhaustively treated the development of case formulation in many psychotherapeutic orientations.

In psychodynamic models, there is obviously case formulation. From our viewpoint, is that in psychodynamic models it is not shared with the patient in the same way and at the same time as in CBT approaches, particularly in standard cognitive therapy (CT). In CBT approaches, case formulation assumes that the alliance is always possible and is stipulated on the grounds of its practical and operational aspects. Psychological resistances may be present, but in CBT approaches they are not considered to be a key concept for understanding the emotional problems of the patient and formulating the case. Instead, in other paradigms, particularly in some forms of psychodynamic therapy, it is assumed that the patient tends to be resistant to cooperate and sometimes sabotages the therapy (Gazzillo 2012). Further, the very therapeutic work comprises the analysis and relational management of these resistances, which are internal and manifest themselves mainly in the therapeutic relationship.

From the tenets of the psychodynamic paradigm (Luborsky et al. 2008), we can plausibly derive that patients, because of their resistances, defences, and intrapsychic and relational conflicts, are unable to share the case conceptualization from the beginning. Its initial explicit formulation is more of a trigger that starts the therapeutic process rather than a reliable result on which the process is grounded. In addition, we could say that in the psychodynamic paradigm the precise therapeutic process involves accompanying the patient as he or she discovers these resistances and—by overcoming and understanding them—only at the end of the process and therapy can the case formulation really be shared with the therapist. Therefore, case formulation comprises the shared formulation of resistances.

It is a conception of mental and human life that basic mental states are assumed to be governed by motivational drives, either sexual—as in the case of classical Freudian psychoanalysis (Strachey 1953–1974)—or aggressive—as in the case of Kleinian models (Klein 2017)—up until Lichtenberg et al. (2011) further developed the model into a theory that includes five *motivational systems. According to these models*, emotional states are believed to be dominated by unconscious desires, anger and other motivational signals that are not easily confessed to the therapist.

This hypothesis is partially applicable, albeit with a number of limitations, to modern psychodynamic models such as the transference focused therapy (TFP) model of Otto Kernberg (Clarkin et al. 1999), the aforementioned CMT (Weiss et al. 1986; Silberschatz 2005) or integrated models such as the ruptures and repairs model (Safran and Muran 2000), which includes a case formulation procedure that is clearly present but—from our viewpoint—not fully shared with the patient from the beginning. On the contrary, these models assume that the formulation is shared only after the client has unconsciously tested the therapist in the therapeutic interaction and revived in the actual relationship with the therapist previous painful interpersonal experiences.

For example, in CMT if the therapist passes the test without falling into the relationship trap and disconfirms the negative expectations of the patient, then he or she allows the patient to acquire new experiences and emotional knowledge that will help to disconfirm the pathogenic beliefs (Gazzillo 2016; Silberschatz 2005). Similar considerations can be made for the ruptures and repairs model (Safran and Muran 2000). In this model, case formulation is not a work explicitly shared from the beginning of the treatment as an opening move of the therapeutic process. Rather, it emerges explicitly only from the shared analysis of the repaired ruptures in the sessions.

Classic Psychodynamic Models

Eells (2007, 2009, 2011, 2015) composed a comprehensive case formulation manual that also includes a historical section. This historical part is instructive but not exhaustive because it has a partial shortcoming: It tells the historical development of case formulation in psychotherapy from an unbalanced point of view that does not provide sufficient credit to the contribution of CBT approaches. It is true that in Eells' book there are sections devoted to the CBT contribution. However, Eells aims to outline an atheoretical story of case formulation that differs from the behavioral tradition of case formulation that Meyer and Turkat began and that influenced traditional CBT.

Eells' version of the case formulation history is particularly useful to understand how it developed outside the behavioral and CBT traditions. It investigates the need in modern psychodynamic practice to place more emphasis upon the sharing of case formulation and to counter the traditional psychodynamic tendency of therapists to infer psychological structures that were only remotely related to observable clinical phenomena. In the psychodynamic tradition, the first models of case formulation were, among others, the Core Conflictual Relationship Theme (CCRT; Luborsky et al. 1994; Luborsky 1997), the Configurational Analysis (Horowitz and Eells 2007) and the Plan Formulation Method (Curtis and Silberschatz 2007). Many of these methods share common characteristics: They identify problems; they infer maladaptive relationships and patterns of self, others and the world; and they are grounded primarily on clinical observations. Furthermore, they imply a relatively low level of inference, arrange the formulation task into operational sequences and reveal a tendency towards psychotherapy integration.

These models do not aim to explore the absolute unconscious of the classical Freudian psychodynamic tradition. For example, the CCRT aims to identify a patient's core problematic relational pattern by focusing on the conscious narratives that the patient discusses in therapy and assessing three key components within these narratives: a wish to be gained, the expected responses of others and the responses of the patients themselves. The method is based on Freud's concept of transference, which argues that innate characteristics and early interpersonal experiences predispose a person to lead close relationships in particular repetitive ways learned from significant relationships. A common CCRT configuration may be that a person wants to be close and accepting, expects rejection from others and then becomes depressed or angry.

As Eells (2011) writes, both the classical psychodynamic tradition and these modern psychodynamic models greatly influenced the development of the psychotherapy case formulation process because they proposed sophisticated models of the psychopathology of personality that encouraged emphasizing the study of case formulation. The psychoanalytical concepts that have most contributed to case formulation development are the notion of the dynamic motivation (considered unconscious in the classical model); the psychological, emotional and symbolic meaning of symptoms; the formation of symptoms as a semi-dysfunctional compromise formation; defense mechanisms as advocates of psychic balance; and the psychodynamic Freudian tripartite structural model of the mind. These concepts have also influenced other psychotherapy paradigms, including CBT.

These contributions are significant and yet differ from the main feature of case formulation in CBT terms, i.e. sharing the case in informed terms from the very beginning of the therapeutic process. Notably, case formulation is not shared in classical psychoanalysis. As we have already discussed, sharing throughout both psychoanalysis and modern psychodynamic models is a process that develops during the procedure and represents an outcome only at the end of the process. This hypothesis emerges from what Eells himself writes, namely that both psychoanalysis and modern psychodynamic models assume that patients can often recognize their psychological problems, and in particular their interpersonal problems, into action only when putting them into action in the therapeutic relationship.

On the other hand, it is also false that in CBT case formulation is built once only at the beginning of the process. Further, case formulation in CBT is a work in progress. However, in CBT the procedure, the provisional state and above all the rationale of the case formulation assessment is unceasingly and explicitly shared, in the sense that the therapist always formulates an explicit hypothesis of the functioning of the patients for which feedback from the patient is steadily required. Without an explicit confirmation, the formulation is rejected, and the patient's rejection of the hypothesis confirmation is not—at least tendentially—considered a resistance that could be part of the case formulation itself. The psychodynamic idea that resistance opens up the assessment itself is in turn a good idea that is part of the contribution of psychoanalytic tradition and its particular view of emotional disorders but—from a CBT viewpoint—is not without risks. Specifically, it is vulnerable to the risk of generating hypotheses with a high level of inference and can allow the therapist to apply incongruous formulations to the patient; a significant example was Freud's case of Dora (Lakoff 1990).

In addition, the radical definition of psychodynamic unconscious, particularly in early psychoanalytic models, would tend to suggest that any claim to develop an initial consciously shared formulation during the initial steps of the therapeutic process is misleading. On the contrary, in the psychodynamic paradigm, it is expected that during the initial steps of the therapeutic process the patient tends to unconsciously and instinctively express his or her dysfunctional, sexual or aggressive patterns. Besides, if conscious activities in the psychodynamic paradigm are considered to be defensive formations, it would derive that any conscious formulation shared with the patient is, at least in its first appearances in sessions, deceptive and could even lead one to think that the content of the formulation must focus not on this defensive process behind the surfaced and only apparently shared cognitive content. It is a further confirmation of the aforementioned hypothesis that in psychodynamic models a case formulation procedure that is clearly present but—from our viewpoint—not fully shared with the patient from the beginning.

Things did not change when Freud was succeeded by the model of Melanie Klein or, to quote a more recent model formulated in operational and replicable terms, by the TFP model of Otto Kernberg (Clarkin et al. 1999). In those cases, sexual drives are replaced by aggressive ones—if possible even more unconscious and unconfessable. This conception assumes that mental states are regulated by competitive and overwhelming representations. TFP regards the conflictual mind as being dominated by drive states of anger, envy, hatred and rivalry; these mental representations are split and disintegrated—or rather extremely dichotomous and contradictory—between poles of extreme positivity and idealization and at the same time or immediately following extreme negativity and devaluation. In more cognitive terms, in this model people would perceive themselves and others as continually swinging between the extremes of goodness and evil, of absolute and symbiotic closeness, and contemptuous and neglectful estrangement that results in either emotional negligence or aggressivity and active violence. In comparison to CBT approaches, there are technical, theoretical, and even cultural differences that lead to intrinsically distinct case conceptualizations.

In TFP, the therapeutic relationship is the key for everything but not—at least initially—a cooperative alliance. Rather, it embodies the opposite form: At the beginning, the patient by definition would sabotage the relationship according to its split and aggressive nature. The treatment would strictly involve the therapist's explicit interpretation of episodes of conflictual tension in sessions as an example of the patient's angry states, which would then be the grounds of the symptoms. Instead of a vaguely welcoming alliance, TFP negotiates a contract which implies that the therapeutic process comprises encouraging the patient to recognize his or her pulsional condition of conflict and anti-alliance with the world as a whole, including the therapist. This initially unconscious condition is made conscious by TFP through the unceasing negotiation and reiteration of a therapeutic contract. This modality implies that the major required task is for the patient to accept the explicit and verbal interpretations of the conflicting interactions which happen during sessions. These are classic transference interpretations (Gazzillo 2012).

In psychoanalysis, however, it is also possible to follow an opposing path that is closer to the CBT conception. It is the conception derived from both the neo-Freudian ego psychology model developed by Anna Freud (1936) and Hartmann (1964); Hartmann et al. (1946)—which favored conscious ego functions at the expense of the unconscious ego and id—and the interpersonal tradition dating back to Alfred Adler (1964) and arriving at Karen Horney (1950) and Harry Stack Sullivan (1947). This concept emphasizes the importance of understanding and treating patients' conscious experiences. It is the same environment in which Beck was later trained, and not coincidentally.

This model attributed a growing importance and autonomy to the ego functions and, therefore, in cognitive terms to the functions that will be called the executive attention (Wells and Mathews 1994). These models assumed the existence of a conflict-free sphere of the ego, i.e. that there are executive functions of the consciousness that act according to non-conflictual purposes. There is still a difference with CBT, which assumes that even emotional suffering can develop in the absence of conflict, but this is a convergence between psychoanalysis and CBT.

The Psychoanalytic Relational Model

The relational psychoanalytic model has separated itself from the pulsional and conflictual model and, similar to what we have seen for the constructive model in the CBT paradigm, it assumes that emotional disorders depend on the impaired development of psychological functioning that in turn depends on unmet relational human needs. These needs were unmet in a traumatic and cumulative way. In developmental terms, the Oedipal conflict between fathers and children of classical psychoanalysis has been replaced by a more romantic and quieter scenario, the so-called attachment relationship between parents and children. Here, the lack of love and care (especially maternal) takes the place of the Oedipal conflict. Winnicot (1965) provided clinical terms and Bowlby (1969, 1973, 1980) experimental terms. With these efforts, clinicians began to consider that the development of the psyche and its deviations would sprout not from a clash between Oedipus and Laius, but from safe and stable care, ensured above all by the mother.

From this theoretical and clinical terrain, Stephen Mitchell (Mitchell and Aron 1999) proposed a new psychotherapeutic model, i.e. relational psychoanalysis. It was no longer a question of reproducing and interpreting the sexual and conflictual Oedipal triangulations during sessions, but rather of living a less tragic, kinder and more courteous relationship between patient and therapist. This cultural change is profound. The tragic Freudian Torah had been replaced by the loving Gospels of Winnicot and John Bowlby, and a gentle Marian cult took over the archaic tragedies. The absolute Freudian unconscious vanished, to be replaced by a hazy state of all-encompassing semi-consciousness and semi-unconsciousness in which what is unresolved can be understood and mentalized and defined as a dream or *reverie* by Wilfred Bion (1962, 1967, 1970), the theorist who came closest to defining a description of the Freudian unconscious that is compatible with the CBT approach.

In Mitchell's relational model, the focus of analytical therapy becomes the construction of a meaningful new interpersonal experience that allows the patient to assimilate new relational models. Mitchell criticizes the analytical "neutrality", which implies the naive hypothesis that it is possible to avoid the influence of the analyst's countertransferential affections, facilitating an "objective" knowledge in the patient. Moreover, the call for a neutral attitude risks inducing the analyst to use an inauthentic mode of behavior. Mitchell suggests replacing the concept of neutrality with that of self-reflexive responsiveness, which is vital for case management and corresponds to immersing oneself in a constant process of understanding the patient's and one's own responses. On the clinical level, authenticity in the emotional relationship, co-construction of the analytical relationship, mutuality, and intersubjectivity became the foundations of the relational model, replacing the traditional classical principles of neutrality, abstinence and anonymity that attempted to protect the integrity of the patient as a monadic or monopersonal system. The analytical work delivers compensation for the environmental deficit that underscored the failure of the system to mature. It is not coincidental to notice the importance of authenticity in the evolutionary cognitive model of Gianni Liotti (Onofri and Tombolini 1997).

It must be said, however, that in the relational model, and unlike in the classical psychoanalytic drive model—either sexual Freudian or aggressive Kleinian—Mitchell does not believe that the patient unconsciously sabotages therapy and deceives the therapist. However, he still thinks that the patient does not have the relational skills to succeed in achieving a satisfactory and cooperative alliance. Therefore, in this case there is a relational difficulty grounded on an impairment and not on an active and aggressive sabotage. Even the conception of the patient changes. There is a conception of the patient as an emotionally neglected and deprived being in whom affective impairments have prevented the development of the higher introspective abilities that are used in psychotherapy. The patient is not unconsciously unreliable but emotionally and relationally impaired.

Hence, the patient is considered to be a difficult person, but he or she is not a deceiver, albeit unconsciously. In this case, the therapeutic work would not include dealing with the patient's sabotage and deception but with his or her failings and limitations by building emotional compensation that would cover basic relational insufficiency. The treatment in this case does not foresee, as in Kernberg's TFP, an emergence to the awareness of split tendencies but rather a corrective relational experience of emotional compensation.

In summary, it seems to us that in the case of Mitchell's relational psychoanalysis there is also an uneven compatibility with the possibility of early shared case formulation, as in the CBT approaches that are not primarily focused on the relational aspect. From our viewpoint, in Mitchell's relational psychoanalysis, as well as in the constructivist relational models explored in chapter "Strengths and Limitations of Case Formulation in Constructivist Cognitive Behavioral Therapies", the shared formulation appears to be more of an outcome at the end of a fascinating path of growth and discovery than a move that sets the rules in the field of play. In Mitchell's relational model, the authenticity of the relationship as a totalizing and therapeutic experience looks to go beyond any explicit sharing of the case formulation, which is conceived as a mere conceptual and abstract tool that cannot be object of experience.

The Mentalization Based Therapy Model

Another step of psychoanalysis toward the CBT approach was taken by Fonagy with his *mentalization based therapy* (MBT, Bateman and Fonagy 2006) model and his concept of mentalization, in which the state of self-reflective awareness has much in common with CBT metacognitive skills. Fonagy has psychoanalytic training and yet his model is partly cognitive, placing at the grounds of emotional disorders an impairment of cognitive or rather metacognitive processes, the so-called mentalization. Besides, Fonagy assumes that at the base of the impaired mentalization there is a relational and interpersonal deficiency during childhood. Once a person pays his or her debt to childhood, Fonagy elaborates a therapeutic model in the cognitive terms of an explicit intervention within a process. The therapy comprises a meticulous work of promotion and encouragement to "mentalize", which is a continuous push to the patient to become aware of his or her mental activity and the possibility to master it.

When Fonagy speaks of mentalization, he always favors an all-encompassing and evocative approach that is not particularly focused on the pragmatic intervention within the cognitive functions, as in the CBT models. Bion's influence on Fonagy can be felt in this aspect. Indeed, it cannot be denied that Fonagy's psychodynamic model and CBT approaches have achieved maximum convergence.

Nevertheless, the differences are not negligible. The most evocative definition of mental functions in Fonagy (and in Bion, who from our point of view foreruns Fonagy) leads, in his model, to case formulation as more experienced in real life and in the actual relationship between the patient and therapist than expressed and explicitly shared in verbal terms, as in CBT approaches. For Fonagy, the encouragement to mentalize does not seem to happen in a frame of shared case formulation: At the beginning, the therapist seems to limit themselves to promoting mentalization without conceptualizing it to the patient; conceptualization seems to happen. It is not coincidental that Fonagy bans any transference analysis. It is another confirmation that the MBT intervention is experienced and not verbally expressed for either case formulation or transference analysis. The regulation of the relationship, of which Fonagy also speaks, seems to be always and only a side product of an intervention that technically is focused on promoting mentalization, i.e. a cognitive attitude of openness and curiosity (Allen et al. 2003).

In addition, in MBT the experience of mentalization happens in the therapeutic relationship. The therapist works mainly in the relationship and uses it in a way that is not wholly shared on an explicit and conceptual level. Instead, the process is experienced with the patient, i.e. without necessarily communicating by words the complete meaning of the therapeutic work but nevertheless fully living it in the emotional experience, in a state of *reverie* or dream that is again reminiscent of Bion's model. Notably, in this case there are analogies with some but not all CBT approaches, such as the constructive and relational models especially of Mahoney, Guidano, Liotti and Bara, to which we refer in chapter "Strengths and Limitations of Case Formulation in Constructivist Cognitive Behavioral Therapies". In both cases, the therapy is conceived as an emotionally charged experience because it takes place in the real and therefore meaningful relationship.

The Rupture and Repairs Model

Safran and Muran's (2000) ruptures and repairs model on the one hand accepts the CBT paradigm of the mind as an information processor, and on the other attempts an integration with relational and psychodynamic concepts. The relational concepts are focused on the analysis of the so-called episodes of rupture of the therapeutic alliance. According to the authors, encouraging the patient to analyze the ruptures and negotiate the repairs in the alliance is crucial to the process of change. Psychotherapists should be aware that patients often have negative feelings about therapy or the therapeutic relationship and are reluctant to share them for fear of the therapist's reaction. It is therefore essential that therapists pay attention to any small signs of rupture in the alliance so that they can take the initiative in exploring them with the patient.

As already described in chapter "Strengths and Limitations of Case Formulation in Constructivist Cognitive Behavioral Therapies", in order to manage these critical episodes, Safran and Muran developed a protocol for monitoring, recognizing and dealing with the ruptures in the alliance in order to achieve repairs. For this reason, patients are allowed to share their point of view on what has emerged during therapy, when it differs from the therapist's point of view and express their negative feelings about the therapy. When this happens, it is important for therapists to respond openly—without being defensive—and accept responsibility for their role in the negative aspects of the relationship.

The strength of Safran and Muran's model is that it offers an operational model of crisis management. It is not the usual wisdom but instead a concrete guideline. In terms of shared case formulation, however, the question is whether the ruptures and repairs are just a possible event or are the unavoidable bottleneck that the therapist must meet in order to reach the healing turning point. In the second case, everything happens in the relational event of rupture and repair: The normal mind develops and matures in tolerable ruptures followed by rewarding repairs, emotional disorders are borne from disturbed ruptures without possible repairs and therapy takes place in the context of relational ruptures and repairs.

The consequences for the function of case formulation in the therapeutic process are significant. If the real therapeutic event is only ruptures and repairs, it follows that every initial episode of shared formulation and negotiation of the therapeutic plan is illusory because it has not yet undergone the decisive test: The rupture. The relational rupture is an indispensable condition for a real understanding and change of the relational dysfunctions that underline the emotional pain. The consequence is that at the bottom of Safran and Muran's conception there remains the psychodynamic conception for which every initial therapeutic alliance is always a defense, an illusory mask, a false self as defined by Winnicot (1965), waiting for the emergence of the true face of the patient: Envious and angry in the Kleinian conception, but more tolerably conflictual and impulsive in that of Safran and Muran. The clinical consequences of this hypothesis are that the relationship, far from just being the framework and the contractual premise of the therapeutic intervention, as in CBT approaches, becomes its only resolutive aspect.

The Control Mastery Theory Model

Another model that integrates cognitive and psychodynamic components is the plan formulation method (Curtis and Silberschatz 2007), a method based on a theoretical paradigm, the CMT (Weiss et al. 1986; Silberschatz 2005), an interesting model that has happily integrated in its psychodynamic framework cognitive concepts such as goals, tests and pathogenic beliefs (or obstructions). CMT explains psychopathology as a result of pathogenic beliefs and therapeutic successes as a result of the disconfirmation of pathogenic beliefs and stresses the need to arrive at a shared case formulation in the initial sessions.

On the other hand, it proposes a theory of therapy in which the interpersonal dimension is pivotal. It comprises a strategic and specific therapeutic use of the relationship that targets the patient's pathogenic beliefs. This idea is highly intriguing: In CMT, cognitive and relational interventions are not put side by side; instead, they are entwined. CMT rigorously defines the concept of *testing* pathogenic beliefs in the relationship with the therapist, making it measurable in the therapeutic process and, finally, it supports this hypothesis with numerous empirical results (O'Connor et al. 1997, Silberschatz 2008, 2015).

In CMT, tests are episodes triggered by the patients during which therapists observe the tested persons' behavior to determine whether they confirm or do not confirm their negative expectations or beliefs. Fundamentally, the patient triggers an emotionally demanding interaction that encourages dysfunctional reactions in the therapist who, if he or she passes the test, gains the necessary confidence for the therapy to begin and the alliance to be established.

From the viewpoint of shared case formulation, despite all its similarities with CBT approaches, the tests and pathogenic beliefs in the CMT model are not ascertained and dealt with at the level of conscious representations, at least from our CBT viewpoint. Instead, these issues occur during episodes in sessions in which the patient does not intentionally test the therapist. The patient unconsciously uses his or her own pathogenic beliefs and unintentionally expects the therapist to react to them in a non-collusive or reactive way (Gazzillo 2016).

This fact clarifies the differences between a CBT case formulation approach, which presumes a functionalist vision of mental activity that privileges intervention on executive functions that are accessible to the consciousness, and another approach, such as CMT, which instead focuses on interpersonal and experiential factors triggered by relational processes that are not fully representable in a patient's consciousness but instead are only emotionally and motivationally perceived.

The clinical differences implied by these distinct approaches are that sharing the case formulation in CMT is actually sharing the passing of the test. Therefore, by definition, it cannot be implemented at the beginning of the process, as per CBT. In CMT, sharing the case formulation is the final outcome of a complex interpersonal therapeutic process that is not immediately accessible to the executive consciousness except after a painful relational process that is not free of misunderstandings and conflicts. From our viewpoint, it remains a specificity of CBT approaches—at least those that are not predominantly focused on the relational and constructivist aspect—that sharing the case formulation is possible from the very beginning. This sharing is of course never definitive; instead, it is incessantly negotiated and reformulated. It is nevertheless explicitly expressed as soon as possible from the very first therapy session and intended to act as the main operational tool for the management of the therapeutic process, also in its aspecific aspects, such as the management of the alliance and the therapeutic relationship.

Conclusion

Shared Case Formulation in Cognitive and Psychodynamic Models

In summary, non-CBT models frequently seem to hold the tenet that sharing the case formulation is often not enough to organize the psychotherapeutic process. This phenomenon can occur because the patient, in spite of any agreement about the case formulation, admittedly does not accept it or because he or she openly opposes it and dismantles the foundation on which the entire therapeutic process should stand. From this point of view, the CBT position would provide a reductive and insufficient solution to the problem of the alliance.

In short, the concepts of alliance and therapeutic relationship come from psychotherapeutic paradigms other than CBT, especially the psychodynamic and the humanistic, and end up obeying different scientific hypotheses. It is not just a question of greater emphasis: The difference is qualitative. In the psychodynamic paradigm, or at least in some of its developments, and in the humanistic one, therapeutic relationships and alliances are not only possible fields of application of the therapeutic process, they are the real units of the analysis of the process itself. The therapeutic change occurs in the relationship and is above all a relational event. In turn, the clinical theory of these paradigms is largely grounded on relational concepts that in turn are connected with the neurobiology of interpersonal experience (Siegel 1999): It is only in the relationship that the mind develops; it is in the relationship that the conditions at the basis of emotional dysfunctions are created; and it is in the relationship that the conditions for therapeutic compensation are sought and created (Mitchell and Aron 1999; Rogers 1951, 1957).

On the other hand, in CBT approaches, everything begins with the explicit agreement by both the patient and the therapist on the shared acceptance of the case formulation. The therapeutic contract and alliance are stipulated on this acceptance, and it is also the pivot around which the therapeutic relationship revolves and is managed. Of course, no CBT therapist would deny that there are patients who sabotage the agreement on case formulation and, hence, the entire therapeutic process. With these patients, any CBT therapist knows that it is necessary to take care of the relationship in order to create and negotiate the conditions of treatment work. The divide between CBT and relationship-focused paradigms is placed between the incompatible ideas that consider this work as either only preparatory and limited to some cases or unavoidable, indispensable and conclusive, whereas the analysis of resistance—or, in more modern terms, the exploration of sabotage—would be the real key intervention of the therapy (Gazzillo 2012).

These reasons clarify the theoretical and clinical differences between shared case formulation in CBT approaches and the conception of the therapeutic alliance and therapeutic relationship in relational-focused therapies, mainly psychodynamic—although there are cognitive treatments that attribute a key role to the relationship as those of constructive ascendancy discussed in chapter "Strengths and Limitations of Case Formulation in Constructivist Cognitive Behavioral Therapies" of this book. Once it is clearly established that shared case formulation is the key aspect of the therapeutic alliance in CBT approaches, we understand why the use of terms such as "therapeutic alliance" or even "therapeutic relationship", terms that are also common in other psychotherapeutic orientations, may be somewhat confusing. We believe that "shared case formulation" may be specific to indicate the CBT conception of the therapeutic alliance.

As a closing remark, it is worth emphasizing that perhaps the real divide that helps to understand the difference between shared case formulation and the therapeutic relationship relies upon the difference between choice and experience. The role attributed in some treatments to the function of free choice significantly distinguishes them from other treatments whose psychotherapeutic process is largely the result of corrective relational experiences. The "choice", i.e. the voluntary executive function, is the human ability to choose despite everything, despite our emotions, even despite our reasoning (which can only be a worry), despite our experiences, our attachments and rejections, despite our relationships, and despite our avoidances, as opposed to the "experience", i.e. the irreplaceable role of experiential learning that always maintains a margin of executive uncontrollability (Wells 2008).

The Risks of the Relational Models

Some critical remarks about the role of the relational factors in the therapeutic process are useful to close this chapter. Clearly, the empirical results in favor of relational factors in the therapeutic process are solid and have their own clinical fertility. There are a number of papers summarizing all the research dedicated to this important factor, including the works of Horvath (Bachelor and Horvath 1999; Horvath 2005; Horvath and Symonds 1991) and the latest book by Wampold and Imel (2015).

These critical remarks regard how these results are used, i.e. for what purposes and with what consequences for the development of psychotherapy, including both CBT and non-CBT approaches. One of the main problems of the literature in favor of the relational factor is its tendency to overlap with the common factors studied by Michael Lambert; these would explain 70% of the clinical change (Lambert and Barley 2001). This overlap between common and relational factors, confirmed by Lambert himself when he writes "common factors largely in the form of relationship variables" (Lambert and Ogles 2014 p. 500), shows the risk of research about the therapeutic relationship to a vague ecumenism that could appear to not be very promising in terms of its clinical progress.

In fact, the overlap between common and relational factors on the one hand suggests that the relational components of the therapeutic process play a resolutive key role; on the other hand, this overlap does not define the relationship as an isolable element specifically present in relational protocols, a factor whose action can be somehow purified in order to make it more and more effective, more governable in therapy and teachable during training in order to increase the effectiveness of treatments. Rather, it is an aspecific, universal element that is spontaneously present in all psychotherapies, an element that in reality was already present and functioning before it was discovered and that was already responsible for the therapeutic successes of Freud's psychoanalysis and Beck's CT. These authors erroneously defined specific (but actually imaginary) mechanisms for their psychotherapies: The interpretation of the drives in psychoanalysis or the work on beliefs in CBT.

This trend is particularly patent in the book recently published by Wampold and Imel (2015). They provide a medical model so that psychotherapy grounded on factors specific to the various orientations is contrasted with a contextual, social and psychological model in which the key factors are presented as aspecific, relational and common to all therapies. As is well known, empirical work on the therapeutic relationship too often presents itself as a confirmation of the equivalence between all psychotherapies, the so-called Dodo verdict (Budd and Hughes 2009; Luborsky et al. 1975, 2002) and as a devaluation of the specific factors of single psychotherapies, reduced to illusory ideologies, as well as their specific increases in therapeutic efficacy, similarly to those shown by CT for depression (Rush et al. 1977). From this viewpoint, the results in favor of the overlapped relational and common factors, far from being a step forward and a discovery capable of ensuring an increase in the effectiveness of the psychotherapy, seem to aspire to play the sterile role of justifying what has already been achieved.

In conclusion, Wampold and Imel have definitively linked the perspective of common factors in the therapeutic relationship to a so-called contextual view of psychotherapy as a socially constructed curative practice in which change depends on:

Psychotherapy is a primarily interpersonal treatment that is a) based on psychological principles; b) involves a trained therapist and a client who is seeking help for a mental disorder, problem, or complaint; c) is intended by the therapist to be remedial for the client disorder, problem, or complaint; and d) is adapted or individualized for the particular client and his or her disorder, problem, or complaint (Wampold and Imel 2015, p. 37).

It follows that the relationship risks becoming a sort of ingredient that is simultaneously decisive and already guaranteed at the beginning without being connected to the professional competence of the therapist reduced to a ritualized ideology: 'a set of procedures or rituals' (Laska et al. 2014, p. 467).

References

Adler, A. (1964). In H. L. Ansbacher & R. R. Ansbacher (Eds.), *The individual psychology of Alfred Adler*. New York, NY: Harper Torchbooks.

Allen, J., Haslam-Hopwood, T., & Strauss, J. S. (2003). Mentalizing as a compass for treatment. *Bulletin of the Menninger Clinic, 67*, 1–11.

Bachelor, A., & Horvath, A. (1999). The therapeutic relationship. In M. A. Hubble, B. L. Duncan, & S. D. Miller (Eds.), *The heart and soul of change: What works in therapy* (pp. 133–178). Washington, DC: American Psychological Association.

Bateman, A., & Fonagy, P. (Eds.). (2006). *Mentalization based treatment: A practical guide*. Oxford: Oxford University Press.

Bion, W. R. (1962). *Learning from experience*. London: William Heinemann.

Bion, W. R. (1967). *Second thoughts*. London: William Heinemann.

Bion, W. R. (1970). *Attention and interpretation*. London: Tavistock Publications.

Bowlby, J. (1969). *Attachement and loss* (Vol. 1). New York, NY: Basic Books.

Bowlby, J. (1973). *Attachement and loss* (Vol. 2). New York, NY: Basic Books.

Bowlby, J. (1980). *Attachement and loss* (Vol. 3). New York, NY: Basic Books.

Budd, R., & Hughes, I. (2009). The dodo bird verdict—Controversial, inevitable and important: A commentary on 30 years of meta-analyses. *Clinical Psychology & Psychotherapy, 16*, 510–522.

Clarkin, J. F., Yeomans, F. E., & Kernberg, O. F. (1999). *Psychotherapy for borderline disorders*. New York, NY: Wiley.

Curtis, J. T., & Silberschatz, G. (2007). Plan formulation method. In T. D. Eells (Ed.), *Handbook of psychotherapy case formulation* (2nd ed., pp. 198–220). New York, NY: Guilford Press.

Eells, T. D. (2007). *Handbook of psychotherapy case formulation*. New York, NY: Guilford Press.

Eells, T. D. (2009). Contemporary themes in case formulation. In P. Sturmey (Ed.), *Clinical case formulation. Varieties of approaches*. Chichester: Wiley-Blackwell.

Eells, T. D. (2011). *Handbook of psychotherapy case formulation* (2nd ed.). New York, NY: Guilford Press.

Eells, T. D. (2015). *Psychotherapy case formulation*. Arlingtion, VI: American Psychological Association.

Freud, A. (1936). *Ego and the mechanisms of defense*. New York, NY: International Universities Press.

Gazzillo, F. (2012). *I sabotatori interni. Il funzionamento delle organizzazioni patologiche di personalità [Internal saboteurs. The functioning of pathological organizations of personalities]*. Milano: Cortina.

Gazzillo, F. (2016). *Fidarsi dei pazienti. Introduzione alla Control-Mastery Theory [Trusting patients. Introduction to control-mastery theory]*. Milano: Cortina.

Hartmann, H. (1964). *Essays on ego psychology*. New York, NY: International Universities Press.

Hartmann, H., Kris, E., & Loewenstein, R. M. (1946). Comments on the formation of psychic structure. *The Psychoanalytic Study of the Child, 2*, 11–38.

Horney, K. (1950). *The collected works of Karen Horney* (Vol. 2 vols). New York, NY: Norton.
Horowitz, M., & Eells, T. (2007). Configurational analysis. States of mind, person schemas, and the control of ideas and affect. In T. Eells (Ed.), *Handbook of psychotherapy case formulation* (pp. 136–163). New York, NY: Guilford Press.
Horvath, A. O. (2005). The therapeutic relationship: Research and theory: An introduction to the special issue. *Psychotherapy Research, 15*, 3–7.
Horvath, A. O., & Symonds, B. D. (1991). Relation between working alliance and outcome in psychotherapy: A meta-analysis. *Journal of Counseling Psychology, 38*, 139.
Klein, M. (2017). *The collected works of Melanie Klein 1921–1963*. London: Karnac Books.
Lakoff, R. T. (1990). *Talking power: The politics of language*. New York, NY: Basic Books.
Lambert, M. J., & Barley, D. E. (2001). Research summary on the therapeutic relationship and psychotherapy outcome. *Psychotherapy: Theory, Research, Practice, Training, 38*, 357.
Lambert, M. J., & Ogles, B. M. (2014). Common factors: Post hoc explanation or empirically based therapy approach? *Psychotherapy, 4*, 500–504.
Laska, K. M., Gurman, A. S., & Wampold, B. E. (2014). Expanding the lens of evidence-based practice in psychotherapy: A common factors perspective. *Psychotherapy, 51*(4), 467.
Lichtenberg, J. D., Lachmann, F. M., & Fosshage, J. L. (2011). *Psychoanalysis and motivational systems: A new look*. London: Routledge.
Luborsky, L. (1997). The core conflictual relationship theme: A basic case formulation method. In T. D. Eells (Ed.), *Handbook of psychotherapy case formulation* (pp. 58–83). New York, NY: Guilford Press.
Luborsky, L., Singer, B., & Luborsky, L. (1975). Comparative studies of psychotherapies: Is it true that everyone has won and all must have prizes? *Archives of General Psychiatry, 32*(8), 995–1008.
Luborsky, L., Popp, C., Luborsky, E., & Mark, D. (1994). The core conflictual relationship theme. *Psychotherapy Research, 4*, 172–183.
Luborsky, L., Rosenthal, R., Diguer, L., Andrusyna, T. P., Berman, J. S., Levitt, J. T., et al. (2002). The dodo bird verdict is alive and well—mostly. *Clinical Psychology: Science and Practice, 9*, 2–12.
Luborsky, E., O'Reilly-Landry, M., & Arlow, J. (2008). Psychoanalysis. In R. J. Corsini & D. Wedding (Eds.), *Current psychotherapies* (pp. 15–62). Belmont, CA: Thomson Higher Education.
Mitchell, S. A., & Aron, L. E. (1999). *Relational psychoanalysis: The emergence of a tradition*. Hillsdale, NJ: Analytic Press.
O'Connor, L. E., Berry, J. W., Weiss, J., Bush, M., & Sampson, H. (1997). Interpersonal guilt: The development of a new measure. *Journal of Clinical Psychology, 53*, 73–89.
Onofri, A., & Tombolini, L. (1997). Il se autopoietico e il se-con-l'altro [The autopoietic self and the self-with-the-other]. *Psicobiettivo, 17*, 35–51.
Rogers, C. (1951). *Client-centered therapy: Its current practice, implications and theory*. London: Constable.
Rogers, C. R. (1957). The necessary and sufficient conditions of therapeutic personality change. *Journal of Consulting and Clinical Psychology, 21*, 95–103.
Rush, A. J., Beck, A. T., Kovacs, M., & Hollon, S. D. (1977). Comparative efficacy of cognitive therapy and pharmacotherapy in the treatment of depressed outpatients. *Cognitive Therapy and Research, 1*, 7–37.
Safran, J. D., & Muran, J. C. (2000). *Negotiating the therapeutic alliance: A relational treatment guide*. New York, NY: Guilford Press.
Siegel, D. (1999). *The developing mind: Toward a neurobiology of interpersonal experience*. New York, NY: Guilford Press.
Silberschatz, G. (2005). The control-mastery theory: An integrated cognitive-psychodynamic-relational theory. In G. Silberschatz (Ed.), *Transformative relationships: The control-mastery theory of psychotherapy* (pp. 219–235). New York, NY: Routledge.

Silberschatz, G. (2008). How patients work on their plans and test their therapists in psychotherapy. *Smith College Studies In Social Work, 78*, 275–286.

Silberschatz, G. (2015). Improving the yield of psychotherapy research. *Psychotherapy Research, 11*, 1–13.

Strachey, J. (Ed.). (1953–1974). *The standard edition of the complete psychological works of Sigmund Freud*. London: Hogarth Press.

Sullivan, H. S. (1947). *Conceptions of modern psychiatry*. Washington, DC: William Alanson White Psychiatric Foundation.

Wampold, B. E., & Imel, Z. E. (2015). *The great psychotherapy debate: The evidence for what makes psychotherapy work*. London: Routledge.

Weiss, J., Sampson, H., & The Mount Zion Psychotherapy Research Group. (1986). *The psychoanalytic process: Theory, clinical observations, and empirical research*. New York, NY: Guilford Press.

Wells, A. (2008). *Metacognitive therapy for anxiety and depression*. London: Guilford Press.

Wells, A., & Mathews, G. (1994). *Attention and emotion: A clinical perspective*. Hove; Hillsdale, NJ: Erlbaum.

Winnicot, D. W. (1965). Ego distortions in terms of true and false self. In D. W. Winnicot (Ed.), *The maturational process and the facilitating environment: Studies in the theory of emotional development* (pp. 140–152). New York: International UP.

Commentary to Chapter "Case Formulation as an Outcome and Not an Opening Move in Relational and Psychodynamic Models": Plan Formulation Vs. Case Formulation: The Perspective of Control-Mastery Theory

Francesco Gazzillo and George Silberschatz

Contents

Plan Formulation in Control Mastery Theory

In order to better shed light on the differences between the Control-Mastery Theory (CMT; Gazzillo 2016; Silberschatz 2005; Weiss 1993; Weiss et al. 1986) and the CBT perspective on case formulation it is probably useful to say that in the former perspective we talk about *plan formulation* and not case formulation. This difference is not simply a matter of words because CMT assumes that patients come to therapy with a plan, which is generally unconscious. A plan formulation includes a description of adaptive *goals* that patients wish to achieve; in order to achieve their goals, they need to disprove *pathogenic beliefs*, which are typically unconscious, and that derive from early attempts to deal with *traumatic and adverse developmental experiences*. Moreover, patients come to therapy because they want to better master these traumatic and adverse experiences, and they often do so by posing *tests of the therapists*, which are unconscious strategies aimed at disproving their

F. Gazzillo (✉)
Department of Dynamic and Clinical Psychology, Sapienza University of Rome, Rome, Italy
e-mail: francesco.gazzillo@uniroma1.it

G. Silberschatz
University of California, San Francisco, CA, USA
e-mail: George.Silberschatz@ucsf.edu

G. M. Ruggiero et al. (eds.), *CBT Case Formulation as Therapeutic Process*,
https://doi.org/10.1007/978-3-030-63587-9_23

pathogenic beliefs and mastering their traumas. Finally, plan formulations include a description of *new experiences* or *insights* patients would like to have in order to better understand their problems. So, the plan that we need to formulate at the beginning of a treatment is the plan of the patient we are going to treat - not our way to understand and make sense of her/his problems according to our favorite theory.

Given these premises, the task of the therapist is *to help patients to carry out their plans* in the way they want to carry them out. In other words, the therapist should help patients pursue their adaptive goals, disprove pathogenic beliefs, and master their traumas and adverse experiences. The therapist needs to provide the patient with the corrective emotional experiences they need (i.e., passing tests) and help the patient to better understand her/himself.

A number of empirical research studies support the idea that it is possible to reliably formulate the plan of a patient on the basis of the contents of the very first sessions of therapy (see, for example, Curtis and Silberschatz 2007) and that patients have an autonomous striving to master their traumas, disprove their pathogenic beliefs and develop insight about themselves and their problems (Curtis et al. 1986; Gassner et al. 1986; Shilkret et al. 1986). Other research studies support the idea that patients test their therapists in order to disprove their pathogenic beliefs and that if therapists pass their tests patients tend to get better (Silberschatz et al. 1986; Silberschatz and Curtis 1993). An overview is in Gazzillo et al. (2019a). Empirical studies have also shown that therapist interventions that support patients in carrying out their plans are predictive of treatment outcome (Silberschatz 2017).

Sharing the Formulation: Conscious and Unconscious

The decision about whether or not to share the plan formulation is, according to CMT, case specific and must be made only on the basis of one criterion: is it pro-plan or not to do so. In fact, the criterion used to evaluate the "correctness" of the plan formulation is whether the patient is getting better and not whether the patient consciously agrees with the plan formulation. In some cases, sharing the formulation with patients may be greatly beneficial because doing so makes the patient feel that the therapist is able to understand them and support their strivings. However, in other cases sharing the formulation with the patient may be detrimental because it could be experienced as the therapist lecturing the patient or showing how brilliant the therapist's insights are.

We would like to briefly comment on the CBT argument that the formulation must be consciously accessible to the patient. Clinical and research studies have shown that the human mind is unconsciously able to perform many of the same complex mental functions that can be performed consciously: we can appraise reality, set goals, develop and test plans, make decisions and so on. Weiss (1986) referred to this as the "higher mental functioning paradigm", which is now supported by an increasing number of cognitive and evolutionary research studies (Bargh 2017; Kenrick 2013; Weinberger and Stoycheva 2019) and inadequately considered by CBT theorists. For instance, the CBT view that that a case formulation *must* be consciously and explicitly articulated to the patient early in the treatment seems to leave no room for unconscious appraisal, testing, planning, or thinking. And, in our opinion, CBT does not adequately consider the emotional relevance of the therapist-patient relationship, which is widely recognized as the major change factor in psychotherapy (Wampold and Imel 2015). In short, CMT is more closely aligned with contemporary research in cognition showing that a great deal of cognitive work goes on unconsciously, and with contemporary research in psychotherapy. Moreover, CMT provides reliable tools to the clinician for understanding how to relate and respond optimally to each specific patient (Gazzillo et al. 2019b).

We end our commentary with a clinical vignette written by Joseph Weiss (1994, pp. 245–246):

Before his first interview with Mr. T. C., the analyst had heard from the referring family physician that Mr. T. C. was depressed and having difficulty working. Mr. T. C.'s parents, siblings, and wife all worked hard themselves and all were worried about his not working. However, during his first session Mr. T. C., a computer programmer, who knew that the analyst had been informed by the referring physician of his difficulty working, did not talk about this problem. Instead he chatted informally about the computer he saw in the secretary's office. He talked about its capabilities and discussed various programs that the secretary might find useful. He also talked about several friends and acquaintances whom the analyst knew.

The analyst became aware that Mr. T. C. was doing the same thing in analysis as in everyday life, that is, making a point of not working. The analyst was tempted to point this out. However, he suspected the patient's wife and parents had been nagging him to work, that he resented this, and that he was testing the analyst to determine whether the analyst would also try to induce him to work. Therefore the analyst decided not to question him and indeed not to offer any interpretations until the patient gave some indication that he wanted to be helped interpretively. The analyst simply showed interest in whatever topic the patient introduced. About 2 weeks after Mr. T. C.'s first session the analyst received a call from the referring physician stating that Mr. T. C. was feeling better and beginning to work more enthusiastically. (Mr. T. C. made no mention of his working.) The analyst inferred from this that he was on the right track and continued his noninterpretive approach. Over a period of time the patient began to talk more freely about himself. After several months he talked about the high value he placed on a sense of freedom. He stated that he felt constrained by a schedule and he linked his need for freedom to the constraints his parents had placed on him. They worked all the time and were uncomfortable when he did not. If he watched T.V. they would remind him of tasks that he had not completed.

At this point the analyst told Mr. T. C. that he had apparently accepted his parents' opinion that he should work all the time and was now struggling against believing this. Mr. T. C. seemed pleased and agreed. As a consequence of these and other comments the patient became less averse to interpretation. Though the analyst continued to treat the patient mainly by his attitude, he made a number of comments designed to help Mr. T. C. fit his memories and his current problems into a broad explanatory framework, thereby enabling him to understand himself better and to see himself more sympathetically. Mr. T C.'s difficulty working was rooted in the pathogenic belief that he should work very hard and should not enjoy leisure or freedom. In childhood he had felt so burdened by his parents' insistence that he always be working that he had become averse to doing any work. In his analysis he feared that the analyst would insist that he work continuously on his problems and so confirm his pathogenic belief that he should not feel free in treatment to talk about whatever he wanted. When the analyst did not insist on his working Mr. T. C. permitted himself to become more relaxed both in his everyday life and in his treatment. As he felt more free and began to enjoy his leisure he found work less burdensome.

This case illustrates that sharing the case formulation early in treatment or requiring explicit agreement about how therapy should proceed can be counterproductive. We believe that sharing the formulation, agreeing on therapeutic tasks, or any other aspects of treatment must be based on an accurate formulation of the patient's plan.

References

Bargh, J. (2017). *Before you know it: The unconscious reasons we do what we do*. New York, NY: Simon and Schuster.

Curtis, J. T., & Silberschatz, G. (2007). Plan formulation method. In T. D. Eells (Ed.), *Handbook of psychotherapy case formulation* (2nd ed., pp. 198–220). New York, NY: Guilford Press.

Curtis, J. T., Ransohoff, P., Sampson, F., Brumer, S., & Bronstein, A. A. (1986). Expressing warded-off contents in behavior. In J. Weiss, H. Sampson, & The Mount Zion Psychotherapy Research Group (Eds.), *The psychoanalytic process: Theory, clinical observation, and empirical research* (pp. 171–186). New York: Guilford Press.

Gassner, S., Sampson, H., Brumer, S., & Weiss, I. (1986). The emergence of warded-off contents. *I. Weiss, 6*, 171–186.

Gazzillo, F. (2016). *Trusting patients. Introduction to control-mastery theory*. Milan, Italy: Raffaello Cortina.

Gazzillo, F., Dimaggio, G., & Curtis, J. T. (2019a). Case formulation and treatment planning: How to take care of relationship and symptoms together. *Journal of Psychotherapy Integration*.

Gazzillo, F., Genova, F., Fedeli, F., Curtis, J. T., Silberschatz, G., Bush, M., & Dazzi, N. (2019b). Patients' unconscious testing activity in psychotherapy: A theoretical and empirical overview. *Psychoanalytic Psychology, 36*(2), 173–1984.

Kenrick, D. T. (2013). *The rational animal: How evolution made us smarter than we think*. Basic Books.

Shilkret, C., Isaacs, M., Drucker, C., & Curtis, J. T. (1986). The acquisition of insight. In J. Weiss, H. Sampson, & The Mount Zion Psychotherapy Research Group (Eds.), *The Psychoanalytic Process: Theory, clinical observation, and empirical research* (pp. 206–217). New York: Guilford Press.

Silberschatz, G. (2005). *Transformative relationships: The control mastery theory of psychotherapy*. New York, NY: Routledge Press.

Silberschatz, G. (2017). Improving the yield of psychotherapy research. *Psychotherapy Research, 27*(1), 1–13.

Silberschatz, G., & Curtis, J. T. (1993). Measuring the therapist's impact on the patient's therapeutic progress. *Journal of Consulting and Clinical Psychology, 61*(3), 403.

Silberschatz, G., Sampson, H., & Weiss, J. (1986). Testing pathogenic belief versus seeking transference gratifications. In J. Weiss, H. Sampson, & The Mount Zion Psychotherapy Research Group (Eds.), *The psychoanalytic process: Theory, clinical observation, and empirical research* (pp. 267–276). New York: Guilford Press.

Wampold, B. E., & Imel, Z. E. (2015). *The great psychotherapy debate. The evidence for what makes psychotherapy work*. New York, NY: Routledge.

Weinberger, J., & Stoycheva, V. (2019). *The Unconscious: Theory, Research, and Clinical Implications*. New York, NY: Guilford Press.

Weiss, J. (1986). Theory and clinical observation. In J. Weiss, H. Sampson, & The Mount Zion Psychotherapy Research Group (Eds.), *The psychoanalytic process: Theory, clinical observation, and empirical research* (pp. 3–138). New York: Guilford Press.

Weiss, J. (1993). *How psychotherapy works: Process and technique*. New York, NY: Guilford Press.

Weiss, J. (1994). The analyst task to help the patient carry out his plan. *Contemporary Psychoanalysis, 30*(2), 236–254.

Weiss, J., Sampson, H., & Mount Zion Psychotherapy Research Group. (1986). *The psychoanalytic process: Theory, clinical observation and empirical research*. New York, NY: Guilford Press.

Some Historical and Theoretical Remarks About Psychodynamic Assessment. Commentary on Chapter "Case Formulation as an Outcome and Not an Opening Move in Relational and Psychodynamic Models"

Marco Innamorati and Mariano Ruperthuz Honorato

Contents

Terminology

For clarity, a brief preliminary terminological explanation is required. In the course of this chapter some terms will be used that need definition. The term *paradigm* will be used, in the meaning introduced by Kuhn (1962), to refer to general systems of thought, such as the psychodynamic/psychoanalytic paradigm or the cognitive-behavior paradigm. We take it for granted that one can speak of a cognitive-behavior paradigm, even if it could be questioned whether it is legitimate to define it a single paradigm, and not the combination (perhaps not universally accepted) of two different ones (cognitive and behaviorist). Sharing a paradigm means sharing compatible foundations and presuppositions. For example, the concept of the unconscious and its relevance for psychotherapeutic practice is supported within the psychodynamic paradigm and denied within the cognitive-behavior paradigm. From a historical

M. Innamorati (✉)
Università degli Studi di Roma "Tor Vergata", Rome, Italy

M. R. Honorato
Andrés Bello University, School of Psychology, Santiago del Cile, Chile
e-mail: mariano.ruperthuz@unab.cl

G. M. Ruggiero et al. (eds.), *CBT Case Formulation as Therapeutic Process*,
https://doi.org/10.1007/978-3-030-63587-9_24

point of view, psychotherapists working with the same paradigm tend, at least partially, to have some common ground and to cite each other, while they generally do not do the same with therapists working in another paradigm.

It must be stressed that our use of the term paradigm lacks an aspect of complete legitimacy in terms of Kuhn's definition in *The Structure of Scientific Revolutions*. There, Kuhn clarifies that a paradigm is a system of thought that, for some time, dominates a certain scientific field. In this sense, maybe, only Freud's psychoanalysis could, briefly, have aspired to such a title, while the world of clinical psychology today should be defined as characterized by being in an inter-paradigmatic phase, that is to say, in a transition where no real paradigm exists (Innamorati et al. 2018).

With the term *theory*, we mean the various at least partially compatible approaches within a paradigm. For example, Freud's Id psychology, Hartmann's Ego psychology, and Kohut's Self psychology within the psychodynamic paradigm. With the term model we mean, in a more idiosyncratic way, the specific clinical applications of theories. Integration in psychotherapy is probably easier between models than between theories, and easier between theories than between paradigms. Elsewhere, one of us (Innamorati 2020) distinguished between inter-paradigmatic dialogue (i.e., between authors from different paradigms) and intra-paradigmatic dialogue (i.e., between authors sharing the same paradigm). Inter-paradigmatic integration seems to be easier on the level of models, namely, the application of specific practical techniques. Specifically, the first efforts at integration came from sharing the same epistemological attitudes, between theories on which different models were based: specifically, constructivist epistemology. The work of Guidano (1991) and Liotti (1994), for instance, starting from the 1990s, can be interpreted in this context.

Aims of This Commentary

On these premises, it is possible to specify the basic thesis of this commentary: chapter "Case Formulation as an Outcome and Not an Opening Move in Relational and Psychodynamic Models" of this book about case formulation is based on some assumptions we would like to discuss: (1) it is possible to define a common attitude shared by every psychodynamic model regarding case formulation; (2) such an attitude is tied to a pessimistic conception of man, related both to (2.1) motivation theory, based on sexuality and aggression, and (2.2) the concept of resistance to therapy; (3) it is also possible to define a common attitude of cognitive-behavior models regarding case formulation.

In our comment we would like to—point (1) and (3)—argue that the difference of attitude, with respect to case formulation, is tied to further factors: (a) the general setting of therapy, which historically divided psychodynamic and cognitive-behavior models, the first being oriented to a global change of personality (to be achieved with relatively long psychotherapeutic work), while the second were focused on solving specific problems (modifying specific themes); (b) the theorists' epistemological attitude, which can be more or less realist, or, on the contrary, more or less hermeneuticist or constructionist; (c) theorists' beliefs about the effect of case formulation, which presuppose (or are at least are linked to) (d) beliefs about *when* or even *if* it is possible to verbalize a case formulation to the patient; (e) different ideas about the conception of transference, its direct influence on therapy and the opportunity, timing, and effects of its interpretation.

It can be observed (a) that some remarks that might be correct in comparing a standard psychoanalytic approach and a standard CBT approach are not necessarily valuable in the same way for all the models within the psychodynamic and cognitive-behavior paradigms respectively. In recent times, the psychodynamic world has been characterized by a more and more open availability to propose treatments focused on specific problems, linked to the effort of also treating people considered un-analyzable in the past, including ones who found it difficult to undergo long treatments (Gabbard 2014). From this point of view, brief treatments, intended for borderline personalities (e.g., Bateman et al. 2004; Clarkin et al. 1999) have been created, sometimes providing an explicit case formulation at the beginning of treatment.

Case Formulation in Psychoanalysis

A point that appears crucial about formulating a case from classical psychoanalysis is that it traditionally implies the relation (as Sigmund Freud himself stated in his technical writings of 1912) between *time* and *repression*. From a psychodynamic perspective, these two variables are intimately in solidarity with the operation of the mind. In this sense, the work of conceptualizing a case, in diagnostic terms, thinking about the Freudian psychopathological pictures of neurosis (hysteria and obsession), psychosis and perversion, is always a tentative and transitory act that only manages to be finally clarified at the end of the resolution of a clinical case. The historicity of a case in psychodynamic terms, unlike cognitive-behavioral approaches, implies the notion of psychic conflict of forces that repress and others that censure, but is closely linked to the personal and family history of a subject. In this way, the work of conceptualization, akin to the work of an archaeologist of the mind, according to Freud, would imply a historical reconstruction of the individual's life. This *official story of the one person*, thanks to unconscious action, would be full of omissions, distortions, and censorship. Therefore, thanks to clinical work, the self that relates will be able to integrate more significant portions of the repressed unconscious contents. It should not be forgotten that in the first Freudian era, the reconstruction of censured chapters was the therapeutic agent *par excellence*. Then, the recognition of the presence of the limited action of the pleasure principle made the analysis of resistances an indispensable clinical objective.

From this point of view, a clinical case is not only related to what happens to someone specific in an intrapsychic way—an issue that takes an important distance from cognitive-behavioral approaches—but, as authors such as Jacques Lacan (1953) have suggested, would exist in the dimension of the Other that precedes the subject, placing it in a genealogy of desires and determining its existence as a symbolic, imaginary and real subject. Therefore, a psychodynamic model would imply always considering the relationships of individuals in the long term, going far beyond an exclusively symptomatic approach. Although the first analyses that were carried out outside the Freudian circle—in public hospital contexts, for example, did not have the specific facilitating conditions to do a "complete analysis"—they reflected a not insignificant investment of time. Reports like those of C.G. Jung at the Burghölzli University Clinic (Freud and Jung 1994) and several of Freud's Latin American representatives confirm this (Plotkin and Ruperthuz 2017). Therefore, it can be affirmed that historicity, in regressive terms, is linked to overcoming the amnesias that all psychodynamic treatment implies, overcoming the resistances that configure the psychic domains of the ego and the reconstruction of a past that has all its influence in the present.

Probably, nonetheless, it was not a first. As is well known, a couple of first-generation pupils of Freud, namely Otto Rank and Sandor Ferenczi (1925), developed a technique, afterwards called active analysis, which entailed: (1) a more frequent rhythm of interpretation; (2) explicitly asking the patient for information about specific topics (contradicting the classic fundamental rule of free association); setting a deadline for treatment (at least in cases where the analysis was in a stalemate situation). A similar attitude can be seen in Wilhelm Reich's character analysis. Somehow, then, the attempts of shorten therapy through more directivity made by Ellis (1955) in his brief career as a psychoanalyst had precedents. As far as Reich and Ferenczi are concerned, there is no specific record of how their cases were assessed (except for Ferenczi's *Clinical Diary* (1988), which was, however, a unique case), in order to understand if an early formulation of the case could be shared with patients, at least sometimes, but, in our opinion, this cannot be completely ruled out. As far as Rank is concerned, this can be almost certainly affirmed, at least since he formulated the theory of the trauma of birth. Actually Rank (1924, 1926), towards the end of his theoretical path, was convinced that every single neurotic problem should be tied to the trauma of birth, and every psychotherapy should aim to let the patient re-live that trauma. Even if Rank did not leave unequivocal indications on this point, such idea was probably communicated at the beginning of therapy, which is equivalent to a shared case formulation. In any case, Rank was subject to overt disapproval form Freud (1936) as well as progressive isolation from the whole psychoanalytic movement.

A glance to Case Formulation in the Cognitive-Behavior Paradigm

Within the cognitive-behavior paradigm, it seems difficult to propose clinical models implying a long-term treatment, especially without a termination established in advance. Nevertheless, (b), a constructivist attitude, if completely consistent, precludes that the therapist could know the "truth" about the case, which means excluding that one could state at the beginning of the therapy *what* is to be changed and *how*. Guidano (1991) even denied that the ABC technique could culminate in *disputing effects*, exactly because a therapist could not have more information than the patients about the means of a therapeutic change.

It also should be noted, incidentally, that a paradox could emerge if the case formulation, which has in fact been made at the beginning of treatment, according to CBT conventions, should therapy have an unexpected ending. A classic example—and not a "negative" one, in a general sense—is a therapy that does not really follow the original path foreseen by the therapist achieving a good result anyway (say, the patient "feels better" than at the beginning of therapy). It was actually Giovanni Maria Ruggiero (2011), to say that many cases of standard CBT therapy—meaning here "second wave" cognitive therapies—achieved improvements in patients without obtaining what the therapist aimed for: that the patient would gain knowledge of his schemes and modify them. In such a situation, the value of the initial case formulation could not be considered higher than the one of the *interpretazione di prova* (trial interpretation) (Semi 1985) or the *summary statement* (Sullivan 1954) of the first session of an analytical psychotherapy: a provisional formulation, based on the material at disposal, that is intended to evolve.

When Case Formulation Is Possible in the Psychodynamic Paradigm

Within the psychodynamic paradigm there are indeed various positions about when and if a case formulation is possible. However, there is at least one theorist who argues that it is simply not appropriate to communicate anything to the analyzand about one's case formulation *at all*: we are speaking of French analyst Jacques Lacan. In his opinion, in fact, the ethics of psychoanalysis (Lacan 2013) forbids such a communication, which would tie the patient to a specific signifying (S_1), preventing him from freely shifting to subsequent sygnifyings (S_2, S_3 etc.). This means that the analysis could not event begin. Moreover, in (Lacan 1967) theoretical proposal, only the analyzand can achieve a case formulation, only at the very end of the analysis, and only if he/she is able to successfully undergo the control procedure, which Lacan himself proposed and defined as *passe*. It should be highlighted that it is a very particular and, so to speak, esoteric procedure: one has to communicate the content and meaning of his/her own analysis to witnesses (*passants*), who, in their turn, will tell to a group of experts (*cartel de la passe*) what they have heard. If the experts certify a positive result, one officially "passes" from the position of analyzand to the position of analyst, namely of *analyste de l'école* (analyst of the School), which is a sort of acknowledgement that still marks the cooption into the elite of the lacanian analysts in the European School of

Psychoanalysis. Moreover, one stays in charge as *analyste de l'école* for just 3 years. Afterwards the title changes to *analyste membre de l'école* (analyst, member of the School), which means a little less: it would seem to imply a provisional condition of self-case formulation.

According to Kohut (1971, 1977, 1984), the patient—especially if suffering from narcissistic personality disorders—is considered to go through a period when it is necessary that no real interpretation be given, in order to let him live the experience of idealizing the analyst, to compensate for what he/she probably lacked during infancy from caregivers. This means that an explicit case formulation would simply have a negative effect on the course of therapy.

Within the psychodynamic paradigm, in a general sense, case formulation should generally be considered a point of arrival rather than a starting point. From this point of view, we would like to reconsider the meaning of the term *pessimism* (2), as proposed in chapter "Case Formulation as an Outcome and Not an Opening Move in Relational and Psychodynamic Models" of this book. It is important here to distinguish between epistemic and existential pessimism, the first referring to knowledge, the second to man's nature.

Epistemic Pessimism in Psychodynamic and Cognitive Behavioral Paradigms

Of course, it is possible to speak of more epistemic pessimism on the side of psychoanalysts than on the side of cognitive-behavior therapists, with respect to the possibility of knowing all the relevant aspects of the clinical case, linked to the idea of unconscious, which is, as we have already recalled, irrelevant to the latter. However, constructionist epistemology, which is shared by theorists on both sides (as we have also recalled), implies by itself a certain pessimism about the possibility of recovering the historical truth. It is worth noting that, before the notorious book by Spence (1984) on the difference between historical and narrative truth, Freud himself expressed such pessimism at the end of his life (Freud had always a very negative idea of man's nature, but is often considered to be optimistic about the scientific enterprise and the possibilities of analytic knowledge). The Viennese patriarch, in *Constructions in Analysis* (Freud 1938), hypothesized that the patient's past could not always be completely recovered, but the narrative content could be completed (constructed), thanks to psychoanalytic theory.

It is, in our opinion, highly disputable that the implied metaphysics (in the sense of Lakatos 1976) underlying the psychodynamic paradigm, is more pessimistic than that of cognitive-behavior therapy. Stoic philosophy has been often identified as a precursor of Ellis' and Beck's theories (e.g., Montgomery 1993). It should be noted that Stoic philosophy is not necessarily less pessimistic than Freud's anthropology, which has itself often been defined as Stoic (e.g., Kirsner 2006; Rorty 1996; Ure 2005). As far as the roots of pessimism, described by Ruggiero, are concerned,

Libido theory (2.1), is not an element that is part of the necessary structure of the psychodynamic paradigm. On the contrary, Stephen Mitchell (1988), one of the most influential analysts of the last 50 years, expressly asked for its definitive refutation, exactly in order to promote the foundation of a new psychoanalytic paradigm. Regarding resistance (2.2), the observation that some patients would not change their schemes led cognitive-behavior therapists to explain such a fact in different ways (Mancini and Gangemi 2002), which are in the end all amenable to the general concept of resistance, drawn from psychoanalytic theories (Foschi and Innamorati 2020).

References

Bateman, A., Peter (Psychoanalysis Unit Fonagy), & Fonagy, P. (2004). *Psychotherapy for borderline personality disorder* (pp. 529–532). Oxford, UK: Oxford University Press.

Clarkin, J. F., Yeomans, F. E., & Kernberg, O. F. (1999). *Psychotherapy for borderline personality*. New York, NY: Wiley.

Ellis, A. (1955). New approaches to psychotherapy techniques. *Journal of Clinical Psychology, 11*, 207–260.

Ferenczi, S. (1988). *The clinical diary of Sándor Ferenczi* (J. Dupont, Ed.; M. Balint and N. Zarday Jackson, Trans.). Cambridge, MA: Harvard University Press.

Foschi, R., & Innamorati, M. (2020). *Storia critica della psicoterapia (Critical history of psychotherapy)*. Milan, Italy: Raffaello Cortina.

Freud, S. (1912). *The Case of Schreber, Papers on Technique and Other Works (1911–1913). The Standard Edition of the Complete Psychological Works of Sigmund Freud* (Vol. XII). London, UK: The Hogarth Press.

Freud, S. (1936). Inhibitions, symptoms and anxiety. *The Psychoanalytic Quarterly, 5*(1), 1–28.

Freud, S. (1938). Constructions in analysis. *International Journal of Psycho-Analysis, 19*, 377–387.

Freud, S., & Jung, C. G. (1994). *The Freud/Jung letters*. New Jersey, NJ: Princeton University Press.

Gabbard, G. O. (2014). *Psychodynamic psychiatry in clinical practice*. Washington, DC: American Psychiatric Pub.

Guidano, V. F. (1991). *The self in process: Toward a post-rationalist cognitive therapy*. New York, NY: Guilford.

Innamorati, M. (2020). Dialogo inter-paradigmatico e intra-paradigmatico (Inter-paradigmatc and intra-paradigmatic dialogue). *Psicoterapia cognitiva e comportamentale* (in press).

Innamorati, M., Pergola, F., & Sarracino, D. (2018). Psychoanalysis and the demarcation criterion: Epistemological criticism revisited and new paradigm. *World Futures, 74*(5), 297–320.

Kirsner, D. (2006). Freud's stoic vision. *Australasian Journal of Psychotherapy, 25*(1), 57–81.

Kohut, H. (1971). *The analysis of the self*. London, UK: Hogarth Press.

Kohut, H. (1977). *The restoration of the self*. Chicago, IL: University of Chicago Press.

Kohut, H. (1984). *How does analysis cure?* Chicago, IL: University of Chicago Press.

Kuhn, T. (1962). *The Structure of Scientific Revolutions*. Chicago, IL, USA: University of Chicago Press.

Lacan, J. (1953). *Ecrits: The First Complete Edition in English*. New York, NY: W. W. Norton & Company.

Lacan, J. (1967). *Proposal of 9 October 1967 on the psychoanalyst of the school*. Retrieved from www.lacaninireland.com

Lacan, J. (2013). *The ethics of psychoanalysis 1959–1960: The seminar of Jacques Lacan [VII]*. London, UK: Routledge.

Lakatos, I. (1976). *Proofs and Refutations*. Cambridge, NY, USA: Cambridge University Press.

Liotti, G. (1994). *La dimensione interpersonale della coscienza The interpersonal dimension of consciousness*. Rome, Italy: NIS.
Mancini, F., & Gangemi, A. (2002). Ragionamento e irrazionalità [Reasoning and irrationality]. In C. Castelfranchi, F. Mancini and M. Miceli (a cura di). *Fondamenti di Cognitivismo Clinico [Fundamentals of Clinical Cognitivism]* (pp. 156–199). Torino, Italy: Bollati Boringhieri.
Mitchell, S. A. (1988). *Relational concepts in psychoanalysis*. Cambridge, MA: Harvard University Press.
Montgomery, R. W. (1993). The ancient origins of cognitive therapy: the reemergence of Stoicism. *Journal of Cognitive Psychotherapy, 7*, 5.
Plotkin, M., & Ruperthuz, M. (2017). *Estimado Dr. Freud. Una historia cultural del psicoanálisis en América Latina*. Buenos Aires, Argentina: Edhasa.
Rank, O. (1924). The trauma of birth in its importance for psychoanalytic therapy. *Psychoanalytic Review, 11*(3), 241–245.
Rank, O. (1926). *Technik der Psychoanalyse (Technique of psychoanalysis)*. Leipzig, Germany/Vienna, Austria: Deuticke.
Rank, O., & Ferenczi, S. (1925). *The development of psychoanalysis*. New York, NY: NNM Publishing.
Rorty, A. (1996). The two faces of Stoicism: Rousseau and Freud. *Journal of the History of Philosophy, 34*(3), 335–356.
Ruggiero, G. M. (2011). *Terapia cognitiva: una storia critica [Cognitive therapy: A critical history]*. Milan, Italy: R. Cortina.
Semi, A. A. (1985). *Tecnica del colloquio [Technique of the interview]*. Milano, Italy: Cortina.
Spence, D. P. (1984). *Narrative truth and historical truth: Meaning and interpretation in psychoanalysis*. New York, NY: Norton & Company.
Sullivan, H. S. (1954). *The psychiatric interview*. New York, NY: Norton & Company.
Ure, M. V. (2005). Stoic comedians. Nietzsche and Freud on the art of arranging one's humours. *Nietzsche-Studien, 34*(1), 186–216.

Case Formulation in Psychoanalysis and in Cognitive-Behavioral Therapies: Commentary on Chapter "Case Formulation as an Outcome and Not an Opening Move in Relational and Psychodynamic Models"

Paolo Migone

Contents

Case Formulation in Psychoanalysis

The central thesis of chapter "Case Formulation as an Outcome and Not an Opening Move in Relational and Psychodynamic Models", and also of the book, is that a shared case formulation from the beginning of therapy characterizes cognitive behavior therapy (CBT) compared with other approaches, and it is a useful therapeutic tool with implications regarding the alliance. But what does "case formulation" mean? As the editors of the book rightly point out, all psychotherapeutic approaches, including CBT, cannot ignore case formulation. For example, in psychodynamic therapy (PDT), which from a theoretical viewpoint should be very different from CBT, case formulation is of seminal importance. It is always present and can be defined as an understanding of the patient's history, a reconstruction of his or her life narrative, and the implementation of interpretation itself—a central concept of psychoanalysis—i.e., the explanation to the patient of the meaning of his or her symptoms, the reason why the patient asked for help. The heart of Freudian enterprise is precisely to understand and formulate the true meaning of the patient's life, to reconstruct his or her story (and, importantly, not to "construct" his or her story,

P. Migone (✉)
Psicoterapia e Scienze Umane ["Psychotherapy and the Human Sciences"], Parma, Italy
e-mail: migone@unipr.it

G. M. Ruggiero et al. (eds.), *CBT Case Formulation as Therapeutic Process*,
https://doi.org/10.1007/978-3-030-63587-9_25

as according to a constructivist approach, which is very much alive in both cognitivist and psychoanalytic traditions; in the latter, it is also called "hermeneutics").

In the psychoanalytic tradition, this work of reconstruction—or, if you prefer, this shared case formulation—is a therapeutic task to the extent that the patient, having better learned to master the meanings of his or her own existence, has less need to express them (symbolized, modified, etc.) through symptoms. Let us think of depression, one of the most common emotional disorders: If we help a patient to talk in detail about his- or herself, and moreover to explore painful themes that he or she has tried to avoid (i.e., working on defenses, modifying them, and so on), it can happen that the level of depression decreases, even in few sessions, because the patient resolves conflicts that were previously experienced as very acute, and reorganizes his or her inner meanings. This phenomenon is basically the famous Freudian *Junktim*, the "inseparable bond" (Freud 1927, p. 256) between the search for truth and therapy.

Case Formulation: Comparison Between Psychoanalysis and Cognitive Therapy

Regarding this aspect, therefore, we could say that there is no substantial difference between CBT and psychoanalysis. A point of apparent divergence arises when the editors state that in CBT the work of self-awareness and conscious sharing must be done as soon as possible in therapy, indeed even at the beginning. It is possible that this insistence on the early sharing of case formulation arises from the need to find a precise difference between CBT and psychoanalysis because there are no other strong aspects or concepts that differentiate these two approaches. We might also suspect that behind this need to find—at all costs—a difference between the two approaches comes from the fear of not having a strong identity. This eventuality is especially true today after the great change we have witnessed in the field of psychotherapy, in which various approaches have hybridized and fertilized each other and sometimes have even assimilated terms and concepts from each other; a similarity is also welcome because by proceeding to find more and more similarities, real differences may emerge, but not the same in which we believed before.

Indeed, sharing the case formulation at the beginning of therapy is present in many models. For instance, in Eric Berne's transactional analysis, which is an approach that is derived from psychoanalysis, a central aspect is the establishment of an initial contract based on the patient's "script": in other words, and in the terms used in this book, on a shared case formulation. There are also some psychoanalytical models adapted to borderline patients whose manuals formulated for empirical research prescribe the establishment of a precise therapeutic contract at the beginning of therapy. These techniques are, for example, Fonagy's *mentalization-based treatment* (MBT) (Bateman and Fonagy 2004) and Kernberg's *transference-focused psychotherapy* (TFP) (Clarkin et al. 1999, 2006), the latter even called *contract-*

based approach (Yeomans et al. 1992). In these psychodynamic models, however, it is argued—contrary to the CBT proposed here where it is suggested that early shared case formulation already contains therapeutic aspects in itself—that the initial contract is useful for the therapy that will take place later, in the subsequent months or years. I believe instead, in agreement with the editors of this book, that this idea is naive, and that the formulation of the initial contract—in cases where, of course, it is possible to establish it—is a *strategic* intervention, endowed with important therapeutic aspects in itself, even if, of course, further improvement may also occur later in therapy (for a discussion of this aspect, see Migone 1999).

The editors also suggest that an early shared case formulation can be therapeutic because it helps build a therapeutic alliance, which has a central role in every therapy, as confirmed by empirical research. I argue, however, that an insistence on the early shared—i.e., conscious—case formulation might be counterproductive and hinder the therapeutic alliance rather than favor it. Given that the aim of therapy—both psychodynamic and CBT—is to share the case formulation, that is to make the patient aware of our hypotheses, we must distinguish a scenario in which we allow the patient to come to accept case formulation in his or her own time (obviously encouraged by the therapist as best he or she can) from another scenario in which we insist that the patient must accept our case formulation when he or she is not yet able to do so, which could interfere with the alliance and even encourage him or her to leave therapy. It comes to mind here that third wave CBT (Migone 2010) has tried to address precisely this type of traditional CBT error that implies risks of drop-out: for example, the introduction of the concepts of "acceptance" in Hayes' *acceptance and commitment therapy* (ACT; Hayes et al. 2011) or of "validation" in Marsha Linehan's (1993) *dialectical behavior therapy* (DBT).

In other words, we can imagine two scenarios: either the patient is able to formulate the case by him- or herself, or he or she is not. If a patient is able to formulate the case, one wonders why he or she would need a therapist to do something the patient already knows how to do, or at least can comfortably do. If this were true, psychotherapy would be much easier. If, instead, the patient is not capable of formulating the case by him- or herself, then he or she must be helped by the therapist, who puts forward his or her hypothesis on the case formulation and shares it with the patient, who is always an active collaborator. Let us not forget that the patient is a fully active agent not only in CBT, as written by the editors, but also in psychoanalysis and almost all psychotherapies, so that this aspect does not characterize CBT; perhaps the only case in which the patient is "passive" is traditional hypnosis, not even Ericksonian hypnosis.

Early Case Formulation in Cognitive-Behavioral Therapy: Critical Remarks

What should be explored in detail is how a CBT therapist manages to persuade the patient to formulate the case with him or her when he or she is incapable or disagrees with the therapist's formulation. There are countless cases that could be cited. For example, some borderline patients (and, for that matter, some adolescents) typically oppose what the therapist says. Indeed, the therapist is seen as almost an enemy, and specific techniques have been identified to reach an agreement, to get the therapy contract accepted, a work that can take several sessions. Another example is the paranoid patient, who has convictions obviously opposed to those of the therapist, who knows that, if at the beginning of the treatment the therapist insists on a shared case formulation, simply loses the patient; therefore, specific techniques are necessary. This commentary is not the place to describe some of these techniques and the theories that underlie them, but for the purpose of curiosity I mention a psychoanalytic hypothesis derived from Kleinian ideas: It is assumed that the patient operates unconsciously (for defensive purposes or—in the cognitive view—for a deficit of cognitive integration) a split within him- or herself. Hence, on the one hand, he or she sees the therapist as an enemy, and on the other hand, he or she cares a lot about therapy and the sessions (which he or she always goes to regularly and on time!), and perhaps precisely to contradict the therapist. In fact, because of this psychopathology, the patient has a deep need for the therapist in order to have an enemy, that is, the patient needs paranoia in order to function, to maintain his or her psychological equilibrium (other people are "bad," while he or she is "good"), and if we demolish this defense or prematurely make the patient aware of his or her contradictions (or if we try to find an agreement with the patient, proposing a shared formulation), the patient might feel a great anger or even quit therapy. For this reason, it is postulated that this splitting should be temporarily accepted and then gradually, step by step, modified over the course of therapy (for further details, see Migone 1988, 1995c, pp. 621–629).

But I do not want to dwell on these clinical examples because they are the daily bread and butter of every therapist. What I want to emphasize is that sometimes it is necessary first to do psychotherapy, and later to share the case formulation, meaning that often the shared—i.e., conscious—formulation of the case is the outcome of therapy and not its premise; furthermore, this initial part of the therapy that precedes the shared formulation can be the most important part of the entire treatment. In my opinion, there is no alternative for the therapist unless, of course, he or she chooses not to treat difficult patients. In this regard, the problem of the so-called "indications for analysis" comes to mind, i.e., the naive way in which certain psychoanalysts of the past handled difficult cases, those who did not comply with the ground rules of therapy: They were simply considered "not analyzable," not suited for psychoanalysis, so that only patients who were, so to speak, already cured were taken into therapy. Patients who were not accepted were sent to other therapists, who faced the same difficulty with the difference that they were willing to treat these patients, also because they knew techniques that those "orthodox" psychoanalysts had not been taught. Traditionally, psychoanalysts used to say that these therapists did not do "psychoanalysis" but "psychoanalytic psychotherapy." They were, in short, sort of second class psychoanalysts, when in reality they were better psychoanalysts because they were able to adapt psychoanalytic theory to the needs of single patients and better understood the relationship between theory and technique. I will not go into this problem here, which also has important sociological implications. For further details, see Migone (1991b, 2000a, 2020).

What should be discussed in detail is the way CBT therapists face the difficulty that some patients have in sharing case formulation. This is from my viewpoint the most interesting aspect, also because we could make discoveries that would surprise us. For instance, we may realize that some supposed differences between CBT and psychodynamic therapy, which we believed as true, would melt like snow in the sun. Let us not forget that often, when we are faced with difficult patients, it is a naive illusion to think that we apply the technique we have learned during our training, because it is the patient who largely suggests what technique to use, who even imposes it on us, who forces us to do certain things and not others. It is no coincidence that the more difficult the patients are, the more similar the therapeutic approaches become, beyond the terminology used. An exploration of strong similarities between the clinical practices of DBT and TFP, two techniques that in theory should be opposite—the first a cognitive-behavioral approach and the second a psychoanalytic approach—is reported in Migone (2004).

I conclude with some reflections regarding the editors' viewpoint that, despite many similarities, it is important to distinguish CBT approaches from other psychotherapeutic treatments—such as psychoanalysis—in which conscious cognition is an important variable but is not the pivotal mediator of emotional suffering and the main goal of therapeutic intervention. It is true that in non-CBT approaches, for example in psychoanalysis, in order to explain both the onset and disappearance of symptoms, and also to maximize the therapeutic process, importance is given to unconscious cognition. However, conscious cognition is never underestimated; on the contrary, in traditional psychoanalysis, as it is well known, it has a central role. Let us think not only of the key concept of verbal interpretation (which is a conscious cognitive intervention and which characterizes psychoanalysis *par excellence*), but also of insight, which, according to the conceptions of classical psychoanalysis, guarantees the stability of change, in opposition to the more experiential approaches. Herein I cannot discuss in depth the heated debate of the 1940s and 1950s on corrective emotional experience, an intervention that could work well without conscious understanding and interpretation, and I refer to the classic contribution of Alexander et al. (1946) and to the critique of Eissler (1950).

On the other hand, the role of the unconscious—understood as "non-conscious," i.e., not as a dynamic or psychoanalytic unconscious but as a cognitive, tacit, procedural unconscious—is a crucial issue. Today, more than ever before, it is an important focus of research and reflections in the cognitive movement, in a way that it would never have been imagined. Since the 1980s, studies on unconscious processes in cognitive psychology, neuroscience, psychopathology, and social and developmental psychology have increased 20 fold (Migone 2013, p. 537; Shevrin 2012, p. 496). In CBT, conscious cognition as well as unconscious cognition are emphasized, given the great importance that CBT assigns to the role of behavior as such. Let us think of behavioral exercises, which are one of the distinctive features of CBT and whose effectiveness is independent of conscious cognition, especially in the light of the crisis that CBT is going through in terms of effectiveness, which has also been admitted by important representatives of CBT itself (e.g., Kazdin 2007, p. 8).

And, conversely, within the psychoanalytic movement, the downsized role of awareness in promoting the therapeutic change has been increasingly understood; let us think of concepts such as insight not as content but as *function*, as if there could be a sort of unconscious insight, or of Ernst Kris's (1952, 1975) line of research (see also Rapaport et al. 1999), which goes back to the 1930s, and so on. Even the recent interest in the topics of mentalization and metacognition—which has brought the attention to issues that in the psychoanalytic movement had been dealt with a long time ago (Fonagy himself sometimes recalls that mentalization is basically old wine in new barrels; see Migone 2000b)—helped many colleagues, both psychoanalysts and cognitivists, to understand how the thought *process* is much more important than its *content*, especially in personality disorders.

A final reflection concerns constructivist approaches. The editors state that in their book they sometimes use the term "constructivist approaches" as distinct from the term "standard CBT approaches," but at the same time we are aware that the constructivist approaches belong to the CBT domain. I have always thought that the constructivist movement falls within the CBT domain only from a sociological viewpoint (e.g., tradition of "schools"): In fact, from the point of view of the history of ideas in psychotherapy we know that constructivism antecedes CBT. It is apparent that the constructivist tradition adopts central ideas of the psychodynamic tradition, often using new terms to allude to the same concepts. For example, let us consider the concept of transference, which is intrinsically a constructivist concept. In this regard, an amusing and enlightening episode comes to my mind. Years ago at a congress I listed the seven principles of psychodynamic therapy as described by Shedler (2010, pp. 98–100), who in turn took them from Blagys and Hilsenroth (2000), who had identified them on a non-theoretical but empirical basis, in order to reliably distinguish CBT from psychodynamic therapy in empirical research; these principles had been described without using a psychoanalytic jargon, but only through clinical language. After I read these seven principles, a well-known exponent of the cognitive movement, director of one of the most important schools of cognitive-constructivist psychotherapy in Italy, raised his hand and said that those principles are exactly what he had always taught in his school.

I cannot here discuss in more depth certain aspects of the cognitive therapy movement, for example the contributions of Vittorio Guidano who, in my opinion, revisited key psychoanalytic concepts without always recognizing his intellectual debt (Migone 1991, 2018) or the developments of the third wave CBT (Migone 2010), which can be seen also as the expression of a crisis of the CBT movement and of the need to go back to old psychodynamic ideas because there is greater awareness that it is not easy to make changes in patients using only classical CBT techniques.

For more in depth discussion of the relationship between cognitive-behavioral and psychodynamic approaches I refer to other papers (Migone 1991, 1991a, 1995b, 2001, 2004, 2007, 2010, 2013, 2018, 2019).

References

Alexander F., & French T.M. et al. (1946). *Psychoanalytic therapy: Principles and applications*. New York, NY: Ronald Press. Internet edition of Chapters 2, 4, and 17: The corrective emotional experience, www.psychomedia.it/pm/modther/probpsiter/alexan-2.htm.

Bateman, A., & Fonagy, P. (2004). *Psychotherapy for borderline personality disorder. Mentalization-based treatment*. New York, NY: Oxford University Press.

Blagys, M. D., & Hilsenroth, M. J. (2000). Distinctive activities of short-term psychodynamic-interpersonal psychotherapy: A review of the comparative psychotherapy process literature. *Clinical Psychology: Science and Practice, 7*(2), 167–188. https://doi.org/10.1093/clipsy.7.2.167.

Clarkin, J. F., Yeomans, F., & Kernberg, O. F. (1999). *Psychotherapy for borderline personality*. New York, NY: Wiley.

Clarkin, J. F., Yeomans, F., & Kernberg, O. F. (2006). *Psychotherapy for borderline personality. Focusing on object relations*. Washington, DC: American Psychiatric Publishing.

Eissler K.R. (1950). The Chicago Institute of Psychoanalysis and the sixth period of the development of psychoanalytic technique. *Journal of General Psychology, 42*(1), 103–157. https://doi.org/10.1080/00221309.1950.9920150. Internet edition: www.psychomedia.it/pm/modther/probpsiter/eiss50-2.htm.

Freud S. (1927). The question of lay analysis (1926). Postscript (1927). *S.E., 20*, 179–258.

Hayes, S. C., Strosahl, K. W., & Wilson, K. G. (2011). *Acceptance and commitment therapy. The process and practice of mindful change* (2nd ed.). New York, NY: Guilford.

Kazdin, A. E. (2007). Mediators and mechanisms of change in psychotherapy research. *Annual Review of Clinical Psychology, 3*, 1–27. https://doi.org/10.1146/annurev.clinpsy.3.022806.091432.

Kris, E. (1952). *Psychoanalytic explorations on art*. New York, NY: International Universities Press.

Kris, E. (1975). *Selected papers*. New Haven, CT: Yale University Press.

Linehan, M. M. (1993). *Cognitive-behavioral treatment of borderline personality disorder; Skills Training Manual for Treating Borderline Personality Disorder*. New York, NY: Guilford.

Migone P. (1988). *La identificazione proiettiva* [Projective identification]. In: Migone, 1995a, Ch. 7 (New edition: 2010). Internet edition: www.psychomedia.it/pm/modther/probpsiter/ruoloter/rt49ip88.htm.

Migone P. (1991). La nuova terapia cognitiva e la psicoanalisi [The new cognitive therapy and psychoanalysis] (Book Review Essay: "Vittorio F. Guidano, The Complexity of the Self. New York, NY: Guilford, 1987"). *Psicoterapia e Scienze Umane, 25*(1), 125–132. (Presentation of the book at the "Centro Gian Franco Minguzzi", Bologna, Italy, October 29, 1990).

Migone, P. (1991a). Ancora sulla "nuova terapia cognitiva" [Again on the "new cognitive therapy"]. *Psicoterapia e Scienze Umane, 25*(4), 109–112.

Migone P. (1991b). La differenza tra psicoanalisi e psicoterapia: panorama storico del dibattito e recente posizione di Merton M. Gill [The difference between psychoanalysis and psychotherapy: Historical review of the discussion and recent position by Merton M. Gill]. *Psicoterapia e Scienze Umane, 25*(4), 35–65. [see also an intervention in the debate: 1992, 26(4), 135–136]. A new version in: Migone, 1995a, ch. 4. An Internet edition: www.psychomedia.it/pm/modther/probpsiter/ruoloter/rt59pip.htm.

Migone P. (1995a). *Terapia psicoanalitica* [Psychoanalytic therapy]. Milan, Italy: FrancoAngeli (New edition: 2010).

Migone P. (1995b). Le differenze tra psicoanalisi e terapia cognitiva [The differences between psychoanalysis and cognitive therapy]. In: Migone, 1995a, Ch. 5 (New edition: 2010).

Migone, P. (1995c). Expressed emotion and projective identification: A bridge between psychiatric and psychoanalytic concepts? *Contemporary Psychoanalysis, 31*(4), 617–640. https://doi.org/10.1080/00107530.1995.10746929.

Migone, P. (1999). Riflessioni sulla tecnica del contratto nella psicoterapia per i pazienti borderline proposta da Kernberg [Reflections on the contract-based technique in Kernberg's psychotherapy for borderline patients]. *Il Ruolo Terapeutico, 81*, 52–58. Internet edition: www.psychomedia.it/pm/modther/probpsiter/ruoloter/rt81-99.htm.

Migone, P. (2000a). A psychoanalysis on the chair and a psychotherapy on the couch. Implications of Gill's redefinition of the differences between psychoanalysis and psychotherapy. In D. K. Silverman & D. L. Wolitzky (Eds.), *Changing conceptions of psychoanalysis: The legacy of Merton M. Gill* (pp. 219–235). Hillsdale, NJ: Analytic Press. [Spanish translation: El psicoanálisis en el sillón y la psicoterapia en el diván. Implicaciones de la redefinición de Gill sobre las diferencias entre psicoanálisis y psicoterapia. Intersubjetivo. Revista de Psicoterapia Psicoanalitica y Salud, 2000, 2(1), 23–40].

Migone, P. (2000b). Recovery of memories and therapeutic change. *International Journal of Psychoanalysis, 81*(2), 356–357. (with a reply by Peter Fonagy, p. 357).

Migone, P. (2001). Psychoanalysis and cognitive-behavior therapy. *International Journal of Psychoanalysis, 85*(5), 984–988.

Migone, P. (2004). Riflessioni sulla Dialectical Behavior Therapy (DBT) di Marsha Linehan [Reflections of Marsha Lineahan's Dialectical Behavior Therapy (DBT)]. *Psicoterapia e Scienze Umane, 38*(3), 361–378.

Migone, P. (2007). L'inconscio psicoanalitico e l'inconscio cognitivo [The psychoanalytic and the cognitive unconscious]. *Il Ruolo Terapeutico, 105*, 51–61. [Spanish translation: El incosciente psicoanalitico y el incosciente cognitivo. *Clinica e Investigación Relacional*, 2010, 4(3), 505–517. Internet edition: www.psicoterapiarelacional.es/Portals/0/eJournalCeIR/V4N3_2010/01_Migone_Inconsciente_CeIR_V4N3.pdf].

Migone, P. (2010). Il problema della "traduzione" di aspetti delle filosofie orientali nella psicoterapia occidentale [The problem of "translation" of aspects of Oriental philosophies into western psychotherapy]. *Psicoterapia e Scienze Umane, 44*(1), 35–52. https://doi.org/10.3280/PU2010-001003.

Migone, P. (2013). Una rassegna delle ricerche sperimentali sull'inconscio psicoanalitico [A review of experimental research on the psychoanalytic unconscious]. *Sistemi Intelligenti, 25*(3), 537–552. https://doi.org/10.1422/76300.

Migone, P. (2018). Book review eassy: "Bruno G. Bara, Il terapeuta relazionale. Tecnica dell'atto terapeutico. [The relational therapist: Technique of the therapeutic act] Turin: Bollati Boringhieri, 2018". *Psicoterapia e Scienze Umane, 52*(3), 479–484. https://doi.org/10.3280/PU2018-003016.

Migone, P. (2019). La relazione terapeutica nella tradizione psicoanalitica [The therapeutic relationship within the psychoanalytic tradition]. *Quaderni di Psicoterapia Cognitiva, 45*, 83–100. https://doi.org/10.3280/qpcoa.v0i45.8989.g532.

Migone, P. (2020). On the identity of psychoanalysis. *International Journal of Psychoanalysis (IJP) Open, 7*, 92 (www.pep-web.org/document.php?id=ijpopen.007.0092a).

Rapaport, D., Kris, E., Neubauer, P. B., Blum, H. P., & Noy, P. (1999). *Preconscio e creatività* [Preconscious and creativity]. Turin, Italy: Einaudi.

Shedler, J. (2010). The efficacy of psychodynamic therapy. *American Psychologist, 65*(2), 98–109. https://doi.org/10.1037/a0018378.

Shevrin, H. (2012). A contribution towards a science of psychoanalysis. *Psychoanalytic Review, 99*(4), 491–509. https://doi.org/10.1521/prev.2012.99.4.491.

Yeomans, F. E., Selzer, M. A., & Clarkin, J. F. (1992). *Treating the borderline patient: A contract-based approach*. New York, NY: Basic Books.

The Empirical State of Case Formulation: Integrating and Validating Cognitive, Evolutionary and Procedural Elements in the CBT Canse Formulation in the LIBET Procedure

Sandra Sassaroli, Gabriele Caselli, and Giovanni Maria Ruggiero

Contents

The Three Principles of the CBT Case Formulation

Core Beliefs and Coping Strategies: The Two Axes of the Diathesis-Stress Model as First Principle of the CBT Case Formulation

In *cognitive behavioral therapy* (CBT) approaches, the shared case formulation is a primary therapeutic tool. In it, the therapist provides the patient an explanation of his or her vulnerability to emotional disorders and suffering in intelligible terms. These terms are the CBT general model of diathesis-stress of psychological vulnerability proposed by Beck, i.e. the emergence of an emotional disorder from a

S. Sassaroli

Sigmund Freud University, Milan, Italy

Sigmund Freud University, Vienna, Austria

"Studi Cognitivi", Cognitive Psychotherapy School and Research Center, Milan, Italy

G. Caselli
Sigmund Freud University, Milano, Italy

Sigmund Freud University, Wien, Austria

Department of Psychology, London South Bank University, London, UK

G. M. Ruggiero et al. (eds.), *CBT Case Formulation as Therapeutic Process*,
https://doi.org/10.1007/978-3-030-63587-9_26

vulnerability to developmental or even biological triggers precipitated by stressful adverse events and maintained by dysfunctional coping strategies (Beck 1996, 2008; Beck and Bredemeier 2016; Clark et al. 1999; Dobson et al. 2018). In addition, the diathesis-stress hypothesis is assumed by Ellis' *rational emotive behavior therapy* (REBT; Ellis 1955, 1962; Ellis and Grieger 1986), as emphasized by David et al. (2005, pp. 198–199).

Beck's model assumes that people who experience adversity during childhood develop negative patterns of self; these patterns are thought to remain inactive until an individual experiences subjectively stressful life events. At that point, the negative schemes are activated and generate negative knowledge called *core beliefs*—particularly about the self but also about the world and the future with respect to human relationships, in particular in the case of depression or personality disorders, which are destructive and extreme. It is also believed that the activated schemes, verbalized as core beliefs, act as filters that shape the way events are perceived, evaluated, followed, and remembered (Beck 1996, 2008; Beck and Bredemeier 2016; Clark et al. 1999; Dobson et al. 2018). Summing up, the verbalization of emotional vulnerability in terms of core beliefs focused on the self is related to the theoretical cognitive model of emotional disorders premised on the pivotal role of self-knowledge—a knowledge that would provide guidance, consistency, coordination, and integration for mental states (Bandura 1977, 1988; Markus 1977; Neisser 1967). Table 1, already present and discussed in the chapter "Strengths and Limitations of Case Formulation in Constructivist Cognitive Behavioral Therapies", reports again the best classifications of self-knowledge as are in Judith Beck's cognitive self-beliefs (Beck 2011, p. 233) and in the constructivist personality organizations by Guidano and Liotti (1983, pp. 171–306) and Mahoney (2003).

In addition, the activated schemes are maintained by dysfunctional *coping strategies* that keep the patients' attention focused on preventing threats, such as:

1. avoidant safety behaviors in anxiety disorders (Salkovskis 1991; Thwaites and Freeston 2005);
2. controlling strategies aimed at preventing threats, as occurs in obsessive compulsive disorder (Barlow 2002; Moulding and Kyrios 2006; Rachman 1993; Salkovskis 1985) and in eating disorders (Sassaroli et al. 2008a, b);
3. aggressive and reactive strategies aimed at suppressing threats (Critchfield et al. 2008; DiGiuseppe and Tafrate 2001; Martin and Dahlen 2005); and
4. rewarding strategies, such as substance abuse and dependent behaviors, aimed at distracting from threats (Allen et al. 2017; Caselli and Spada 2015; Dragan 2015; Spada et al. 2012, 2013).

G. M. Ruggiero (✉)
"Psicoterapia Cognitiva e Ricerca," Cognitive Psychotherapy School and Research Center, Milan, Italy

Sigmund Freud University, Milan, Italy

Sigmund Freud University, Vienna, Austria
e-mail: gm.ruggiero@milano-sfu.it

Table 1 Self-knowledge in constructive and cognitive therapy approaches

Beck's cognitive therapy self-beliefs (adapted from Beck 2011, p. 233)	Constructive personality organizations (Guidano and Liotti 1983, pp. 171–306; Mahoney 2003)
Helpless self Defective; Failed; Helpless; Incompetent; Ineffective; Loser; Needy; Not good enough; Out of control; Powerless; Trapped; Victim; Vulnerable; Weak	**Phobic personality organization** Being despised; Being ridiculed; Needing protection; Not amiable; Not in control; Unable to cope with; Weak
Unlovable self Bad; Bound to be abandoned; Bound to be alone; Bound to be rejected; Defective; Different; Unattractive; Uncared for; Undesirable; Unlikeable; Unlovable; Unwanted	**Depressed personality organization** Abandoned; Being wrong; Disappointed; Failed; Helpless; Isolated; Missing significant ones (loss); Needing approval; Not loved; Rejected; Separated; Worthless
Worthless self A waste; Dangerous; Do not deserve to live; Evil; Immoral; Toxic; Unacceptable; Worthless	**Obsessive personality organization** Controlled; Detached; Doubtful; Guilty; Judgmental; Looking for certainty; Moral; Perfectionistic; Responsible; Restrained; Unemotional
	Eating disordered personality organization Adhering to others' judgment; Craving emotional contact; Dependent; Self-criticizing; Self-deprecating; Undefined

The Second Principle of CBT Case Formulation: The Change of Cognitive Content as Rationale for the CBT Treatment

In addition, the CBT case formulation includes not only a model of emotional disorders but also a rationale for the CBT treatment. Aaron T. Beck provided this when he hypothesized that the therapeutic mechanism depends on the exploration and change of cognitive content (Lyddon 1990; Wells and Mathews 1994, p. 2) and that negative conscious patterns can be altered through verbal reattribution into therapy (Beck 1996; Beck et al. 1979; Clark et al. 1999; Clark and Beck 2010; Dobson and Khatri 2000; Ellis and Grieger 1986; Kelly 1955; Mahoney 1974; Meichenbaum 1977; Rachman 1977). It should be noted that constructivist models also have emphasized the organizational role played by conscious thoughts related to personal meanings (Bruner 1973; Guidano and Liotti 1983; Kelly 1955; Mahoney 1991). In this model, the stress on personal vulnerability is not sufficient to determine the disorder; on the contrary, if well-managed in a flexible way, it can result in momentary and tolerable discomfort. The transformation of that discomfort into symptoms occurs only if its management takes place in a rigid manner. Patients, instead of aiming to tolerate physiological stress, pursue an illusory final elimination of emotional suffering through the above-mentioned rigid use of coping strategies.

Sharing the CBT Formulation: An Overlooked Third Principle

The possibility of verbally conceptualizing the case along the two axes of core beliefs and coping strategies allows formulation of the case in a shared manner between therapist and patient. This sharing is a fundamental step in the CBT therapeutic process. However, it must be admitted that CBT approaches have developed without an explicit reference to case formulation (Beck 1996). It is only recently that scholars have emphasized the role of explicitly-expressed case formulation in the CBT process as a key procedure (Bieling and Kuyken 2003) that is able to link theory and practice (Butler 1998) and is the principle underlying the clinical practice of CBT (Flitcroft et al. 2007). As Willem Kuyken (2006) writes, we have to be aware of this late conceptual shift of the theoretical importance given to case formulation in CBT, otherwise it risks becoming the Emperor's magnificent new clothes (see also Tarrier 2006).

Despite all these principles, procedures of CBT case formulation have developed without much explicit reference to the explicitly shared component. An exception is Judith Beck, who is among the first scholars to have provided a detailed description and an operational tool of the therapeutic use of case formulation in cognitive therapy (CT) as developed by her father Aaron T. Beck (1996). It is known as the cognitive conceptualization diagram (CCD; Beck 2011, p. 200). In CT, the therapist uses the components of the CCD—core beliefs, intermediate beliefs and coping strategies—in order to provide the patient with a psychopathological interpretation, a rationale, and a plan for the therapeutic reworking of the reported problematic situations by questioning them. The term "sharing" emphasizes the therapist's task of steadily communicating and discussing all emerging aspects of the formulation with the patient and using CCD as a tool to manage the direction of the therapeutic process. Moreover, in CT, the CCD is crucial for the management of the therapeutic relationship in so-called complex cases, i.e. cases that undermine the therapeutic alliance. Judith Beck (2011) not only suggests that the problem in complex cases should be addressed on a relational level, but also that CCD can be used to conceptualize relational obstacles to therapy and find solutions for relational difficulties in a careful analysis of biased interpersonal beliefs (Beck et al. 2015).

Validation of the CBT Case Formulation: A Review

Despite all these principles, measures of validity and reliability either of CBT case formulation or of the diathesis-stress scientific foundation of the CBT approaches are only beginning to be studied and, in addition, have developed without much explicit reference to each other. For example, although the procedure of implementation of the above-mentioned CCD formulation is mature, its validation as well as that of other case formulation procedures remain imperfect, as reported by Eells (2007, 2011, 2015). According to Eells, the validation of the case formulation models remains only partially developed in a still insufficient number of publications—on the order of dozens compared to hundreds of studies (or more) exploring therapeutic procedures and their efficacy. The results of these studies are not conclusive, being limited to inter-rater reliability (Mumma and Smith 2001; Persons and Bertagnolli 1999) and construct validity (Kuyken et al. 2008).

Therefore, measurement of the validity and reliability of the case formulation process and its sharing with the patient in CBT approaches are just beginning. However, there is some emerging evidence that therapist training, experience and competence and the use of structured case formulation procedures improve reliability (Kuyken et al. 2005; Persons and Bertagnolli 1999). More experienced CBT therapists are more likely to produce more consistent, elaborate, and concise case formulations (Kendjelic and Eells 2007; Kuyken et al. 2005; Mumma and Mooney 2007). However, only a minority of formulations are good enough in terms of quality (Kuyken et al. 2005).

Regarding the reliability of the CBT case formulation process, some studies report that a good degree of consensus can be reached (Mumma and Smith 2001; Persons and Bertagnolli 1999). Despite this, there is no evidence of the convergence of formulations between practitioners, clients, and supervisors. Although there are studies (Kuyken et al. 2001; Persons et al. 2006) suggesting that the results of CBT case formulation in real-world contexts are comparable to those observed in randomized controlled trials, there is no conclusive research confirming the convergent validity of CBT case formulation (Kuyken et al. 2008). Furthermore, the existing literature (Chadwick et al. 2003; Nelson-Gray et al. 1989; Schulte et al. 1992) does not support the suggestion that therapeutic approaches based on individualized formulations improve results. On the other hand, as regards reliability among practitioners, the available studies suggest that CBT professionals may agree on the descriptive aspects of a formulation, but agreement on the inferential aspects tends to be moderate or poor (Mumma and Smith 2001; Persons and Bertagnolli 1999).

From a patient perspective, several studies (Ghaderi 2006; Schneider and Byrne 1987; Strauman et al. 2006; Evans and Parry 1996; Pain et al. 2008) have provided support for both the likely benefits and the possible drawbacks of a CBT case formulation. On the other hand, CBT therapists generally consider case formulation to be a vital part of CBT (Flitcroft et al. 2007). In conclusion, strong confirmation that case formulation improves CBT results is surprisingly absent. These results are applicable to J. Beck's CCD (Kuyken et al. 2005).

In summary, while these studies suggest that high-quality case formulation is essential in intervention planning (Needleman 1999) they fail to demonstrate the direct impact of cognitive case formulation on CBT outcomes. They also raise an important conceptual question because these studies on the one hand state that the formulation should be explicitly shared with the client, and on the other also suggest that a large part of professionals' case formulation processes are not explicitly shared and managed on an intuitive level.

Another aspect of the CBT case formulation that remains imperfectly explored and validated is its bidimensional arrangement in core beliefs and coping strategies based on the diathesis-stress model. We would expect to find many in-depth studies on this classification and its validation. However, the reality is unsatisfactory.

Steps Forward in the Validating the CBT Case Formulation: The LIBET Procedure

Aims of the LIBET Procedure

The *Life themes and semi-adaptive plans: Implications of biased Beliefs, Elicitation and Treatment* (LIBET; Sassaroli et al. 2016) is a method aimed to explicitly share a CBT case formulation grounded on the diathesis stress model. In particular, it is a procedure that allows the therapist to understand and share with the patient an explanation of his or her emotional disorder, a rationale for the implementation of the therapeutic procedures selected and a measure for monitoring the progression of the psychotherapy.

From a clinical viewpoint, LIBET is aimed to encourage clinicians to use shared formulation in their practice and help them to avoid the risk to take for granted that the formulation was automatically shared with the patients during the therapeutic process. LIBET aims also to provide a measure of the specific contribution of the shared aspect of case formulation to the therapeutic process in CBT approaches.

In addition, LIBET is designed to be a step forward in the validating process of the CBT case formulation model and, in particular, of its bidimensional arrangement in two axes: emotional vulnerability (expressed in terms of core beliefs in CBT models) and coping strategies. In fact, the LIBET assessment procedure is in line with Judith Beck's CCD, as it maintains the two-axis model of core beliefs and coping strategies.

Integrating and Validating Cognitive, Evolutionary and Procedural Elements in the Formulation of the CBT Case in the LIBET Procedure

The LIBET aims to both validate the standard CBT model and promotes its further development by conceptualizing it not only in terms of classical cognitive contents about self-core beliefs and coping strategies, but also including a developmental aspect that would justify the emotional vulnerability as a learnt experience during the patients' life as well as a process dimension that explains the maintaining role of the coping strategies. In other words, in LIBET, the two dimensions of emotional vulnerability and coping strategies are expressed in terms of the developmental sensitivity precipitated and maintained by dysfunctional process rigidities (Sassaroli et al. 2017a, b).

Actually, these additional aspects and process aspects of LIBET are rooted in the history of the standard CBT model. The developmental vulnerability was already partially present in Beck's model, when it suggested that dysfunctional self-schemata and self-beliefs are rooted in the personal history of the patient (Beck 1996, 2008; Beck and Bredemeier 2016; Clark et al. 1999; Clark and Beck 2010; Dobson et al. 2018) and, in the CCD procedure, this notion was called "relevant childhood data" (Beck 2011, p. 201). As mentioned above, it was also present in other CBT approaches that traditionally cultivated this aspect (Bannister and Fransella 1971; Feixas and Miró 1993; Guidano 1987, 1991; Guidano and Liotti 1983; Lorenzini and Sassaroli 1995; Mahoney 1974, 1991, 2003; Neimeyer 2009; Neimeyer and Mahoney 1995; Winter and Viney 2005). Emotional disorders seem to be contingent on early experiences that leave some of the primary emotional needs of the child unsatisfied and that create psychological vulnerability (Young et al. 2003). However, in the CBT approach such vulnerability is not mechanically doomed to develop into an emotional disorder because early patterns are characterized by a form of adaptability that is only subsequently compromised in dysfunctional reactions to painful experiences. Therefore, unhealthy adult modalities represent a rigid application of functional developmental habits.

Also, LIBET's promotion of the integration of process aspects into standard CBT is rooted in the history of the CBT model itself. Again, the importance of process components had already been identified in CBT standard models, such as by Aaron Beck himself when he described the circle of fear of fear, in his paper claiming the possibility of going beyond beliefs (Beck), or even more sharply by Ellis with his seminal concept of secondary ABC, which was a forerrunner metacognitive concepts (DiGiuseppe et al. 2014, pp. 64–65; Sassaroli et al. 2005). Recently, a similar integration was proposed by Hayes and Hofman (2018) in their process-based CBT model.

On the other hand, it is true that the exploration of processes owes much to the new generation of CBT, which focuses on psychopathological processes—i.e., *acceptance and commitment therapy* (ACT; Hayes and Strosahl 2004), *behavioral activation* (BA; Martell et al. 2001; Kanter et al. 2009), *cognitive behavioral analysis system of psychotherapy* (CBASP; McCullough Jr and Goldfried 1999), *dialectical behavior therapy* (DBT; Linehan 1993), *functional analysis psychotherapy* (FAP; Kohlenberg and Tsai 1991), and *integrative behavioral couples therapy* (IBCT; Christensen et al. 1995)—and metacognitive reflexive mental functioning, i.e., *metacognitive therapy* (MCT; Wells 2008). This kind of functional cognitivism suggests that emotional disorders do not depend exclusively on biased mental representations of the self (i.e. self-knowledge and self-beliefs), as A. T. Beck (1996) held. Rather, they rely on the dysfunctional interaction between voluntary and regulatory processes—for example, attention and executive control—and emotionally charged, automatic associative processes (Hayes and Hofman 2018; Kahneman and Frederick 2002; Martin and Sloman 2013; Sloman 2002; Stanovich 1999; Stanovich and West 2002; Wells and Mathews 1994).

Therefore, the LIBET model attempts to integrate these functionalist principles into the classical CBT diathesis-stress model by assuming that developmental vulnerability is not sufficient to determine the disorder but—if managed in a flexible way by individuals—results in temporary discomfort. By contrast, psychopathology emerges only if the management of the discomfort occurs in rigid ways and when the mind is not aimed at tolerating stress (but has the goal of gaining an illusory, definitive suppression of emotional pain through the rigid use of coping strategies).

Summing up, LIBET is a clinical conceptualization model for emotional disorders that reformulates core beliefs and coping strategies along two process-related dimensions: (1) "life themes," defined as mental states of focused attention to emotional sensitivities represented as self-beliefs in consciousness (Wells 2008) and/or bodily sensations influenced by experiences perceived as intolerably painful and/or dangerous during personal development (Panksepp 1998; Panksepp and Watt 2011; Schore 2012a, b); and (2) "semi-adaptive plans" or rigid management strategies of "life themes," implemented by adopting coping strategies such as anxious safety behaviors (Salkovskis 1991; Thwaites and Freeston 2005), compulsive controls (Salkovskis 1985); and aggressive or rewarding strategies, including desire thinking, anger rumination, impulsive behaviors, and dependent behaviors (Critchfield et al. 2008; DiGiuseppe and Tafrate 2001; Martin and Dahlen 2005; Spada et al. 2012). These strategies are adopted even at the cost of giving up significant areas of personal development. Therefore, in the long term, "semi-adaptive plans" hinder personal development and, beyond a certain level of dysfunctionality, may lead to emotional disorders. Finally, there is (3) a process level that maintains active themes and plans to the extent that they are considered either conditioning, necessary, uncontrollable, or intolerable.

Cognitive and Constructivist Roots of the LIBET Model

The LIBET is not only a response to the need to develop and validate the shared formulation of the case; it is also the historical fruit of the Italian clinical cognitivism tradition—a school of thought that has often integrated both the standard CT model and the constructivist one. This integration is carried out starting from the common view of the pivotal role of the schemes on the self and dysfunctional behaviors in both traditions, and adding to these two parameters other processes that hearken to two other traditions: (1) Ellis' REBT (DiGiuseppe et al. 2014; Ellis and Grieger 1986) which, despite its traditional approach, has always had a process aspect and (2) the recent process-based CBT therapies (Hayes and Hofman 2018). In summary, the LIBET model is a case formulation procedure aimed at conceptualizing coping strategies as partially functional in certain periods of life, but also at the risk of hindering personal development and leading to emotional disorders. The rigidity, in turn, is assessed in terms of processes: intolerability and conditioning of life themes and necessity and uncontrollability of semi-adaptive plans.

Conceptualizing a clinical case in terms of themes and plans allows us to have a broader view of the patient, something that tells us not only about their symptoms but also how his/her emotional suffering is grounded into his or her personal life. Life themes and semi-adaptive plans are process concepts that allow both clinicians and patients to familiarize themselves with the functionalist vision of the mind. On such a view, one overcomes certain limitations of the CBT paradigm—that can be defined as naive computationalism and in which emotional pain is a pure error of evaluation of situations and a defect in the examination of reality.

In the process-based CBT vision, psychopathology can instead be conceived of as a simple mistake of the mind but rather as a dysfunction of mental states grounded in existential, and therefore human, motivations. Of course, in order for existential purposes to be degraded to dysfunctional purposes, dysfunctional processes must intervene, but these dysfunctions are not simple mistakes of evaluation but can be described in motivational terms. In this regard, the motivational cognitive model of Mogg and Bradley (1998) could serve as a link; they propose that, for example, anxiety disorders can be explained not only in process-based terms as an automatic tendency of attention to the threat but also by describing the effects on the motivation of these processes. Specifically, Mogg and Bradley proposed that the degree to which an individual deals with a trigger will depend on his or her currently active target, as well as how he or she evaluates the trigger procedurally. Thus, an anxious person who believes he or she is in danger not only selectively pays attention to threatening triggers, but is also objectively interested in the purpose of self-preservation and prudence, while people with low levels of anxiety would have less interest in this purpose and place less importance on threatening triggers. Likewise, depression leads to the abandonment of motivational self-preservation goals (Mogg and Bradley 1998).

Functionalist and Motivational Aspects in the LIBET Model: Emotional Suffering as Rigid Management of Contradictory Needs

Another aim of LIBET is to integrate functionalist and motivational concepts in a standard CBT framework. According to the functionalist model (Sturmey 1996, 2008), the reasons for psychological suffering are to be sought within mental functioning itself; therefore, emotional disorders are conceived of as a malfunction in the management of mental states in adverse situations. Of course, situations are adverse because they frustrate a human need (basic or culturally developed). Much ethological, psychological, and neurobiological research has defined these basic needs in terms of emotional and motivational systems (Gilbert 1989; Kenrick 2011; Kenrick et al. 2010; Panksepp 1998).

However, from a functionalist point of view, unmet human needs and frustrations are not in themselves the reasons of the psychopathological state. It is rather the inflexible and rigid management of the possible frustration that creates the condition of psychopathology. In fact, a complete elimination of frustration does not seem possible for a number of reasons: the objective limits of material reality, i.e. the hostility of the natural, family and/or social environment and the evolutionary vulnerability of the human species, an inept species with even more inept offspring: Homo is a weak and slow-ripening species in need of a high level of continuing and prolonged social care and protection (Narvaez 2018).

Another reason that suggests that frustration cannot be eliminated but only managed and tolerated is the intrinsic contradictions among the human needs themselves. Subsequently, the satisfaction of a certain need inherently implies the partial frustration of another, at least temporarily. For example, in Maslow's pyramid of needs, the needs of basic protection and safety aim to minimize risk while other needs, such as exploration and personal fulfilment, tend to increase this (Maslow 1943, 1954). These contradictory needs must be balanced in a flexible way taking into account the fact that they can never be fully satisfied at the same time in the same place, thus generating a state of inevitable physiological frustration.

From a clinical viewpoint, we could reduce the possible contradictions between the needs explored in ethological, psychological, neurobiological research (Gilbert 1989; Kenrick 2011; Kenrick et al. 2010; Panksepp 1998) to some main pairs. A first pair of contradictory needs is the tension between the basic needs of protection and safety and those of individual development and personal fulfilment. The first need encourages a watchful attitude and a cautious behavioral mechanism aimed to minimize the risk; the second suggests exploratory and curious behaviors, leading to the investigation of the environment with which the underestimation of risk and the setting aside—at least momentarily—of safety needs is correlated. The second couple includes the needs of social cooperation and collaboration, with their related affective warmth, sympathy, and mutual care ranging from professional collaboration to the most intense friendly and familiar affection. In competition with social cooperation is the individual need for personal development, affirmation, competition and social rank.

These needs are partially contradictory with each other. We cannot take this harmony between safety and development, or between sociality and personal affirmation for granted. Every time that we choose safety, protection and social warm we also decrease our degree of exploration and personal growth and affirmation and vice versa. The partial tension between basic security and social and personal needs suggests that a condition of unsatisfied partial frustration is predominant and compels the mind to embark upon a frustration tolerance task and a hard to maintain balancing effort that never stabilizes. This ongoing balancing and frustration tolerance task could be a good environmental justification for that mental flexibility that has been invoked, in context of the functionalist model, as the main mental function (Hayes and Strosahl 2004) and which in turn is related to that self-directedness that defines individual maturity (Cloninger et al. 1993).

Unfortunately, due to difficult environmental conditions or personal vulnerabilities, the mind may fail to find the compromise between contradictory needs, may stop tolerating partial frustration and ends up abandoning flexibility by opting for a kind of rigidity that privileges only one of the needs at the expense of others and thus favoring emotional disorders. In anxiety, we therefore prefer the need for protection and safety. In the narcissistic personality disorder a need for personal affirmation is interpreted as rank and competition; in depression, on the other hand, it is possible that the rigidification is obtained in the complete repudiation of satisfying needs. In other words, in emotional disorders, the mind would lose flexibility and self-directedness and would give up the objective of balancing needs, choosing to focus on the rigid satisfaction of a single need at the expense of all the others.

The impossibility of fully meeting human needs could be related to the Kellian (Kelly 1955) concept of invalidation. Kelly's view of psychopathology is based on the fundamental concept that "all disorders can be considered to represent strategies by which the individual attempts to cope with invalidation and avoid uncertainty" (Winter 1992, p. 15). During their daily life, people continually face both the validation and invalidation of their goals and expectations. Good mental functioning is the ability to use invalidation to increase complexity and knowledge growth. However, invalidations lead to knowledge growth only if managed through flexibility or, in Kellian terms, "permeability," i.e. the ability of the mental system to admit new elements in its range of constructs (Winter 1992).

Self-Generating Processes: From Dysfunctional Circles to Metacognition

Another mechanism of dysfunctionality of the system is that of the circles of self-regeneration of symptoms. Cognitive clinical theory has a long tradition of studying these self-generating cycles, from the dysfunctional circles of fear described in the standard CT to the concept of "recursive self-validation" in Kelly's model (Lorenzini and Sassaroli 1987) to Ellis with his concept of secondary ABC (DiGiuseppe et al. 2014, pp. 64–65). Finally, these self-generating processes have been promoted to the rank of the main mechanism of mental malfunctioning in metacognitive models, where they are considered to be the main mechanism of producing dysfunctionality through biased metacognitive beliefs of mental functioning (Wells and Mathews 1994).

Process Rigidity and Personal Life Story in the LIBET

Finally, there is another process that leads to rigidification, one that passes through the personal life story of the individual. The environment conditions the way in which a person's own needs are managed individually, which, as long as those environmental conditions are maintained, can be considered adequate. Later, however, those same behaviors if strictly applied to modified scenarios can become dysfunctional. For example, being a perfectionist and hyper-adaptive may work in certain types of families in the growth phase prior to adolescence; however, it can be harmful once the person begins to frequent a peer group outside their family and perceive their first complex social and affective needs. At this point it is necessary to develop different relational skills and styles. Faced with the invalidation of a perfectionistic behavior, the individual may believe that the failure is not due to an incongruity of his or her own conduct but to its insufficient application.

This phenomenon in LIBET goes by the name of rigidification the plan on developmental grounds (Lorenzini and Sassaroli 1995) and is a theoretical bridge between Kellian constructivism and the developmental model. Lorenzini and Sassaroli (1995) have proposed a conceptualization of the attachment relationship as the context in which the child learns the cognitive management of invalidation. A good attachment relationship is not only a secure emotional base but also a kind of learning laboratory in which the child learns both not to be afraid of discomfort generated by invalidations and the skill needed to integrate them into the system. On the other hand, an insecure attachment is also a context in which the child tends to conceive any invalidation as a threatening event to which he or she reacts rigidly through avoidance, controlling behaviors or aggressive counterattacks. In other words, attachment is the central relationship in which the child learns his or her own internal and others' work patterns and preferred strategies.

The Variables of Case Formulation in LIBET: Life Themes

The goal of LIBET is to translate such cognitive clinical concepts into procedural terms. The themes and plans of LIBET are primarily a tool for the representation of mental activity. They facilitate the translation of the old cognitive concepts—catastrophic thinking, loss of confidence in the future of depression, overestimation of risk, fear of judgment, inflated sense of responsibility or perfectionism—into metacognitive representations no longer directed outwards but inwards, towards the regulation of mental representations themselves. While in standard CT, dysfunctionality depends on the mistaken evaluation of realty, e.g., overestimation of risks, in the third wave process paradigm it depends on a biased internal regulation of mental representations themselves of frustration in adverse situations.

"Life themes" represents emotional vulnerability to adversity. It is a term we can find in several authors of Italian cognitivism (Capo et al. 2010; Di Fini and Veglia 2019; Dodet 2010) who had borrowed it from the field of humanistic and existential psychotherapy, namely from Frankl (2006) and Jaspers (1971), and then from the work of Csikszentmihalyi and Beattie (1979). In particular, Capo and Mancini (2008)—following a path already established by Miceli and Castelfranchi (2002)—had sensed that the life themes, although possessing philosophical and existential origins, could be translated in psychological terms if they were connected to the satisfaction of basic needs, such as protection and nutrition, and more evolved ones, such as self-affirmation and exploration of the world.

The results of the analysis of lexical specificities assessed in qualitative interviews with patients and nonclinical individuals has suggested three clusters of life themes.

1. The first cluster may correspond to a vulnerability state of *freezing/panic* (Herman 1992; Ogden et al. 2006; van der Kolk 1996) that we have linked to the life theme of *threat*, or the need to possess a protected place of personal safety, nourishment, and care (Siegel 1999). The absence of security can lead to a self-perception of endlessness and disorganization (Ogden et al. 2006).
2. A second cluster refers to sadness and depression (Bifulco et al. 2006; Huprich 2003; Kiernan and Huerta 2008), linked to a life theme of *disaffection and inadequacy*, in which a protective environment is present and the exploratory needs of the subject are not contrasted. Here, everything is provided in a cold atmosphere of emotional deprivation, dismissing affectivity, and in which bodily contacts are rare and clumsy (Bosquet and Egeland 2006; Woodruff-Borden et al. 2002).
3. The third cluster primarily concerns shame and guilt (Brewin et al. 1992; Huprich 2003; Irons et al. 2006; Kawamura et al. 2001; Vieth and Trull 1999), linked to a life theme of *unworthiness*, where a protective environment is present, exploratory functions are not contrasted and there is some affective warmth, but there is also a severely critical, controlling, and oppressive relational style, in which rules are experienced and transmitted in an oppressive, moralistic, guilty, and punitive manner.

The Variables of the Case Formulation in LIBET: Semi-adaptive Plans

Semi-adaptive plans are ways in which the mind manages its life themes and its vulnerabilities. They are defined as semi-adaptive because they are functional in a given context but can turn into dysfunctional plans if applied inflexibly to another context and favor an emotional disorder when mechanically applied to all contexts. An experience of risk can crystallize into a rigid belief that the world is dangerous and the person is fragile, leading the individual to turn his/her entire life into an avoidance in which the goal of personal safety is constantly at the forefront regardless of context and at the expense of the alternative goals of self-affirmation, personal growth, and risk acceptance. Just as the life themes of LIBET revisit Beck's core beliefs in process terms, semi-adaptive plans rework the other pillar of the CT model—the coping strategies—in process terms.

However, there are differences. In CT, a coping strategy is a conscious effort to solve a personal or interpersonal problem that itself generates a new stress. Coping strategies therefore have an episodic, conscious, and reactive nature to adverse conditions. Instead, semi-adaptive plans are habitual strategies to maintain security and prevent threats to learned vulnerabilities. In this sense, they possess characteristics that differ from coping strategies: (1) they are generalized and pervasive and are therefore independent of circumstances; (2) they have had an adaptive role at least in the phase of life in which they were learned and established and promote learning through reinforcement processes; (3) there is a lack of awareness of their voluntariness, activate by default in a type of passive and automated ego-syntonic state that makes them an aspect of personality; (4) they have a preventive purpose that is active even in conditions of low threat and regardless of the needs of the circumstances. Semi-adaptive plans always show a metacognitive aspect: for example, the over-safety of anxious people's life plan is not only an overestimation of the dangerousness of the world, but also and above all, an over-importance and attention to their anxious states and an overestimation of their intensity and intolerability; the person overestimates the signal, not reality.

The results of the analysis of lexical specificities assessed in qualitative interviews in patients and in nonclinical individuals have suggested three clusters of semi-adaptive plans.

1. The first cluster corresponds to the *prudential plan*, in which people tend to avoid aversive and threatening stimulations. The consequence is a failure to develop explorative and constructive aspects of existence (Barlow 2002; Blalock and Joiner 2000).
2. The second cluster is the *prescriptive plan*, in which the individual steadily attempts to control, prevent, or resolve any adverse stimuli. This preventive plan can be manifested in either simply mingling and worrying about acting on reality and relationships, or in controlling behaviors (Barlow 2002; Moulding and Kyrios 2006; Ruggiero et al. 2012; Sassaroli et al. 2008a, b; Shafran et al. 2002).
3. The third cluster pertains to the *immunizing plan*, in which the subject seeks to exclude from one's conscience any threat related to the painful subject through direct action on its internal state, whether by (1) fostering alternatives and intense emotional states (anger, exciting substances) or (2) reducing consciousness (e.g., taking sedatives such as alcohol). These plans are related to intentional states of anger and/or desire (Critchfield et al. 2008; DiGiuseppe and Tafrate 2001; Mansueto et al. 2019; Martin and Dahlen 2005; Spada et al. 2012).

Implementation of the Shared Formulation and Monitoring of the Case in LIBET

The shared formulation and monitoring diagram of the case in LIBET, as set out in Table 2, has been designed by adapting the CCD case formulation model. As in CCD, in LIBET there is a series of functional analyses of problematic situations, tendentially (but not necessarily) three. From the REBT but not from the CT, however, we have borrowed the ABC framework, which is historically widespread in the clinical practice of Italian cognitivism, and the position of emotions located before thoughts. Moreover, unlike CBT and this time borrowing from the constructivist and developmental tradition of Italian cognitivism, the problem situations are not all located in the present but cover the timeline of the patient's developmental process of the problem.

The first ABC is that of the *present*, the one that characteristically represents the problem that brought the patient into therapy. At the opposite extreme, instead, we find an ABC that represents the *learning* in the past of the problematic cognitive and emotional configuration, where the life theme was fixed in the patient's mind and the elaboration of the protective semi functional plan began. Between these points we find the ABC of *invalidation*, the situation in which the coping plan has gone into crisis, demonstrating its limitations. It is also, however, the situation in which the plan paradoxically became definitively rigid in which the patient, instead of looking for alternative ways and making his or her behavior and thoughts more flexible, thought that he or she should apply the semi functional plan even more rigidly, making it wholly dysfunctional. It is also the situation in which the vulnerabilities have pathologically transformed from painful to intolerable because the patient felt that it had become necessary to avoid any mental contact with them.

The number of three ABCs is not to be considered a prescription; instead the therapist aims to look for examples of at least three general situations. In fact, the three scenarios, present problem, past learning of the problem and invalidation are actually implemented in more than one ABC for each of the three scenarios. Once the ABCs have been collected, they can then be summarized into life themes and semi-adaptive plans.

Life themes and semi-adaptive plans, in addition to their content, have a score that evaluates their process aspect. LIBET monitoring of the course of therapy is implemented by using four process variables: (1) the intolerability and (2) conditioning of the life theme, and (3) the necessity; and (4) uncontrollability of the semi-adaptive plan.

1. The evaluation of intolerability of the theme modifies the value attributed to it as a mental experience and therefore can rigidify the system in a defensive perspective, both in preventive and reactive terms. The experience of intolerability can become worrying, an obligation to keep the attention focused on the pain itself;
2. Conditioning of the life theme means that its experience is evaluated as pivotal for making decisions. It is an indication of how protection from the experience of the life theme is a priority for the individual and becomes a discriminating element for them to organize their daily and long term choices;
3. The necessity of the semi-adaptive plan means that it is evaluated as necessary to protect the person from the life theme. This process organizes the system resources for the planning, activation, and suspension of actions (i.e. cognitive such as worry or behavioral such as withdrawal) on the grounds of internal signals—whether they be bodily or cognitive—associated with the life theme;
4. The fourth and final cognitive regulation variable is the uncontrollability of semi-adaptive plans. Different expressions underline this perspective: "It's just the way I am," "it is my nature." The most studied processes of this kind are beliefs about the uncontrollability of worry and one's behavior (Wells 2008).

Table 2 Formulation and case monitoring diagram in LIBET

DATE:	PATIENT:	THERAPIST:
Life theme(s):		
Process beliefs: Is this theme intolerable? Does it condition you? Do you need the plan? Does the plan seem necessary to you?		
Semi functional plan(s):		
ABC OF THE PRESENT (*current problem*)	**LEARNING ABC** (*episodes of experience and learning about themes and plans*)	**INVALIDATING ABC** (*precipitating episodes and/or onset of the problem*)
ANTECEDENT What is/was the problematic situation?	ANTECEDENT Can you tell me another situation where you felt that way? Where did you learn to feel that way?	ANTECEDENT Can you tell me a situation in which the way you were handling your discomfort started to have a cost?
EMOTION How did you feel in that situation?	EMOTION How did you feel in that situation?	EMOTION How did you feel in that situation?
BEHAVIOR What did you do? Why did you do that? Do you use other strategies?	BEHAVIOR What did you do? Why did you do that? Do you use other strategies?	BEHAVIOR What did you do? Why did you do that? Do you use other strategies?
BELIEF, LADDERING AND SELF BELIEF What was going through your mind at the time? What didn't you like about that? How did you consider yourself?	BELIEF, LADDERING AND SELF BELIEF What was going through your mind at the time? What didn't you like about that? How did you consider yourself?	BELIEF, LADDERING AND SELF BELIEF What was going through your mind at the time? What didn't you like about that? How did you consider yourself?

These four variables characterize the LIBET monitoring in terms of the process of the course of therapy and definitively establishes the LIBET therapeutic contract and the work alliance between patient and therapist in a LIBET framework. This is a contract that encourages the patient to work on the intolerability and conditioning of the life theme and on the necessity and uncontrollability of the semi-adaptive plan. On the basis of this contract, the therapeutic intervention agenda can be discussed and its rationale justified.

The evaluation of the four processes is implemented in a ceaselessly shared monitoring procedure that is renewed at each session and gives direction to the therapeutic agenda. Each session should open with the evaluation of process variables in parallel with a measurement of the degree of psychological, emotional, and behavioral discomfort of the patient, so that he/she is aware of the relationship between process evaluation and improvement of the emotional disorder. Evaluating the four processes and the emotional discomfort each time facilitates comparison of the course of the pathological mechanisms with the symptomatological state and makes the patient aware of the relationship between the two levels. These evaluations, when shared between patient and therapist, increase effectiveness both by directly motivating compliance and by increasing awareness of the therapeutic process (Lambert and Barley 2001).

In an evaluation card called "CORE + LIBET" (displayed in Table 3) the shared measurement of the four process variables and psychological discomfort is carried out.

The card contains the CORE 10 (Barkham et al. 2013) in the upper half, a short measure of psychological distress. The therapist invites the patient to fill in the CORE 10 at the beginning of the session and to evaluate the result together, an elementary sum that the patient and the therapist can perform together. The result should be reported on the evaluation card itself. A simple and friendly way to introduce the operation can be:

T.: I would like to invite you to fill out this simple scale of evaluation with me; it allows us to monitor and understand the progress of this treatment. This tool helps to make the treatment more effective.

Once the CORE has been completed, the four process variables are evaluated. Fulfillment of the analogical scales must be accompanied by a brief joint description of the content of the life theme and the semi-adaptive plan of the patient evaluated by the LIBET diagram in order to allow the therapist and patient to further memorize and share the case formulation. These quantitative assessments are not an end in themselves but aim to increase cooperation between patient and therapist. They become an opportunity for a deepened and shared detachment from the dysfunctional processes: how much the life theme still makes the patient feel conditioned and hurt, and how much the semi-adaptive plan is still considered necessary and uncontrollable.

The evaluations can also be reported on a longitudinal evaluation card (Table 4) that allows the patient to monitor the course of therapy both in terms of distress and processes and makes him/her further aware of the relationship between these variables.

The use of these tools must be intertwined with the management of the sessions. The evaluation of the LIBET process variables is combined with the structure of the CBT session (which opens with review of the homework, followed by sharing of the case formulation and drafting of the agenda, then choice of the interventions and an explanation of their rationale and their implementation, and ends with new homework. A CORE 10 + LIBET process evaluation is implemented at least every 2–3 sessions. With the choice of therapeutic interventions, we definitively enter into the use of LIBET heuristic for strategic choice.

Table 3 CORE-10 (not reported) + LIBET

This questionnaire contains ten statements that can describe *how you felt during the last week*	
Life Theme(s): *indicate with an "X" on this scale your degree of agreement with each statement in relation to the themes identified*	
Content of the theme(s): strongly disagreestrongly agree	
It conditions my choices	I________________________________I
It is intolerable to feel it	I________________________________I
It affects my relationships	I________________________________I
It's painful	I________________________________I
Semi-Adaptive Plan(s): *indicate with an "X" on this scale your degree of agreement with each statement in relation to the plans identified*	
Content of the plan(s): strongly disagreestrongly agree	
It is still necessary for me	I________________________________I
I can't do otherwise	I________________________________I
It is necessary in order to manage difficulties	I________________________________I
I can't change these strategies	I________________________________I

The LIBET Procedure

Preliminary Sharing of the Model

As we have already argued in various parts of the book, sharing the case formulation is vital to building a therapeutic alliance. Therefore, during the assessment phase, the therapist explains the LIBET model to the patient. You can approach the patient with a prompt such as follows:

> *All of us as human beings have vulnerabilities in our life history that we call life themes. This vulnerability is a way of considering reality and feelings that recur in our lives—a way that, in some circumstances, can become painful or even intolerable.*
>
> *Over the course of our life, we have learned strategies that we will call semi-adaptive plans; these have allowed us to manage our life themes. These plans can help us, but when they become rigid and inflexible, they also increase the emotional pain and create other problems because we can no longer adapt to what is happening in our lives. Sometimes that's what we call symptoms.*
>
> *We are going to work together using themes and plans to understand your distress and then find a therapeutic strategy to deal with it.*

Table 4 Overview of progress

Patient: *Theme(s):* *Plan(s):*	Session and/or supervision Date: … … …	Session and/or supervision Date: … … …	Session and/or supervision Date: … … …	Session and/or supervision Date: … … …
Core 10				
Life theme(s)				
It conditions my choices				
It is intolerable to feel it				
It affects my relationships				
It's painful				
Semi-adaptive plan(s)				
It's still necessary for me				
I can't do otherwise				
It's necessary to manage difficulties				
I can't change these strategies				
Interventions				

LIBET Assessment Techniques: ABC and Laddering

The LIBET case formulation procedure refers to the techniques of the main CBT approaches, i.e. standard CBT (Clark and Beck 2010), REBT (DiGiuseppe et al. 2014; Ellis 1962; Ellis and Grieger 1986) and the cognitive therapies of the constructivist tradition (Bannister and Fransella 1971; Feixas and Miró 1993; Guidano and Liotti 1983; Guidano 1987, 1991; Lorenzini and Sassaroli 1995; Mahoney 1974, 1991, 2003; Neimeyer 2009; Winter and Viney 2005). All these use models of cognitive functional analysis that can be traced back to REBT's ABC framework (DiGiuseppe et al. 2014; Ellis and Grieger 1986). They all structure problematic situations into disturbing antecedents (A), dysfunctional thoughts or beliefs (B) and distressing emotions and dysfunctional behaviors (C). The procedure of LIBET also uses the ABC analysis model and calls this basic element "ABC-LIBET" (more briefly, ABC-L) and is reported above in Table 2.

The ABC-L begins with the elicitation of a problematic situation, encouraging the patient to be as specific and concrete as possible:

Can you tell me a specific situation during which your problem arose? An occasion particularly representative for you in which you comprehensively remember the circumstances, the time and place where it happened?

The insistence on precision is necessary because emotional suffering tends to present itself with a vague character (Borkovec and Inz 1990). A way to specifically introduce some LIBET concepts can be:

Can you tell me about an occasion when your problem prevented you from successfully managing a situation—or even getting away with it without too much damage?

The hypothesis is that something new happened during the problematic episode that invalidated a semi-adaptive behavior that the patient had previously adopted. After assessment of the situation, the process follows "C," i.e. addresses emotions and dysfunctional behaviors:

T: What did you feel?

T: What did you do then that didn't help you?

There are various classifications of dysfunctional behaviors. Table 5 illustrates the standard CBT and REBT models of dysfunctional behaviors.

After emotions and behaviors, dysfunctional thoughts are elicited by asking about the immediate conscious thought in the problematic situation:

What was going through your mind at that moment? What did you think at that moment?

The "going through your mind" emphasizes the analysis of the automatic and involuntary aspect of the mental state. Care must be taken so that the patient precisely focuses on those thoughts by suspending rational criticism.

T.: Let's focus on what you thought at that moment that did not help you.

The assessment of the first thought is not enough. It is necessary to go on eliciting the chain of thought until the mental states at the basis of the emotional pain are ascertained. The elicitation of the chain of thought can be carried out using various techniques, from the *downward arrow of the* CT school (Beck 2011, pp. 206–208) to the *chain inference of* the REBT school (DiGiuseppe et al. 2014, pp. 173–174) to the *laddering of the* Kellian constructivist school (Hinkle 1965; Bannister and Mair 1968; Bannister and Fransella 1971). All of them focus primarily on the negative implications of the feared events, situations, or moods. The question is:

T.: What don't you like in this?

This question tends to look for a self-belief. Once we have ascertained the beliefs we reach a hypothesis of the patient's life theme in its self-descriptive component. The life theme, in fact, is comprised of:

- A cognitive and self-descriptive component (e.g. "I see myself as a failure");
- An emotional and viscerally perceptive component, i.e. a prevailing, pervasive and disturbing emotion (e.g., "I feel shame").

Table 5 REBT and CBT dysfunctional behaviors

Dysfunctional behavior in REBT (DiGiuseppe et al. 2014)	Safety behavior in standard CBT (Salkovskis 1991; Thwaites and Freeston 2005)
Social avoidance	Avoidance
Not taking care of yourself	Seeking reassurance
Aggressiveness (being aggressive)	Hypervigilance

Present Problem, Invalidation and Life History: How Many ABCs Are There to Ascertain?

To assess a LIBET case formulation it is necessary to ascertain more than on ABC-L. A single ABC-L provides only an initial hypothesis. As in the CBT's CCD procedure, several problematic situations are assessed and then combined in an overall formulation. In CBT, however, the problematic situations are all located in the present. LIBET, on the other hand, aims to combine case formulation and developmental assessment, erecting a formulation that includes the patient's life history.

More than one ABC is also needed because the invalidation and present problem can either overlap or be separated. In fact, every problematic situation, in itself, is an invalidation. However, if the present problem does not correspond to the onset of the emotional disorder, we can distinguish between invalidation overlap with the onset of the disorder and states of chronic invalidation that occur in the present problem.

As we have already written, the concept of invalidation indicates the moment when a situation unequivocally disconfirms a predictive hypothesis (Kelly 1955). In LIBET, the concept of invalidation is applied to the plan. It is assumed that there was a time when the protective benefits of a semi-adaptive plan outweighed their emotional and behavioral cost. The concept of invalidation helps therapists understand how the patient went from a premorbid personality in which some not yet dysfunctional plans were present to the pathological dysfunctionality of the symptom. For this reason, in order to fully explore the dysfunctional elaboration of an invalidation, it is necessary to focus on the episodes related to the onset of the disorders. The invalidation ABC can be ascertained by asking:

What was changing in your life before you got sick?
What happened before you got sick?
When did this behavior stop being useful to you? How come it didn't work anymore?
When did you realize that doing this was doing you more harm than good?
What happened that broke the plan?

The whole situation is formulated in ABC terms and shared with the patient, including the term "invalidation," and explaining it as an event that changed something—an event in which some usual behavior did not work as well as before. It is important to share the link between invalidation and plan, i.e. between the external situation that had disconfirmed the patient's predictions and the dysfunctional reaction that rigidified the plan in place of the search for flexibility and alternatives. This connection is created by encouraging the patient to reflect on the supposed purposes of his or her rigid behavior:

What was your purpose in doing this?
Why was this goal so important?

Once the episode has been identified, the patient is encouraged to explore the connection between invalidation and symptomatic onset.

Do you see a relationship between this episode and the onset of your problem?

Repeating in a seemingly redundant way:

In this episode, which we could call "invalidation" (a brief explanation of the term follows), *what behavior—which you have always put into practice—has proved to be less useful?*

How come your strategies no longer work today? How come they're not helping you today?

And why did you find it useful to behave in a similar manner even more?

In a simpler and more direct way:

Which of your plans are you most sick of?

The third step is the link between the life theme and life history. The aim is to identify other ABCs, called "life history ABCs," in which the patient is asked for a past situation in which he/she learned to react in a way akin to what would become his/her plan.

There are two main techniques. In one, we do not focus on single episodes but on a more general relational situation, i.e. deriving a broad and detailed description of the quality of the relationship with their significant relationships:

Can you tell me something about your relationship with significant people during your childhood and adolescence? How were your relationships? Can you tell me about any significant episodes at different times in your growth?

And then, more specifically, they ask about situations:

Where did you learn to see yourself like that?

Or you can focus, in a similar way to the ABCs of the present, on individual episodes, even if they belong to the past.

We are now looking for an episode in your past in which you considered yourself as a … (Use the patient's words, e.g. "failure") or experienced this emotion of … (Use the patient's words, e.g. "shame") in a similar way to the present. What are you thinking?

In the analysis of past episodes, it is necessary to focus both on the cognitive component, i.e. how the patient saw and considered him-/herself (self-belief). However, for a child, interactions are problematic either because of objectively traumatic conditions or because certain needs, such as the need for protection or exploration, are frustrated. That's why it's useful to ask:

How did you see that child? What did you want? What did you need?

The questions assessing the development of semi-adaptive coping strategies or plans may then be:

How did you react? Where have you learnt to handle feeling that way? How did it help you? Had somebody in your family similar problems? Or reactions?

In this way, we come to behaviors:

Where did you learn to do that? Where did you learn to believe it was right/convenient to do so and/or that it helped you?

Identify Life Themes and Semi-adaptive Plans

Once a number of ABCs have been identified, they can be summarized into a life theme and a semi-adaptive plan. It is good once again to share it explicitly with the patient:

Can we call your vulnerable way of feeling and judging yourself in problematic situations your "life theme"?

When dealing with the plan, it is also necessary to use more friendly terminology, for example, not only talking about "plans" and "goals" but also more simply about benefits and costs. The term "costs" in particular shows the dysfunctional component of the plan, while "benefits" underlines the advantages—even if temporary—the patient has derived from this rigid method of conduct.

The aspect that leads the patient to prioritize the benefits and underestimate the costs of a plan is that the costs are generally longer-term and therefore underestimated, while the benefits are more immediate. For many patients, it can be difficult to grasp the intentional nature of the plan (thus experiencing it as an uncontrollable symptom). A way to bring the patient closer to the protective intentionality of the plan can be by emphasizing the momentary emotional benefit. An understandable term for many patients is "relief":

What did you do in that situation that gave you relief?

Other useful questions to ascertain the benefits may be:

What do you like about that?
Why do you care so much about being/appearing like that? What does that mean to you?
What does it mean for you to achieve/obtain that relief?

The term "relief" underscores how the aims of this dysfunctional plan, above all, are to avoid emotional distress rather than towards a pragmatic goal. There is, therefore, a dramatic lack of self-directedness in these rigid pursuits. At this point, it is also good to share the terminology with the patient, with a simple suggestion:

Can we call that your "plan"?

Process Evaluations on Topics and Plans: Intolerability, Conditioning, Utility and Uncontrollability

Once the themes and plans and their evolutionary roots have been identified the maintenance processes are assessed. The evaluation of the process variables should be divided into several questions, with at least two for each variable, in order to increase the reliability of the evaluations. The quantitative evaluation can be implemented on the evaluation card above reported in Table 3.

1. The Theme
    (a) *How intolerable is it?*
    (b) *How much does it affect your choices in life?*

2. The Plan
   (a) *How necessary do you think it is to protect yourself?*
   (b) *How uncontrollable is it to react like that? Do you think you can't do otherwise?*

The evaluation can also be done in a more narrative manner, encouraging the patient to comprehensively discuss his or her life and assessing during the conversation the extent to which the themes and the plans have made the patient suffer, have conditioned his or her life and have been considered necessary or uncsontrollable.

Once the case has been formulated in a shared way, LIBET can be used as a planning tool for the intervention agenda. Its themes, plans, and four process variables can be applied as heuristics to guide therapeutic choices. Besides, LIBET is also a tool for evaluating and monitoring therapeutic developments. In particular, the four process variables can be indexes of evaluating the therapeutic response. In short, LIBET means: (1) conceptualization of the case; (2) orientation towards the therapeutic choice; (3) monitoring the effectiveness of the therapy.

An elementary method of looking at LIBET variables as heuristics is grounded in clinical common sense. Every CBT orientation has some theoretical and clinical tenets which are in relation to the process variables of the LIBET. For example, a life theme maintained by a conditioning LIBET process may encourage the use of a constructive cognitive therapy targeted towards a conditioning negative self-belief learned during childhood, while a life theme maintained by an intolerability LIBET process may require a REBT disputing intervention targeting frustration intolerance. REBT may be appropriate where LIBET has reported particularly intense subjective painful—maybe "terrible" or "intolerable"—beliefs about the themes. A semi-adaptive plan maintained by a necessity LIBET process variable may require a CBT assessment targeting evidence for this necessity; finally a semi-adaptive plan maintained by an uncontrollability LIBET process may require a process-based CBT focused on mental control. Besides, the ideas of the necessity and uncontrollability of plans, experienced as particularly rigid and inflexible, could be linked to irrational ideas of demandingness, which is typically REBT. These are just some examples, traced rather roughly, of how LIBET can provide a heuristics to guide therapeutic choices. In short, in order to use LIBET as a frame for treatment choices, the therapist should assess to what extent the theoretical and clinical rationale of the possible interventions is justified by the content of a LIBET variable.

References

Allen, A., Kannis-Dymand, L., & Katsikitis, M. (2017). Problematic internet pornography use: The role of craving, desire thinking, and metacognition. *Addictive Behaviors, 70*, 65–71.

Bandura, A. (1977). Self-efficacy: Toward a unifying theory of behavioral change. *Psychological Review, 84*, 191–215.

Bandura, A. (1988). Self-efficacy conception of anxiety. *Anxiety Research, 1*, 77–98.

Bannister, D. F., & Fransella, F. (1971). *Inquiring man: The psychology of personal constructs* (3rd ed.). Harmondsworth, UK: Penguin.

Bannister, D., & Mair, J. M. M. (1968). *The evaluation of personal constructs*. London, UK: Academic.

Barkham, M., Bewick, B., Mullin, T., Gilbody, S., Connell, J., Cahill, J., et al. (2013). The CORE-10: A short measure of psychological distress for routine use in the psychological therapies. *Counselling and Psychotherapy Research, 13*, 3–13.

Barlow, D. H. (2002). *Anxiety and its disorders: the nature and treatment of anxiety and panic*. New York, NY: Guilford.

Beck, A. T. (1996). Beyond belief: A theory of modes, personality, and psychopathology. In P. M. Salkovskis (Ed.), *Frontiers of Cognitive Therapy* (pp. 1–26). New York, NY: The Guilford Press.

Beck, A. T. (2008). The evolution of the cognitive model of depression and its neurobiological correlates. *American Journal of Psychiatry, 165*, 969–977.

Beck, J. S. (2011). *Cognitive behavior therapy: Basics and beyond*. New York, NY: Guilford.

Beck, A. T., & Bredemeier, K. (2016). A unified model of depression: Integrating clinical, cognitive, biological, and evolutionary perspectives. *Clinical Psychological Science, 4*, 596–619.

Beck, A. T., Rush, A. J., Shaw, B. F., & Emery, G. (1979). *Cognitive therapy of depression*. New York, NY: Guilford Press.

Beck, A. T., Davis, D. D., & Freeman, A. (2015). *Cognitive therapy of personality disorders* (3rd ed.). New, NY: Guilford.

Bieling, P. J., & Kuyken, W. (2003). Is cognitive case formulation science or science fiction? *Clinical Psychology: Science and Practice, 10*, 52–69.

Bifulco, A., Kwon, J., Jacobs, C., Moran, P. M., & Bunn, A. (2006). Adult attachment style as mediator between childhood neglect/abuse and adult depression and anxiety. *Social Psychiatry and Psychiatric Epidemiology, 41*, 796–805.

Blalock, J. A., & Joiner, T. E. (2000). Interaction of cognitive avoidance coping and stress in predicting depression/anxiety. *Cognitive Therapy and Research, 24*, 47–65.

Borkovec, T. D., & Inz, J. (1990). The nature of worry in generalized anxiety disorder: A predominance of thought activity. *Behaviour Research and Therapy, 28*, 153–158.

Bosquet, M., & Egeland, B. (2006). The development and maintenance of anxiety symptoms from infancy through adolescence in a longitudinal sample. *Development and Psychopathology, 18*, 517–550.

Brewin, C. R., Firth-Cozens, J., Furnham, A., & McManus, C. (1992). Self-criticism in adulthood and recalled childhood experience. *Journal of Abnormal Psychology, 101*(3), 561.

Bruner, J. (1973). *Going beyond the information given*. New York, NY: Norton.

Butler, G. (1998). Clinical formulation. In A. S. Bellack & M. Hersen (Eds.), *Comprehensive clinical psychology* (pp. 1–24). New York, NY: Pergamon Press.

Capo, R., & Mancini, F. (2008). Scopi terminali, temi di vita e psicopatologia [Terminal goals, life themes and psychopathology]. In C. Perdighe & F. Mancini (Eds.), *Elementi di psicoterapia cognitiva: II edizione [Elements of cognitive psychotherapy: II edition]* (pp. 39–68). Roma, Italy: Fioriti.

Capo, R., Mancini, F., & Barcaccia, B. (2010). Temi di vita e psicopatologia [Life themes and psychopathology]. In A. Pacciolla & F. Mancini (Eds.), *Cognitivismo Esistenziale: Dal significato del sintomo al significato della vita [Existential Cognitivism: From the meaning of the symptom to the meaning of life]* (pp. 202–226). Milano, Italy: Franco Angeli.

Caselli, G., & Spada, M. M. (2015). Desire thinking: What is it and what drives it? *Addictive Behaviors, 44*, 71–79.

Chadwick, P., Williams, C., & Mackenzie, J. (2003). Impact of case formulation in cognitive behaviour therapy for psychosis. *Behaviour Research and Therapy, 41*, 671–680.

Christensen, A., Jacobson, N. S., & Babcock, J. C. (1995). Integrative behavioral couples therapy. In N. S. Jacobson & A. S. Gurman (Eds.), *Clinical handbook for couples therapy* (pp. 31–64). New York: Guildford.

Clark, D. A., & Beck, A. T. (2010). *Cognitive therapy of anxiety disorders: Science and practice*. New York, NY: Guilford Press.

Clark, D. A., Beck, A. T., & Alford, B. A. (1999). *Scientific foundations of cognitive theory and therapy of depression*. Chichester, UK: Wiley.

Cloninger, C. R., Svrakic, D. M., & Przybeck, T. R. (1993). A psychobiological model of temperament and character. *Archives of General Psychiatry, 50*, 975–990.

Critchfield, K. L., Levy, K. N., Clarkin, J. F., & Kernberg, O. F. (2008). The relational context of aggression in Borderlin-e personality disorder: Using adult attachment style to predict forms of hostility. *Journal of Clinical Psychology, 64*, 67–82.

Csikszentmihalyi, M., & Beattie, O. V. (1979). Life themes: A theoretical and empirical exploration of their origins and effects. *Journal of Humanistic Psychology, 19*, 45–63.

David, D., Freeman, A., & DiGiuseppe, R. (2005). Rational and irrational beliefs: Implications for mechanisms of change and practice in psychotherapy. In D. David, S. J. Lynn, & A. Ellis (Eds.), *Rational and irrational beliefs: Research, theory and clinical practice* (pp. 195–217). Oxford, UK: Oxford University Press.

Di Fini, G., & Veglia, F. (2019). Life themes and attachment system in the narrative self-construction: Direct and indirect indicators. *Frontiers in Psychology, 10*, 1393–1406.

DiGiuseppe, R., & Tafrate, R. C. (2001). A comprehensive treatment model for anger disorders. *Psychotherapy: Theory, Research, Practice, Training, 38*, 262–271.

DiGiuseppe, R., Doyle, K. A., Dryden, W., & Backx, W. (2014). *A practioner's guide to Rational Emotive Behavior Therapy*. New York, NY: Oxford University Press.

Dobson, K. S., & Khatri, N. (2000). Cognitive therapy: Looking backward, looking forward. *Journal of Clinical Psychology, 56*, 907–923.

Dobson, K. S., Poole, J. C., & Beck, J. S. (2018). The fundamental cognitive model. In R. L. Lehay (Ed.), *Science and practice in cognitive therapy: Foundations, mechanisms, and applications* (pp. 29–47). New York, NY: Guilford.

Dodet, M. (2010). Self meaning e tema di vita [Self meaning and life theme]. In A. Pacciolla & F. Mancini (Eds.), *Cognitivismo Esistenziale: Dal significato del sintomo al significato della vita [Existential Cognitivism: From the meaning of the symptom to the meaning of life]* (pp. 148–169). Milano, Italy: Franco Angeli.

Dragan, M. (2015). Difficulties in emotion regulation and problem drinking in young women: The mediating effect of metacognitions about alcohol use. *Addictive Behaviors, 48*, 30–35.

Eells, T. D. (2007). *Handbook of psychotherapy case formulation*. New York, NY: Guilford Press.

Eells, T. D. (2011). *Handbook of psychotherapy case formulation* (2nd ed.). New York, NY: Guilford Press.

Eells, T. D. (2015). *Psychotherapy case formulation*. Arlingtion, VI: American Psychological Association.

Ellis, A. (1955). New approaches to psychotherapy techniques. *Journal of Clinical Psychology, 11*, 207–260.

Ellis, A. (1962). *Reason and emotion in psychotherapy*. New York, NY: Stuart.

Ellis, A., & Grieger, R. M. (Eds.). (1986). *Handbook of rational-emotive therapy*. New York, NY: Springer.

Evans, J., & Parry, G. (1996). The impact of reformulation in cognitive-analytic therapy with difficultto-help clients. *Clinical Psychology and Psychotherapy, 3*, 109–117.

Feixas, G., & Miró, M. (1993). *Aproximaciones ala Psicoterapia. Una Introducción a los Tratamientos Psicológicos [Approaches to Psychotherapy. An Introduction to Psychological Treatments]*. Barcelona, Spain: Paidós.

Flitcroft, A., James, I. A., Freeston, M., & Wood-Mitchell, A. (2007). Determining what is important in a good formulation. *Behavioural and Cognitive Psychotherapy, 35*, 325–333.

Frankl, V. (2006). *Man's search for meaning. An Introduction to Logotherapy. Originally published in 1946*. Boston, MA: Beacon Press.

Ghaderi, A. (2006). Does individualization matter? A randomized trial of standardized (focused) versus individualized (broad) cognitive behavior therapy for bulimia nervosa. *Behavior Research and Therapy, 44*, 273–288.

Gilbert, P. (1989). *Human nature and suffering*. London, UK: Earlbaum.

Guidano, V. F. (1987). *Complexity of the Self.* New York, NY: Guilford Press.

Guidano, V. F. (1991). *The self in process: toward a post-rationalist cognitive therapy*. New York, NY: Guilford Press.

Guidano, V. F., & Liotti, G. (1983). *Cognitive processes and emotional disorders: A structural approach to psychotherapy*. New York, NY: Guilford.

Hayes, S. C., & Hofman, S. G. (2018). *Process-based CBT. The science and core clinical competencies of cognitive behavioral therapy*. Oakland, CA: Context Press, New Harbinger.

Hayes, S. C., & Strosahl, K. D. (2004). *A practical guide to acceptance and commitment therapy*. New York, NY: Guildford Press.

Herman, J. (1992). *Trauma and recovery: The aftermath of violence—from domestic abuse to political terror*. New York, NY: Perseus.

Hinkle, D. N. (1965). *The change of personal constructs from the viewpoint of a theory of construct implications*. Unpublished PhD dissertation, Ohio State University, Columbus, OH.

Huprich, S. K. (2003). Depressive personality and its relationship to depressed mood, interpersonal loss, negative parental perceptions, and perfectionism. *Journal of Nervous & Mental Disease, 191*, 73–79.

Irons, C., Gilbert, P., Baldwin, M. W., Baccus, J. R., & Palmer, M. (2006). Parental recall, attachment relating and self-attacking/self-reassurance: their relationship with depression. *British Journal of Medical Psychology, 45*, 297–308.

Jaspers, K. (1971). *Philosophy of existence*. Filadelfia, PA: University of Pennsylvania Press.

Kahneman, D., & Frederick, S. (2002). Representativeness revisited: Attribute substitution in intuitive judgment. In T. Gilovich, D. Griffin, & D. Kahneman (Eds.), *Heuristics and biases* (pp. 49–81). New York, NY: Cambridge University Press.

Kanter, J. W., Bush, A. M., & Rush, L. C. (2009). *Behavioral activation*. New York, NY: Routledge.

Kawamura, K. Y., Frost, R. O., & Harmatz, M. G. (2001). The relationship of perceived parenting styles to perfectionism. *Personality and Individual Differences, 32*, 317–327.

Kelly, G. A. (1955). *The psychology of personal constructs: Vol 1 and 2*. New York, NY: Norton.

Kendjelic, E. M., & Eells, T. D. (2007). Generic psychotherapy case formulation training improves formulation quality. *Psychotherapy: Theory, Research, Practice, Training, 44*, 66.

Kenrick, D. T. (2011). *Sex, murder and the meaning of life*. New York, NY: Basic books.

Kenrick, D. T., Griskevicius, V., Neuberg, S. L., & Schaller, M. (2010). Renovating the pyramid of needs: Contemporary extensions built upon ancient foundations. *Perspectives on Psychological Science, 5*, 292–314.

Kiernan, K. E., & Huerta, M. C. (2008). Economic deprivation, maternal depression, parenting and children's cognitive and emotional development in early childhood. *The British Journal of Sociology, 59*, 783–806.

Kohlenberg, R. J., & Tsai, M. (1991). *Functional analytic psychotherapy: Creating intense and curative therapeutic relationships*. New York, NY: Plenum Press.

Kuyken, W. (2006). Evidence-based case formulation: Is the emperor clothed? In N. Tarrier (Ed.), *Case Formulation in cognitive behaviour therapy. The treatment of challenging and complex cases* (pp. 28–51). Hove, UK/New York, NY: Routledge.

Kuyken, W., Kurzer, N., DeRubeis, R. J., Beck, A. T., & Brown, G. K. (2001). Response to cognitive therapy in depression: The role of maladaptive beliefs and personality disorders. *Journal of Consulting and Clinical Psychology, 69*, 560.

Kuyken, W., Fothergill, C. D., Musa, M., & Chadwick, P. (2005). The reliability and quality of cognitive case formulation. *Behaviour Research and Therapy, 43*, 1187–1201.

Kuyken, W., Padesky, C. A., & Dudley, R. (2008). The science and practice of case conceptualization. *Behavioural and Cognitive Psychotherapy, 36*(6), 757–768.

Lambert, M. J., & Barley, D. E. (2001). Research summary on the therapeutic relationship and psychotherapy outcome. *Psychotherapy: Theory, Research, Practice, Training, 38*, 357.

Linehan, M. M. (1993). *Cognitive-behavioral treatment of borderline personality disorder*. New York, NY: Guilford Press.

Lorenzini, R., & Sassaroli, S. (1987). *La paura della paura [The fear of fear]*. Firenze, Italy: Nuova Italia Scientifica.

Lorenzini, R., & Sassaroli, S. (1995). *Attaccamento, conoscenza e disturbi di personalità [Attachment, knowledge and personality disorders]*. Milano, Italy: Cortina.

Lyddon, W. J. (1990). First- and second-order change: Implications for rationalist and constructivist cognitive therapies. *Journal of Counseling & Development, 69*, 122–127.

Mahoney, M. J. (1974). *Cognition and behavior modification*. Cambridge, MA: Ballinger.

Mahoney, M. J. (1991). *Human change process*. New York, NY: Basic Books.

Mahoney, M. J. (2003). *Constructive psychotherapy: A practical guide*. New York, NY: Guilford.

Mansueto, G., Martino, F., Palmieri, S., Scaini, S., Ruggiero, G. M., Sassaroli, S., & Caselli, G. (2019). Desire Thinking across addictive behaviours: A systematic review and meta-analysis. *Addictive Behaviors, 98*. https://doi.org/10.1016/j.addbeh.2019.06.007.

Markus, H. (1977). Self-schemata and processing information about the self. *Journal of Personality and Social Psychology, 35*, 63–78.

Martell, C. R., Addis, M. E., & Jacobson, N. S. (2001). *Depression in context: Strategies for guided action*. New York, NY: Norton.

Martin, R. C., & Dahlen, E. R. (2005). Cognitive emotion regulation in the prediction of depression, anxiety, stress, and anger. *Personality and Individual Differences, 39*, 1249–1260.

Martin, J. W., & Sloman, S. A. (2013). Refining the dual-system theory of choice. *Journal of Consumer Psychology, 23*, 552–555.

Maslow, A. (1943). A theory of human motivation. *Psychological Review, 50*, 370–396.

Maslow, A. (1954). *Motivation and personality*. New York, NY: Harper & Brothers.

McCullough, J. P., Jr., & Goldfried, M. R. (1999). *Treatment for chronic depression: Cognitive behavioral analysis system of psychotherapy*. New York, NY: Guilford Press.

Meichenbaum, D. H. (1977). *Cognitive behavior modification*. New York, NY: Plenum.

Miceli, M., & Castelfranchi, C. (2002). The mind and the future: The (negative) power of expectations. *Theory and Psychology, 12*, 335–366.

Mogg, K., & Bradley, B. P. (1998). A cognitive-motivational analysis of anxiety. *Behaviour Research and Therapy, 36*(36), 809–848.

Moulding, R., & Kyrios, M. (2006). Anxiety disorders and control related beliefs: the example of Obsessive-Compulsive Disorder (OCD). *Clinical Psychology Review, 26*, 573–583.

Mumma, G. H., & Smith, J. L. (2001). Cognitive–behavioral-interpersonal scenarios: Interformulator reliability and convergent validity. *Journal of Psychopathology and Behavioral Assessment, 23*, 203–221.

Mumma, G. H., & Mooney, S. R. (2007). Incremental validity of cognitions in a clinical case formulation: An intraindividual test in a case example. *Journal of Psychopathology and Behavioral Assessment, 29*, 17–28.

Narvaez, D. (2018). *Basic needs, wellbeing and morality: Fulfilling human potential*. Cham, Switzerland: Springer.

Needleman, L. D. (1999). *Cognitive case conceptualization: A guidebook for practitioners*. Abingdon, UK: Routledge.

Neimeyer, R. A. (2009). *Constructivist psychotherapy. Distinctive features*. London, UK: Routledge.

Neimeyer, R. A., & Mahoney, M. J. (Eds.). (1995). *Constructivism in psychotherapy*. Washington, DC: APA Press.

Neisser, U. (1967). *Cognitive psychology*. Englewood Cliffs, NJ: Prentice-Hall.

Nelson-Gray, R. O., Herbert, J. D., Herbert, D. L., Sigmon, S. T., & Brannon, S. E. (1989). Effectiveness of matched, mismatched, and package treatments of depression. *Journal of Behavior Therapy and Experimental Psychiatry, 20*, 281–294.

Ogden, P., Minton, K., & Pain, C. (2006). *Trauma and the body: A sensorimotor approach to psychotherapy*. New York, NY: Norton.
Pain, C. M., Chadwick, P., & Abba, N. (2008). Clients' experience of case formulation in cognitive behaviour therapy for psychosis. *British Journal of Clinical Psychology, 47*, 127–138.
Panksepp, J. (1998). *Affective neuroscience: The foundations of human and animal emotions*. New York, NY: Oxford University Press.
Panksepp, J., & Watt, D. (2011). Why does depression hurt? Ancestral primary-process separation-distress (PANIC/GRIEF) and diminished brain reward (SEEKING) processes in the genesis of depressive affect. *Psychiatry: Interpersonal & Biological Processes, 74*, 5–13.
Persons, J. B., & Bertagnolli, A. (1999). Inter-rater reliability of cognitive-behavioral case formulations of depression: A replication. *Cognitive Therapy and Research, 23*, 271–283.
Persons, J. B., Roberts, N. A., Zalecki, C. A., & Brechwald, W. A. (2006). Naturalistic outcome of case formulation-driven cognitive-behavior therapy for anxious depressed outpatients. *Behaviour Research and Therapy, 44*, 1041–1051.
Rachman, S. (1977). The conditioning theory of fear acquisition: a critical examination. *Behaviour Research and Therapy, 15*, 375–387.
Rachman, S. (1993). Obsessions, responsibility and guilt. *Behaviour Research and Therapy, 31*, 149–154.
Ruggiero, G. M., Stapinski, L., Caselli, G., Fiore, F., Gallucci, M., Sassaroli, S., & Rapee, R. (2012). Beliefs over control and meta-worry interact with the effect of intolerance of uncertainty on worry. *Personality and Individual Differences, 53*, 224–230.
Salkovskis, P. M. (1985). Obsessive-compulsive problems: A cognitive-behavioural analysis. *Behaviour Research and Therapy, 23*, 571–583.
Salkovskis, P. M. (1991). The importance of behaviour in the maintenance of anxiety and panic: A cognitive account. *Behavioural Psychotherapy, 19*, 6–19.
Sassaroli, S., Lorenzini, R., & Ruggiero, G. M. (2005). Kellian invalidation, attachment and the construct of 'control'. In D. A. Winter & L. L. Viney (Eds.), *Personal construct psychotherapy. Advances in theory, practice and research* (pp. 34–42). London, UK: Whurr Publishers.
Sassaroli, S., Gallucci, M., & Ruggiero, G. M. (2008a). Low perception of control as a cognitive factor of eating disorders. Its independent effects on measures of eating disorders and its interactive effects with perfectionism and self-esteem. *Journal of Behavior Therapy and Experimental Psychiatry, 39*, 467–488.
Sassaroli, S., Romero, L., Ruggiero, G. M., & Frost, R. (2008b). Perfectionism in depression, obsessive compulsive disorder and eating disorders. *Behaviour Research and Therapy, 46*, 757–765.
Sassaroli, S., Caselli, G., & Ruggiero, G. M. (2016). Un modello cognitivo clinico di accertamento e concettualizzazione del caso: Life themes and plans Implications of biased Beliefs: Elicitation and Treatment (LIBET) [A clinical cognitive model of assessment and conceptualization of the case: Life themes and plans Implications of biased Beliefs: Elicitation and Treatment (LIBET)]. *Psicoterapia Cognitiva e Comportamentale, 22*, 183–197.
Sassaroli, S., Caselli, G., & Bassanini. & Ruggiero, G.M. (2017a). Procedure e protocollo di terapia LIBET seconda parte: fasi del protocollo e caso clinico Antonia A [LIBET therapy procedures and protocol second part: protocol phases and clinical case Antonia A]. *Psicoterapia Cognitiva e Comportamentale, 32*, 331–344.
Sassaroli, S., Caselli, G., Redaelli, C., & Ruggiero, G. M. (2017b). Procedure e protocollo di terapia LIBET—prima parte: le procedure ABC-LIBET, laddering e disputing [LIBET procedures and therapy protocol—first part: ABC-LIBET procedures, laddering and disputing]. *Psicoterapia Cognitiva e Comportamentale, 23*, 73–92.
Schneider, B. H., & Byrne, B. M. (1987). Individualizing social skills training for behavior-disordered children. *Journal of Consulting and Clinical Psychology, 55*, 444–445.
Schore, A. N. (2012a). *The science of the art of psychotherapy*. New York, NY: Norton.
Schore, A. N. (2012b). Bowlby's 'environment of evolutionary adaptedness.' Recent studies on the interpersonal neurobiology of attachment and emotional development. In D. Narvaez,

J. Panksepp, A. N. Schore, & T. R. Gleason (Eds.), *Evolution, early experience and human development. From research to practice* (pp. 31–73). New York, NY: Oxford University Press.
Schulte, D., Künzel, R., Pepping, G., & Schulte-Bahrenberg, T. (1992). Tailor-made versus standardized therapy of phobic patients. *Advances in Behaviour Research and Therapy, 14*, 67–92.
Shafran, R., Cooper, Z., & Fairburn, C. G. (2002). Clinical perfectionism: A cognitive-behavioural analysis. *Behaviour Research and Therapy, 40*, 773–791.
Siegel, D. (1999). *The developing mind: toward a neurobiology of interpersonal experience*. New York, NY: Guilford.
Sloman, S. A. (2002). Two systems of reasoning. In T. Gilovich, D. Griffin, & D. Kahneman (Eds.), *Heuristics and biases* (pp. 379–396). Cambridge, UK: Cambridge University Press.
Spada, M. M., Caselli, G., & Wells, A. (2012). *The metacognitive therapy approach to problem drinking. Mindfulness and acceptance for addictive behaviors: Applying contextual CBT to substance abuse and behavioral addictions*. New York, NY: New Harbinger.
Spada, M. M., Caselli, G., & Wells, A. (2013). A triphasic metacognitive formulation of problem drinking. *Clinical Psychology & Psychotherapy, 20*, 494–500.
Stanovich, K. E. (1999). *Who is rational? Studies of individual differences in reasoning*. Mahwah, NJ: Erlbaum.
Stanovich, K. E., & West, R. F. (2002). Individual differences in reasoning: Implications for the rationality debate. In T. Gilovich, D. Griffin, & D. Kahneman (Eds.), *Heuristics and biases* (pp. 421–440). Cambridge, UK: Cambridge University Press.
Strauman, T. J., Vieth, A. Z., Merrill, K. A., Kolden, G. G., Woods, T. E., Klein, M. H., Papadakis, A., Schneider, K. L., & Kwapil, L. (2006). Self-system therapy as an intervention for self-regulatory dysfunction in depression: a randomized comparison with cognitive therapy. *Journal of Consulting and Clinical Psychology, 74*, 367–376.
Sturmey, P. (1996). *Functional analysis in clinical psychology*. Chicester, UK: Wiley.
Sturmey, P. (2008). *Behavioral case formulation and intervention: A functional analytic approach*. Chicester, UK: John Wiley & Sons.
Tarrier, N. (Ed.). (2006). *Case Formulation in Cognitive Behaviour Therapy. The treatment of challenging and complex cases*. Hove, UK, New York, USA: Routledge.
Thwaites, R., & Freeston, M. H. (2005). Safety-seeking behaviours: fact or function? How can we clinically differentiate between safety behaviours and adaptive coping strategies across anxiety disorders? *Behavioural and Cognitive Psychotherapy, 33*, 177–188.
van der Kolk, B. A. (1996). The complexity of adaptation to trauma: Self-regulation, stimulus discrimination, and characterological development. In B. A. van der Kolk, A. C. McFarlane, & L. Weisaeth (Eds.), *Traumatic stress: The effects of overwhelming experience on mind, body, and society* (pp. 182–213). New York, NY, US: Guilford Press.
Vieth, A. Z., & Trull, T. J. (1999). Family patterns of perfectionism: an examination of college. *Journal of Personality Assessment, 72*, 49–67.
Wells, A. (2008). *Metacognitive therapy for anxiety and depression*. London, UK: Guilford Press.
Wells, A., & Mathews, G. (1994). *Attention and emotion: A clinical perspective*. Hove, UK/ Hillsdale, NJ: Erlbaum.
Winter, D. A. (1992). Personal construct psychology in clinical practice. In *Theory, research and applications*. London, UK: Routledge.
Winter, D. A., & Viney, L. L. (Eds.). (2005). *Personal construct psychotherapy. Advances in theory, practice and research*. London, UK: Whurr Publishers.
Woodruff-Borden, J., Morrow, C., Bourland, S., & Cambron, S. (2002). The behavior of anxious parents: Examining mechanisms of transmission of anxiety from parent to child. *Journal of Clinical Child & Adolescent Psychology, 31*, 364–374.
Young, J. E., Klosko, J. S., & Weishaar, M. (2003). *Schema therapy: A practitioner's guide*. New York, NY: Guilford.

Commentary on Chapter "The Empirical State of Case Formulation: Integrating and Validating Cognitive, Evolutionary and Procedural Elements in the CBT Case Formulation in the LIBET Procedure": A Constructivist Perspective on LIBET

David A. Winter

Contents

Principal Features of Formulation

The editors and authors of Chapter "The Empirical State of Case Formulation: Integrating and Validating Cognitive, Evolutionary and Procedural Elements in the CBT Case Formulation in the LIBET Procedure" of this book state that shared case formulation is the main therapeutic tool by which the therapist provides the patient with an explanation of his or her vulnerability to emotional pain in intelligible terms. This statement rightly indicates that a case formulation should be *shared*. Furthermore, this sharing should not simply be a matter of the clinician presenting to the client a fully formed construction of the client's problems (as could be implied by 'provides the patient with an explanation') but should characterize the *process* of formulation, in which both the clinician's and client's and perhaps significant others' and other professional team members' (Johnstone 2014a) hypotheses are considered, tested, and refined in a collaborative manner. Secondly, the authors' statement rightly views formulation as a (indeed, the main) therapeutic tool rather than merely an initial and fixed diagnostic construction that may prescribe, but is

D. A. Winter (✉)
University of Hertfordshire, Hertfordshire, UK
e-mail: d.winter@herts.ac.uk

G. M. Ruggiero et al. (eds.), *CBT Case Formulation as Therapeutic Process*,
https://doi.org/10.1007/978-3-030-63587-9_27

otherwise divorced from, the process of therapeutic intervention. Thirdly, I would agree that the reason why formulation is central to the therapeutic process is that it offers the client a comprehensible construction of their predicament. In contrast to a rationalist cognitive approach, I would consider that the terms in which this construction is provided are of no great relevance. What really matters is that the client, who is likely to be trapped in a particular construction of their problem, is shown that alternative constructions by which they may make sense of it are possible. This process of considering and testing alternative constructions may then extend to other areas of the client's life.

In considering constructivist models, the chapter's authors go on to say that these 'have also emphasized the organizational role played by conscious thoughts related to personal meanings' and that 'the transformation of discomfort into symptoms occurs only if the management of the discomfort takes place in a rigid manner. Patients, instead of aiming to tolerate physiological stress, pursue an illusory final elimination of suffering through the rigid use of *coping* strategies'. I would, of course, agree with the emphasis that is given to personal meanings, particularly in regard to the client's identity, but would consider that the constructions and strategies concerned, rather than being 'conscious thoughts', may often not be at a high level of awareness. Indeed, as in dilemma-focused intervention (Feixas and Compañ 2016), a central component of therapy may be to help the client become more aware of these constructions. I would also agree with the authors' emphasis on clients' rigidity and inflexibility. This is exemplified in George Kelly's (1955) definition of a disorder as '*any personal construction which is used repeatedly in spite of consistent invalidation*' (p. 831, italics in original) and in the view that the client's use of strategies to avoid or cope with invalidation is imbalanced (Walker and Winter 2005; Winter 2003).

The authors also rightly point to the dearth of empirical evidence on case formulation and its effectiveness in facilitating positive therapeutic outcome (Bieling and Kuyken 2003; Johnstone 2014b). There is sometimes a tendency in the clinical field (and indeed other fields) to assume that it is self-evident that a particular approach should be followed, and that evaluation of the approach is scarcely necessary. For example, how much evidence is there on the effectiveness of evidence-based practice? The authors provide a timely reminder that a similar view should not be taken of formulation, research on which should be of high priority.

The LIBET model can be considered to focus upon the features of formulation discussed above in that it facilitates the sharing with the client of the formulation and its implications for treatment; it considers not only painful themes but also 'semi-adaptive' strategies for dealing with these, as well as the processes by which these themes and plans are maintained; and it is well geared to research, coming complete with a system for rating the progress of, and providing feedback to, the client.

Axes of a LIBET Formulation

The first axis of a LIBET formulation concerns painful life themes, 'i.e. attentional focus on vulnerable negative mental states articulated in automatic beliefs in the self and/or emotional and bodily perceptions influenced by developmental experiences and relationships evaluated as intolerably painful'. These could be considered to reflect the individual's superordinate and core constructs (Kelly 1955), those which are central to the person's view of the world and of their identity. A major factor in their development will have been the person's main 'validating agents' (Landfield 1988), often members of their family, and, going beyond a sole focus on the individual client, they may reflect shared family constructs (Procter 1981; Procter and Winter 2020) or even the constructs of a broader social system. In the LIBET model, though, the focus in considering a person's 'painful themes' is not so much on the content of their construing as on metacognitive processes.

The next axis considers semi-adaptive plans, which are rigid strategies for managing life themes by adopting rigid coping strategies even at the cost of giving up significant areas of personal development. Importantly, it is stated that these strategies can be 'partly functional'. Therefore, the strategies are not dismissed as irrational processes but their adaptive value in certain areas of the client's life, or at particular times, is acknowledged. The approach taken is essentially a *credulous* one (Kelly 1955), which, by not regarding the client as committing cognitive errors, increases the likelihood of the development of a collaborative therapeutic relationship and a strong therapeutic alliance. However, the difficulty of completely shedding a more traditional, rationalist cognitive approach is perhaps indicated by the authors' occasional use of terms such as 'psychopathology' and 'dysfunction'.

The third axis concerns 'a process level that maintains active themes and plans to the extent that they are considered either conditioning, necessary, uncontrollable or intolerable'. This axis includes consideration of the motivational aspects of the client's processes, and in particular contradictions between needs, which are reduced to 'two main pairs': 'protection and safety' and 'individual development and personal fulfilment'. Whilst I would certainly regard contradictory directions of movement of the self towards its ideals, as for example expressed in *implicative dilemmas* (Feixas et al. 2009), as often being central to psychological problems, and while I would agree that there may be some common themes in such dilemmas (Feixas et al. 2014), I would consider these to span very many areas of human experience and personal meaning, rather than being limited to dilemmas of just two main types. As the authors indicate, one way (although not the only way) of resolving such contradictions and dilemmas is by the use of superordinate constructs that are sufficiently permeable to subsume the two poles of the dilemma. For example, in the person who wishes to be kind but sometimes also not to meet their child's every expressed need, despite this seeming to be unkind, the dilemma may be resolved by the application of a superordinate construct concerning responsible child-rearing which implies that one sometimes has to be cruel to be kind.

The authors also indicate that the client's life themes may be maintained by recursive cycles of construing. A central process in such cycles may be *hostility*, in Kelly's (1955) sense of extorting evidence for a failed construction. A cyclical process of hostility may involve not only the client but also other significant people, each extorting from the other evidence that validates their constructions (Aldridge 1998; Winter 2020). The chapter's authors, in considering interpersonal relationships that may contribute to a process of 'stiffening' the client's constructions, pay particular attention to attachment patterns and the ways in which these may be reflected in characteristic ways of dealing with invalidation of construing.

Implementation of the LIBET Procedure

The formulation and case monitoring diagram used in LIBET provides a systematic way of analysing not only the client's current problem but also the development of the client's ways of construing and their experiences of invalidation. I would not agree with the chapter's authors that all cognitive therapies of the constructivist tradition (a cognitive label that many personal construct psychotherapists would consider is inappropriately applied to them) use models of cognitive functional analysis that can be traced back to REBT's ABC framework, which is used in the author's diagram. Indeed, I would not subscribe to the separation of cognition and emotion that is implied by this framework. Nevertheless, I do endorse the authors' use of a system for rating of aspects of the client's life themes and semi-functional plans. The session-by-session use of this system, coupled with symptom measures, provides a basis for demonstration of links between processes of construing and symptoms, for quality management of therapy, and for patient-focused research (Lambert et al. 2001). I would agree with the authors that the formulation process could be supplemented by the use of other assessment techniques including those from the constructivist tradition. One of these that is mentioned by the authors is laddering (Hinkle 1965) but others, that could, for example, identify and monitor conflicts and dilemmas in construing, are repertory grid technique (Fransella et al. 2004) and personal construct psychology's own ABC model (Tschudi and Winter 2011).

The authors provide numerous useful forms of words and questions that may be used to explain the LIBET model to, and develop a formulation with, a client. Finally, they provide valuable indications of how the model may be used to guide choices of therapeutic interventions.

Conclusions

LIBET provides an impressive means of formulating the processes and strategies that are central to a client's presenting complaint, as well as considering the developmental history of these. It not only informs the selection of therapeutic techniques but is itself central to the therapeutic process, and includes methods which facilitate both the collaborative sharing of the formulation with the client and the monitoring of therapeutic progress. Areas in which it could perhaps be developed further include consideration of the construing and strategies of the client's significant others (which may involve shifting from a view of the problem as located in the individual client); the co-construction of formulations; and the use of additional assessment methods in the formulation process.

References

Aldridge, D. (1998). *Suicide: The tragedy of hopelessness*. London: Jessica Kingsley.

Bieling, P. J., & Kuyken, W. (2003). Is cognitive case formulation science or science fiction? *Clinical Psychology: Science and Practice, 10*, 52–69.

Feixas, G., & Compañ, V. (2016). Dilemma-focused intervention for unipolar depression: A treatment manual. *BMC Psychiatry, 16*, 1–28.

Feixas, G., Montesano, A., Erazo-Caicedo, M. I., Compañ, V., & Pucurull, O. (2014). Implicative dilemmas and symptom severity in depression: A preliminary and content analysis study. *Journal of Constructivist Psychology, 27*, 31–40.

Feixas, G., Saúl, L. A., & Ávila-Espada, A. (2009). Viewing cognitive conflicts as dilemmas: Implications for mental health. *Journal of Constructivist Psychology, 22*, 141–169.

Fransella, F., Bell, R., & Bannister, D. (2004). *A manual for repertory grid technique*. Chichester: Wiley.

Hinkle, D. N. (1965) The change of personal constructs from the viewpoint of a theory of construct implications. Unpublished PhD thesis, Ohio State University.

Johnstone, L. (2014a). Using formulation in teams. In L. Johnstone & R. Dallos (Eds.), *Formulation in psychology and psychotherapy* (2nd ed., pp. 216–242). London: Routledge.

Johnstone, L. (2014b). Controversies and debates about formulation. In L. Johnstone & R. Dallos (Eds.), *Formulation in psychology and psychotherapy* (2nd ed., pp. 260–289). London: Routledge.

Kelly, G. A. (1955). *The psychology of personal constructs. Vol. I, II*. New York: Norton. (2nd printing1991 London: Routledge.

Lambert, M. J., Hansen, N. B., & Finch, A. E. (2001). Patient-focused research: Using patient outcome data to enhance treatment effects. *Journal of Consulting and Clinical Psychology, 69*, 159–172.

Landfield, A. (1988). Personal science and the concept of validation. *International Journal of Personal Construct Psychology, 1*, 237–249.

Procter, H. G. (1981). Family construct psychology: An approach to understanding and treating families. In S. Walrond-Skinner (Ed.), *Developments in family therapy: Theories and applications since 1948* (pp. 350–366). London: Routledge and Kegan Paul.

Procter, H. & Winter, D.A. (2020). Personal and relational construct psychotherapy. London: Palgrave Macmillan.

Tschudi, F., & Winter, D. (2011). The ABC model revisited. In P. Caputi, L. L. Viney, B. M. Walker, & N. Crittenden (Eds.), *Personal construct methodology* (pp. 89–108). Chichester: Wiley-Blackwell.

Walker, B., & Winter, D. (2005). Psychological disorder and reconstruction. In D. A. Winter & L. L. Viney (Eds.), *Personal construct psychotherapy: Advances in theory, practice and research* (pp. 21–33). London: Whurr.

Winter, D. A. (2003). Psychological disorder as imbalance. In F. Fransella (Ed.), *International handbook of personal construct psychology* (pp. 201–209). London: Wiley.

Winter, D. A. (2020). Sociality and hostility: A pernicious mix. *Journal of Constructivist Psychology*. Published online, 11 Aug, 2020, from: http://doi-org-443.webvpn.fjmu.edu.cn/10.1080/10720537.2020.1805062.

New Dimensions in Case Planning: Integration of E-Mental Health Applications

Christiane Eichenberg

Contents

Aims of the Chapter

The growing digitization, which is also finding its role in psychotherapy, makes it indispensable for psychotherapy schools to include it as another dimension in the case formulation. In my opinion, the possibility of integrating digital technology into psychotherapy nowadays makes the case formulation complementary to this aspect. Digital extensions entail a modality change, e.g., online video sessions, therapy-related mail communication between sessions, and comprehensive case planning for online exclusively sessions. The adoption of digital media has (in some cases clinically relevant) effects and correlations concerning human behavior and experience (for a detailed description of Internet-related disorders and problems see Eichenberg 2017). Case conceptualization should also cover this feature.

This paper presents different scenarios for the integration of digital support into psychotherapy, suggestions on its impact on past case formulations, and, in conclusion, a comprehensive overview of recommendations for practitioners on effective implementation of digital technology in their field. The increasing need for mental

C. Eichenberg (✉)
Faculty of Medicine, Sigmund Freud University, Wien, Austria
e-mail: christiane@rz-online.de

G. M. Ruggiero et al. (eds.), *CBT Case Formulation as Therapeutic Process*,
https://doi.org/10.1007/978-3-030-63587-9_28

health services in the population demands the integration of a digital offer into everyday care (e.g., Eichenberg et al. 2013; Waligóra and Bujnowska-Fedak 2019). The goal would be to establish practical guidelines further to support therapists guarantee reliability in the delivery of their services.

Overview: E-Mental Health Treatment Scenarios

Definition of E-Health

E-Health is the use of information and communication technologies (ICT) to facilitate prevention, diagnosis, treatment, monitoring, and administration in the healthcare system. The domain has further differentiated to encompass *E-Mental Health,* involving digital media in prevention, self-help, counseling, therapy, and rehabilitation from psychological and psychosomatic disorders, and *M-Health*, referring to the practice supported by mobile devices.

A systematization of patient-centered E-mental Health offers can respond to the following criteria (for a different systematization, see Eichenberg and Kühne 2014): (1) Type of device, (2) The number of participants (e.g., individual or group sessions), (3) Disorders and problems referred (e.g., acute or chronic) and (4) Therapeutic intervention time (e.g., preventive or curative). The spectrum of these offers is proportionately broad, ranging from individual self-management to therapy support, and rehabilitation groups. Hereafter, the assistance scenarios directly relevant to outpatient and inpatient psychotherapy.

First and foremost, it is essential to define whether sessions take place exclusively online or supplement the traditional setting (so-called blended therapy).

Online Therapy

Online therapy pertains to autonomous programs following a defined treatment protocol. The structure of these programs can envisage autonomous online training for self-help (so-called internet-based, unassisted self-help) to online psychotherapy units managed by patients along with supplementary consultation with the psychotherapist, e.g., via E-mail, telephone or short messages (so-called internet-based guided self-help) (Andersson et al. 2014). Consultations involve, in most cases, minimal contact, as it was proven to be the most effective method. Most of these offers are relevant to cognitive-behavioral therapy with more than 100 studies (Andersson et al. 2014; Peñate and Fumero 2016), typically relating to depressive and anxiety disorders (Stein et al. 2018). Currently, there are support offers for virtually all issues and disorders, among which favorably assessed services provided within the psychodynamics field targeted to individual (e.g., "KEN-Online," Zwerenz et al. 2017) and group sessions alike (Lemma and Fogany 2013).

An alternative can be remote therapy, where sessions take place exclusively via video conference—also proven a valid digital resource in psychodynamic therapy (Eichenberg and Hübner 2018).

Blended Therapy

Blended therapy combines conventional therapy with digital sessions. In this context, a further distinction is necessary. E-health applications can apply (1) prior to therapy/at the beginning of therapy (e.g., to bridge the waiting time for a therapy environment or in preparation for the therapy), (2) during therapy, (e.g., E-mental health units completed alongside or in alternation with face-to-face sessions), (3) in aftercare (e.g., as post-inpatient management programs to maximize the therapeutic effects).

Setting changes impact the therapeutic relationship. While there is extensive literature on the crucial role of the therapeutic relationship in face-to-face psychotherapy, research on the therapeutic alliance in Internet interventions is still insufficient. Notoriously, with the support of a therapist, online psychotherapy can build a sound and positive therapeutic relationship (for an overview of the current studies on the therapeutic relationship in the online setting and the differences between cognitive-behavioral and psychodynamic online therapy see Eichenberg and Hübner 2019a, b).

Case Formulation in E-Mental Health

Case formulation also poses a focus on modality. Patients address to practitioners with their concerns, refer to psychotherapists to inquire about E-mental health applications to utilize between sessions, and report by SMS on critical situations or in case attending regular face-to-face sessions is impracticable due to specific circumstances. Digital options and modality changes should be incorporated in the case formulation. In the course of the treatment planning phase, it lies with the therapist to present the potential digital options to integrate therapy, based on the "media anamnesis" and the case formulation:

Media Anamnesis

Considering the prevalence of digital media, it strongly advisable to trace a history of their use at the beginning of psychotherapy (PwC 2018). The purpose of this preliminary step is to ascertain potential challenges. Notably, addictive uses, also within the family circle (Müller and Wölfling 2017), dysfunctional uses or

"Cyberchondria," the delusional persuasion of suffering from a disease, especially in hypochondriacal subjects, with the risk of aggravating anxiety (Eichenberg and Schott 2019). Also, uses that might hinder psychotherapy (e.g., suicide forums, see Eichenberg 2008). Therefore, it is vital to determine the type of content and platforms that might assist patients in their self-help journey (forums, blogs, video channels revolving around mental illness, or a second opinion online). This stride can give the therapist insight into the nature of the patient's approach in order to allow the progression of psychotherapy. The anamnesis also clarifies if resorting to digital offers is relevant to the case formulation, regardless of whether it might originate from the patient's or therapist's suggestion, and in consideration of treatment-related factors.

Case Formulation in Online Therapy

Online therapy implies the challenge of determining, in virtue of online diagnostics, the validity of this option, and its therapeutic plan for the patient. Internet-based cognitive-behavioral therapy mostly includes pre-use questionnaires. In tackling depressive disorders, this means a rating scale and the evaluation of suicidal tendencies are fundamental to exclude participants with such inclinations. However, currently, there are no reports on how to deal with subjects who develop suicidal thoughts only in the course of online therapy or manifest such drive at a later time. Treatment planning should cover not only this aspect but also contingency strategies considering what can therapist and patient do in the event of technical issues (e.g., switching to alternative communication channels) or if the symptoms exacerbate making online therapy insufficient. It is at this stage that precise agreements are necessary to define the appropriate actions to take if a consistent supervision of symptoms calls for further therapeutic measures.

Case Formulation in Blended Therapy

The shared decision between therapist and patient, to support face-to-face therapy with online treatment, should contemplate two aspects. The first aspect touches the communication set-up: on which platform will the therapist be available? Are between-sessions contacts feasible to discuss organizational matters only or for treatment-related topics as well? Will the therapist be accessible outside of sessions, and how, in the event of a crisis? These boundaries apply in both directions and also pertain to the patient's preferred modalities. Therefore, transparency is necessary to avoid any violations (for detailed information on boundaries violations in the online setting, see Eichenberg and Küsel 2017).

Prerequisites for the Integration of Digital Media in Therapy

Therapist's Prerequisites

(a) *Socio-technical proficiency and equipment*. The therapist must have appropriate devices, e.g., for video sessions: headset, webcam, a video application certified for therapeutic purposes. The integration of E-mental health units such as unassisted self-help programs for inpatient or outpatient therapy requires a compatible application with definite evidence of evaluation in line with the standards of psychotherapy research. With video telephony, it is a good practice for the therapist to test functionality beforehand with someone who is not a patient.
(b) *Legal framework*. The compliance with the current data protection regulations across jurisdictions, along with the diverse professional regulations regimenting whether and how digital media can complement psychotherapy and potential refunds criteria.

The therapist has to guarantee proficiency in the field of E-mental health to meet prime therapy standards.

Patient's Prerequisites

(a) *Socio-technical proficiency and equipment*. The patient must be equally willing to resort to digital media and adequately equipped.

Therapeutic Alliance

(a) *Context rules*. Before the first video session, both therapist and patient should agree on specific rules, e.g., both parties will participate alone, sessions will take place behind-closed-doors, will not be recorded, and interference sources (such as cell phones) will be deactivated. Moreover, each client's personality, background, disorder, and the structural level are fundamental to evaluate the pertinence of digital media from a treatment perspective.
(b) *Treatment aspects*. The following considerations offer recommendations - indications and contraindications—on the integration of digital options into the case formulation. These reflections rest on media integration both in psychodynamic and cognitive-behavioral therapy, which, according to an adaptive treatment process, remains subject to consistent evaluation.

Use of Technology: Specific Recommendations

Treatment Phase

The treatment phase is strongly case-specific. Can a given patient also establish a relationship throughout video sessions? Are unassisted online self-help units effective, or are they more indicated as a "follow-up measure"? Does E-mental health encourage therapy and promote improvement? How frequent is regression after inpatient treatment? Do post-inpatient chat groups prevent reversion?

Patient's Background

A "media anamnesis"(see above) should take into account the patient's current media consumption and document its history. What role did the media play in the patient's childhood? In patients who experienced media as a factor alienating them from caregivers, the therapist's suggestion to use unassisted self-help programs will have a different impact than on patients who have not experienced a similar deprivation.

Symptoms

Therapists should always check the availability of disorder-specific online self-help programs before recommending their integration into conventional treatment. While Serious Games (The purpose of a "serious game" is twofold: to be fun, entertaining and engaging, and to develop new knowledge, train new skills and change behavior) can support therapy for several disorders in children and adolescents (Eichenberg and Schott 2017), options targeting different age groups are limited. The same applies to unassisted online tools for self-help. Despite covering a broad spectrum of disorders, translation in different languages is only available for the most common ones.

Personality Traits

The offer and the introduction of media offers in therapy should take into account the patient's specific personality traits. A patient with a compulsive disorder will perceive and use the media offer with a radically different approach compared to a narcissist or a subject with histrionic personality. The risk in compulsive patients lies in the excessive use of unassisted online self-help tools, in a person with a histrionic personality disorder, the risk is triggering an attention-seeking behavior. As for narcissistic personalities, the challenge resides in the potential undermining of the therapist's role. In general, monitoring the use of online tools seems essential to uphold a complementary relationship with the therapist (self-help books, or dedicated online-modules). Narcissistic patients can, for instance, resort to programs featuring the opportunity to check the appropriate usage for the progress of therapy.

Structural Level

The patient's structural level also determines whether the context rules also apply in a virtual space, e.g., in video telephony. In neurotic patients, Email or chat-based exchange can increase the transmission process and positively affect therapy (Colon 1999). In patients with a lower structural level, however, the lack of physical proximity can also destabilize. An accurate selection of the appropriate communication tools and their timely application will endorse the patient's development.

Adaptation of the Treatment Methods to Technology

Conclusively, therapy schools also specify the extent of conventional therapy adaptability and what methods better conform to digital options. Indeed, behavioral therapy better combines with E-mental health programs than psychoanalysis or Gestalt therapy. The essential elements of client-centered psychotherapy better facilitate Email-based communication than creative therapy, and, on the other hand, systematic programs necessitate specific technical requirements to work online with a group of family members.

Empirical Evidence on the Inclusion of E-Mental Health in the Case Formulation

To my knowledge, no research addresses specifically whether case formulation incorporates E-mental health applications. However, three of our current studies provide a starting point. Eichenberg et al. (2019) for instance, have interviewed $N = 160$ psychotherapists from Germany and Austria (female: 75%, male: 25%, age: M: 45.4; $SD = 18.9$) on their therapeutic approach involving digital media. The vast majority (63%) reported not speaking to their patients about the circumstances determining the pertinence of digital media to their case. Factors such as gender, age, and the different schools had no implications. One of the prerequisites for the inclusion of digital media in the case formulation is to understand the patient's relationship with such tool. In our survey, however, 63.2% of psychotherapists stated they were not aware of what role digital media plays in their patients' lives, regardless of the therapist's school. Only 15% was accurate about how their patients deal with digital media. The larger share (72.5%) stated they had not previously participated in any advanced training on the association of psychotherapy and media, but 61.9% said they would find such subject-specific studies beneficial.

A study (Eichenberg and Hübner 2019a, b) on $N = 50$ participants at the congress of the International Psychoanalytical Association in London in July 2019 (female: 56%, male: 44%, age: $M = 48.6$; $SD = 12.7$), 62% had completed psychoanalytic studies, 38% still in training) showed that: 48% used Skype, 30% phone calls, 14% WhatsApp, 8% SMS and 4% Email (multiple answers questionnaire). As for online therapy, 12% utilize Skype, 8% resort to telephone calls, and 2% participate via WhatsApp. According to the psychoanalysts' self-assessment portion, 30% reported integrating digital media and conventional therapy from the outset, 32% declared turning to applications following a patient's request, and 38% indicated regulations on the use of digital media as not relevant.

In an ongoing study, we questioned a group of in-training psychotherapists from different countries (Italy: in collaboration with SFU Milano, Prof. Dr. Borlimi; UK: in collaboration with the University of Plymouth, Dr. Cattani) about their view on media as a segment of therapy. Among German and Austrian participants (currently $N = 154$), those who are already treating patients ($N = 83$, 53.9%) revealed that 24.1% prefer phone calls, 8.4% video conferences (Skype), 7.2% SMS and 6.0% Emails to plan face-to-face sessions. As for therapy held exclusively online, 6% meet on Skype, and 4% choose other applications. A total of 50.6% planned the use of communication channels at the beginning of therapy with each patient; 47.0% only discuss this option when patients raise the subject. Overall, 41% discuss the use of media in psychotherapy with their supervisor first, and 7.2% answered their supervisor decided about it.

The current corona crisis suggests that the approach to E-mental health applications in psychotherapy is bound to change. Several countries with restrictive policies for the delivery of ad hoc video therapy have eased their legislation in support of this practice (Eichenberg 2020). In this circumstance, psychotherapists are facing the complexity of embracing online psychotherapy, and pondering on the standardization of case formulation to encompass the aspect of E-mental health.

References

Andersson, G., Cuijpers, P., Carlbring, P., Riper, H., & Hedman, E. (2014). Guided Internet-based vs. face-to-face cognitive behavior therapy for psychiatric and somatic disorders: A systematic review and meta-analysis. *World Psychiatry, 13*, 288–295.

Colon, Y. (1999). *Chatte(er)ring through the fingertips: Doing group therapy online.* Retrieved March 29, 2020, from http://web.archive.org/web/20040616205705/www.echonyc.com/~women/Issue17/public-colon.html

Eichenberg, C. (2008). Internet message boards for suicidal people: A typology of users. *Cyberpsychology & Behavior, 11*, 98–104.
Eichenberg, C. (2017). Internetassoziierte Störungen und Probleme [Internet associated disorders and problem]. *Sozialpsychiatrische Informationen, 1*, 37–40.
Eichenberg, C. (2020). Online-Psychotherapie in Zeiten der Corona-Krise [Online psychotherapy in the Coronavirus crisis age]. In R. Bering & C. Eichenberg (Eds.), Die Psyche in Zeiten der Corona-Krise [The mind in the Coronavirus crisis age]. (pp. 69–82) Stuttgart: Klett-Cotta.
Eichenberg, C., & Hübner, L. (2018). Psychoanalyse via Internet: Ein Überblick zum aktuellen Stand der Diskussion um Möglichkeiten und Grenzen [Psychoanalysis via the Internet: An overview of the current state of the discussion about possibilities and limits]. *Psychotherapeut, 63*, 283–290. https://doi.org/10.1007/s00278-018-0294-0.
Eichenberg, C., & Hübner, L. (2019a). Internet presence of psychoanalysts and digitally boundary violations in psychoanalytic treatment.. Submitted manuscript.
Eichenberg, C. & Hübner, L. (2019b). *Therapeutische Beziehung im Zeitalter digitaler Medien: Perspektiven und Ergebnisse aus Verhaltenstherapie und psychodynamischer Psychotherapie. [Therapeutic relationship in the age of digital media: Perspectives and results from behavioral therapy and psychodynamic psychotherapy].* Submitted manuscript.
Eichenberg, C., & Kühne, S. (2014). *Einführung Online-Beratung und –therapie. Grundlagen, Interventionen und Effekte der Internetnutzung [Introduction to online counseling and therapy. Basics, interventions and effects of internet use].* München: UTB.anderss.
Eichenberg, C., & Küsel, C. (2017). E-Mental Health: Potenzielle Grenzverletzungen [E-Mental Health: Potential borderline injuries]. *Deutsches Ärzteblatt, Ausgabe PP, 12*, 590–592.
Eichenberg, C., Piening, K. & van Loh, J. (2019). Therapeutische Haltung zu digitalen Medienstörungen in der Psychotherapie [Therapeutic stance on digital media disorders in psychotherapy]. Submitted manuscript.
Eichenberg, C., & Schott, M. (2017). Serious games for psychotherapy: A systematic review. *Games for Health*, (3), 127–135.
Eichenberg, C., & Schott, M. (2019). Use of online health services in individuals with and without symptoms of hypochondria: Survey Study. *Journal of Medical Internet Research, 21*, e10980. https://doi.org/10.2196/10980.
Eichenberg, C., Wolters, C., & Brähler, E. (2013). The internet as a mental health advisor in Germany—Results of a national survey. *PLoS One, 8*(11), e79206. https://doi.org/10.1371/journal.pone.0079206.
Lemma, A., & Fogany, P. (2013). Feasibility study of a psychodynamic online group intervention for depression and anxiety. *Psychoanalytic Psychology, 30*(3), 367–380.
Müller, K. W., & Wölfling, K. (2017). *Pathologischer Mediengebrauch und Internetsucht.* Stuttgart: Kohlhammer.
Peñate, W., & Fumero, A. (2016). A meta-review of Internet computer-based psychological treatments for anxiety disorders. *Journal of Telemedicine and Telecare, 22*, 3–11.
PwC. (2018). *Future Health. Bevölkerungsumfrage zur Digitalisierung und Technologisierung im Gesundheitswesen [Future health. Population survey on digitization and technology in healthcare].* Retrieved March 29, 2020, from https://www.pwc.de/de/gesundheitswesen-und-pharma/ future-health-berichtsband.pdf.
Stein, J., Röhr, S., Luck, T., Löbner, M., & Riedel-Heller, S. (2018). Indikationen und Evidenz von international entwickelten Online-Coaches zur Intervention bei psychischen Erkrankungen—ein Meta-Review [Indications and evidence from internationally developed online coaches for intervention in mental illnesses—A meta-review]. *Psychiatische Praxis, 45*, 7–15. https://doi.org/10.1055/s-0043-117050.
Waligóra, J., & Bujnowska-Fedak, M. M. (2019). Online health technologies and mobile devices: Attitudes, needs, and future. *Advances in Experimental and Medical Biology*. https://doi.org/10.1007/5584_2019_335.

Zwerenz, R., Becker, J., Johansson, R., Frederick, R. J., Andersson, G., & Beutel, M. E. (2017). Transdiagnostic, psychodynamic web-based self-help intervention following inpatient psychotherapy: Results of a feasibility study and Randomized Controlled Trial. *Journal of Medical Internet Research Mental Health, 4*, e41. https://doi.org/10.2196/mental.7889.

Now's the Time: CBT Shares Case Formulation More (but Not *Too*) Easily

Giovanni Maria Ruggiero, Gabriele Caselli, and Sandra Sassaroli

Contents

G. M. Ruggiero (✉)
"Psicoterapia Cognitiva e Ricerca," Cognitive Psychotherapy School and Research Center, Milan, Italy

Sigmund Freud University, Milan, Italy

Sigmund Freud University, Vienna, Austria
e-mail: gm.ruggiero@milano-sfu.it

G. Caselli
Sigmund Freud University, Milan, Italy

Sigmund Freud University, Wien, Austria

Department of Psychology, London South Bank University, London, UK

S. Sassaroli
Sigmund Freud University, Milan, Italy

Sigmund Freud University, Vienna, Austria

"Studi Cognitivi", Cognitive Psychotherapy School and Research Center, Milan, Italy

G. M. Ruggiero et al. (eds.), *CBT Case Formulation as Therapeutic Process*,
https://doi.org/10.1007/978-3-030-63587-9_29

Let's Fall in Love: Initial or Gradual Sharing of *Case Formulation*

At the end of this walk-through among the forms of case formulation in psychotherapy, it is necessary to revisit the initial question: Is sharing case formulations the initial move and main operational tool of a significant number of cognitive behavioral therapy (CBT) approaches? And is it true that this peculiar way of using case formulations is the specific way in which CBT approaches theoretically define and clinically handle non-specific factors of the therapeutic process—i.e., the therapeutic relationship and alliance?

In the many commentaries on the chapters of this book, the most recurrent criticism of our hypothesis is that the case formulation can never really be defined and shared from the beginning; it is not an initial declaration of intent or a *gentlemen's agreement* on the rules of the game, but an agreement that is built together with the patient throughout the entire therapeutic process and, therefore, an outcome. We find this criticism not only in all the commentaries relating to cognitive constructivist orientation (Chapters "A Constructivist Pioneer of Formulation: A Commentary on Chapter "Strengths and Limitations of Case Formulation in Constructivist Cognitive Behavioral Therapies"", "Commentary on the Presentation of the Metacognitive Interpersonal Therapy Model in Chapter "Strengths and Limitations of Case Formulation in Constructivist Cognitive Behavioral Therapies"", "The Role of Trauma in Psychotherapeutic Complications and the Worth of Giovanni Liotti's Cognitive-Evolutionist Perspective (cep): Commentary on Chapter "Strengths and Limitations of Case Formulation in Constructivist Cognitive Behavioral Therapies"", "The Case Formulation in the Post-rationalist Constructivist Model: Commentary on Chapter "Strengths and Limitations of Case Formulation in Constructivist Cognitive Behavioral Therapies"", Case Formulation and the Therapeutic Relationship from an Evolutionary Theory of Motivation: Commentary to Chapter "Strengths and Limitations of Case Formulation in Constructivist Cognitive Behavioral Therapies"", and "Emotion, Motivation, Therapeutic Relationship and Cognition in Giovanni Liotti's Model: Commentary on Chapter "Strengths and Limitations of Case Formulation in Constructivist Cognitive Behavioral Therapies"") and psychodynamic orientation (Chapters "Commentary to Chapter "Case Formulation as an Outcome and not an Opening Move in Relational and Psychodynamic Models": Plan Formulation Vs. Case Formulation—The Perspective of Control-Mastery Theory", "Some Historical and Theoretical Remarks About Psychodynamic Assessment: Commentary on Chapter "Case Formulation as an Outcome and not an Opening Move in Relational and Psychodynamic Models"", and "Case Formulation in Psychoanalysis and in Cognitive-Behavioral Therapies: Commentary on Chapter "Case Formulation as an Outcome and not an Opening Move in Relational and Psychodynamic Models""), but also—in a more moderate version—those of behavioral orientation (Chapter "Some Thoughts on Chapter "Case Formulation in the Behavioral Tradition: Meyer, Turkat, Lane, Bruch, and Sturmey" *Case Formulation in the Behavioral Tradition: Meyer, Turkat, Lane,*

Bruch, and Sturmey by Giovanni Maria Ruggiero, Gabriele Caselli and Sandra Sassaroli") and neo-behavioral and experiential orientation—largely called "third wave" orientation (Chapters "Commentary on Chapter "Case Formulation in Process-Based Therapies": Process Based CBT as an Approach to Case Conceptualization", "Clinical Behavior Analysis, ACT and Case Formulation: A Commentary on Chapter "Case Formulation in Process-Based Therapies"", and "Schema Therapy, Contextual Schema Therapy and Case Formulation: Commentary on Chapter "Case Formulation in Process-Based Therapies"").

How Deep Is the Ocean? Sharing the Content or Process of the *Case Formulation*

This criticism can be accepted when one admits that the specific content of the case formulation changes along the course of treatment, even in CBT approaches, and often significantly. What is always shared from the outset is not the specific content but the principle that the treatment works through immediate agreement on the equally immediate shareability of (a) a hypothesis, albeit provisional, of (dis)functioning based on emotional vulnerabilities and semi-adaptive rigidified behaviors and (b) an attitude of critical detachment toward the level of intolerability of emotional vulnerability and uncontrollability of rigidified behaviors—an attitude not to be discovered as the therapy proceeds but to be rapidly assumed. It is therefore a sharing of the process but not always of the content. At the end of this historical and critical *promenade*, we accept from our commentators this adjustment of our definition of a shared formulation of the case. However, we would like to reiterate that, from our viewpoint, sharing the case formulation from the outset is also possible in terms of content in many cases, at least in the target disorders of CBT approaches—i.e., anxiety disorders and depression. It is also plausible to think that, in the case of personality disorders, CBT approaches should in some cases—but not always—share the case formulation from the outset in terms of process, but not necessarily in terms of content.

Night and Day. Distinction Between CBT and Other Approaches

This concession to the gradualist conception of shared case formulation proposed by psychodynamic and constructivist therapies does not mean that the distinction between CBT and other approaches disappears into the usual *continuum* concept. In our opinion, the theoretical and clinical approaches of the psychodynamic and constructivist orientations intrinsically imply that the sharing of the case formulation is always only gradually implemented and eventually implemented in the form of sharing the patient's functioning and the treatment's process, and not only the content. This is because of many theoretical and clinical reasons that have already been extensively explained and discussed in the chapters of the book and that, from our point of view, have been accepted and claimed in many *commentaries*. This difference between CBT and both psychodynamic and constructivist approaches is not meant to be a value judgement but a *de facto* distinction between theoretical and clinical approaches that are not compatible with each other, and which helps us to understand the differences between these approaches and their theoretical and clinical pros and cons. In summary, the distinction makes it possible to distinguish between CBT approaches that focus on the clinical possibility of quick agreement and explicit alliance with the executive functions of the mind on the basis of a theoretical principle of reasonably rapid conscious representability of hypotheses of emotional and behavioral dysfunction and approaches that believe that this agreement must be the result of a complex and even conflictual process in which the conscious representation of the function is only the final outcome of a process not immediately representable to consciousness of which the agreement is continuously subject to relational crises between therapist and patient and conflictual turns which are then the real critical episodes which reveal the patient's own dysfunction.

Tea for Three. The Position of *Behavior Therapy* and Third Wave Cognitive Psychotherapy

As Sturmey pointed out in his *commentary*, the position of behavior therapy (BT) is not reducible to that of CBT approaches, and this is perhaps also the case for some experiential aspects of the so-called "third wave" cognitive-behavioral psychotherapies, which in some respects could also be defined as neo-behavioral therapies. However, they remain, in our opinion, close to the CBT approach. It is true that this proximity still needs to be better explored and that this imperfect understanding is probably also due to a lack of knowledge on the part of those scholars of CBT who have superficially assumed the harmonic filiation of CBT from BT. It is necessary to rethink CBT concepts in more rigorous behavioral terms. For example, dysfunctional rigidification of maladaptive plans is defined in BT terms as behavioral reinforcement—a term that may help to better distinguish the CBT *coping strategies* (Chapter "Case Formulation in Standard Cognitive Therapy") or semi-adaptive plans proposed in the LIBET procedure (Chapter "The Empirical State of Case Formulation: Integrating and Validating Cognitive, Evolutionary and Procedural Elements in the CBT Case Formulation in the LIBET Procedure") from psychodynamic defenses, in order to avoid eclectic conceptual confusion. It is our intention to explore the integration between BT and CBT theories in less simplistic terms than done so far and, as written in Chapter "Case Formulation in Process-Based Therapies", we believe that the basis for this integration may be metacognition.

Just Friends. *Case Formulation* and Therapeutic Alliance

Finally, it seems to us that, at least provisionally, it is possible to confirm the feasibility of our proposal that the shared formulation of the case may be the specific way in which CBT approaches can define and handle the concepts of aspecific factors of the therapeutic process—i.e., the therapeutic relationship and the alliance. This does not mean that CBT cannot recognize the contribution of reflection on the therapeutic relationship proposed by the model of aspecific factors or psychodynamic models. On the contrary, it can also be admitted that the contributions of these theoretical reflections were partly neglected in the first formulations of CBT models. However, once these stimuli are admitted, we believe that they should be used to develop a specific CBT path of theorizing the therapeutic alliance in order to avoid the risk of simplistic eclecticism and superficial integrations. Shared formulation of the case may be one of these paths.

The End of a Love Affair. Final Remarks

The review of case formulation models in this book allows us to propose some *final remarks* on the vicissitudes of cognitive models and some hypotheses on future directions. Beck's CBT model (Chapters "Case Formulation in Standard Cognitive Therapy", "The Conceptualization Process in Cognitive Behavioral Therapy: Commentary on Chapter "Case Formulation in Standard Cognitive Therapy"", and "Case Formulation in Standard Cognitive Therapy: A Commentary on Chapter "Case Formulation in Standard Cognitive Therapy"") identified dysfunctions as cognitive biases and he was scientifically satisfied with those explanations. That model granted centrality to psychological dysfunctions and defined them in cognitive terms, a simplification that allowed formalizing the psychological biases and operationalizing the psychotherapeutic intervention in an economic way. The efficient simplicity of the model consciously avoided investigating the reasons for the dysfunctions themselves, correctly believing that such an investigation could lead to the risk of identifying extra-psychological causes, such as environmental, evolutionary, or genetic vulnerabilities, factors that were naturally plausible from a scientific point of view but which risked requiring non-psychotherapeutic treatments, treatments that might be appropriate that were clinically off-topic in a psychotherapy research. The price of the simplicity of the classical CBT model was of course the simplism of narrowing mental states to explicit cognitive processes.

Both constructivist (Chapters "Strengths and Limitations of Case Formulation in Constructivist Cognitive Behavioral Therapies", "A Constructivist Pioneer of Formulation: A Commentary on Chapter "Strengths and Limitations of Case Formulation in Constructivist Cognitive Behavioral Therapies"", "Commentary on the Presentation of the Metacognitive Interpersonal Therapy Model in Chapter "Strengths and Limitations of Case Formulation in Constructivist Cognitive

Behavioral Therapies"", "The Role of Trauma in Psychotherapeutic Complications and the Worth of Giovanni Liotti's Cognitive-Evolutionist Perspective (Cep): Commentary on Chapter "Strengths and Limitations of Case Formulation in Constructivist Cognitive Behavioral Therapies"", "The Case Formulation in the Post-rationalist Constructivist Model: Commentary on Chapter "Strengths and Limitations of Case Formulation in Constructivist Cognitive Behavioral Therapies"", "Case Formulation and the Therapeutic Relationship from an Evolutionary Theory of Motivation: Commentary to Chapter "Strengths and Limitations of Case Formulation in Constructivist Cognitive Behavioral Therapies"", and "Emotion, Motivation, Therapeutic Relationship and Cognition in Giovanni Liotti's Model: Commentary on Chapter "Strengths and Limitations of Case Formulation in Constructivist Cognitive Behavioral Therapies"") and psychodynamic orientations (Chapters "Case Formulation as an Outcome and not an Opening Move in Relational and Psychodynamic Models", "Commentary to Chapter "Case Formulation as an Outcome and not an Opening Move in Relational and Psychodynamic Models": Plan Formulation Vs. Case Formulation—The Perspective of Control-Mastery Theory", "Some Historical and Theoretical Remarks About Psychodynamic Assessment: Commentary on Chapter "Case Formulation as an Outcome and not an Opening Move in Relational and Psychodynamic Models"", and "Case Formulation in Psychoanalysis and in Cognitive-Behavioral Therapies: Commentary on Chapter "Case Formulation as an Outcome and not an Opening Move in Relational and Psychodynamic Models"") instead accepted the challenge of complexity, exploring the evolutionary basis of cognitive dysfunctions. The risk that the corresponding constructivist and psychodynamic treatments would become non-psychological was avoided by widening the area of intervention to the relational domain, seen as the place where evolutionary influence could be compensated in psychological terms, although not cognitive but emotional. The problems of those proposals were the difficulty of operationalizing the emotional states and the generation of less economical and efficient treatments than the classic CBT model which, not by chance, did not lead to an increase in effectiveness but to the flattening of Dodo's verdict and of the model of common factors.

Lately, the psychodynamic and constructivist fields have been trying to get out of the problems of their relational direction by focusing on experiential interventions, which would have the advantage of being emotionally experienced and not only cognitively thought. An apparently similar direction has also been taken in the cognitive-behavioral field with process "third wave" therapies (Chapters "Case Formulation in Process-Based Therapies", "Commentary on Chapter "Case Formulation in Process-Based Therapies": Process Based CBT as an Approach to Case Conceptualization", "Clinical Behavior Analysis, ACT and Case Formulation: A Commentary on Chapter "Case Formulation in Process-Based Therapies"", and "Schema Therapy, Contextual Schema Therapy and Case Formulation: Commentary on Chapter "Case Formulation in Process-Based Therapies""). However, while the direction is similar, the theoretical and clinical approach is different. The experiential intervention in the psychodynamic and constructivist field seems to draw inspiration from the gestaltic and humanistic-experiential interventions whose main defect, in our opinion, remains the tendency to rely on a conception of non-cognitive mental states not easily formalizable in efficient and economic terms and—sometimes—deliberately not formalized, risking ending up outside the space delimited by Occam's razor.

On the other hand, the openness to the experiential aspect in the cognitive-behavioral field takes place in terms of the mentioned process "third wave" models (Chapters "Case Formulation in Process-Based Therapies", "Commentary on Chapter "Case Formulation in Process-Based Therapies": Process Based CBT as an Approach to Case Conceptualization", "Clinical Behavior Analysis, ACT and Case Formulation: A Commentary on Chapter "Case Formulation in Process-Based Therapies"", and "Schema Therapy, Contextual Schema Therapy and Case Formulation: Commentary on Chapter "Case Formulation in Process-Based Therapies"") partly preceded by Albert Ellis' REBT model (Chapters "How B-C Connection and Negotiation of F Allow the Design and Implementation of a Cooperative and Effective Disputing in Rational Emotive Behavior Therapy", "Commentary to Chapter VIII. REBT's B–C Connection and Negotiation of F", and "Commentary to Chapter "How B–C Connection and Negotiation of F Allow the Design and Implementation of a Cooperative and Effective Disputing in Rational Emotive Behavior Therapy": Commentary on Chapter VIII: REBT Provides a Firm Basis for Case Formulation by Employing an Ongoing, Implicit and Hypothetico-Deductive Form of Data Collection in Critical Collaboration, Negotiation and an Equal Relationship with the Client") which broaden the definition of mental state beyond cognitive content and which clinically make use of behavioral interventions that have already been operationalized (Chapters "Case Formulation in the Behavioral Tradition: Meyer, Turkat, Lane, Bruch, and Sturmey" and "Some Thoughts on Chapter "Case Formulation in the Behavioral Tradition: Meyer, Turkat, Lane, Bruch, and Sturmey" *Case Formulation in the Behavioral Tradition: Meyer, Turkat, Lane, Bruch, and Sturmey* by Giovanni Maria Ruggiero, Gabriele Caselli and Sandra Sassaroli"). Moreover, the theoretical node is solved at the metacognitive level, where dysfunctions are no longer mistakes in the evaluation of reality but biases in the functional management of internal states. In this way, it also becomes possible to insert evolutionary aspects into the theoretical model, defining them as predisposing but not causal conditions of metacognitive dysfunction, avoiding the risk that they will replace the centrality of psychological dysfunctions, both in the psychopathological and therapeutic processes. The final proposal of our LIBET model of case formulation is at the provisional end of this path (Chapters "The Empirical State of Case Formulation: Integrating and Validating Cognitive, Evolutionary and Procedural Elements in the CBT Case Formulation in the LIBET Procedure" and "Commentary on Chapter "The Empirical State of Case Formulation: Integrating and Validating Cognitive, Evolutionary and Procedural Elements in the CBT Case Formulation in the LIBET Procedure": A Constructivist Perspective on LIBET").

Index

G. M. Ruggiero et al. (eds.), *CBT Case Formulation as Therapeutic Process*,
https://doi.org/10.1007/978-3-030-63587-9

The manufacturer's authorised representative in the EU is Springer Nature Customer Service Centre GmbH, Europaplatz 3, 69115 Heidelberg, Germany. If you have any concerns regarding our products, please contact ProductSafety@springernature.com

Printed and bound by CPI Group (UK) Ltd, Croydon, CR0 4YY
22/09/2026
02221061-0015